Rick.

D0357447

FRANCE
BELGIUM &
THE NETHERLANDS
2001

Rick Steves and Steve Smith

AVALON
TRAVEL
publishing

Other ATP travel guidebooks by Rick Steves
Rick Steves' Europe Through the Back Door
Rick Steves' Europe 101: History and Art for the Traveler
  (with Gene Openshaw)
Rick Steves' Mona Winks: Self-Guided Tours of Europe's Top Museums
  (with Gene Openshaw)
Rick Steves' Postcards from Europe
Rick Steves' Best of Europe
Rick Steves' Germany, Austria & Switzerland
Rick Steves' Great Britain & Ireland
Rick Steves' Italy
Rick Steves' Scandinavia
Rick Steves' Spain & Portugal
Rick Steves' London (with Gene Openshaw)
Rick Steves' Paris (with Steve Smith and Gene Openshaw)
Rick Steves' Rome (with Gene Openshaw)
Rick Steves' Phrase Books: German, French, Italian, Spanish/Portuguese,
  and French/Italian/German

Thanks to Steve's wife, Karen Lewis, for her help on covering the
cuisine of France.

Avalon Travel Publishing, 5855 Beaudry Street, Emeryville, CA 94608

Printed in the United States of America
First printing December 2000

For the latest on Rick's lectures, guidebooks, tours, and public television
series, contact Europe Through the Back Door, Box 2009, Edmonds, WA
98020, tel. 425/771-8303, fax 425/771-0833, www.ricksteves.com, or
e-mail: rick@ricksteves.com.

ISSN 1084-4406
ISBN 1-56691-231-8

Europe Through the Back Door Editors Risa Laib, Jacquie Maupin
Avalon Travel Publishing Editor Kate Willis
Copy Editor Chris Hayhurst
Production & Typesetting Kathleen Sparkes, White Hart Design
Design Linda Braun
Cover Design Janine Lehmann
Maps David C. Hoerlein
Printer Publishers Press
Cover Photo Arc d' Triomphe, Paris, France; © Jeff Greenberg/
  Unicorn Stock Photos

Distributed to the book trade by Publishers Group West
Berkeley, California

CONTENTS

Top Destinations in France, Belgium, and the Netherlands

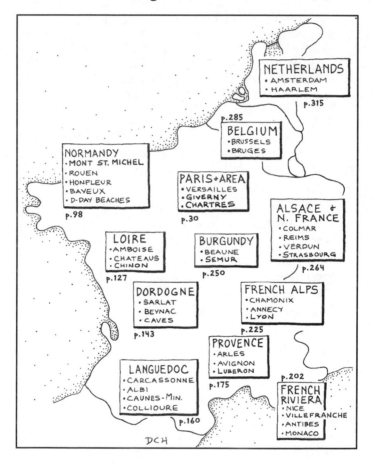

NETHERLANDS
• AMSTERDAM
• HAARLEM
p.315

p.285

BELGIUM
• BRUSSELS
• BRUGES

NORMANDY
• MONT ST. MICHEL
• ROUEN
• HONFLEUR
• BAYEUX
• D-DAY BEACHES
p.98

PARIS & AREA
• VERSAILLES
• GIVERNY
• CHARTRES
p.30

ALSACE &
N. FRANCE
• COLMAR
• REIMS
• VERDUN
• STRASBOURG
p.264

LOIRE
• AMBOISE
• CHATEAUS
• CHINON
p.127

BURGUNDY
• BEAUNE
• SEMUR
p.250

DORDOGNE
• SARLAT
• BEYNAC
• CAVES
p.143

FRENCH ALPS
• CHAMONIX
• ANNECY
• LYON
p.225

PROVENCE
• ARLES
• AVIGNON
• LUBERON
p.175

p.202

LANGUEDOC
• CARCASSONNE
• ALBI
• CAUNES-MIN.
• COLLIOURE
p.160

FRENCH
RIVIERA
• NICE
• VILLEFRANCHE
• ANTIBES
• MONACO

DCH

INTRODUCTION

You've made a great choice. France is Europe's most diverse, tasty, and, in many ways, exciting country to explore. And for extra travel thrills, this book takes you north through the best of Belgium and the Netherlands.

France is nearly as big as Texas, with 58 million people and 400 different cheeses. *Diversité* is a French forte. This country features three distinct mountain ranges (the Alps, the Pyrénées, and the Central), the different-as-night-and-day Atlantic and Mediterranean coastlines, cosmopolitan cities (such as Paris, Lyon, and Nice, all featured in this book), and sleepy villages. From its Swisslike Alps to its *molto* Italian Riviera and from the Spanish Pyrénées to *das* German Alsace, you can stay in France, feel like you've sampled much of Europe, and never be more than a short stroll from a good *vin rouge*.

Belgium and the Netherlands, called the Low Countries because nearly half their land is below sea level, are easy to over-look, surrounded by mega-Europe. We've spliced these into our France guide so that your memories can include some Bruges lace, Belgian waffles, a dike hike, and a few Dutch masters. If ever an area was a travel cliché come true, it's the Low Countries.

After years of researching and tour guiding together, Rick Steves and Francophile Steve Smith have teamed up to write this book. For 13 years we have worked hard every year to discover and describe France's most interesting destinations and give you tips on how to use your time and money most efficiently. France, Belgium, and the Netherlands are a many-faceted cultural fondue. Each of our recommended destinations is a dripping forkful (complete with instructions on how to enjoy the full flavor without burning your tongue).

This book covers the predictable biggies and mixes in a healthy dose of "Back Door" intimacy. Along with the Eiffel Tower, Mont St. Michel, and the French Riviera, you'll take a bike tour of the Loire, marvel at 15,000-year-old cave paintings, and take a canoe ride down the lazy Dordogne River. You'll find a *magnifique* hill-town perch to catch a Provencal sunset, ride Europe's highest mountain lift, and touch the quiet Romanesque soul of village Burgundy. Just as important, you'll meet the intriguing people who run your hotel or bed-and-breakfast.

Rick Steves' France, Belgium & the Netherlands is a tour guide in your pocket—actually, two tour guides in your pocket. Places covered are balanced to include the most famous cities and inti-mate villages, from jet-setting beach resorts to the traditional heartland. We've been selective, including only the most exciting sights and romantic villages. For example, there are *beaucoup* beau-tiful châteaus in the Loire region. We recommend just the best.

And while there are dozens of Loire towns to base in, we recommend the top two. The best is, of course, only our opinion. But after more than 25 busy years of travel writing, lecturing, tour guiding, and Francophilia between us, we've developed a sixth sense for what tickles the traveler's fancy.

This Information Is Accurate and Up-to-Date

This book is completely updated every year. Most publishers of guidebooks that cover a region from top to bottom can afford an update only every two or three years (and even then it's often by letter). Since this book is selective, covering only the places we think make the top month of sightseeing, we can update it each summer. Of course, even with an annual update, things change. But if you're traveling with the current edition of this book, we guarantee you're using the most up-to-date information available. This book will help you have an inexpensive, hassle-free trip. Use this year's edition. Saving a few bucks by traveling on old information is not smart. If you're packing an old book, you'll learn the seriousness of your mistake . . . in Europe. Your trip costs at least $10 per waking hour. Your time is valuable. This guidebook saves lots of time.

Planning Your Trip

This book is organized by destinations. Each of these destinations is a mini-vacation on its own, filled with exciting sights and homey, affordable places to stay. For each chapter, you'll find the following:

Planning Your Time, a suggested schedule with thoughts on how to best use your limited time.

Orientation material, including tourist information, city transportation, and an easy-to-read map designed to make the text clear and your arrival smooth.

Sights with ratings: ▲▲▲—Don't miss; ▲▲—Try hard to see; ▲—Worthwhile if you can make it; No rating—Worth knowing about.

Sleeping and **Eating**, with addresses, phone and fax numbers, and, when available, e-mail addresses of our favorite hotels and restaurants, from budget bargains to worthwhile splurges.

Transportation Connections to nearby destinations by train and route tips for drivers.

The handy **Appendix** includes telephone tips, a festival calendar, a climate chart, and French survival phrases.

Browse through this book, choose your favorite destinations, and link them up. You'll travel like a temporary local, getting the absolute most out of every mile, minute, and dollar. You won't waste time on mediocre sights because, unlike other guidebooks, we cover only the best. Since your major financial pitfall is lousy, expensive hotels, we've worked hard to assemble the best accommodation values for each stop. As you travel the route we know and love, we're happy you'll be meeting some of our favorite Europeans.

Trip Costs

Five components make up your total trip cost: airfare, surface transportation, room and board, sightseeing/entertainment, and shopping/miscellany.

Airfare: Don't try to sort through the mess. Find and use a good travel agent. A basic round-trip United States-to-Paris flight costs $700 to $1,100, depending on where you fly from and when. Always consider saving time and money in Europe by flying "open jaw" (into one city and out of another). Flying into Amsterdam and out of Paris costs roughly the same as flying round-trip to Paris. You can get cheaper round-trip flights to London or Amsterdam, but the cost of train tickets (to get you back to London or Amsterdam for your flight home) will eliminate most of your savings.

Surface Transportation: For a three-week whirlwind trip of our recommended destinations in France, allow $500 per person for public transportation (trains and key buses), or $600 per person (based on 2 people sharing) for a three-week car rental, tolls, gas, and insurance. Car rental is cheapest if arranged from the United States. Train passes are normally available only outside of Europe. You may save money by simply buying tickets as you go (see "Transportation," below).

Room and Board: You can thrive in France and the Low Countries on $65 a day per person for room and board (allow $75 a day for Paris). A $65-a-day budget allows $10 for lunch, $20 for dinner, and $35 for lodging (based on 2 people splitting the cost of a $70 double room that includes breakfast). That's doable. Students and tightwads do it on $35 to $40 ($20 per bed, $15–20 for meals and snacks). Budget sleeping and eating require the skills and information covered later in this chapter (and in far more depth in *Rick Steves' Europe Through the Back Door*).

Sightseeing and Entertainment: In big cities, figure $5 to $8 per major sight (Louvre-$8, Anne Frank House-$6), $2 for minor ones (climbing church towers), $10 for guided walks, and $25 for bus tours and splurge experiences (concerts in Paris' Sainte-Chapelle or a ride on the Chamonix gondola). An overall average of $15 a day works for most. Don't skimp here. After all, this category directly powers most of the experiences all the other expenses are designed to make possible.

Shopping and Miscellany: Figure $2 per ice-cream cone, coffee, or soft drink. Shopping can vary in cost from nearly nothing to a small fortune. Good budget travelers find that this category has little to do with assembling a trip full of lifelong and wonderful memories.

Prices, Times, and Discounts

The prices in this book, as well as the hours and telephone numbers, are accurate as of late 2000. Europe is always changing, and we know you'll understand that this, like any other guidebook, starts to yellow even before it's printed.

In Europe—and in this book—you'll be using the 24-hour clock. After 12:00 noon, keep going—13:00, 14:00, and so on. For anything over 12, subtract 12 and add p.m. (for example, 14:00 is 2 p.m.).

While discounts for sights and transportation are generally not listed in this book, seniors (60 and over), students (with International Student Identification Cards), and youths (under 18) often get big discounts—but only by asking.

Exchange Rates

We've priced things in this book in the local currency.

> **About $1 equals…**
> 6.50 French francs (F). One franc is worth about 15 cents.
> 45 Belgian francs (BF). One Belgian franc is worth less than 2 cents.
> 2.50 Dutch guilders (f). One guilder is worth about 40 cents.

To convert prices in francs into dollars, divide by six (160F = about $27). To convert Belgian francs into dollars, knock off the last digit and divide by two (235BF = about $12). For Dutch guilders, divide by two, then subtract 10 percent (f98 = about $40).

Euro: The euro, adopted as a currency by 11 countries in Europe, won't concern you until 2002, when it materializes into actual bills and coins. For a preview, France, Belgium, and the Netherlands will all convert to euros.

When to Go

Late spring and fall are best. Wildflowers proliferate in May and June, while September brings the grape harvest and drier weather. In late October France glistens in fall colors. Europeans vacation in July and August, jamming the Riviera and the Alps (August is worst), leaving the rest of the country reasonably tranquil. And while many French businesses close in August, the traveler hardly notices. Winter travel is OK—you'll find gray, generally mild weather in the south (unless the wind is blowing), cold weather in the north, and rain everywhere. While Holland is a festival of flowers in the spring, the Low Countries have considerably shorter summers and drearier winters than southern France. Sights and tourist information offices keep shorter hours, and some tourist activities (like English-language castle tours) vanish altogether.

Sightseeing Priorities

Depending on the length of your trip, here are our recommended priorities. The material in this book could keep you wonderfully entertained for at least a month in France, Belgium, and the Netherlands.

France:

3 days:	Paris and maybe Versailles
5 days, add:	Normandy
7 days, add:	The Loire
10 days, add:	Dordogne, Carcassonne
14 days, add:	Provence, the Riviera
18 days, add:	Burgundy, Chamonix
21 days, add:	Alsace, Champagne

For a day-by-day itinerary for this three-week trip, geared for drivers and train travelers, see the appendix (route map included).

Belgium and the Netherlands:

With cheap flights from the United States, minimal culture shock, almost no language barrier, and a well-organized tourist trade, the Low Countries are a good place to start a European trip.

2 days:	Amsterdam, Haarlem
3–4 days, add:	Bruges
5–6 days, add:	Brussels
7 days, add:	Side trips from Amsterdam (e.g., Enkhuisen, The Hague)

Red Tape and Business Hours

You need a passport but no visa or shots to travel in France, Belgium, and the Netherlands.

You'll find much of rural France closed weekdays from noon to 14:00 (lunch is sacred). On Sunday most French businesses are closed (family is sacred), though small markets such as *boulangeries* (bakeries) are open Sunday morning until noon, and museums are open all day. On Monday many businesses are closed until 14:00 and often all day. Saturdays are like weekdays. Beware: Many sights stop admitting people 30 to 60 minutes before they close.

PTT (Postal, Telegraph, and Telephone) offices' hours vary, though most are open weekdays from 8:00 to 19:00 and Saturday from 8:00 to noon. (Small-town PTTs close for lunch 12:00–14:00.) Stamps and phone cards are also sold at the *tabac* (tobacco shop). It costs 4.40F to mail a postcard to the United States.

Banking

Bring your ATM, credit, or debit card and some traveler's checks in dollars. Listed hotels rarely accept American Express.

The best and easiest way to get cash in French francs is to

use the omnipresent French bank machines (always open, lower fees, quick processing; you'll need a four-digit PIN—numbers only, no letters—with your Visa or MasterCard). Some ATM bankcards will work at some banks, though Visa and MasterCard are more reliable. Before you go, verify with your bank that your card will work. Bring two cards; demagnetization can be a problem. "Cash machine" in French is *"distributeur automatique des billets,"* or *D.A.B.* (day-ah-bay).

Regular banks usually have the best rates for cashing traveler's checks. For a large exchange it pays to compare rates and fees. Exchange rates and transaction fees can vary wildly. The Bank of France (Banque de France) offers the best rates but has branches only in larger cities. French banking hours vary, though most are open Monday through Friday from 9:00 to 16:30. Some branches open Saturday morning, and many are closed on Monday. Post offices, train stations, and tourist offices usually change money if you can't get to a bank. Post offices (which take cash or American Express traveler's checks) give a good rate, have longer hours, and charge no fee. Don't be petty about changing traveler's checks. The greatest avoidable money-changing expense is having to waste time every few days returning to a bank. Change 10 days' or two weeks' worth of money, get big bills, stuff them in your money belt, and travel!

Just like at home, credit (or debit) cards work easily at hotels, restaurants, and shops, but small businesses (like bed-and-breakfasts) accept payment only in local currency. Smart travelers function with hard local cash.

The Language Barrier

You've no doubt heard that the French are "mean and cold and refuse to speak English." This is an out-of-date preconception left over from the de Gaulle days. The French are as friendly as any other people. Parisians are no more disagreeable than New Yorkers. And, without any doubt, the French speak more English than Americans speak French. Be reasonable in your expectations: Waiters are paid to be efficient, not chatty. And small-town French postal clerks are every bit as speedy, cheery, and multi-lingual as ours are back home.

With an understanding of French culture, you're less likely to misinterpret the French people. The French take great pride in their culture, clinging to their belief in cultural superiority despite the fact that they're no longer a world superpower. Let's face it—it's tough to keep on smiling when you've been crushed by a Big Mac, Mickey-Moused by Disney, and drowned in instant coffee. To the French, Americans must seem a lot like Doris Day. The French are cold only if you decide to see them that way. Polite and formal, they respect the fine points of culture. In France,

strolling down the street with a big grin on your face is a sign
of senility, not friendliness (seriously). The French think that
Americans, while friendly, are hesitant to pursue more serious
friendships. Recognize sincerity and look for kindness. Give the
French the benefit of the doubt.

Communication difficulties in France are exaggerated.
To hurdle the language barrier, bring a small English/French
dictionary, a phrase book (look for ours), a menu reader, and a
good supply of patience. If you learn only five phrases, learn and
use these: *bonjour* (good day), *pardon* (pardon me), *s'il vous plaît*
(please), *merci* (thank you), and *au revoir* (goodbye). The French
place great importance on politeness. Begin every encounter
with *"Bonjour madame/monsieur"* and end every encounter with
"Au revoir madame/monsieur."

The French are language perfectionists—they take their
language (and other languages) seriously. Often they speak
more English than they let on. This isn't a tourist-baiting tactic
but is timidity on their part to speak another language less
than fluently. Start any conversation with *"Bonjour, madame/
monsieur. Parlez-vous anglais?"* and hope they speak more English
than you speak French. In transactions, a small notepad and
pen minimize misunderstandings about prices. Have vendors
write the price down.

In Belgium and the Netherlands, forget the language barrier.
Except in smaller, nontouristy towns, most young or well-
educated people speak English (along with other languages).
In southern Belgium, French is foremost; in northern Belgium
and the Netherlands it's Dutch, but English is a close second.

Travel Smart

Upon arrival in a new town, lay the groundwork for a smooth
departure. Reread this book as you travel and visit local tourist
information offices. Enjoy the friendliness of the local people.
Ask questions. Most locals are eager to tell you about their town's
history and point you in their idea of the right direction. Buy a
phone card and use it for reservations and confirmations. Wear
your money belt. Those who expect to travel smart, do.

Train travelers: Look for the tips on trains and buses later
in this chapter. Drivers: Read our driving tips and study the
examples of road signs in this chapter.

Maximize rootedness by minimizing one-night stands. Mix
intense and relaxed periods. Every trip (and every traveler) needs
at least a few slack days. Pace yourself. Assume you will return.

As you read through this book, note special days (festivals,
market days, and days when sights are closed). Plan ahead for
banking, laundry, post office chores, picnics, and Sundays
(particularly if traveling by train). Sundays have pros and cons,

as they do for travelers in the United States (special events and weekly markets, limited hours, shops and banks closed, limited public transportation, no rush hours). Saturdays are virtually weekdays. Popular places are even more popular on weekends and inundated on three-day weekends (most common in May).

Tourist Information

The tourist information office is your best first stop in any new city. If you're arriving in town after the office closes, try calling ahead or picking up a map in a neighboring town. In this book we refer to tourist offices as TIs (for Tourist Information). Through-out France and the Low Countries you'll find TIs are usually well organized and have English-speaking staffs. Most will help you find a room by calling hotels (for a small fee) or giving you a complete listing of available bed-and-breakfasts. Towns with a lot of tourism generally have English-speaking guides available for private hire (about $100 for a 90-minute guided town walk).

The French call their TIs by different names. Office de Tourisme and Bureau de Tourisme are used in cities, while Syndicat d'Initiative or Information Touristique are used in small towns. French TIs are often closed from noon to 14:00.

Tourist Offices, U.S. Addresses

Each country's national tourist office in the United States is a wealth of information. Before your trip, request any specific information you may want (such as city maps and schedules of upcoming festivals).

French Government Tourist Office: For general information, call 410/286-8310, check their Web site (www .francetourism.com), or contact the nearest office...

In New York: 444 Madison Avenue, 16th floor, New York, NY 10022, tel. 212/838-7800, e-mail: info@francetourism.com.

In Illinois: 676 North Michigan Avenue #3360, Chicago, IL 60611, brochure hotline tel. 312/751-7800, fax 312/337-6339, e-mail: fgto@mcs.net.

In California: 9454 Wilshire Boulevard #715, Beverly Hills, CA 90212, brochure hotline tel. 310/859-3486, fax 310/276-2835, e-mail: fgto@gte.net.

Belgian National Tourist Office: 780 Third Avenue #1501, New York, NY 10017, tel. 212/758-8130, fax 212/355-7675, www .visitbelgium.com, e-mail: info@visitbelgium.com. They have hotel and city guides, plus brochures for ABC lovers: antiques, beer, and chocolates.

Netherlands Board of Tourism: 355 Lexington Avenue, 19th floor, New York, NY 10017, tel. 888/GO-HOLLAND or 212/370-7360, fax 212/370-9507, www.holland.com, e-mail: info @goholland.com. Donation requested for information delivered within two weeks; materials delivered in three to four weeks are free. Ask for their great country map.

Recommended Guidebooks

Consider some supplemental travel information, especially if you're traveling beyond our recommended destinations. Considering the improvements they'll make in your $3,000 vacation, $25 or $35 for extra maps and books is money well spent. One simple budget tip can easily save the price of an extra guidebook.

France: Lonely Planet's *France* is well researched and packed with good maps and hotel recommendations for low- to moderate-budget travelers (but it's not updated annually). The highly opinionated, annually updated *Let's Go: France* (St. Martin's Press) is ideal for students and vagabonds. The popular skinny green Michelin guides are dry but informative, especially if you're driving. They're known for their city and sightseeing maps and for their concise and helpful information on all major sights. English editions, covering most of the regions you'll want to visit, are sold in France for about $12 (or $20 in the United States). Consider *Rick Steves' Paris* (see below). Of the multitude of other guidebooks on France and Paris, many are high on facts and low on opinion, guts, or personality. For background reading, consider *French or Foe* (by Polly Platt) and *Fragile Glory* (by Richard Bernstein).

Belgium and the Netherlands: For the same reason that this region only appears as an add-on to our France book, the Low Countries seem to fall through the cracks in most travel publishers' catalogs. You'll find skimpy chapters in the big all-Europe books or too much information in the various city or country guidebooks covering the region.

Rick Steves' Books and Videos

Rick Steves' Europe Through the Back Door 2001 gives you budget travel tips on minimizing jet lag, packing light, planning your itinerary, traveling by car or train, finding budget beds without reservations, changing money, avoiding rip-offs, outsmarting thieves, hurdling the language barrier, staying healthy, taking great photographs, using your bidet, and lots more. The book also includes chapters on 35 of Rick's favorite "Back Doors," three of which are in France and Belgium.

Rick Steves' Country Guides are a series of seven guidebooks—including this book—covering the Best of Europe; Britain/Ireland; Germany/Austria/Switzerland; Italy; Scandinavia; and Spain/Portugal. All are updated annually and come out in December.

Rick Steves' City Guides for Paris, London and Rome annually updated and available in January) give you all you'll need to make your trip a success: in-depth information on the sights, hotels, restaurants, and nightlife in these grand cities along with illustrated tours of their great museums.

Europe 101: History and Art for the Traveler (with Gene Openshaw, 2000) gives you the story of Europe's people, history, and art. Written for smart people who were sleeping in their history and art classes before they knew they were going to Europe, *101* really helps Europe's sights come alive.

Rick Steves' Mona Winks (with Gene Openshaw, 1998) gives you fun, easy-to-follow self-guided tours of Europe's top 20 museums, including Amsterdam's Rijksmuseum and Van Gogh Museum and Paris' Louvre, Orsay, and Palace of Versailles, and a walk through historic Paris.

My rigorously researched *Rick Steves' French Phrase Book* (1999) gives you the words and survival phrases you'll need while traveling in France and much of Belgium.

My public television series, *Travels in Europe with Rick Steves*, includes 11 half-hour shows on France, Belgium, and the Netherlands. A brand-new series, called *Rick Steves' Europe*, airs in 2001 with 16 shows, including one on Paris. All of the shows run throughout the United States on public television stations and on the Travel Channel. The shows are also available as information-packed videotapes, along with my 90-minute slideshow lecture on France, Belgium, and the Netherlands (call us at 425/771-8303 for our free newsletter/catalog).

Rick Steves' Postcards from Europe (1999), my autobiographical book, packs 25 years of travel anecdotes and insights into the ultimate 3,000-mile European adventure. Through my guidebooks, I share my favorite European discoveries with you. *Postcards* (some of which is set in France and the Netherlands) introduces you to my favorite European friends.

All of my books are published by Avalon Travel Publishing (www.travelmatters.com).

Maps

The maps in this book, drawn by Dave Hoerlein, are concise and simple. Dave, who is well traveled in France and the Low Countries, has designed the maps to help you locate recommended places and get to the TIs, where you'll find more in-depth maps (often free) of the cities or regions. For an overall map of Europe, consider my new Rick Steves' Europe Planning Map—geared to travelers' needs—with sightseeing destinations listed prominently (for our free newsletter/catalog, contact us at 425/771-8303 or www.ricksteves.com).

Don't skimp on maps. Michelin maps are available throughout France at bookstores, newsstands, and gas stations (for 26F, half the U.S. price). Train travelers can do fine with Michelin's #989 France map (1:1,000,000). For better detail, pick up the yellow 1:200,000-

scale maps as you travel. Drivers should consider the soft-cover
Michelin France atlas (the entire country at 1:200,000, well organized in a $20 book with an index and maps of major cities). Learn
the Michelin key to get the most sightseeing value out of their maps.

Tours of France by Rick Steves and Steve Smith

Travel agents can tell you about all the normal tours, but they
won't tell you about ours. At Europe Through the Back Door,
we organize and lead tours covering the highlights of this book.
Choose among a 14-day *Feast of the East*, a 14-day *Best of the West*,
or the 20-day *Best of Village France*. These depart each year from
April through October, are limited to 26 people per group, and
have two guides and big roomy buses. We also offer one-week
winter getaways to Paris. For details, call us at 425/771-8303 or
check www.ricksteves.com.

Transportation

By Car or Train?

Cars are best for three or more traveling together (especially
families with small kids), those packing heavy, and those scouring
the countryside. Trains and buses are best for solo travelers,
blitz tourists, and city-to-city travelers. We have significantly
improved information for train travelers in recent editions.

Trains

Train stations are usually centrally located in cities, making hotel
hunting and sightseeing easier. Schedules change by season, weekday, and weekend. Verify train schedules shown in this book (to
study ahead on the Web, check http://bahn.hafas.de/english.html).

For France, the nationwide information line for train schedules
and reservations is 08 36 35 35 35; ask for an English-speaking
agent. This helpful timesaving service costs 2.20F per minute
from anywhere in France (call to confirm schedules and make
TGV reservations, allow 5 minutes per call). The message prompts
you to push "9" for a sales agent and "*" for information only.

France's rail system (SNCF) sets the pace in Europe. Its super
TGV system has inspired bullet trains throughout the world. The
TGV runs at 170 to 220 mph. Its rails are fused into one long, con-
tinuous track for a faster and smoother ride. The TGV has changed
commuting patterns in much of France and put most of the country
within day-trip distance of Paris. The Eurostar English Channel
tunnel train to Britain and the Thalys bullet train to Brussels are two
more links in the grand European train system of the 21st century.

The most economical railpass for a focused tour of France,
Belgium, and the Netherlands is the new Eurail Selectpass for $476,
which gives you 10 travel days (within a 2-month period) in three

The French Rail System

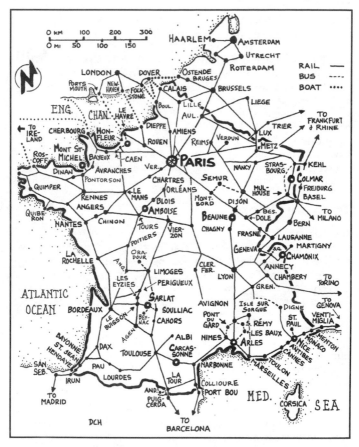

adjacent countries. Other railpass possibilities include a five-country Europass (with BeNeLux added) or a pricey 17-country Eurailpass (best for a whirlwind trip of Europe). All of these passes give a 15 percent discount to two or more companions traveling together.

Those traveling solely in France will save money with a France Railpass (available only outside France, through travel agents or Europe Through the Back Door; call us at 425/771-8303 for our free railpass guide or find it at www.ricksteves.com). For about the cost of a Paris-Avignon-Paris ticket, the France Railpass offers three days of travel (within a month) anywhere in France. Add up to six additional days for the cost of a two-hour ride each. (The Flexi Saver gives two traveling together a

25 percent discount.) Each day of use allows you to take as many trips as you want in a 24-hour period (you could go from Paris to Chartres, see the cathedral, then continue to Avignon, stay a few hours, and end in Nice). Buy second-class tickets in France for shorter trips and spend your valuable railpass days wisely.

If traveling *sans* railpass, inquire about the many point-to-point discount fares possible (for youths, those over 60, married couples, families, travel during off-peak hours, and more). While Eurailers (over 26) automatically travel first class, those buying individual tickets should remember that second-class tickets, available to people of any age, provide the same transportation for 33 percent less.

Reservations are generally unnecessary for local trains but are required for any TGV train (generally 20–60F) and for *couchettes* (berths, 100F) on night trains. Even railpass holders need reservations for the TGV trains. To avoid the more expensive reservation fees, avoid traveling at peak times; ask at the station. Validate (*composter*) all train tickets and reservations in the orange machines located before the platforms. (Watch others and imitate.)

For mixing train and bike travel, ask at stations for information booklets: *Train + Velo* (France) and *Treins en Fiets* (the Netherlands).

Cars, Rail 'n' Drive Passes, and Buses

Car rental is cheapest if arranged in advance through your home-town travel agent. The best rates are weekly with unlimited mileage or leasing (see below). You can pick up and drop off just about anywhere, anytime. Big companies have offices in most cities. Small rental companies can be cheaper but aren't as flexible.

When you drive a rental car you are liable for its replacement value. CDW (Collision-Damage Waiver) insurance gives you the peace of mind that comes with a zero- or low-deductible coverage for about $15 a day. A few "gold" credit cards provide this coverage for free if you use their card for the rental; quiz your credit-card company on the worst-case scenario. Or consider the $6 a day policy offered by Travel Guard (U.S. tel. 800/826-1300, www.travelguard.com).

For a trip of three weeks or more, leasing is a bargain. By technically buying and then selling back the car, you save lots of money on tax and insurance (CDW is included). Leasing, which you should arrange from the United States, usually requires a 22-day minimum contract, but Europe by Car leases cars in France for as few as 17 days for $500 (U.S. tel. 800/223-1516, www.europebycar.com). Belgium and the Netherlands are also particularly good for leasing.

You can rent a car on the spot just about anywhere. In many cases this is a worthwhile splurge. All you need is your American

Cost of Public Transportation

My free *Rick Steves' Guide to European Railpasses* has the latest on 2001 prices. To get the railpass guide, call us at 425/771-8303 or visit www.ricksteves.com/rail (you can order most passes online).

FRANCE FLEXIPASS (2000)

	1st class	2nd class
Any 3 days in a month	$210	$180
France Flexi Saver*	171	146
Any 4 days in 2 months Youth (2nd cl)**		164

Extra days $30 (6 max). Kids 4-11: half adult fare.

*3 days in a month, per person for 2 or more people traveling together on all journeys (no kids discounts). Extra days $30 (6 max).

**Must be under age 26. Extra days $20 (6 max).

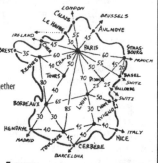

FRANCE RAIL & DRIVE PASS (2000)

Any 3 days of rail and 2 days of Avis rental car in a month.

Car category	1st class	2nd class	Extra car day
Economy	$199	$175	$49
Compact	209	185	55
Intermediate	220	199	70
Small automatic	229	205	79

France:
The map shows approximate point-to-point one-way 2nd class rail fares in $US. Add up fares for your itinerary to see whether a railpass will save you money.

Rail and Drive prices are approximate per person, two traveling together. Solo travelers pay about $100 extra, third and fourth members of a group need only buy the equivalent flexi railpass. Extra rail days (7 max) cost $30 per day for first or second class. You can add up to 6 extra car days. To order a France Rail & Drive pass, call your travel agent or Rail Europe at 800/438-7245.

driver's license and money (about 400F, or $65, for a day, with 100 kilometers included). Campanje, a Dutch company, specializes in used VW campers fully loaded for camping through Europe. Rates run about $470 per week for a four-person camper (less for long-term rentals), including tax and insurance. Ask about discounts for early booking and off-season and long-term rental (P.O. Box 9332, 3506 GH Utrecht, Netherlands, tel. 31/30-244-7070, fax 31/30-242-0981, www.xs4all.nl/~campanje, e-mail: campanje@xs4all.nl).

Rail 'n' drive passes allow you to economically mix car and train travel (available only outside of France, from your travel agent). Generally, big-city connections are best done by train and rural regions are best done by car. With a rail 'n' drive pass you get an economic "flexi" railpass with "flexi" car days. This allows you to combine rail and drive into one pass—you can take advantage of the high speed and comfort of the TGV trains for longer trips and rent a car for as little as one day at a time for those regions that are difficult to get around in without one (like the Loire, the Dordogne, and Provence), all for a very reasonable package price. Within the same country, you can pick a car up in one city and drop it off in another city with no problem. While

Train Tips

- Arrive at the station with plenty of time before your departure to find the right platform, confirm connections, and so on. In small towns, your train may depart before the station opens, in which case you should go directly to the tracks and find the overhead sign that confirms your train stops at that track.
- Check schedules in advance. Upon arrival at a station, find out your departure possibilities. Large stations have a separate information window or office; at small stations, the regular ticket office gives information.
- Write the date on your "flexi" pass each day you travel.
- Validate tickets (not passes) and reservations in orange machines before boarding. If you're traveling with a pass and have a reservation for a particular trip (e.g., TGV), you must validate the reservation.
- When getting on a train, confirm that it's going where you think it is. For example, ask the conductor or any local passenger on the platform, "Ah Bayeux?" (To Bayeux?).
- Some trains split cars en route. Make sure your train car is continuing to your destination by asking, "Set vwa-ture vah ah Bayeux?" ("This car goes to Bayeux?").
- If a seat is reserved, it will be labeled *réservé*, with the cities to and from which it is reserved.
- Verify with the conductor all transfers you must make ("Correspondance ah?" means "Transfer where?").
- To guard against theft, keep your bags right overhead; don't store them on the racks at the end of the car.
- Note your arrival time so you'll be ready to get off.
- Use the trains' free WCs before you get off (a bird in the hand).

Bus Tips

- Year-round, service is sparse on Sunday. Wednesday bus schedules are often different during the school year.
- Be at stops at least five minutes early.
- On schedules, "*en semaine*" means Monday through Saturday.

Key Phrases

- *Bonjour, monsieur/madame, parlez vous anglais?* Phonetics: bohn-zhoor, muhs-yur/mah-dahm, par-lay-voo ahn-glay? Meaning: Hello, sir/madame, do you speak English?
- *Je voudrais un depart pour* ___ (destination), *pour le* ___ (date), *vers* ___ (general time of day), *la plus direct possible*. Phonetics: zhuh voo-dray day-par poor ___ (destination), poor luh ___ (date), vayr ___ (time), lah ploo dee-rek poh-see-bluh. Meaning/Example: I would like a departure for Amboise, on 23 May, about 9:00, the most direct way possible.

you're only required to reserve the first car day, it's safer to reserve all days, as cars are not always available on short notice.

Regional buses take over where the trains stop. You can get almost anywhere by rail and bus if you're well organized and patient. Review our bus schedule information and always verify times at the tourist office or bus station, calling ahead when possible. A few bus lines are run by SNCF (France's rail system) and are included with your railpass, but most bus lines are independent of the rail system and are not covered by railpasses. Train stations often have bus information where train-to-bus connections are important— and vice versa for bus companies. On Sunday regional bus service virtually disappears.

Regional minivan excursions offer organized day tours of regions where bus and train service is useless. For the D-Day beaches, châteaux of the Loire Valley, the *Route du Vin* in the Alsace, and wine tasting in Burgundy, we list companies providing this helpful service at reasonable rates. Some of these minivan excursions offer just transportation between the sights; others add a running commentary and regional history.

Driving

An international driver's license is not necessary for France, Belgium, and the Netherlands. Seat belts are mandatory, and children under age 10 must be in the back seat. Gas (*essence*) is expensive—about $4.50 per gallon. Diesel (*gazole*) is less—about $3.50 per gallon. It's worth renting a diesel car if you can. Gas is most expensive on autoroutes and cheapest at big supermarkets. Many gas stations close on Sunday.

Go metric. A liter is about a quart, four to a gallon. A kilometer is six-tenths of a mile. I figure kilometers to miles by cutting them in half and adding back 10 percent of the original (120 km: 60 + 12 = 72 miles, 300 km: 150 + 30 = 180 miles).

Four hours of autoroute tolls cost about $20, but the alternative to these super "feeways" is often being marooned in rural traffic. Autoroutes usually save enough time, gas, and nausea to justify the splurge. Mix high-speed "autorouting" with scenic country-road rambling (be careful of sluggish tractors on country roads).

Roads in France are classified into departmental (D), national (N), and autoroutes (A). D routes (usually yellow lines on maps) are slow and often the most scenic. N routes (usually red lines) are the fastest after autoroutes (orange lines). Green road signs are for national routes; blue are for autoroutes. There are plenty of good facilities, gas stations, and rest stops along most French roads.

Here are a few French road tips: In city centers, traffic merging from the right normally has the right of way (*priorité à droite*). Approach intersections cautiously. When navigating through cities, stow the map and follow the signs to *centre-ville* (downtown)

Standard European Road Signs

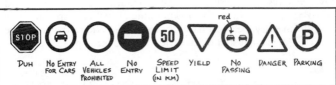

and from there to the tourist information office (*Office de Tourisme*). When leaving (or just passing through), follow the signs for *Toutes Directions* or *Autres Directions* (meaning anywhere else) until you see a sign for your specific destination. While the French are eating (12:00–14:00), many sights (and gas stations) are closed, so you can make great time driving. The French drive fast and live to tailgate.

Parking is a headache in the larger cities, and theft is a problem throughout France. Ask your hotelier for ideas, and pay to park at well-patrolled lots (blue "P" signs direct you to parking lots in French cities). Or use the parking meters, which are usually free 12:30 to 14:00 and 19:00 to 9:00 and in August. Individual meters don't exist. Look instead for the small machine selling time (called *horadateur*), plug in a few coins (about 5F gets an hour), push the

Quick-and-Dirty Road Sign Translation

Céder le Passage: Yield
Centre Commercial: Grouping of large, suburban stores (not city center)
Centre-Ville: City center
Doublage Interdit: No passing
Feu: Traffic signal
Horadateur: Remote parking meter, usually at the end of the block
Parc de Stationnement: Parking lot
Parking/Stationnement Interdit: No parking
Priorité à Droite: Right of way
Rue Pietonne: Pedestrian-only street
Sauf Riverains: Local access only

Signs Unique to Autoroutes:

Bouchon: Traffic jam ahead
Fluide: No slowing ahead, fluid conditions
Peage: Toll
Telepeage: Toll booths—for locals with automatic toll payment only
Toutes/Autres Directions: All/other directions (leaving city)

green button and get a receipt showing the amount of time you have, then display it inside your windshield. Keep a pile of 1F and 2F coins in your ashtray for parking meters, public restrooms, and Laundromat dryers. Most parking structures require that you take a ticket and pre-pay at a machine just before leaving.

Biking

Throughout France and the Low Countries you'll find areas where public transportation is limited and bicycle touring is an excellent idea. We've listed bike-rental shops where appropriate. The TI will always have addresses. For a good touring bike, allow about $12 for a half day and $18 for a full day. You're always better off paying a bit more for better equipment; generally the best is available through bike shops, not at TIs or train stations. Before committing to an extensive ride, think how long it's been since you've spent all day on a bike. It can make sense to start with an easy ride.

Telephones, Mail, and E-mail

An efficient card-operated system has virtually replaced coin-operated public phones throughout Europe. Each country offers phone cards good for use only in telephones within its borders (though you can use it for international calls). Insert the card in the phone and dial away.

France: Buy a phone card (*une télécarte*) from any post office or train station or from most newsstands and tobacco shops (*tabac*). Pick up a *télécarte* at the beginning of your trip and use it for hotel reservations, calling TIs, and phoning home. France has two denominations of phone cards: *une petite* costs 48F; *une grande* is 99F. When you use the *télécarte* (simply take the phone off the hook, insert the card, and wait for a dial tone) the price of the call (local or international) is automatically deducted. France's latest phone card (KOSMOS) is not inserted into the phone but allows you to dial from the comfort of your hotel (or anywhere) and charge the call to the card for lower rates than with a *télécarte* (50F and 100F cards available). It's simple to use, instructions are provided in English, and the card is sold wherever *télécartes* are sold. And while per-minute rates are cheaper with KOSMOS than a *télécarte*, it's slower to use (more numbers to dial), so local calls are quicker with a *télécarte* from a phone booth.

Despite the expense, some travelers prefer to use American calling cards (AT&T, MCI, and Sprint numbers listed in appendix). Calling-card calls were a fine deal until direct-dial rates were cut in half. Now it's cheaper to make your international calls using a European phone card (whether French or KOSMOS, Belgian, or Dutch). Definitely avoid using your American calling card for calls between European countries; it's far cheaper to call direct.

France has a dial-direct 10-digit telephone system. There are no area codes. To call to or from anywhere in France, including Paris, you dial the 10 numbers directly.

To call France from another country, start with the international access code of the country you're calling from (00 for European countries and 011 from the United States and Canada), dial France's country code (33), and then drop the initial zero of the 10 digit local number and dial the remaining nine digits. For example, the phone number of one of our favorite hotels in Paris is 01 47 05 49 15. To call it from home, dial 011-33-1 47 05 49 15.

To dial out of France, start your call with its international code (00), then dial the country code of the country you're calling. To call our office in the United States, dial 00 (France's international access code), 1 (U.S. country code), then 425/771-8303 (our area code plus local number). For a list of international access codes and country codes, see the appendix. European time is six/nine hours ahead of the east/west coast of the United States.

Belgium and the Netherlands: Both countries use area codes throughout. For instance, Bruges' area code is 050. To call Bruges long distance from within Belgium, dial 050, then the local number. When calling from another country, drop the first zero in the area code. Calling Bruges from Amsterdam, you'd dial 00 (the Netherlands' international access code), 32 (Belgium's country code), 50 (Bruges' area code without the zero), then the local number.

Mail: To arrange for mail delivery, reserve a few hotels along your route in advance and give their addresses to friends. Or you can use American Express Company's mail services (available to anyone who has at least one American Express traveler's check). Allow 10 days for a letter to arrive. Phoning is so easy that we've dispensed with mail stops altogether.

E-mail: E-mail use among European hoteliers is increasing. We've listed e-mail addresses whenever available. Cybercafés are popular in most cities, giving you reasonably inexpensive and easy Internet access.

Sleeping

In France and the Low Countries, accommodations are a good value and easy to find. Choose from one- or two-star hotels, bed-and-breakfasts, hostels, and campgrounds. We like places that are clean, small, central, traditional, inexpensive, friendly, and not listed in other guidebooks. Most places we list have at least five of these seven virtues.

Hotels

In this book the price for a double room will normally range from $30 (very simple, toilet and shower down the hall) to $140 (maximum plumbing and more), with most clustering around $60. Rates

Sleep Code

To give maximum information in a minimum of space, we use these codes to describe accommodations listed in this book. Prices listed are per room, not per person.

   S = Single room (or price for one person in a double).
   D = Double or Twin. French double beds can be very small.
   T = Triple (generally a double bed with a single).
   Q = Quad (usually two double beds).
   b = Private bathroom with toilet and shower or tub.
   t = Private toilet only. (The shower is down the hall.)
   s = Private shower or tub only. (The toilet is down the hall.)
 CC = Accepts credit cards (**V**isa, **M**asterCard, **A**merican Express). If CC isn't mentioned, assume you'll need to pay cash.
 SE = Speaks English. This code is used only when it seems predictable that you'll encounter English-speaking staff.
NSE = Does not speak English. Used only when it's unlikely you'll encounter English-speaking staff.
   * = French hotel rating system, ranging from zero to four stars.

According to this code, a couple staying at a "Db-450F, CC:V, SE" hotel would pay a total of 450 French francs (or about $70) for a double room with a private bathroom. The hotel accepts Visa or French cash in payment, and the staff speaks English.

are higher in Paris and other popular cities. A triple and a double are often the same room, with a small double bed and a sliver single, so a third person sleeps very cheaply. Most hotels have a few singles, triples, and quads. While groups sleep cheap, traveling alone can be expensive—a single room usually costs about the same as a double.

French receptionists often don't mention the cheaper rooms. Study the room price list posted at the desk. Understand it. You'll save an average of $15 if you get a room with a shower "down the hall" rather than in your room; ask for a room without a shower (*sans douche*) rather than with a shower (*avec douche*). A room with a bathtub (*salle de bain*) costs $5 to $10 more than a room with a shower (*douche*) and is generally larger. A double bed (*grand lit*) is $5 to $10 cheaper than twins (*deux petits lits*), though rooms with twin beds tend to be larger and French double beds are generally smaller than American double beds. Queen-size beds are rare. Hotels often have more rooms with tubs than showers and are inclined to give you a room with a tub (which the French prefer). If you prefer a double bed and a shower, you need to ask for it—and you'll save up to $20. If you'll take twins or a double, ask for a *chambre pour deux* (room for two) to avoid being needlessly turned away.

The French have a simple hotel rating system (0–4 stars) that depends on the amenities offered. We like the one- or two-star hotels and the occasional three-star hotel. More than two stars generally gets you expensive and unnecessary amenities. Unclassified hotels (no stars) can be bargains or depressing dumps. Look before you leap and lay before you pay (upon departure). Hotels in France must charge a daily tax (*tax du séjour*) that is normally added to the bill. It varies from 3F to 6F per day depending on the number of stars the hotel has. While some hotels include it in the price list, most add it to your bill.

You'll have the option of breakfast at your hotel, which is pleasant and convenient, but paying 35F for coffee, croissant, and bread is not a great value. Some hotels offer a buffet breakfast (about 50F), adding cereals, fruit, cheese, and yogurt alongside the bread and croissants. While it's pricey, we usually spring for it. Hotels rarely require you to have breakfast and many travelers enjoy their coffee and croissant for less at the corner café.

Some hotels strongly encourage their peak-season guests to take half-pension; that is, breakfast and either lunch or dinner. By law, they can't require you to take half-pension unless you are staying three or more nights, but in effect, many do. While the food is usually good, it limits your ability to shop around. We've indicated where we think *demi-pension* is a good value.

France is littered with inexpensive, sterile, ultramodern hotels, usually located on cheap land just outside of town, providing drivers with low-stress accommodations. The antiseptically clean and cheap Formule 1 chain (150–250F per room for up to 3 people) and the more hotelesque Ibis hotels (330–430F for a double, www.ibishotel.com) are most popular. While far from quaint, these can be a fine value.

Rooms are safe. Still, keep cameras and money out of sight. Towels aren't routinely replaced every day; drip-dry and conserve. If that French Lincoln-log pillow isn't your idea of comfort, American-style pillows (and extra blankets) are usually in the closet or available on request. For a pillow, ask for "*un oreiller, s'il vous plaît*" (un oar-ray-yay, see-voo-play). Many hotels will ask you to sign their *Livre d'Or* (a book for client comments). They take this seriously and enjoy reading your comments.

Making Reservations

It's possible to travel at any time of year without reservations, but given the high stakes, erratic accommodations values, and the quality of the gems we've found for this book, we'd highly recommend calling ahead for rooms several days in advance.

If you know exactly which dates you need and really want a particular place, reserve before you leave home. This is especially important for Paris, which can be tight anytime (May, June, September, and October are worst).

If you prefer to book rooms as you go, make a habit of calling between 10:00 and 11:00 on the day you plan to arrive, when the hotelier knows who'll be checking out and just which rooms will be available.

Don't be afraid to call. We've taken great pains to list telephone numbers with long-distance instructions (see "Telephones and Mail," above, and the appendix). Most hotels listed are accustomed to English-only speakers. A hotel receptionist will trust you and hold a room until 16:00 without a deposit, though some will ask for a credit-card number. Please honor (or cancel by phone) your reservations. *If you must cancel, give at least two days notice.* These family-run businesses lose money if they turn away customers while holding a room for someone who doesn't show up. Long distance is cheap and easy from public phone booths. Don't let these people down—we promised you'd call and cancel if for some reason you won't show up. Don't needlessly confirm rooms through the tourist office; they'll take a commission.

When reserving from home, phone and fax costs are reasonable, e-mail is a steal, and simple English works. To fax, use the form in the appendix (online at www.ricksteves.com/reservation). If you're writing a letter, add the zip code and confirm the need and method for a deposit. A two-night stay in August would be "two nights, 16/8/01 to 18/8/01"—Europeans write the date as day/month/year, and European hotel jargon uses your day of departure.

If you send a reservation request and receive a response with rates stating that rooms are available, this is not a confirmation. You must confirm that the rates are fine and that indeed you want the room. One night's deposit is generally required. A credit card will usually be accepted as a deposit, though you may need to send a signed traveler's check or a bank draft in the local currency. If you give your credit-card number for the deposit, the hotel may bill one night's stay to your card (most let you know this in advance). Don't give your credit card number as a deposit unless you're absolutely sure you want to stay there on the dates you requested and are clear that they have a room available. If you don't show up, you'll be billed for one night, and if you cancel in advance, you may not receive your entire deposit back. Reconfirm your reservations a few days in advance for safety.

Bed-and-Breakfasts

B&Bs offer double the cultural intimacy for a good deal less than most hotel rooms. This book and local TIs list B&Bs.

France: *Chambres d'hôte* (CH) are found mainly in the smaller towns and the countryside. They are listed by the owner's family name. While some post small *"Chambres"* or *"Chambres d'hôte"* signs in their front windows, many are found only through the local tourist office. We list reliable CHs that offer a good value and/or unique experience (such as CHs in renovated mills, châteaus, and wine *domaines*). Doubles with breakfast generally cost between 200F and 300F (breakfast may or may not be included—ask). While your hosts will rarely speak English, they will almost always be enthusiastic and delightful.

Belgium and the Netherlands: B&Bs in the Low Countries are common in well-touristed areas. Hosts usually speak English and are interesting conversationalists. Local TIs can book you into a B&B much cheaper than a hotel (though it's even cheaper to use our B&B listings and book direct). B&Bs are more important for budget travelers here than in France.

Hostels

Hostels charge about $14 per bed. Get a hostel card before you go (contact Hostelling International, tel. 202/783-6161, www .hiayh.org). Travelers of any age are welcome if they don't mind dorm-style accommodations or meeting other travelers. Travelers without a hostel card can generally spend the night for a small extra "one-night membership" fee. Cheap meals are sometimes available, and kitchen facilities are usually provided for do-it-yourselfers. Expect youth groups in spring, crowds in the summer, snoring, and incredible variability in quality from one hostel to the next. Family rooms are sometimes available on request, but it's basically boys' dorms and girls' dorms. You usually can't check in before 17:00 and must be out by 10:00. There is often a 23:00 curfew. Official hostels are marked with a triangular sign that shows a house and a tree. In France ask for an *auberge de jeunesse*.

Camping

In Europe camping is more of a social than an environmental experience. It's a great way for American travelers to make European friends. Camping costs about $12 per campsite per night, and almost every destination recommended in this book has a campground within a reasonable walk or bus ride from the town center and train station. A tent and sleeping bag are all you need. Many campgrounds have small grocery stores and washing machines, and some even come with discos and miniature golf. Hot showers are better at campgrounds than at many hotels. Local TIs have camping information. You'll find more detailed information in the *Michelin Camping Guide* (available at most French bookstores) or the thorough *Guide Officiel Camping/Caravaning* (Fédération Française de Camping et de Caravaning).

Eating in France

The French eat long and well. Relaxed lunches, three-hour dinners, and endless hours sitting in outdoor cafés are the norm. They have a legislated 35-hour workweek and a self-imposed 36-hour eat-week. Local cafés, cuisine, and wines become a highlight of any French adventure—sightseeing for your palate. Even if the rest of you is sleeping in cheap hotels, let your taste buds travel first-class in France. (They can go coach in England.) You can eat well without going broke—but choose carefully: You're just as likely to blow a small fortune on a mediocre meal as you are to dine wonderfully for $15.

Breakfast

Petit déjeuner (puh-tee day-zhu-nay) is typically *café au lait*, hot chocolate, or tea; a roll with butter and marmalade; and a croissant. We carry fruit and a package of Vache Qui Rit (Laughing Cow) cheese to supplement the morning marmalade. While breakfasts are available at your hotel (about 35F), they're cheaper at corner cafés (no coffee refills). It's fine to buy a croissant or roll at a bakery and eat it with your cup of coffee at a café. If your hotel offers a buffet breakfast (usually cereal, yogurt, cheese, fruit, and bread), spring for it. If the morning egg urge gets the best of you, drop into a café and order *une omelette* or *oeufs sur le plat* (fried eggs). You could also buy or bring plastic bowls and spoons from home, buy a box of French cereal and a small box of milk, and eat in your room before heading out for coffee.

Picnics

For most lunches—*déjeuner* (day-zhu-nay)—we picnic or munch a take-away sandwich from a *boulangerie* (bakery), or a crepe from a crêperie.

French picnics can be first-class affairs and adventures in high cuisine. Be daring. Try the smelly cheeses, ugly pâtés, sissy quiches, and minuscule yogurts. Local shopkeepers are accustomed to selling small quantities of produce. Try the tasty salads to go and ask for a plastic fork (*une fourchette en plastique*; oon foor-shet en plah-steek).

Gather supplies early; you'll want to visit several small stores to assemble a complete meal, and many close at noon. Look for a *boulangerie*, a *crémerie* (cheeses), a *charcuterie* (deli items, meats, and pâtés), an *épicerie* or *alimentation* (small grocery with veggies, drinks, and so on), and a *pâtisserie* (delicious pastries). Open-air markets (*marchés*) are fun and photogenic and close about noon (local TIs have details). Local *supermarchés* offer less color and cost, more efficiency, and adequate quality. Department stores often have supermarkets in the basement. On the outskirts of cities you'll find the monster *hypermarchés*. Drop in for a glimpse of hyper-France in action.

Café Culture

French cafés (or brasseries) provide light meals and a refuge from museum and church overload. They are carefully positioned spots from which to watch the river of local life flow by. It's easier to sit and feel comfortable in a café when you know the system.

Check the price list first. Prices, which must be posted prominently, vary wildly between cafés. Cafés charge different prices for the same drink depending upon where you want to be seated. Prices are posted: *comptoir* (counter/bar) and the more expensive *salle* (seated). Don't pay for your drink at the bar if you want to sit at a table (as you might do at home).

Your waiter won't overwhelm you with friendliness. Notice how hard they work. They almost never stop. Cozying up to clients (French or foreign) is probably the last thing on their minds.

The standard menu items are the *croque monsieur* (grilled ham and cheese sandwich) and *croque madame* (*monsieur* with a fried egg on top). The *salade composée* (sah-lahd com-po-zay) is a hearty chef's salad. Sandwiches are least expensive but plain unless you buy them at the *boulangerie* (bakery). To get more than a piece of ham (*jambon*) on a baguette, order a sandwich *jambon-crudité* (crew-dee-tay), which means garnished with lettuce, tomatoes, cucumbers, and so on. Omelets come lonely on a plate with a basket of bread. The *plat du jour* (daily special) is your fast, hearty 50F-to-60F hot plate. Regardless of what you order, bread is free; to get more, just hold up your bread basket and ask, "*Encore, s'il vous plaît.*" While prices include service, tip, and tax, it's polite to round up for a drink or meal well served (e.g., if your bill is 24F, leave 25F).

If you order coffee, here's the lingo:

- *un express* (uh nex-press) = shot of espresso
- *une noisette* (oon nwah-zette) = espresso with a shot of milk
- *café au lait* = coffee with lots of milk. Also called *un grand crème* (uh grahn krem; big) or *un petit crème* (uh puh-tee krem; average)
- *un café allongé* (uh kah-fay ah-low-zhay) = cup of coffee, closest to American-style
- *un décaffiné* (uh day-kah-fee-nay) = decaf; can modify any of the above drinks

Note: By law the waiter must give you a glass of tap water with your coffee if you request it; ask for "*Un verre d'eau, s'il vous plaît*" (uh vayr dough, see voo play).

Restaurants

Choose restaurants filled with locals, not places with big neon ∎∎∎s boasting, "We Speak English." Consider our suggestions and your hotelier's opinion but trust your instinct. If the menu (*la carte*) isn't posted outside, move along. Refer to our restaurant recommendations to get a sense of what a reasonable meal should cost.

La carte is the menu; if you ask for *le menu*, you'll get a fixed-price meal. This fixed-price *menu* gives you a choice of soup, appetizer, or salad (*entrée*); a choice of three or four main courses (*plat principal*) with vegetables; plus a cheese course and/or a choice of desserts. (The same *menu* can cost 40F more at dinner.) Most restaurants offer a reasonable *menu-enfant* (kids' menu). Service is included, but wine or drinks are generally extra. Wines are often listed in a separate *carte des vins*; ask for *un vin ordinaire* (van or-din-air) if all you want is table wine. Tipping (*pourboire*) is unnecessary as service is always included, though if you enjoyed the service it's polite to leave a few francs (10F per person if you really appreciated the service, none if you didn't).

If you'd prefer ordering *à la carte*, ask the waiter for help in deciphering *la carte*. Go with the waiter's recommendations and anything *de la maison* (of the house), unless it's organ meat (*tripes, rognons, andouillette*). Galloping gourmets should bring a menu translator (the *Marling Menu Master* is excellent).

Remember, the *entrée* is the first course and *le plat principal* is the main course. *Le plat du jour* (plate of the day) is usually a one-course (main) daily special served with vegetables (usually 50–70F), served all day at bistros and cafés but only at lunch (when available) at restaurants. Soft drinks and beer cost 8F to 20F ($1.50–3.50), and a bottle or carafe of house wine—which is invariably good enough for Rick, if not always Steve—costs 30F to 70F ($6–14). To get a waiter's attention, simply say, "*S'il vous plaît.*"

Restaurants are generally a far better value in the country-side than in Paris. If you're driving, look for red-and-blue *Relais Routier* decals, indicating that the place is recommended by the truckers' union.

Drinks

In stores, unrefrigerated soft drinks and beer are one-third the price of cold drinks. Milk and boxed fruit juice are the cheapest drinks. Avoid buying drinks to go at streetside stands; you'll find them far cheaper in a shop. Try to keep a water bottle with you. Water quenches your thirst better and cheaper than anything you'll find in a store or café. We drink tap water throughout France and the Low Countries.

The French often order bottled water with their meal (*eau minérale*; oh mee-nay-rahl). If you'd rather get a free pitcher of tap water, ask for *une carafe d'eau* (oon kah-rahf doh). Otherwise, you may unwittingly buy bottled water.

To save money when ordering a beer at a café or restaurant, ask for a beer on tap (*une pression*; oon pres-yon) or a draft beer (*un demi;* uh duh-mee); either is less expensive than a bottled beer. House wine is cheaper by the "pitcher" (*pichet*; pee-shay) than a bottle (*bouteille;* boo-teh-ee). If all you want is a glass of wine (about 5–14F), ask for *un verre de vin* (uh vehr duh van).

You could drink away your children's inheritance if you're not careful. The most famous wines are the most expensive, while lesser-known taste-alikes remain a bargain (see our regional suggestions in each chapter). If you like brandy, try a *marc* (regional brandy, e.g., *marc de Bourgogne*) or an Armagnac, cognac's cheaper twin brother. *Pastis*, the standard *apéritif*, is a sweet anise or licorice drink that comes on the rocks with a glass of water. Cut it to taste with lots of water. France's best beer is Alsatian; also try Krônenburg or the heavier Pelfort. *Une panaché* (pan-a-shay) is a very refreshing French shandy (lemonade and beer). For a fun, bright, nonalcoholic drink, order *un diabolo menthe* (7-Up with mint syrup). The ice cubes melted after the last Yankee tour group left.

Traveling with Kids

France is kid friendly, partly because so much of it is rural. It's easy to find restaurants with kids' menus and hotels with pools. Choose hotels with attached restaurants so the kids can go back to the room and play while you finish a pleasant dinner. Minimize hotel changes by planning three-day stops.

To make your trip fun for everyone in the family, mix heavy-duty sights with kids' activities (playing miniature golf, renting bikes, and riding the little tourist trains popular in many French towns). Swap baby-sitting duties with your partner if one of you wants to take in an extra sight. Our kids' favorite places were Mont St. Michel, the Alps, the Loire châteaus, Carcassonne, and Paris (especially the Eiffel Tower and Seine River boat ride).

Stranger in a Strange Land

We travel all the way to Europe to enjoy differences—to become temporary locals. You'll experience frustrations. Certain truths that we find "God-given" or "self-evident," like cold beer, ice in drinks, bottomless cups of coffee, hot showers, body odor smelling bad, and bigger being better, are suddenly not so true. One of the benefits of travel is the eye-opening realization that there are logical, civil, and even better alternatives. The fact that Americans treat time as a commodity can lead to frustrations when dealing with other cultures. For instance, while an American "spends" or "wastes" time, a French person merely "passes" it. A willingness to go local (and at a local tempo) ensures that you'll enjoy a full dose of European hospitality.

If there is a negative aspect to the European image of Americans, we can appear big, loud, aggressive, impolite, rich, and a bit naive. While Europeans look bemusedly at some of our Yankee excesses—and worriedly at others—they nearly always afford us individual travelers all the warmth we deserve.

Back Door Manners

While updating this book, we heard over and over again that our readers are considerate and fun to have as guests. Thank you for traveling as temporary locals who are sensitive to the culture. It's fun to follow you in our travels.

Send Us a Postcard, Drop Us a Line

If you enjoy a successful trip with the help of this book and would like to share your discoveries, please fill out and send the survey at the end of this book to us at Europe Through the Back Door, Box 2009, Edmonds, WA 98020. We personally read and value all feedback. Thanks in advance—it helps a lot.

For our latest travel information, tap into our Web site: www.ricksteves.com. For any updates to this book, check www.ricksteves.com/update. Rick's e-mail address is rick@ricksteves.com. Anyone is welcome to request a free issue of our *Back Door* quarterly newsletter.

Judging from all the positive feedback and happy postcards we receive from travelers who have used this book, it's safe to assume you'll enjoy a great, affordable vacation—with the finesse of an independent, experienced traveler.

From this point, "we" (your coauthors) will shed our respective egos and become "I."

Thanks, and *bon voyage*!

BACK DOOR TRAVEL PHILOSOPHY
As Taught in *Rick Steves' Europe Through the Back Door*

Travel is intensified living—maximum thrills per minute and one of the last great sources of legal adventure. Travel is freedom. It's recess, and we need it.

Experiencing the real Europe requires catching it by surprise, going casual... "Through the Back Door."

Affording travel is a matter of priorities. (Make do with the old car.) You can travel—simply, safely, and comfortably—anywhere in Europe for $70 a day plus transportation costs. In many ways, spending more money only builds a thicker wall between you and what you came to see. Europe is a cultural carnival; time after time you'll find that its best acts are free and the best seats are the cheap ones.

A tight budget forces you to travel close to the ground, meeting and communicating with the people, not relying on service with a purchased smile. Never sacrifice sleep, nutrition, safety, or cleanliness in the name of budget. Simply enjoy the local-style alternatives to expensive hotels and restaurants.

Extroverts have more fun. If your trip is low on magic moments, kick yourself and make things happen. If you don't enjoy a place, maybe you don't know enough about it. Seek the truth. Recognize tourist traps. Give a culture the benefit of your open mind. See things as different but not better or worse. Any culture has much to share.

Of course, travel, like the world, is a series of hills and valleys. Be fanatically positive and militantly optimistic. If something's not to your liking, change your liking. Travel is addicting. It can make you a happier American as well as a citizen of the world. Our Earth is home to 6 billion equally important people. It's humbling to travel and find that people don't envy Americans. They like us but, with all due respect, they wouldn't trade passports.

Globe-trotting destroys ethnocentricity. It helps you understand and appreciate different cultures. Travel changes people. It broadens perspectives and teaches new ways to measure quality of life. Many travelers toss aside their hometown blinders. Their prized souvenirs are the strands of different cultures they decide to knit into their own character. The world is a cultural yarn shop. And Back Door Travelers are weaving the ultimate tapestry. Come on, join in!

PARIS

Paris offers sweeping boulevards, sleepy parks, world-class art galleries, chatty crepe stands, Napoleon's body, sleek shopping malls, the Eiffel Tower, and people watching from outdoor cafés. Climb the Notre-Dame and the Eiffel Tower, cruise the Seine and the Champs-Élysées, and master the Louvre and Orsay Museums. Save some after-dark energy for one of the world's most romantic cities. Many people fall in love with Paris. Some see the essentials and flee, overwhelmed by the huge city. With the proper approach and a good orientation, you'll fall head over heels for Europe's capital city.

Planning Your Time
Paris in One, Two, or Three Days

Day 1
Morning: Follow "Historic Core of Paris Walk" (see "Sights," below) featuring Île de la Cité, Notre-Dame, Latin Quarter, and Sainte-Chapelle.
Afternoon: Tour Louvre Museum.
Evening: Cruise Seine River or take illuminated Paris by Night bus tour.

Day 2
Morning: Métro to l'Arc de Triomphe and saunter down the Champs-Élysées.
Midday: Tour Orsay Museum.
Afternoon: Catch RER from Orsay to Versailles. To avoid crowds, see the park first and the palace late.
Evening: Enjoy Trocadero scene and ride up Eiffel Tower.

Daily Reminder

Monday: These museums are closed today—Orsay, Rodin, Marmottan, Montmartre, Carnavalet, and Versailles. The Louvre is especially crowded today, but the Richelieu wing stays open until 21:45. Many small stores don't open until 14:00. Some restaurants are closed today. It's discount night at most cinemas.

Tuesday: Many museums are closed today, including the Louvre, Picasso, Cluny, and Pompidou Center. The Eiffel Tower, Versailles, and the Orsay are particularly busy today.

Wednesday: All museums are open, the Louvre until 21:45. The weekly *Pariscope* magazine comes out today.

Thursday: All museums are open (the Orsay until 21:45). The Sewer Tour is closed. Department stores are open late.

Friday: All sights are open (except the Sewer Tour). Afternoon trains and roads leaving Paris are crowded; TGV reservation fees are much higher.

Saturday: All sights are open (except the Jewish Art and History Museum), and the fountains run at Versailles (July–Sept). Paris department stores are busy.

Sunday: Some museums are two-thirds price all day (Louvre, Orsay, Cluny, and Picasso). The fountains run at Versailles (early April–early Oct). Most stores are closed today, but shoppers will find relief in the lively Marais neighborhood—the Jewish Quarter—where many stores are open. Look for organ concerts at St. Sulpice and possibly other churches. The American Church usually offers a free evening concert (18:00).

Day 3
Morning: Follow "Marais Walk" (below).
Afternoon: Either stay in Marais neighborhood (for Pompidou Center and Museum of Art and History of Judaism) or tour Rodin Museum and nearby Napoleon's Tomb and Military Museum.
Evening: Explore Montmartre and Sacre Coeur.

Orientation

Paris is split in half by the Seine River, divided into 20 *arrondissements* (proud and independent governmental jurisdictions), and circled by a ring-road freeway (the *périphérique*). You'll find Paris easier to negotiate if you know which side of the river you're on, which arrondissement you're in, and which subway (Métro) stop you're closest to. If you're north of the river (above on any city map), you're on the Right Bank (*rive droite*). If you're south of it, you're on the Left Bank (*rive gauche*).

Paris Overview

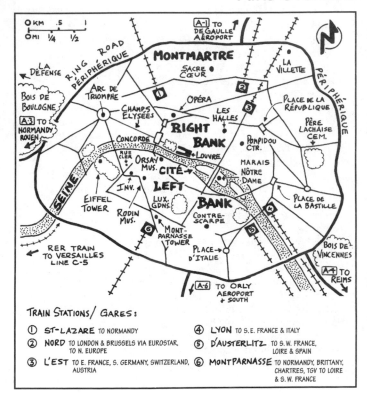

O KM .5   1
O MI ¼   ½

MONTMARTRE

A-1 TO DE GAULLE AÉROPORT

RING ROAD PÉRIPHÉRIQUE

LA DÉFENSE

SACRÉ CŒUR

LA VILLETTE

PÉRIPHÉRIQUE

BOIS DE BOULOGNE

ARC DE TRIOMPHE

OPÉRA

PLACE DE LA RÉPUBLIQUE

A-3 TO NORMANDY ROUEN

CHAMPS ELYSÉES

LES HALLES

PÈRE LACHAISE CEM.

RIGHT

POMPIDOU CTR.

CONCORDE

LOUVRE

BANK

MARAIS

RUE CLER

ORSAY MUS.

NÔTRE DAME

SEINE

CITÉ

LEFT

INV.

LUX. GDNS.

PLACE DE LA BASTILLE

EIFFEL TOWER

RODIN MUS.

BANK

CONTRE-SCARPE

MONT-PARNASSE TOWER

PLACE D'ITALIE

BOIS DE VINCENNES

RER TRAIN TO VERSAILLES LINE C-5

A-4 TO REIMS

A-6 TO ORLY AÉROPORT & SOUTH

TRAIN STATIONS / GARES:

① **ST-LAZARE** TO NORMANDY

② **NORD** TO LONDON & BRUSSELS VIA EUROSTAR, TO N. EUROPE

③ **L'EST** TO E. FRANCE, S. GERMANY, SWITZERLAND, AUSTRIA

④ **LYON** TO S.E. FRANCE & ITALY

⑤ **D'AUSTERLITZ** TO S.W. FRANCE, LOIRE & SPAIN

⑥ **MONTPARNASSE** TO NORMANDY, BRITTANY, CHARTRES, TGV TO LOIRE & S.W. FRANCE

Arrondissements are numbered, starting at Notre-Dame (ground zero) and moving in a clockwise spiral out to the ring road. The last two digits in a Parisian zip code are the arrondissement number, and the notation for the Métro stop is "Mo." In Parisian jargon, Napoleon's tomb is on *la rive gauche* (the Left Bank) in the *7ème* (seventh arrondissement), zip code 75007, Mo: Invalides. Paris Métro stops are used as a standard aid in giving directions, even for those not using the Métro.

Tourist Information

Avoid the Paris tourist offices—long lines, short information, and a 5F charge for maps. This book, the *Pariscope* magazine (described below), and one of the freebie maps available at any hotel are all you need. The main TI is at 127 avenue des Champs-Élysées (daily 9:00–20:00, tel. 08 36 68 31 12 or 01 49 52 53 10), but the TIs at the Gare de Lyon (daily 8:00–20:00, tel. 01 43 43 33 24, answered

by live English-speaker), Eiffel Tower (daily May–Sept 11:00–
18:00), and Louvre (Wed–Mon 10:00–19:00) are less crowded. For
a complete list of museum hours and scheduled English-language
museum tours, pick up the free "Musées, Monuments Historiques,
et Expositions" booklet from any museum.

Pariscope: The *Pariscope* weekly magazine (or one of its
clones, 3F at any newsstand) lists museum hours, art exhibits,
concerts, music festivals, plays, movies, and nightclubs.

Maps: While Paris is littered with free maps, they don't show
all the streets. You may want the huge Michelin #10 map of Paris.
For an extended stay, consider the pocket-size and street-indexed
Paris Pratique (40F).

Bookstores: There are many English-language bookstores
in Paris where you can pick up guidebooks (for nearly double
their American price). A few are: Shakespeare & Company (daily
12:00–24:00, some used travel books, 37 rue de la Boucherie,
across the river from Notre-Dame), W. H. Smith (248 rue de
Rivoli, Mo: Concorde, tel. 01 44 77 88 99), and Brentanos
(37 avenue de L'Opéra, Mo: Opéra, tel. 01 42 61 52 50).

American Church: The American Church is a nerve center
for the American émigré community. It distributes a free, handy,
and insightful monthly English-language newspaper, called the
Free Voice, with useful reviews of concerts, plays, and current
events (available at around 200 locations in Paris), and an adver-
tisement paper called *France—U.S.A. Contacts*, full of helpful
information for those looking for work or long-term housing.
The church faces the river between the Eiffel Tower and Orsay
Museum (reception open Mon–Sat 9:30–22:30, Sun 9:00–19:30,
65 quai d'Orsay, Mo: Invalides, tel. 01 40 62 05 00).

Arrival in Paris

By Train: Paris has six train stations, all connected by Métro,
bus, and taxi. All have ATMs, banks or change offices, information
desks, telephones, cafés, lockers (*consigne automatique*), newsstands,
and clever pickpockets. Hop the Métro to your hotel (see "Getting
around Paris," below).

By Plane: For detailed information on getting from Paris'
airports to downtown Paris (and vice versa), see "Transportation
Connections" at the end of this chapter.

Helpful Hints

Theft Alert: Use your money belt and never carry a wallet in your
back pocket or a purse over your shoulder. Thieves thrive
in tourist areas and the Métro (at stations and in subway cars).

Museums: Most museums offer reduced prices and shorter
hours on Sunday. Many begin closing rooms 45 minutes before
the actual closing time. For the fewest crowds, visit very early, at

lunch, or very late. The best Impressionist art museums are the Orsay and Marmottan (another, L'Orangerie, is closed for renovation). Most museums have slightly shorter hours October through March. French holidays can really mess up your sightseeing plans (Jan 1, May 1, May 8, July 14, Nov 1, Nov 11, and Dec 25). See "Daily Reminder," above, for other "closed" days.

Paris Museum Pass: In Paris there are two classes of sightseers: those with a museum pass and those without. Serious sightseers save time and money by getting this pass. Sold at museums, main Métro stations, and TIs, it pays for itself in two admissions and gets you into sights with no lining up (1 day-80F, 3 consecutive days-160F, 5 consecutive days-240F; no discounts for kids). Included sights (and admission prices without the pass) you're likely to visit: Louvre (45F), Orsay (40F), Sainte-Chapelle (35F), l'Arc de Triomphe (40F), Napoleon's Tomb (38F), Carnavalet Museum (35F), Conciergerie (35F), Sewer Tour (25F), Cluny Museum (38F), Pompidou Center (50F), Notre-Dame towers (35F) and crypt (35F), Picasso Museum (30F), Rodin Museum (28F), and the elevator to the top of the Grand Arche de la Defense (46F). Outside Paris, the pass covers the Palace of Versailles (46F), its Grand Trianon (25F), and Château Chantilly (43F). Notable sights not covered: Marmottan Museum, Jewish Art and History Museum, Eiffel Tower, Montparnasse Tower, the ladies of Pigalle, and Disneyland Paris. Tally it up—but remember, an advantage of the pass is that you skip to the front of the line, saving hours of waiting in the summer (though everyone must pass through the slow-moving metal-detector lines at a few sights). With the pass, you'll pop painlessly into sights (even for a few minutes) that you're walking by that might otherwise not be worth the expense (e.g., Notre-Dame crypt, Cluny Museum, Conciergerie, Victor Hugo's House). The free directory that comes with your pass lists the latest hours, phone numbers, and prices for kids (the cutoff age for free entry varies from 5 to 18). Most major art museums let in young people up to age 18 for free. If you're buying a pass at a museum with a long line, skip to the front and find the sales window.

Telephone Cards: Pick up the essential France *télécarte* or a KOSMOS card at any *tabac* (tobacco shop), post office, or tourist office (*une petite télécarte* is 49F; *une grande* is 98F). Smart travelers check things by telephone. Most public phones use *télécartes* (KOSMOS cards work at any phone).

Useful Telephone Numbers: American Hospital—01 46 41 25 25, American pharmacy— 01 47 42 49 40 (Mo: Opéra), Police—17, U.S. Embassy—01 43 12 22 22, Paris and France directory assistance—12, AT&T operator—0800 99 00 11, MCI—0800 99 00 19, Sprint—0800 99 00 87. (See appendix for additional numbers.)

Toilets: Carry small change for pay toilets, or walk into any outdoor café like you own the place and find the toilet in the back. Remember, the toilets in museums are free and generally the best you'll find. Modern super-sanitary street-booth toilets provide both relief and a memory (2F coin required, don't leave small children inside unattended).

Getting around Paris

By Métro: Europe's best subway is divided into two systems—the Métro (for puddle-jumping everywhere in Paris) and the RER (which connects suburban destinations with a few stops within central Paris). You'll be using the Métro for almost all your trips. Occasionally you'll find the RER more convenient as it makes fewer stops (like an express bus).

In Paris you're never more than a 10-minute walk from a Métro station. One ticket takes you anywhere in the system with unlimited transfers. Save 40 percent by buying a *carnet* (car-nay) of 10 tickets for 54F at any Métro station (a single ticket is 8F). Métro tickets work on city buses, though one ticket cannot be used as a transfer between subway and bus.

The *Mobilis* ticket (moh-bee-lee) allows unlimited travel for a single day on all bus and Métro lines (30F). If you're staying longer, the *Carte Orange* (pron: kart oh-rahnzh) pass gives you free run of the bus and Métro system for one week (80F, ask for the *Carte Orange Coupon Vert*, supply a photo) or a month (280F, ask for the *Carte Orange Coupon Orange*, supply a photo). These pass prices cover only central Paris; you can pay more for passes covering regional destinations (e.g., Versailles).

The weekly pass begins Monday and ends Sunday, and the monthly pass begins the first day of the month and ends the last day of that month, so midweek or midmonth purchases are generally not worthwhile. The passes are officially only for Parisian residents. While the purchase of these passes by tourists is rarely an issue, be aware that a ticket seller might refuse to sell you this pass. In this case you have three options: (1) Tell them you are living in Paris for a temporary period; (2) Go to another station to buy your pass; (3) Use carnets of 10 tickets instead. All passes can be purchased at any Métro station (most have photo booths).

To get to your destination, determine which "Mo" stop is closest to it and which line or lines will get you there. The lines have numbers, but they're best known by their direction or end-of-the-line stop. (For example, the La Defense/Château de Vincennes line runs between La Defense in the west and Vincennes in the east.)

Once in the Métro station, you'll see blue-and-white signs directing you to the train going in your direction (e.g., "direction: La Defense"). Insert your ticket in the automatic turnstile, pass through, and reclaim and keep your ticket until you exit the

Paris

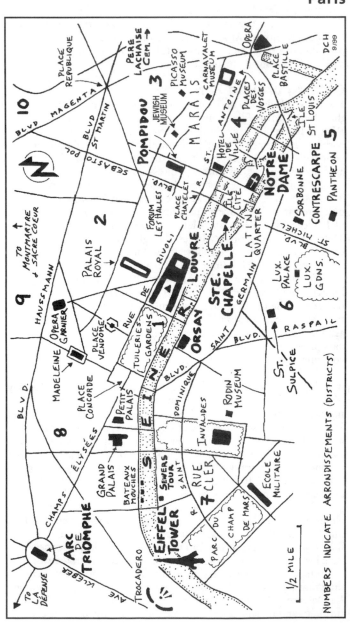

Key Words for the Métro and RER

- *direction* (dee-rek-see-ohn): direction
- *ligne* (lean-yuh): line
- *correspondance* (kor-res-pohn-dahns): transfer
- *sortie* (sor-tee): exit
- *carnet* (kar-nay): cheap set of 10 tickets
- *Pardon, madame/monsieur* (par-dohn, mah-dahm/mes-yur): Excuse me, lady/bud.
- *Je descend* (juh day-sahn): I'm getting off.
- *Donnez-moi mon porte-monnaie!*: Give me back my wallet!

Etiquette

- When waiting at the platform, get out of the way of those exiting their train. Board only once everyone is off.
- Avoid using the hinged seats when the car is jammed; they take up valuable standing space.
- When in a crowded train, try not to block the exit. If you're blocking the door when the train stops, step out of the car and to the side, let others off, then get back on.
- Talk softly in the cars. Listen to how quietly Parisians can communicate and follow their lead.
- On escalators, stand on the right, pass on the left.

system. Fare inspectors regularly check for cheaters and accept absolutely no excuses from anyone. I repeat, keep that ticket until you leave the Métro system.

Transfers are free and can be made wherever lines cross. When you transfer, look for the orange *correspondance* (connections) signs when you exit your first train, then follow the proper direction sign.

Before you *sortie* (exit), check the helpful *plan du quartier* (map of the neighborhood) to get your bearings, locate your destination, and decide which *sortie* you want. At stops with several *sorties*, you can save lots of walking by choosing the best exit.

Thieves spend their days in the Métro. Be on guard. For example, a pocket picked as you pass through a turnstile leaves you on the wrong side and the thief strolling away. Any jostle or commotion (especially when boarding or leaving trains) is likely the sign of a thief or team of thieves in action.

Paris has a huge homeless population and over 11 percent unemployment; expect a warm Métro welcome by panhandlers, musicians, and those selling magazines produced by the homeless community.

By RER: The RER (Réseau Express Régionale, air-ay-air) is the suburban train system, indicated by thick lines on your subway map and identified by letters A, B, C, and so on. The RER works like the Métro but can be speedier (if it serves your destination directly) because it makes only a few stops within the city. One Métro ticket is all you need for RER rides within central Paris. You can transfer between the Métro and RER systems with the same ticket. Unlike the Métro, you need to insert your ticket in a turnstile to exit the RER system. To travel outside the city (to Versailles or the airport, for example), you'll need to buy a separate, more expensive ticket at the station window before boarding. Make sure your stop is served by checking the signs over the train platform (not all trains serve all stops).

By City Bus: The trickier bus system is worth figuring out. Métro tickets are good on both bus and Métro, though you can't use the same ticket to transfer between the two systems. One ticket gets you anywhere in central Paris, but if you leave the city center (shown as section 1 on the diagram onboard the bus), you must validate a second ticket. While the Métro shuts down about 00:30, some buses continue much later. Schedules are posted at bus stops. Handy bus-system maps (*plan des autobus*) are available in any Métro station and are provided in your *Paris Pratique* map book if you invest (40F).

Big system maps, posted at each bus and Métro stop, display the routes. Individual route diagrams show the exact routes of the lines serving that stop. Major stops are painted on the side of each bus. Enter through the front doors. Punch your Métro ticket in the machine behind the driver, or pay the higher cash fare. Get off the bus using the rear door. Even if you're not certain you've figured it out, do some joyriding (outside of rush hour). Lines #24, #63, and #69 are Paris' most scenic routes and make a great introduction to the city. Bus #69 is particularly handy, running between the Eiffel Tower, rue Cler (recommended hotels), Orsay, Louvre, Marais (recommended hotels), and Père Lachaise Cemetery. The most handy bus routes are listed for each hotel area recommended (see "Sleeping," near end of chapter).

By Taxi: Parisian taxis are almost reasonable. A 10-minute ride costs about 50F (versus 5.50F to get anywhere in town on the Métro). You can try waving one down (a glowing white light on the roof means it's free, an orange light means occupied), but it's easier to ask for the nearest taxi stand (*Où est une station de taxi?*; oo ay oon stah-see-ohn duh taxi) or ask your hotel to call for you. Higher rates are charged at night from 19:00 to 7:00, all day Sunday, and to either airport. There's a 6F charge for each piece of baggage. A 3- to 5F-tip is generally plenty. If you call from your hotel, the meter starts as soon as the call is received. Taxis are tough to find on Friday and Saturday night, especially after the Métro closes (around 00:30). If you need a taxi for a morning trip to the airport or train station, consider booking the night before.

By Foot: Be careful! Parisian drivers are notorious for ignoring pedestrians. Never assume you have the right of way, even in a crosswalk. When crossing a street, keep your pace constant and don't stop suddenly. Drivers carefully calculate your speed and will miss you, providing you don't alter your route or pace.

Organized Tours of Paris

Bus Tours: Paris Vision offers handy bus tours of Paris, day and night (advertised in hotel lobbies); their "Illuminated Paris" tour is far more interesting (see "Nightlife in Paris," below). A better daytime bus tour is the hop-on hop-off double-decker bus service called **Open Deck Tours**, offering three different routes covering most of the important sights in Paris (the Paris Grand Tour is the best to start with). Use these buses to connect the major sights (with a running commentary) and get a good city-orientation tour at the same time. Expect to wait 15 to 20 minutes for a bus at each stop. Buy your tickets from the driver (135F/one day, 150F/two days, 2 buses/hrly about 10:00–18:00, you can hop off at various sights then catch a later bus). You'll see these bright yellow topless double-decker buses all over town—pick one up at the first important sight you visit, or start your tour at the Eiffel Tower stop (the first street on the non-river side of the tower).

Boat Tours: Several companies offer one-hour boat cruises on the Seine (by far best at night; see "Nightlife in Paris," below). The huge, mass-production **Bateaux-Mouches** boats depart every 30 minutes from Pont de l'Alma's right bank and are convenient to rue Cler hotels (40F, 20F under 14, daily 10:00–23:00, useless taped explanations in 6 languages and tour groups by the dozens, tel. 01 42 25 96 10). The much smaller and more intimate **Vedettes de Pont Neuf** boats depart only once an hour from the center of the Pont Neuf but come with a live guide giving explanations in French and English only and are convenient to Marais and Contrescarpe hotels (50F, 25F under age 14, tel. 01 46 33 98 38). From April to October, **Bateau-Bus** operates boats on the Seine, connecting six key stops about every 25 minutes: Eiffel Tower, Orsay/place de la Concorde, Louvre, Notre-Dame, Hôtel de Ville, and St. Germain-des-Près. Pick up their schedule at any stop (or TI) and use them as a scenic alternative to the Métro. Tickets are available for single trips (20F), one day (60F), and two days (90F). Boats run from 10:00 to 19:00, until 22:00 in summer. **Paris Canal** boats depart twice daily for three-hour cruises between the Orsay and the Parc de la Vilette. You'll cruise up the Seine then along a quiet canal through untouristed Paris, accompanied by English explanations (100F-adults, 75F-ages 12–25, 55F-ages 4–11, one-way departures from the Orsay at 9:30 and from Parc de la Vilette at 14:30, tel. 01 42 40 96 97).

Walking Tours: Paris Walking Tours offers a variety of

excellent two-hour walks nearly daily for 60F (tel. 01 48 09 21 40, fax 01 42 43 75 51, http://pariswalkingtours.com). They focus on the Marais, Luxembourg Gardens, Opéra Garnier, Montmartre, and Hemingway's Paris. Call a day or two ahead to learn their schedule and starting point. No reservations are required. These are thoughtfully prepared, humorous, and relaxing walking tours led by British or American guides. Don't hesitate to stand close to the guide to hear. For Lost Generation fans, **Paris Literary Promenades** takes you through areas once popular with literary giants from Joyce to Beckett to Hemingway (60F, 2 hrs, late May–mid-Oct, tours depart from place de l'Odeon daily except Wed at 14:30 and 19:00, tel. 01 48 07 80 72 or cellular 06 03 27 73 52). You can also hire a Parisian as your personal guide. Arnaud Servignat (tel. 01 42 57 03 35, fax 01 42 62 68 62, e-mail: arnotour@cybercable.fr) and Marianne Siegler (tel. 01 42 52 32 51) are licensed local guides who freelance for individuals and families ($150/4 hrs, $250/day).

Bike Tours: Bullfrog Bike Tours will show you Paris on two wheels at a relaxed pace (120F, 3–4-hr tours in English May–mid-Sept 11:00 and 15:30, no bikes or reservations needed, meet at fountain on avenue Joseph, 100 meters from Eiffel Tower in Champ de Mars park, ask about new evening tours, cellular 06 09 98 08 60, http://BullfrogBikes.com.

Sights—The "Historic Core of Paris" Walk

(This information is distilled from the Historic Paris Walk chapter in *Rick Steves' Mona Winks*, by Gene Openshaw and Rick Steves.)

Allow four hours for this self-guided tour, including sight-seeing. Start where the city did—on the Île de la Cité. Face Notre-Dame and follow the dotted line on the "Core of Paris" map (within this chapter). To get to Notre-Dame, ride the Métro to Cité, Hôtel de Ville, or St. Michel and walk to the big square facing the ...

▲▲**Notre-Dame Cathedral**—This 700-year-old cathedral is packed with history and tourists. Study its sculpture and windows, take in a Mass, eavesdrop on guides, and walk all around the outside (free, daily 8:00–18:45, 15F for treasury open daily 9:30–17:30, free English tours normally Wed and Thu at 12:00 and Sat at 14:30, Sun Masses at 8:00, 8:45, 10:00, 11:30, 12:30, and 18:30). Climb to the top for a great view of the city; you get 400 steps for only 35F (entrance outside, north tower open 9:30–17:30, closed at lunch and earlier off-season). There are clean 2.70F toilets in front of the church near Charlemagne's statue.

The **cathedral facade** is worth a close look. The church is dedicated to "Our Lady" (Notre-Dame). Mary is center stage—cradling Jesus, surrounded by the halo of the rose window. Adam is on the left and Eve is on the right.

Core of Paris

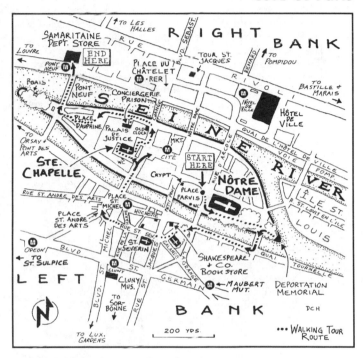

Below Mary and above the arches is a row of 28 statues known as the Kings of Judah. During the French Revolution, these Biblical kings were mistaken for the hated French kings. The citizens stormed the church, crying, "Off with their heads!" All were decapitated but have since been recapitated.

Speaking of decapitation, look at the carving above the doorway on the left. The man with his head in his hands is St. Denis. Back when there was a Roman temple on this spot, Christianity began making converts. The fourth-century bishop of Roman Paris, Denis, was beheaded. But these early Christians were hard to keep down. The man who would become St. Denis got up, tucked his head under his arm, and headed north until he found just the right place to meet his maker: Montmartre, which means "mountain of the martyr." The Parisians were convinced of this miracle, Christianity gained ground, and a church soon replaced the pagan temple.

Medieval art was OK if it embellished the house of God and told Bible stories. For a fine example, move to the base of the central column (at the foot of Mary, about where the head of St. Denis could spit if he was real good). Working around from the left, find God telling a barely created Eve, "Have fun but no apples." Next, the sexiest serpent I've ever seen makes apples à la mode. Finally, Adam and Eve, now ashamed of their nakedness, are expelled by an angel. This is a tiny example in a church covered with meaning.

Now move to the right and study the carving above the **central portal**. It's the end of the world, and Christ sits on the throne of Judgment (just under the arches, holding his hands up). Below him an angel and a demon weigh souls in the balance. The "good" stand to the left, looking up to heaven. The "bad" ones to the right are chained up and led off to . . . Versailles on a Tuesday. The "ugly" ones must be the crazy sculpted demons to the right, at the base of the arch.

Wander through the interior. You'll be routed around the ambulatory, much as medieval pilgrims would have been. Don't miss the rose windows filling each of the transepts. Back outside, walk around the church through the park on the riverside for a close look at the flying buttresses.

The neo-Gothic 90-meter **spire** is a product of the 1860 reconstruction. Around its base are apostles and evangelists (the green men) as well as Viollet-le-Duc, the architect in charge of the work. Notice how the apostles look outward, blessing the city, while the architect (at top, seen from behind the church) looks up, admiring his spire.

The archaeological **crypt** is a worthwhile 15-minute stop with your museum pass (35F, 50F with Notre-Dame's tower, daily 10:00–18:00, closes at 17:00 Oct–April, enter 100 meters in front of church). You'll see Roman ruins, trace the street plan of the medieval village, and see diagrams of how the earliest Paris grew and grew, all thoughtfully explained in English.

If you're hungry near Notre-Dame, the nearby Île St. Louis has inexpensive *crêperies* and grocery stores open daily on its main drag. Plan a picnic for the quiet bench-filled park immediately behind the church (public WC).

Behind Notre-Dame, squeeze through the tourist buses, cross the street, and enter the iron gate into the park at the tip of the island. Look for the stairs and head down.

▲▲**Deportation Memorial (Mémorial de la Déportation)**— This memorial to the 200,000 French victims of the Nazi concentration camps draws you into their experience. As you descend the steps, the city around you disappears. Surrounded by walls, you have become a prisoner. Your only freedom is your view of the sky and the tantalizing glimpse of the river below.

Enter the single-file chamber ahead. Inside, the circular plaque in the floor reads, "They descended into the mouth of the earth and they did not return." A hallway stretches in front of you, lined with 200,000 lighted crystals, one for each French citizen that died. Flickering at the far end is the eternal flame of hope. The tomb of the unknown deportee lies at your feet. Above, the inscription reads, "Dedicated to the living memory of the 200,000 French deportees sleeping in the night and the fog, exterminated in the Nazi concentration camps."

Above the exit as you leave is the message you'll find at all Nazi sights: "Forgive but never forget." (Free, Mon–Fri 8:30–21:45, Sat–Sun and holidays from 9:00, sometimes closes 12:00–14:00, shorter hours off-season, east tip of the island near Île St. Louis, behind Notre-Dame, Mo: Cité.)

Île St. Louis—Look across the river to the Île St. Louis. If the Île de la Cité is a tug laden with the history of Paris, it's towing this classy little residential dinghy laden only with boutiques, famous sorbet shops, and restaurants (see "Eating in Paris," below). This island wasn't developed until much later (18th century). What was a swampy mess is now harmonious Parisian architecture. The pedestrian bridge, Pont Saint Louis, connects the two islands, leading right to rue Saint Louis en l'Île. This spine of the island is lined with interesting shops. A short stroll takes you to the famous Bertillon ice-cream parlour (#31). Loop back to the pedestrian bridge along the parklike quays (walk north to the river and turn left). This walk is about as peaceful and romantic as Paris gets.

Before walking to the opposite end of the Île de la Cité, loop through the Latin Quarter (as indicated on the map). From the Deportation Memorial cross the bridge onto the Left Bank and enjoy the riverside view of the Notre-Dame and window shop among the green book stalls, browsing through used books, vintage posters, and souvenirs. At the little park and church (over the bridge from the front of Notre-Dame), venture inland a few blocks, basically arcing through the Latin Quarter and returning to the island two bridges down at place St. Michel.

▲Latin Quarter—This area, which gets its name from the language used here when it was an exclusive medieval university district, lies between the Luxembourg Gardens and the Seine, centering around the Sorbonne University and boulevards St. Germain and St. Michel. This is the core of the Left Bank—it's crowded with international eateries, far-out bookshops, street singers, and jazz clubs. For colorful wandering and café sitting, afternoons and evenings are best (Mo: St. Michel).

Along rue Saint-Severin you can still see the shadow of the medieval sewer system (the street slopes into a central channel of bricks). In the days before plumbing and toilets, when people still went to the river or neighborhood wells for their water, "flushing" meant throwing it out the window. Certain times of day were flushing times. Maids on the fourth floor would holler "*Garde de l'euu!*" ("Look out for the water!") and heave it into the streets, where it would eventually be washed down into the Seine.

Consider a visit to the Cluny Museum for its medieval art and unicorn tapestries (listed under "Sights—Southeast Paris," below).

Place St. Michel (facing the St. Michel bridge) is the traditional core of the Left Bank's artsy, liberal, hippie, Bohemian district of poets, philosophers, winos, and tourists. In less-commercial times, place St. Michel was a gathering point for the city's malcontents and misfits. Here, in 1871, the citizens took the streets from the government troops, set up barricades *Les Mis*–style, and established the Paris Commune. In World War II the locals rose up against their Nazi oppressors (read the plaques by the St. Michel fountain). And in the spring of 1968, a time of social upheaval all over the world, young students—battling riot batons and tear gas—took over the square and demanded change.

From place St. Michel, look across the river and find the spire of Sainte-Chapelle church and its weathervane angel (below). Cross the river on the Pont St. Michel and continue along boulevard du Palais. On your left you'll see the high-security doorway to Sainte-Chapelle. But first, carry on another 30 meters and turn right at a wide pedestrian street, the rue de Lutece.

Cité "Métropolitain" Stop—Of the 141 original turn-of-the-19th-century subway entrances, this is one of 17 survivors now preserved as a national art treasure. The curvy, plantlike iron work is a textbook example of Art Nouveau, the style that rebelled against the erector-set squareness of the Industrial Age (e.g., Mr. Eiffel's tower).

The flower market right here on place Louis Lepine is a pleasant detour. On Sundays this square chirps with a busy bird market. And across the way is the Prefecture de Police, where Inspector Clouseau of *Pink Panther* fame used to work and where the local resistance fighters took the first building from the Nazis in August 1944, leading to the Allied liberation of Paris a week later.

Pause here to admire the view. Sainte-Chapelle is a pearl in an ugly architectural oyster, part of a complex of buildings that includes the Palace of Justice (to the right of Sainte-Chapelle, behind the fancy gates). Return to the entrance of Sainte-Chapelle. You'll need to pass through a metal detector to get in. Free toilets are ahead on the left. The line into the church may be long. (Museum-card holders can go directly in; pick up the excellent English info sheet.) Enter the humble ground floor of...

▲▲▲Sainte-Chapelle—The triumph of Gothic church architecture is a cathedral of glass like no other. It was speedily built from 1242 to 1248 for St. Louis IX (France's only canonized king) to house the supposed Crown of Thorns. Its architectural harmony is due to the fact that it was completed under the direction of one architect in only six years—unheard of in Gothic times. (Notre-Dame took more than 200 years to build.)

The design clearly shows an Old Regime approach to worship.

The basement was for staff and other common folk. Royal Christians worshiped upstairs. The ground-floor paint job, a 19th-century restoration, is a reasonably accurate copy of the original.

Climb the spiral staircase to the **Chapelle Haute**. Fill the place with choral music, crank up the sunshine, face the top of the altar, and really believe that the Crown of Thorns was there, and this becomes one awesome space.

"Let there be light." In the Bible, it's clear: Light is divine. Light shining through stained glass was a symbol of God's grace shining down to earth. Gothic architects used their new technology to turn dark stone buildings into lanterns of light. The glory of Gothic shines brighter here than in any other church.

There are 15 separate panels of stained glass (6,500 square feet—two-thirds of it 13th-century original), with more than 1,100 different scenes, mostly from the Bible. In medieval times, scenes like these helped teach Bible stories to the illiterate.

The altar was raised up high to better display the relic—the Crown of Thorns—around which this chapel was built. The supposed crown cost King Louis three times as much as this church. Today it is kept in the Notre-Dame Treasury and shown only on Good Friday.

Louis' little private viewing window is in the wall to the right of the altar. Louis, both saintly and shy, liked to go to church without dealing with the rigors of public royal life. Here he could worship still dressed in his jammies.

Lay your camera on the ground and shoot the ceiling. Those ribs growing out of the slender columns are the essence of Gothic.

Books in the gift shop explain the stained glass in English. There are concerts (120F) almost every summer evening (35F, daily 9:30–18:00, off-season 10:00–16:30, call 01 48 01 91 35 for concert information, Mo: Cité).

Palais du Justice—Back outside, as you walk around the church exterior, look down and notice how much Paris has risen in the 800 years since Sainte-Chapelle was built. You're in a huge complex of buildings that has housed the local government since ancient Roman times. It was the site of the original Gothic palace of the early kings of France. The only surviving medieval parts are the Sainte-Chapelle church and the Conciergerie prison.

Most of the site is now covered by the giant Palais de Justice, home of France's supreme court (built in 1776). "Liberté, Egalité, Fraternité" over the doors is a reminder that this was also the headquarters of the revolutionary government.

Now pass through the big iron gate to the noisy boulevard du Palais and turn left (toward the Right Bank). On the corner is the site of the oldest public clock (built in 1334) in the city. While the present clock is said to be Baroque, it somehow still manages to keep accurate time.

Turn left onto quai de l'Horologe and walk along the river. The round medieval tower just ahead marks the entrance to the Conciergerie. Pop in to visit the courtyard and lobby (free). Step past the serious-looking guard into the courtyard.

Conciergerie—The Conciergerie, a former prison, is a gloomy place. Kings used it to torture and execute failed assassins. The leaders of the Revolution put it to similar good use. The tower next to the entrance, called "the babbler," was named for the painful sounds that leaked from it.

Look at the stark lettering above the doorways. This was a no-nonsense revolutionary time. Everything, even lettering, was subjected to the test of reason. No frills or we chop 'em off.

Step inside; the lobby, with an English-language history display, is free. Marie Antoinette was imprisoned here. During a busy eight-month period in the Revolution, she was one of 2,600 prisoners kept here on the way to the guillotine. The interior, with its huge vaulted and pillared rooms, echoes with history but is pretty barren (35F, daily 9:30–18:30, 10:00–17:00 in winter, good English descriptions). You can see Marie Antoinette's cell, housing a collection of her mementos. In another room, a list of those made "a foot shorter at the top" by the "national razor" includes ex-King Louis XVI, Charlotte Corday (who murdered Marat in his bathtub), and the chief revolutionary who got a taste of his own medicine, Maximilien Robespierre.

Back outside, wink at the flak-proof vested guard, fake right, and turn left. Listen for babbles and continue your walk along the river. Across the river you can see the rooftop observatory—flags flapping—of the Samaritaine department store, where this walk will end. At the first corner, veer left past France's supreme-court building and into a sleepy triangular square called place Dauphine. Marvel at how such quaintness could be lodged in the midst of such greatness as you walk through the park to the end of the island. At the equestrian statue of Henry IV, turn right onto the bridge and take refuge in one of the nooks on the Eiffel Tower side.

Pont Neuf—This "new bridge" is now Paris' oldest. Built during Henry IV's reign (around 1600), its 12 arches span the widest part of the river. The fine view includes the park on the tip of the island (note Seine tour boats), the Orsay Museum, and the Louvre. These turrets were originally for vendors and street entertainers. In the days of Henry IV, who originated the promise of "a chicken in every pot," this would have been a lively scene.

Directly over the river, the first building you'll hit on the Right Bank is the venerable old department store, Samaritaine.

▲**Samaritaine Department Store Viewpoint**—Enter the store and go to the rooftop. Ride the glass elevator from near the Pont Neuf entrance to the ninth floor (you'll be greeted by a WC—check out the sink). Pass the 10th-floor *terrasse* for the 11th-floor panorama (tight spiral staircase; watch your head). Quiz yourself. Working counterclockwise, find the Eiffel Tower, Invalides/ Napoleon's Tomb, Montparnasse Tower, Henry IV statue on the tip of the island, Sorbonne University, the dome of the Panthéon, Sainte-Chapelle, Notre-Dame, Hôtel de Ville (city hall), Pompidou Center, Sacré-Coeur, Opéra, and Louvre. The Champs-Élysées leads to the Arc de Triomphe. Shadowing that—even bigger, while two times as distant—is the Grand Arche de la Défense. You'll find light, reasonably priced, and incredibly scenic meals on the breezy terrace and a supermarket in the basement. (Rooftop view is free, daily 9:30–19:00, Mo: Pont Neuf, tel. 01 40 41 20 20.)

Sights—Paris' Museums near the Tuileries Gardens

The newly renovated Tuileries Gardens was once private property of kings and queens. Paris' grandest public park links these museums.

▲▲▲Louvre—This is Europe's oldest, biggest, greatest, and maybe most-crowded museum. There is no grander entry than through the pyramid, but metal detectors create a long line at times. To avoid the line, you have two choices. Museum-pass holders can use the group entrance in the pedestrian passageway between the pyramid and rue de Rivoli (facing the pyramid with your back to the Tuileries Gardens, go to your left, which is north; under the arches you'll find the entrance and escalator down). Or anyone can get into the Louvre from the slick underground shopping mall that connects with the museum; enter the mall either at 99 rue de Rivoli at the door with the red awning or get off the Métro at the "Palais Royal Musée du Louvre" stop and follow signs to "Musée du Louvre" (don't get off at the "Louvre Rivoli" Métro stop, which is farther away).

Pick up the free "Louvre Handbook" in English at the information desk under the pyramid as you enter. Don't try to cover the entire museum. The 90-minute English-language tours, which leave six times daily except Sunday, boil this overwhelming museum down to size (35F, tour tel. 01 40 20 52 09). Clever 30F digital audioguides (after ticket booths, at top of stairs) give you a receiver and a directory of about 130 masterpieces, allowing you to dial a (rather dull) commentary on included works as you stumble upon them. Rick Steves' and Gene Openshaw's museum guidebook, *Rick Steves' Mona Winks* (buy in United States), includes a self-guided tour of the Louvre.

If you can't get a guide, start in the Denon wing and visit these **highlights**, in this order: Michelangelo's *Slaves*, Ancient Greek and Roman works (Parthenon frieze, *Venus de Milo*, Pompeii mosaics, Etruscan sarcophagi, Roman portrait busts, *Nike of Samothrace*); Apollo Gallery (jewels); French and Italian

Paris Museums near Tuileries Gardens

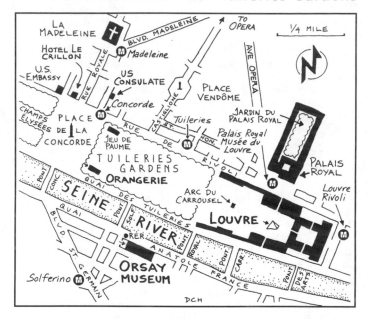

paintings in the Grande Galerie (a quarter-mile long and worth the hike); the *Mona Lisa* and her Italian Renaissance roommates; the nearby neoclassical collection (*Coronation of Napoleon*); and the Romantic collection, with works by Delacroix (*Liberty at the Barricades*) and Géricault (*Raft of the Medusa*).

Cost: 45F, 26F after 15:00 and on Sunday, those under 18 enter free; free on first Sunday of the month. Tickets good all day. Reentry allowed.

Hours: Wednesday through Monday 9:00 to 18:00, closed Tuesday, all wings open Wednesday until 21:45, Richelieu Wing open until 21:45 on Monday. Galleries start closing 30 minutes early. Closed January 1, Easter, May 1, November 1, and Christmas Day. Crowds are worst on Sunday, Monday, Wednesday, and mornings. Save money by visiting after 15:00. (You can enter the pyramid for free until 21:30. Go in at night and see it glow.) Tel. 01 40 20 51 51 or 01 40 20 53 17 for recorded information (www.louvre.fr).

The newly renovated Richelieu wing and the underground shopping-mall extension add the finishing touches to Le Grand Louvre Project (which started in 1989 with the pyramid entrance). To explore this most recent extension of the Louvre, enter through the pyramid, walk toward the inverted pyramid, and

uncover a post office, a handy TI and SNCF office, glittering
boutiques and a dizzying assortment of good-value eateries (up the
escalator), and the Palais-Royal Métro entrance. Stairs at the far
end take you right into the Tuileries Gardens, a perfect antidote
to the stuffy, crowded rooms of the Louvre.

Jeu de Paume—This one-time home to the Impressionist art
collection (now located in the Musée d'Orsay) hosts rotating
exhibits of top contemporary artists (38F, not covered by museum
pass, Tue 12:00–21:30, Wed–Fri 12:00–19:00, Sat–Sun 10:00–
19:00, closed Mon, on place de la Concorde, just inside Tuileries
Gardens on the rue de Rivoli side, Mo: Concorde).

L'Orangerie—Closed for renovation until 2002.

▲▲▲Orsay Museum—Paris' 19th-century art museum (actually,
art from 1848–1914) includes Europe's greatest collection of
Impressionist works. The museum is housed in a former train
station (Gare d'Orsay) across the river and 10 minutes down-
stream from the Louvre. (The RER-C train line zips you right
to "Musée d'Orsay;" the Métro stop Solferino is three blocks
south of the Orsay.)

Start on the ground floor. The "pretty" conservative-
establishment art is on the right. Then cross left into the brutally
truthful and, at that time, very shocking art of the realist rebels
and Manet. Then ride the escalators at the far end (detouring at
the top for a grand museum view) to the series of Impressionist
rooms (Monet, Renoir, Dégas, et al). Don't miss the Grand
Ballroom (room 52, Arts et Decors de la IIIème République)
and Art Nouveau on the mezzanine level.

Cost: 40F, 30F on Sun and for people ages 18 to 25 or over 60,
free for those under 18 and for anyone first Sun of month; tickets
good all day. The booth near the entrance gives free floor plans in
English. English-language tours usually run daily except Sunday at
11:30, cost 36F, take 90 minutes, and are also available on audioguide (30F). Paris museum passes are sold in the basement; if there's
a long line you can skip it by buying one there, but you can't skip
the metal-detector line into the museum. Tel. 01 40 49 48 48.

Hours: Tuesday through Saturday 10:00 to 18:00, Thursday
until 21:45, Sunday 9:00 to 18:00, closed Monday. The museum
opens at 9:00 June 20 through September 20. Last entrance is 45
minutes before closing. Galleries start closing 30 minutes early.
The Orsay is very crowded on Tuesday, when the Louvre is closed.

Sights—Southwest Paris:
The Eiffel Tower Neighborhood

▲▲▲Eiffel Tower—It's crowded and expensive but worth the
trouble. Go early (arrive by 9:15) or late in the day (after 18:00)
to avoid most crowds. Weekends are worst. Pilier Nord (the north
pillar) has the biggest elevator and, therefore, the fastest-moving

Eiffel Tower to Invalides

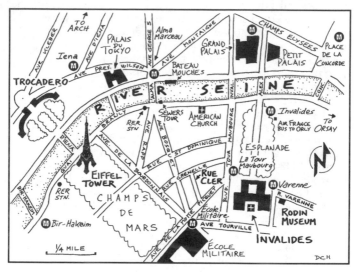

line. The stairs (yes, you can walk up) are next to the Jules Verne restaurant entry.

It's 1,000 feet tall (6 inches taller in hot weather), covers two and one-half acres, and requires 50 tons of paint. The tower's 7,000 tons of metal are spread out so well at the base that it's no heavier per square inch than a linebacker on tiptoes. Visitors to Paris may find *Mona Lisa* to be less than expected, but the Eiffel Tower rarely disappoints, even in an era of skyscrapers.

Built a hundred years after the French Revolution (and in the midst of an industrial one), the tower served no function but to impress. Gustave Eiffel won an architectural contest at the 1889 centennial world's fair by beating out such rival proposals as a giant guillotine. To a generation hooked on technology, the tower was the marvel of the age, a symbol of progress and of man's ingenuity. To others it was a cloned-sheep monstrosity. The writer de Maupassant routinely ate lunch in the tower just so he wouldn't have to look at it.

Delicate and graceful when seen from afar, it's massive—even a bit scary—from close up. You don't appreciate the size until you walk toward it—like a mountain, it seems so close but takes forever to reach. There are three observation platforms, at 200, 400, and 900 feet. The higher you go the more you pay. Each requires a separate elevator (and a line), so plan on at least 90 minutes if you want to go to the top and back. The view from the 400-foot-high second level is plenty. Begin at the first floor, read the informative signs (in English) describing the major monuments, see the entertaining free movie on the history of the tower, and consider a drink overlooking all of Paris at the café or at Paris' best view/bar restaurant, Altitude 95 (260F meals, seatings at 19:00 and 21:00, reserve well ahead for a view table, tel. 01 45 55 20 04). Take the elevator to the second floor for even greater views. As you ascend through the metal beams, imagine being a worker, perched high above nothing, riveting this giant erector set together.

On top you can see all of Paris, aided by a panorama guide. On a good day you can see 40 miles. It costs 22F to go to the first level, 44F to the second, and 62F to go all the way for the 1,000-foot view (not included with museum pass). On a budget? You can climb the stairs to the second level for only 18F (summers daily 9:00–24:00, off-season 9:30–23:00, tel. 01 44 11 23 23, Mo: Trocadero, RER: Champs de Mars, tel. 01 44 11 23 23).

For a great view, especially at night, enjoy the tower—and the wild in-line-skating scene on Trocadero square—by approaching via the Trocadero Métro stop (from here the tower is a 10-min walk north, across the river). Another super view is from the long, grassy fields of the Champs du Mars (to the south). After about 21:00 the gendarmes look the other way as Parisians stretch out or picnic on the grass. However impressive it may be by day, it's an awesome thing to see at twilight, when the tower becomes engorged with light and virile Paris lies back and lets night be on top.

▲**Paris Sewer Tour (Égouts)**—This quick and easy visit takes you along a few hundred meters of underground water tunnel lined with interesting displays, well described in English, explaining the evolution of the world's longest sewer system. (If you lined up Paris' sewers they would reach beyond Istanbul.) Don't miss the slideshow, the fine WCs just beyond the gift shop, and the occasional tours in English (25F, Sat–Wed 11:00–17:00, closed Thu–Fri, where the Pont de l'Alma hits the Left Bank, tel. 01 47 05 10 29).

▲▲**Napoleon's Tomb and Army Museum (Les Invalides)**—The emperor lies majestically dead inside several coffins under a grand dome—a goose-bumping pilgrimage for historians. Napoleon is surrounded by the tombs of other French war heroes and a fine military museum in Hôtel des Invalides (check out the new World War II wing). Follow signs to the "crypt" to find Roman Empire–style reliefs listing the accomplishments of Napoleon's administration. The restored dome glitters with 26 pounds of gold (38F, students and kids 12–17 pay 28F, under 12-free, daily 10:00–17:45, closes off-season at 16:45, tel. 01 44 42 37 67, Métros: La Tour Maubourg or Varennes).

▲▲**Rodin Museum**—This user-friendly museum is filled with passionate works by the greatest sculptor since Michelangelo. See *The Kiss*, *The Thinker*, *The Gates of Hell*, and many more. Don't miss the room full of work by Rodin's student and mistress,

Camille Claudel (28F, 18F on Sun, free for those under 18 and
for anyone first Sun of month; 5F for gardens only, which may be
Paris' best deal, as many works are well displayed in the beautiful
gardens; Tue–Sun 9:30–17:45, closed Mon and at 17:00 off-
season, 77 rue de Varennes, Mo: Varennes, near Napoleon's
Tomb, tel. 01 44 18 61 10). There's a good self-serve cafeteria as
well as idyllic picnic spots in the family-friendly back garden.
▲▲**Marmottan**—In this private, intimate, less-visited museum
you'll find more than 100 paintings by Claude Monet (thanks to
his son Michel), including the *Impressions of a Sunrise* painting that
gave the movement its start—and name (40F, not covered by
museum pass, Tue–Sun 10:00–17:30, closed Mon, 2 rue Louis
Boilly, Mo: La Muette, follow the museum signs 6 blocks through
a park to the museum, tel. 01 42 24 07 02). Combine this fine
museum with a stroll down one of Paris' most pleasant shopping
streets, the rue de Passy (from la Muette Mo. stop).

Sights—Southeast Paris: The Latin Quarter
▲**Latin Quarter**—This Left Bank neighborhood just opposite the
Notre-Dame is the Latin Quarter. (For more information and a
walking tour, see "Historic Core of Paris Walk," above.) This was
a center of Roman Paris. But its touristic fame relates to the Latin
Quarter's intriguing artsy, bohemian character. This was perhaps
Europe's leading university district in the Middle Ages—home,
since the 13th century, to the prestigious Sorbonne University.
Back then, Latin was the language of higher education. And, since
students here came from all over Europe, Latin served as their
linguistic common denominator. Locals referred to the quarter by
its language: Latin. In modern times this was the center of Paris'
café culture. The neighborhood's main boulevards (St. Michel and
St. Germain) are lined with cafés—once the haunts of great poets
and philosophers but now the hangout of tired tourists. While still
youthful and artsy, the area has become a tourist ghetto filled with
cheap North African eateries.
▲**Cluny Museum (Musée National du Moyen Age)**—This treasure trove of medieval art fills the old Roman baths, offering close-up
looks at stained glass, Notre-Dame carvings, fine goldsmithing and
jewelry, and rooms of tapestries—the best of which is the exquisite
Lady with the Unicorn. In five panels, a delicate-as-medieval-can-be
noble lady introduces a delighted unicorn to the senses of taste, hearing, sight, smell, and touch (38F, 28F on Sun, Wed–Mon 9:15–
17:45, closed Tue, 6 place Paul-Painlevé, near the corner of boulevards St. Michel and St. Germain, Mo: Cluny, tel. 01 53 73 78 00).
St. Germain des Prés—A church was first built on this site in
A.D. 452. The church you see today was constructed in 1163. The
area around the church hops at night with fire eaters, mimes, and
scads of artists (Mo: St. Germain-des-Prés).

▲**St. Sulpice Organ Concert**—For pipe-organ enthusiasts, this is a delight. The Grand-Orgue at St. Sulpice has a rich history, with a line of 12 world-class organists (including Widor and Dupre) going back 300 years. Widor started the tradition of opening the loft to visitors after the 10:30 service on Sundays. Daniel Roth continues to welcome guests in three languages while playing five keyboards at once. The 10:30 Sunday Mass is followed by a 25-minute recital at 11:40. If you're lucky, at 12:00 the small unmarked door will open (left of entry as you face the rear) and allow visitors to scamper like sixteenth notes up spiral stairs to a world of 7,000 pipes, where they can watch the master perform the next Mass, friends warming his bench, and a committee scrambling to pull and push the 102 stops (Mo: St. Sulpice or Mabillon).

▲▲**Luxembourg Gardens**—Paris' most beautiful, interesting, and enjoyable garden/park/recreational area is a great place to watch Parisians at rest and play. The brilliant flower plantings are completely changed three times a year, and the boxed trees are brought out of the *orangerie* in May. Challenge the card and chess players to a game (near the tennis courts), or find a free chair near the main pond and take a breather. Notice any pigeons? A poor Ernest Hemingway used to hand-hunt (read: strangle) them here. Paris Walks offers a good tour of the park (see "Organized Tours," above). The grand neoclassical-domed Panthéon, now a mausoleum housing the tombs of several great Frenchmen, is a block away and is only worth entering if you have a museum pass. The park is open until dusk (Mo: Odéon, RER: Luxembourg). If you enjoy the Luxembourg Gardens and want to see more, visit the elegant Parc Monceau (Mo: Monceau) and the colorful Jardin des Plantes (Mo: Jussieu or Gare d'Austerlitz, RER: Luxembourg).

Montparnasse Tower—This 59-floor superscraper—it's cheaper and easier to get to the top than to that of the Eiffel Tower—offers one of Paris' best views, since the Eiffel Tower is in it and Montparnasse Tower isn't. Buy the photo guide to the city, then go to the rooftop and orient yourself (46F, daily in summer 9:30–23:00, off-season 10:00–22:00, disappointing after dark, entrance on rue l'Arrivé, Mo: Montparnasse). This is efficient when combined with a day trip to Chartres, which begins at the Montparnasse train station.

Sights—Northwest Paris

▲▲**Place de la Concorde and the Champs-Élysées**—This famous boulevard is Paris' backbone and greatest concentration of traffic. All of France seems to converge on the place de la Concorde, the city's largest square. It was here that the guillotine took the lives of thousands—including King Louis XVI and Marie Antoinette. Back then it was called the place de la Revolution.

Catherine de Médici wanted a place to drive her carriage,

so she started draining the swamp that would become the Champs-
Élysées. Napoleon put on the final touches, and it's been the place
to be seen ever since. The Tour de France bicycle race ends here,
as do all parades (French or foe) of any significance. While the
boulevard has become a bit hamburgerized, a walk here is a must.
Take the Métro to the Arc de Triomphe (Mo: Étoile) and saunter
down the Champs-Élysées (Métro stops every few blocks: FDR,
George V, and Étoile).

▲▲▲Arc de Triomphe—Napoleon had the magnificent Arc de
Triomphe commissioned to commemorate his victory at the Battle
of Austerlitz. There's no triumphal arch bigger (50 meters high,
40 meters wide). And, with 12 converging boulevards, there's no
traffic circle more thrilling to experience—either behind the wheel
or on foot (take the underpass). An elevator or a spiral staircase
leads to a cute museum about the arch and a grand view from the
top, even after dark (40F, June–Sept daily 9:30–23:00, Oct–May
daily 9:30–22:00, Mo: Étoile, tel. 01 43 80 31 31).

▲Grande Arche de La Défense—The centerpiece of Paris'
ambitious skyscraper complex (La Défense) is the Grande Arche.
Built to celebrate the 200th anniversary of the 1789 French Revolution, the place is big—38 floors on more than 200 acres. It holds
offices for 30,000 people. Notre-Dame Cathedral could fit under
its arch. The La Défense complex is an interesting study in 1960s
land-use planning. More than 100,000 workers commute here
daily, directing lots of business and development away from downtown and allowing central Paris to retain its more elegant feel.
This aspect makes sense to most Parisians, regardless of whatever
else they feel about the controversial complex. You'll enjoy city
views from the Arche elevator (46F includes a film on its construction and art exhibits, daily 10:00–19:00, Métro or RER: La
Défense, follow signs to Grande Arche, tel. 01 49 07 27 57).

Sights—Northeast Paris:
Marais Neighborhood and More

To better appreciate this area and connect its sights, take the
"Marais Walk," described later in this chapter.

▲▲Pompidou Center—Europe's greatest collection of far-out
modern art, the Musée National d'Art Moderne, is housed on the
top floor of this newly renovated and colorful exoskeletal building.
Once ahead of its time, this 20th-century art (remember that
century?) has been waiting for the world to catch up with it. After
so many Madonnas and Children, a piano smashed to bits and
glued to the wall is refreshing (50F, audioguide-25F, Wed–Mon
11:00–22:00, closed Tue, to ride escalator you need a museum
ticket or pass, café on mezzanine level is cheaper than cafés outside, Mo: Rambuteau, tel. 01 44 78 12 33).

The Pompidou Center and its square are lively, with lots of

people, street theater, and activity inside and out—a perpetual
street fair. Kids of any age enjoy the fun, colorful fountain (called
Homage to Stravinsky) on the square.

▲▲**Museum of Art and History of Judaism (Hotel
d'Aignan)**—This remarkable museum, located in a beautifully
restored Marais mansion, tells the story of *Judaism* throughout
Europe, from the Roman destruction of Jerusalem to the theft of
famous artwork during World War II. Helpful audioguides and
many English explanations make this an enjoyable history lesson.
Move along at your own speed. The emphasis of the museum is
to illustrate the cultural unity maintained by this continually
dispersed population. You'll learn about the history of Jewish
traditions, from bar mitzvahs to menorahs, and see exquisite traditional costumes and objects around which daily life revolved. Don't
miss the explanation of the Dreyfus affair, a major event in early-
1900 French politics.You'll also see photographs of and paintings
by famous Jewish artists, including Chagall, Modigliani, and
Soutine. The small section devoted to the deportation of Jews
from Paris is very moving (40F, not covered with museum pass,
Sun 10:00–18:00, Mon–Fri 11:00–18:00, closed Sat, 71 rue du
Temple, tel. 01 53 01 86 53).

▲**Picasso Museum (Hôtel Salé)**—This is the world's largest
collection of Pablo Picasso's paintings, sculpture, sketches, and
ceramics and includes his personal collection of Impressionist art.
It's well explained in English and worth ▲▲▲ if you're a fan
(30F, Wed–Mon 9:30–18:00, closed Tue, 5 rue Thorigny, Mo:
St. Paul or Chemin Vert, tel. 01 42 71 25 21).

▲**Carnavalet Museum**—The tumultuous history of Paris is well
displayed in this converted Marais mansion. Unfortunately, explanations are in French only, but many displays are fairly self-explanatory.
You'll see paintings of Parisian scenes, French Revolution paraphernalia, old Parisian store signs, a small guillotine, a model of 16th-
century Île de la Cité (notice the bridge houses), and rooms full of
15th-century Parisian furniture (35F, Tue–Sun 10:00–17:00, closed
Mon, 23 rue de Sévigné, Mo: St Paul, tel. 01 42 72 21 13).

Victor Hugo's House—France's literary giant lived in this fine
house on the place des Vosges from 1832 to 1848. Inside you'll
find many posters advertising theater productions of his works,
paintings of some of his most famous character creations, and a
few furnished rooms (22F, Tue–Sun 10:00–17:40, closed Mon,
6 place des Vosges).

Promenade Plantée Park—This three-kilometer narrow
garden walk, once a train track and now a joy, runs from
place de la Bastille (Mo: Bastille) along avenue Daumesnil to
Saint-Mandé (Mo: Michel Bizot). Part of the park is elevated.
At times you'll walk along the street till you pick up the next
segment. From place de la Bastille, take avenue Daumesnil

(past Opéra building) to the intersection with avenue Ledru Rollin. Walk up the stairs and through the gate (free, hours vary with season, open roughly 8:00–20:00).

▲**Père Lachaise Cemetery**—Littered with the tombstones of many of the city's most illustrious dead, this is your best one-stop look at the fascinating, romantic world of permanent Parisians. The place is confusing, but maps will direct you to the graves of Chopin, Molière, Edith Piaf, Oscar Wilde, Gertrude Stein, Héloïse, and Abelard. In section 92, a series of statues memorializing the war makes the French war experience a bit more real (helpful 10F maps at the flower store near the entry, across the street from Métro stop, closes at dusk, Mo: Père Lachaise or bus #69).

Sights—North Paris: Montmartre

▲**Sacré-Coeur and Montmartre**—This Byzantine-looking church, while only 130 years old, is impressive. It was built as a "praise the Lord anyway" gesture after the French were humiliated by the Germans in a brief war in 1871. The church is open daily until 23:00. One block from the church, the place du Tertre was the haunt of Toulouse-Lautrec and the original Bohemians. Today it's mobbed by tourists and unoriginal bohemians but still fun (go early in the morning to beat the crowds). Wander down the rue Lepic to the two remaining windmills (once there were 30). Rue des Saules leads to Paris' only vineyard. Métros: Anvers (an extra Métro ticket buys your way up the funicular and avoids the stairs) or the closer but less scenic Abbesses. A taxi to the top of the hill saves time and sweat.

Pigalle—Paris' red-light district, the infamous "Pig Alley," is at the foot of Butte Montmartre. *Ooh la la*. More shocking than dangerous. Walk from place Pigalle to place Blanche, teasing desperate barkers and fast-talking temptresses. In bars a 1,000F bottle of cheap champagne comes with a friend. Stick to the bigger streets, hang on to your wallet, and exercise good judgment. Cancan can cost a fortune, as can con artists in topless bars. After dark, tour buses line the streets. Tour guides make big bucks by bringing their groups to touristic nightclubs like the Moulin Rouge (Mo: Pigalle and Abbesses).

Best Shopping

Forum des Halles is a huge subterranean shopping center. It's fun, mod, and colorful but lacks a soul (Mo: Les Halles). The **Galeries Lafayette** behind the old Opéra Garnier is your best elegant, Old World, one-stop Parisian department store/shopping center (Mo: Opéra). Also visit the adjacent **Printemps** store and the historic (as well as handy) **Samaritaine** department store in several buildings near Pont Neuf (Mo: Pont Neuf). Ritzy shops surround the Ritz Hotel at place Vendôme (Mo: Tuileries).

Disappointments de Paris

While Paris can drive you in-Seine with superlatives, here are a few negatives to help you manage your limited time:

La Madeleine is a big, stark, neoclassical church with a post-card facade and a postbox interior. The famous aristocratic deli behind the church, Fauchon, is elegant, but so are many others handier to your hotel

Paris' Panthéon (nothing like Rome's) is another stark, neo-classical edifice filled with mortal remains of great Frenchmen who mean little to the average American tourist.

The Bastille is Paris' most famous nonsight. The square is there, but confused tourists look everywhere and can't find the famous prison of Revolution fame. The building's gone, and the square is good only as a jumping-off point for the "Marais Walk" (see below) or the Promenade Plantée Park (see "Sights—Northeast Paris," above).

The Latin Quarter is a frail shadow of its characteristic self. It's more Tunisian, Greek, and Woolworth's than old-time Paris. The café life that turned on Hemingway and endeared boul' Miche and boulevard St. Germain to so many poets is also trampled by modern commercialism.

Marais Walk

This walk takes you through one of Paris' most characteristic quarters. When you're in Paris, the natural inclination is to con-centrate only on the big sights. But to experience Paris you need to experience a vital neighborhood. This is a good one, containing more pre-Revolutionary buildings than anywhere else in town.

Ride the Métro to Bastille and follow the dotted path outlined on the Marais map in this chapter. This walk is about five kilome-ters (3 miles) long. Allow two hours and add another hour if you visit the Carnavalet Museum. For more information on the sights mentioned, see "Sights—Northeast Paris," above.

At **place de la Bastille** there are more revolutionary images in the Métro station murals than on the square. Exit the Métro following signs to rue Saint Antoine (not the signs to rue Saint Antoine du Faubourg). Ascend onto a noisy square dominated by the bronze *Colonne de Juillet* (July Column). Victims of the uprisings of 1830 and 1848 are buried in a vault 55 meters below this gilded statue of liberty. The actual **Bastille**, a royal fortress-then-prison that once symbolized old regime tyranny and now symbolizes the Parisian emancipation, is long gone. While only a brick outline of the fortress' round turrets survives (under the traffic where rue Saint Antoine hits the square), the story of the Bastille is indelibly etched on the city's psyche.

For centuries the Bastille was used to defend the city (mostly from its own people). On July 14, 1789, the people of Paris

Marais Walk

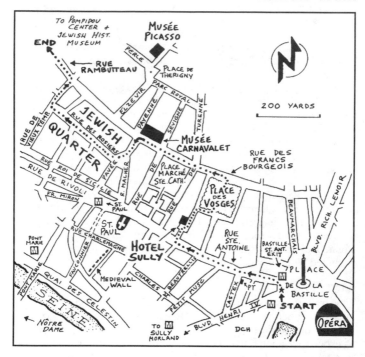

stormed the prison, releasing its seven prisoners and hoping to find arms. They demolished the brick fortress and decorated their pikes with the heads of a few bigwigs. By shedding blood, the leaders of the gang made sure it would be tough to turn back the tides of revolution. Ever since, the French have celebrated July 14th as their independence day—Bastille Day.

The flashy, glassy-gray, and controversial **Opéra-Bastille** dominates—some say overwhelms—the square. Designed by the Canadian architect Carlos Ott, this latest Parisian grand project was opened with great fanfare by François Mitterrand on the 200th Bastille Day, July 14, 1989, and follows in the footsteps of other "grand projects" like the Louvre Pyramid, the Grande Arche at La Défense, and the Pompidou Center. (For ticket information, see "Nightlife in Paris," below.)

Turn your back to the statue and, passing the Banque de France on your right (good rates, long lines, opposite a fine map of the area on your left), head straight down the busy rue Saint Antoine about four blocks into the Marais.

The Marais neighborhood, still filled with pre-Revolutionary lanes and buildings, is more characteristic than touristy (unlike the Latin Quarter). It's medieval Paris. This is how much of the city looked until, in the mid-1800s, Napoleon III had Baron Haussmann blast out the narrow streets to construct broad boulevards (wide enough for the guns and marching ranks of the army but too wide for revolutionary barricades).

Leave rue Saint Antoine at #62 and turn right through two elegant courtyards of Hôtel de Sully (62 rue Saint Antoine, open until 19:00, good Marais map on corridor wall). Originally a swamp (*marais*), during the reign of Henry IV it became the hometown of the French aristocracy. In the 17th century big shots built their private mansions (*hôtels*) like this one—close to Henry's place des Vosges. Hôtels that survived the revolution now house museums, libraries, and national institutions. The aristocrats may be gone, but the Marais—which until recently was a dumpy Bohemian quarter—is today a thriving, trendy, but real community and a joy to explore.

To get to the **place des Vosges park**, continue through Hôtel de Sully (if it's closed, backtrack to rue Biraque to reach place des Vosges). The small door on the far-right corner of the second courtyard pops you out into one of Paris' finest squares (closes at dusk). Walk to the center, where Louis XIII sits on a horse surrounded by locals enjoying their community park. Children frolic in the sandbox, lovers warm benches, and pigeons guard their fountains, while trees shade this retreat from the glare of the big city. Henry IV built this centerpiece of the Marais in 1605. As hoped, this turned the Marais into Paris' most exclusive neighborhood. **Victor Hugo's House** is at #6 (22F, Tue–Sun 10:00–17:40, closed Mon, 6 place des Vosges, corner closest to the Bastille).

To leave the square, walk behind Louis' horse to the arcade. Follow it left past art galleries and antique shops onto the boutique-filled rue des Francs Bourgeois. Browse two blocks off place des Vosges to the corner of rue de Sévigné, where you'll see the Musée Carnavalet (on right).

The **Carnavalet Museum**, focusing on the history of Paris, is housed inside a Marais mansion with classy courtyards and statues (35F, Tue–Sun 10:00–17:00, closed Mon, 23 rue de Sévigné).

To continue the Marais walk, go another block along rue des Francs Bourgeois (peeking through the gate on the right) and turn left at the post office. (The **Picasso Museum** is up one block to the right; 30F, Wed–Mon 9:30–18:00, closed Tue, 5 rue Thorigny.) From rue Pavée, bend right onto rue Rosiers, which runs straight through Paris' Jewish Quarter. It's lively every day except Saturday.

The **Jewish Quarter** is lined with colorful shops and kosher eateries. Jo Goldenberg's delicatessen/restaurant (first corner on ‏t, at #7—scene of a terrorist bombing in darker times) is worth king into. You'll be tempted by kosher pizza and plenty of 20F

falafel-to-go (*emporter* = to go) joints. Rue Rosiers dead-ends into
rue du Vieille du Temple. Turn right.

Frank Bourgeois is waiting at the corner postcard/print shop.
Turn left on rue des Francs Bourgeois. This road leads past the
national archives (peek inside the courtyard) and turns into rue
Rambuteau. The **Museum of Art and History of Judaism** (40F,
Mon–Fri 11:00–18:00, Sun 10:00–18:00, closed Sat, 71 rue de
Temple) is a block before the Pompidou Center.

The pipes and glass of the **Pompidou Center** reintroduce
you to this century (50F, Wed–Mon 11:00–22:00, closed Tue).
Pass that huge building on your left to join the fray in front of
the center (also called the Centre Beaubourg). Survey this popular
spot from the top of the sloping square. A tubular series of escalators leads up the building.

The Pompidou Center follows with gusto the modern-
day architectural axiom "form follows function." To get a more
spacious and functional interior, the guts of this exoskeletal building are draped on the outside and color coded: vibrant red for
people lifts, cool blue for air-conditioning, eco-green for plumbing, don't-touch-it yellow for electrical stuff, and white for bones.
Enjoy the adjacent *Homage to Stravinsky* **fountain**. Jean Tingley
designed this new-wave fountain as a tribute to the composer.
Every fountain represents one of his hard-to-hum scores.

With your back to the Pompidou Center's escalators, walk the
cobbled pedestrian mall and cross the busy boulevard Sebastopol to
the ivy-covered pavilions of **Les Halles**. After 800 years as Paris'
down-and-dirty central produce market, this was replaced by a
glitzy but soulless modern shopping center in the late 1970s. The
most endearing layer of the mall is its grassy rooftop park. The
Gothic Saint Eustache church overlooking this contemporary scene
seems ignored but has a famous 8,000-pipe organ. The Louvre and
Notre-Dame are just a short walk away. The mall is served by Paris'
busiest Métro hub (the Chatelet-Les Halles station).

Palace of Versailles

Every king's dream, Versailles was the residence of the French
king and the cultural heartbeat of Europe for about 100 years—
until the Revolution of 1789 ended the notion that God deputized
some people to rule for Him on Earth. Louis XIV spent half a
year's income of Europe's richest country turning his dad's hunting lodge into a palace fit for a divine monarch. Louis XV and
Louis XVI spent much of the 18th century gilding Louis XIV's
lily. In 1837, about 50 years after the royal family was evicted,
King Louis Philippe opened the palace as a museum. Europe's
next-best palaces are Versailles wanna-bes.

Information: A helpful TI is just past the Sofitel Hôtel
on your way from the station to the palace (tel. 01 39 24 88 88).

Versailles

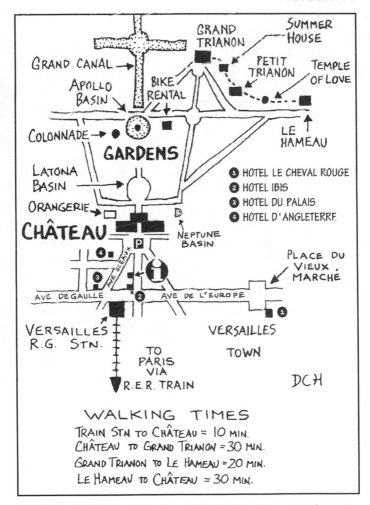

GRAND TRIANON

SUMMER HOUSE

GRAND CANAL →

APOLLO BASIN

BIKE RENTAL

PETIT TRIANON

TEMPLE OF LOVE

COLONNADE →

GARDENS

LE HAMEAU

LATONA BASIN →

❶ HOTEL LE CHEVAL ROUGE

❷ HOTEL IBIS

❸ HOTEL DU PALAIS

❹ HOTEL D'ANGLETERRE

ORANGERIE →

CHÂTEAU

NEPTUNE BASIN

PLACE DU VIEUX MARCHÉ

❹

❸

AVE. SEAUX

AVE DE GAULLE

❷

AVE DE L'EUROPE

❶

VERSAILLES R.G. STN.

VERSAILLES TOWN

TO PARIS VIA R.E.R. TRAIN

DCH

WALKING TIMES
TRAIN STN TO CHÂTEAU = 10 MIN.
CHÂTEAU TO GRAND TRIANON = 30 MIN.
GRAND TRIANON TO LE HAMEAU = 20 MIN.
LE HAMEAU TO CHÂTEAU = 30 MIN.

You'll also find information booths inside the château (at doors A, B-2, and C). The useful brochure, "Versailles Orientation Guide," explains your sightseeing options.

Ticket Options: The self-guided one-way romp through the State Apartments, including the Hall of Mirrors, costs 46F (covered by museum pass, 36F after 15:30, on Sun, or for those over 60 or ages 18–25, under 18 free). The entry fee is payable at doors A, C, or D. If you want a guided tour through the other sections, you need to pay the 46F base price, then pay extra for the tour.

Entrances to Versailles

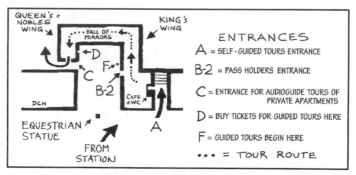

Tours: Add 25F for a 60-minute guided tour (of lesser-known nobles' apartments, like those of the well-coiffed Madame Pompadour) or 37F for a 90-minute guided tour of the King's Private Apartments (Louis XV, Louis XVI, and Marie-Antoinette), the chapel, and Opera House. Pay and get your tour appointment at entrance D. Tour times are normally all allotted for the day by 13:00. Tours leave from door F (across the courtyard from door D). Audioguides are available for 30F (choose between Louis XIV's Private Apartments at door C, or the State Apartments and Hall of Mirrors at doors A or B-2). Tours aren't covered by the museum pass. If you have extra time before your tour, wander through the state apartments or gardens.

Hours: May through September Tuesday through Sunday 9:00 to 18:30, October through April Tuesday through Sunday 9:00 to 17:30, closed Monday, last entry 30 minutes before closing. Versailles is especially crowded around 10:00 and 13:00, Tuesday, and Sunday. To minimize crowds, either arrive by 9:00 or after 15:30 (admission is cheaper after 15:30, but you'll miss the last guided tours of the day, which generally depart around 15:00); tour the gardens after the palace closes. The palace is great late. On my last visit, at 18:00, I was the only tourist in the Hall of Mirrors...even on a Tuesday.

Time to Allow: Six hours round-trip from Paris (1 hour each way in transit, 2 hours for palace, 2 for gardens).

Self-Guided Tour: For the basic self-guided tour, join the line at entrance A. Those with a museum pass are allowed in through entrance B-2 without a wait. Enter the palace and take a one-way walk through the State Apartments from the "King's Wing," through the magnificent Hall of Mirrors, and out via the "Queen's Wing."

The Hall of Mirrors was the ultimate hall of the day—250 feet long, 17 arched mirrors matching 17 windows with royal garden views, 24 gilded candelabra, eight busts of Roman emperors, and eight classical-style statues (7 are ancient originals). The ceiling is decorated with stories of Louis' triumphs. Imagine this place filled with silk gowns and powdered wigs, lit by thousands of candles. The mirrors—a luxurious rarity at the time—were a reflection of a time when aristocrats felt good about their looks and their fortunes. In another age altogether, this was the room in which the Treaty of Versailles was signed, ending World War I.

Before going downstairs at the end, take a stroll clockwise around the long room filled with the great battles of France murals. If you don't have *Rick Steves' Paris* or *Rick Steves' Mona Winks*, the guidebook called *The Châteaux, The Gardens, and Trianon* gives a room-by-room rundown.

Palace Gardens: The gardens offer a world of royal amusements. Outside the palace is L'Orangerie. Louis, the only one who could grow oranges in Paris, had an orange grove on wheels that could be wheeled in and out of his greenhouses according to the weather. A promenade leads from the palace to the Grand Canal, an artificial lake that, in Louis' day, was a mini-sea with nine ships, including a 32-cannon warship. France's royalty used to float up and down the canal in Venetian gondolas.

While Louis cleverly used palace life at Versailles to "domesticate" his nobility, turning otherwise meddlesome nobles into groveling socialites, all this pomp and ceremony hampered the royal family as well. For an escape from the public life at Versailles, they built more intimate palaces as retreats in their garden. Before the revolution there was plenty of space to retreat—the grounds were enclosed by a 25-mile-long fence.

The beautifully restored **Grand Trianon Palace** is as sumptuous as the main palace but much smaller. With its pastel-pink colonnade and more human scale, this is a place you'd like to call home. The nearby **Petit Trianon**, which has a fine neoclassical exterior with a skippable interior, was Marie Antoinette's favorite residence (25F-Grand Trianon, 15F-Petit Trianon, 30F for both, covered by museum pass, May–Sept Tue–Sun 10:00–18:00, closed Mon, Oct–April 10:00–17:00).

You can almost see princesses bobbing gaily in the branches as you walk through the enchanting forest, past the white marble temple of love (1778) to the queen's fake-peasant **Hamlet** (*Hameau*; interior not tourable). Palace life really got to Marie Antoinette. Sort of a back-to-basics queen, she retreated further and further from her blue-blooded reality. Her happiest days were at the hamlet, under a bonnet, tending her perfumed sheep and her manicured gardens in a thatch-happy wonderland.

Getting around the Gardens: It's a 30-minute hike from the palace, down the canal, past the two mini-palaces to the hamlet. You can rent bikes (30F/hr). The pokey tourist train, which costs only 10F, runs between the canal and château (30F, 5/hrly,

4 stops, you can hop on and off as you like; nearly worthless commentary).

Garden Hours: Except for fountain-filled weekends (see below), the gardens are free and open from 7:00 to sunset (as late as 21:30). There's a sandwich kiosk and a decent restaurant at the canal.

Fountain Spectacles: Classical music fills the king's backyard and the garden's fountains are in full squirt on Saturdays from July through September and on Sundays from early April through early October (schedule for both days: 11:00–12:00, 15:30–17:00, and 17:20–17:30). On these "spray days," the gardens cost 30F (not covered by museum pass). Louis had his engineers literally reroute a river to fuel these fountains. Even by today's standards they are impressive. For more information, pick up the map of the fountain show (*Les Grandes Eaux Musicales*) at any information booth.

Getting There: Take the RER-C train (29F round-trip, 30 min one-way) to Versailles R.G. or "Rive Gauche" (not Versailles C.H., which is farther from the palace). Trains, usually named "Vick," leave about five times an hour for the palace. RER-C trains leave from these RER/Métro stops: Invalides, Champ de Mars, Musée d'Orsay, St. Michel, and Gare d'Austerlitz. Get off at Versailles Rive Gauche (the end of the line), turn right out of the station, then left at the first boulevard. It's a 10-minute walk to the palace.

Your Eurailpass covers this inexpensive trip, but it uses up a valuable "flexi" day; consider seeing Versailles on your way in or out of Paris. To get free passage, show your railpass at an SCNF ticket window (for example, at the Les Invalides or Musée d'Orsay RER stops) and get a *contremarque de passage*; keep this ticket to exit the system.

When returning from Versailles, look through the windows past the turnstiles for the departure board. Any train leaving Versailles goes as far as downtown Paris (they're marked "all stations until d'Austerlitz"). If you're uncertain, confirm with a local by asking, "*À Paris?*" ("To Paris?").

Allow 225F (each way) for a taxi from Paris to Versailles. To cut your park walking by 50 percent, consider having the taxi drop you at the Hamlet (*Hameau*).

Town of Versailles (zip code: 78000): After the palace closes and the tourists go, the prosperous, wholesome town of Versailles feels a long way from Paris. The central market thrives on place du Marché on Tuesday, Friday, and Saturday until 13:00 (leaving the RER station, turn right and walk 10 min). Consider the wisdom of picking up or dropping your rental car in Versailles rather than in Paris. In Versailles, the Hertz and Avis offices are at the Gare des Chantiers (Versailles C.H., served by Paris' Montparnasse station). Versailles makes a fine home base; see Versailles accommodations under "Sleeping," below.

Paris Day Trips

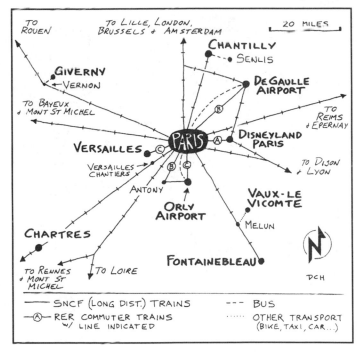

More Day Trips from Paris

▲▲▲**Chartres**—In 1194 a terrible fire destroyed the church at Chartres that housed the much-venerated veil of Mary. With almost unbelievably good fortune, the monks found the veil miraculously preserved in the ashes. Money poured in for the building of a bigger and better cathedral—decorated with 2,000 carved figures and some of France's best stained glass. The cathedral feels too large for the city because it was designed to accommodate huge crowds of pilgrims. One of those pilgrims, an impressed Napoleon, declared after a visit in 1811: "Chartres is no place for an atheist." Rodin called it "the Acropolis of France." British Francophile Malcolm Miller or his assistant give great "Appreciation of Gothic" tours Monday through Saturday, usually at noon and 14:45 (verify times in advance, no tours off-season, call TI at 02 37 18 26 26). Each 40F tour is different, many people stay for both tours. Just show up at the church (daily 7:00–19:00).

Explore Chartres' pleasant city center and discover the picnic-friendly park behind the cathedral. The helpful TI, next to the cathedral, has a map with a self-guided tour of Chartres (daily

Chartres

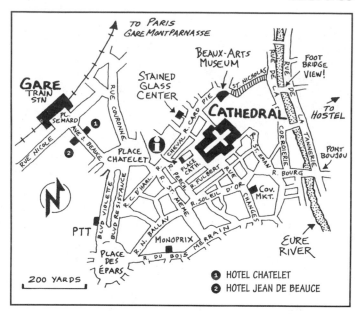

- ① HOTEL CHATELET
- ② HOTEL JEAN DE BEAUCE

9:30–18:45). Chartres is a one-hour train trip from the Gare
Montparnasse (about 75F one-way, 10/day). To stay overnight, try
the comfy **Hôtel Chatelet***** (Db-430–510F, CC:VM, 6 avenue
Jehan de Bruce, tel. 02 37 21 78 00, fax 02 37 36 23 01) or the
basic **Hôtel Jehan de Beauce**** (Db-240–310F, 19 avenue Jehan
de Beauce, tel. 02 37 21 01 41, fax 02 37 21 59 10).

▲**Giverny**—Monet spent 43 of his most creative years here (1883–
1926). Monet's gardens and home are unfortunately split by a busy
road and very popular with tourists. Buy your ticket, walk through
the gardens, and take the underpass into the artist's famous lilypad
land. The path leads you over the Japanese Bridge, under weeping
willows, and past countless scenes that leave artists aching for an
easel. Back on the other side, stroll through his more robust, struc-
tured garden and his mildly interesting home. The jammed gift shop
at the exit is Monet's actual skylit studio.

While lines may be long and tour groups may trample the
flowers, true fans still find magic in those lilypads. Minimize
crowds by arriving before 10:00 (get in line) or after 16:00 (35F,
25F for gardens only, April–Oct Tue–Sun 10:00–18:00, closed
Mon and Nov–March, tel. 02 32 51 94 65). Take the Rouen-
bound train from Paris' Gare St. Lazare station to Vernon (about
140F round-trip, long gaps in service, know the schedule before

you go). To get from the Vernon train station to Monet's garden (4 kilometers away), take the Vernon-to-Giverny bus (5/day, scheduled to meet most trains), hitch, taxi (60F), or rent a bike at the station (60F, busy road). Get return bus times from the ticket office in Giverny or ask them to call a taxi. Big tour companies do a Giverny day trip from Paris for around $60.

The new **American Impressionist Art Museum** is devoted to American artists who followed Claude to Giverny. This bright, modern gallery is well explained in English, has a good little Mary Cassatt section, and gives Americans a rare chance to see French people appreciating our artists (same price and hours as Monet's home, pleasant café, 100 meters from Monet's place).

To sleep two blocks from Monet's home, try the adorable **Hôtel La Musardiere**** (Db-400F, 132 rue Claude Monet, tel. 02 32 21 03 18, fax 02 32 21 60 00).

▲▲**Disneyland Paris**—Europe's Disneyland is basically a modern remake of California's, with most of the same rides and smiles. The main difference is that Mickey Mouse speaks French (and you can buy wine with your lunch). My kids went ducky. Locals love it. It's worth a day if Paris is handier than Florida or California. If possible, avoid Saturday, Sunday, Wednesday, school holidays, and July and August. The park can get very crowded. When 60,000 have entered, they close the gates (tel. 01 64 74 30 00 for the latest). After dinner, crowds are gone, and you'll walk right onto rides that had a 45-minute wait three hours earlier. Food is fun but expensive. Smuggle in a picnic.

Disney brochures are in every Paris hotel. The RER (about 43F each way, direct from downtown Paris to Marne-la-Vallee in 30 minutes) drops you right into the park. The last train back to Paris leaves shortly after midnight. (220F for adults, 170F for kids ages 3–11, 25F less in spring and fall, daily 9:00–23:00 late June–early Sept and Sat–Sun off-season, shoulder-season Mon–Fri 9:00–19:00, off-season 10:00–18:00, tel. 01 60 30 60 30.)

To sleep reasonably at the huge Disney complex, try Hotel Sante Fe (780F family rooms for 2–4 people includes breakfast, less off-season; ask for their hotel-and-park package deal, tel. 01 60 30 60 30, fax 01 60 30 60 65). If all this ain't enough, a new Planet Hollywood restaurant opened just outside the park.

Nightlife in Paris

Paris is brilliant after dark. Save energy from your day's sight-seeing and get out at night. Whether it's a concert at Sainte-Chapelle, an elevator up the Arc de Triomphe, or a late-night café, experience the city of light lit. If a night bus tour or a Seine River cruise appeals, see "Organized Tours of Paris," above.

The *Pariscope* magazine (3F at any newsstand) offers a complete weekly listing of music, cinema, theater, opera, and other special events; we decipher this useful periodical for you below. The *Free Voice* newspaper, in English, has a monthly review of Paris entertainment (available at any English-language bookstore, French-American establishments, or the American Church).

A Tour of Pariscope

The weekly *Pariscope* (3F) or *L'Officiel des Spectacles* (2F) are both cheap and essential if you want to know what's happening. For a head start, *Pariscope* has a Web site: www.pariscope.fr.

Each begins with culture news. Skip the "Theatres" and "Dîners/Spectacles" sections and anything listed as "*des environs*" (outside of Paris). "Musique" or "Concerts Classiques" list each day's events (with location, time, and price). Venues with phone numbers and addresses are listed in an "Adresses des Salles de Concerts" sidebar. Touristic venues (Sainte-Chapelle, Église de la Madeleine) are often featured in display ads. "Opéras," "Musique Traditionelle," "Ballet/Danse," and "Jazz/Rock" listings follow.

Half of these magazines are devoted to cinema—a Paris forte. After the "Films Nouveaux" section trumpets new releases, the "Films en Exclusivite" pages list all the films playing in town. While a code marks films as "Historique," "Karate," "Erotisme," and so on, the key mark for tourists is "v.o.," which means *version original* (American films have their English soundtracks and French subtitles). Films are listed alphabetically, with theaters and their arrondissements at the end of each entry. Later films are listed by neighborhood ("Salles Paris") and by genre. First runs are shown at cinemas on the Champs-Élysées and on place de l'Odeon; art films and older films are best found in the Latin Quarter. To find a showing near your hotel, simply match the arrondissement (but don't hesitate to hop on the Métro for the film you want). "Salles Périphérie" is out in the suburbs. Film festivals are also listed.

Pariscope has a small English "Time Out" section listing the week's events. The "Musées" sections (Monuments, Jardins, Autres Curiosites, Promenades, Activites Sportives, Piscines) give hours of sights, gardens, curiosities, boat tours, sports, pools, and so on. "Clubs de Loisirs" are athletic and social clubs. "Pour les Jeunes" is for young people (kids' films, cartoons, marionettes, circuses, and amusement parks, such as Asterix and Disney). "Conferences" are mostly lectures. For cancan mischief, look under "Paris la Nuit," "Cabarets," or the busty "Spectacles Erotiques."

Finally, you'll find a TV listing. Paris has four country-wide stations: TF1, France 2, France 3, and the new Arte station (a German/French cultural channel). M6 is filled with American series. Canal Plus (channel 4) is a cable channel that airs an American news show at 7:00 and an American sports event on Sunday evening.

Music

Jazz Clubs

With a lively mix of American, French, and international musicians, Paris has been an internationally acclaimed jazz capital since World War II. You'll pay from 40F to 160F to enter a jazz club (a drink may be included; if not, expect to pay 30–60F per drink; beer is cheapest). See *Pariscope* under "Musique" for listings or, better, the American Church's *Free Voice* paper for a good monthly review (in English)—or drop by to check out their calendars posted on the front door. Music starts after 22:00 in most clubs. Some offer dinner concerts from about 20:30 on. Here are a few good bets:

Caveau de la Huchette, a characteristic old jazz club for visitors, fills an ancient Latin Quarter cellar with live jazz and frenzied dancing every night (65F weekday, 80F weekend admission, 30F drinks, 21:30–02:30 or later, closed Mon, 5 rue de la Huchette, recorded info tel. 01 43 26 65 05).

For a hotbed of late-night activity and jazz, go to the two-block-long rue des Lombards, at boulevard Sebastopol, midway between the river and Pompidou Center (Mo: Chatelet). **Au Duc des Lombards**, right at the corner, is one of the most popular and respected jazz clubs in Paris with concerts generally at 21:30 (42 rue des Lombards, tel. 01 42 33 23 88, www.jazzvalley.com/duc). **Le Sunset** is a block west and offers more traditional jazz and fewer crowds with concerts around 21:00 (60 rue des Lombards, Mo: Chatelet, tel. 01 40 26 46 60).

At the down-to-earth and mellow **Le Cave du Franc Pinot**, you can enjoy a glass of chardonnay at the main-floor wine bar then drop downstairs for a cool jazz scene (1 quai de Bourbon, good dinner values as well, located on Île St. Louis where the Pont Marie meets the island, Mo: Pont Marie, tel. 01 46 33 60 64).

The **American Church** regularly plays host to fine jazz musicians for the best price in Paris (free, 65 quai d'Orsay, Mo: Invalides, RER-C: Pont de l'Alma, tel. 01 40 62 05 00).

Classical Concerts

For classical music on any night, consult *Pariscope* magazine; the "Musique" section under "Concerts Classique" lists concerts (free and fee). Look for posters at churches. Churches that regularly host concerts include St. Sulpice, St. Germain-des-Près, Basilique de Madeleine, St. Eustache, and Sainte-Chapelle. It's worth the 100F to 150F to hear Mozart while you're surrounded by the stained glass of the tiny Sainte-Chapelle. Even the Galeries Lafayette department store offers concerts. Many are free (*entree libre*), such as the Sunday Atelier concert sponsored by the American Church (18:00, 65 quai d'Orsay, Mo: Invalides, RER: Pont de l'Alma, tel. 01 47 05 07 99).

Opera

Paris is home to two well-respected operas. The **Opéra Garnier**, Paris' first opera house, hosts opera and ballet performances. Come here for less-expensive tickets and grand belle epoque decor (Mo: Opéra, tel. 01 44 73 13 99). The **Opéra de la Bastille** is the massive modern opera house that dominates place de la Bastille. Come here for state-of-the-art special effects and modern interpretations of classic ballets and operas (Mo: Bastille, tel. 01 43 43 96 96). For tickets, either call 01 44 73 13 00, go to the opera ticket offices (open 11:00–18:00), or, best, reserve on the Web at www .ticketavenue.com (for both operas).

Seine River Cruises

The Bâteaux-Mouches offer one-hour cruises on huge glass boats with departures (every 30 min from 10:00–23:00) from the Pont de l'Alma, the centrally located Pont Neuf, and right in front of the Eiffel Tower (see "Organized Tours of Paris," above).

Bus Tours

Paris Illumination Tours, run by Paris Vision, connect all the great illuminated sights of Paris with a 100-minute bus tour in 12 languages. Double-decker buses have huge windows, but Moulin Rouge customers get the most desirable front seats. You'll stampede on with a United Nations of tourists, get a hand-held audioguide, and listen to a tape-recorded spiel (interesting but occasionally hard to hear). Uninspired as it is, this provides a fine first-night overview of the city at its floodlit scenic best. Visibility is fine in the rain. You're entirely on the bus except for one five-minute cigarette break at the Eiffel Tower viewpoint (150F-adult, 75F-ages 4–11, free-under 3, departures at 20:30 nightly all year plus 22:00 Apr–Oct, departs from Paris Vision office at 214 rue de Rivoli, across street from Mo: Tuileries). These trips are sold through your hotel (brochures in lobby) or direct at the address listed above. Look also for the same tour by minivan—pickup is at your hotel, the driver is a qualified guide, and there's a maximum of seven clients (295F per person, for bus and minivans tel. 01 42 60 30 01, fax 01 42 86 95 36, www.parisvision.com).

Sleeping in Paris
(6.50F = about $1, country code: 33)

Sleep Code: **S** = Single, **D** = Double/Twin, **T** = Triple, **Q** = Quad, **b** = bathroom, **t** = toilet only, **s** = shower only, **CC** = Credit Card (**V** = Visa, **M** = MasterCard, **A** = Amex), * = French hotel rating system (0–4 stars).

I've focused on three safe, handy, and colorful neighborhoods: rue Cler, Marais, and Contrescarpe. For each, I list good hotels, helpful hints, and restaurants (see "Eating," below). Before reserving, read the descriptions of the three neighborhoods closely. Each offers different pros and cons, and your neighborhood is as important as your hotel to the success of your trip.

Reserve ahead for Paris, the sooner the better. Conventions clog Paris in September (worst), October, May, and June. In August, when Paris is quiet, some hotels offer lower rates to fill their rooms (if you're planning to visit Paris in the summer, the extra expense of an air-conditioned room can be money well spent). Most hotels accept telephone reservations, require prepayment with a credit-card number, and prefer a faxed follow-up to be sure everything is in order. For more information, see "Making Reservations" in this book's introduction.

French hotels are rated by stars (indicated in this book by an *). One star is simple, two has most of the comforts, and three generally just adds a mini-bar and fancier lobby (though I've tried to find three-star hotels that merit the extra expense).

Old, characteristic, budget Parisian hotels have always been cramped. Retrofitted with elevators, toilets, and private showers (as most are today), they are even more cramped. Even three-star hotel rooms are small and often not worth the extra expense in Paris. Some hotels include the hotel tax (*taxe du séjour*, about 5F per person per day), though most will add this to your bill. Two- and three-star hotels are required to have an English-speaking staff. Nearly all hotels listed will have someone who speaks English.

Quad rooms usually have two double beds. Recommended hotels have an elevator unless otherwise noted. Because rooms with double beds and showers are cheaper than rooms with twin beds and baths, room prices vary within each hotel.

You can save as much as 100F by finding the increasingly rare room without a private shower, though some hotels charge for down-the-hall showers. Singles (except for the rare closet-type rooms that fit only one twin bed) are simply doubles used by one person. They rent for only a little less than a double. Continental breakfasts cost 25F to 35F, buffet breakfasts (baked goods, cereal, yogurt, and fruit) cost 50F to 60F. Café or picnic breakfasts are cheaper, but hotels usually give unlimited coffee.

Get advice from your hotel for safe parking (consider long-term parking at Orly Airport and taxi in). Meters are free in August. Garages are plentiful (90–140F/day, with special rates through some hotels). Self-serve Laundromats are common; ask your hotelier for the nearest one (*Où est un laverie automatique?*; ooh ay uh lah-vay-ree auto-mah-teek).

Rue Cler Orientation

Rue Cler, a village-like pedestrian street, is safe, tidy, and makes me feel like I must have been a poodle in a previous life. How such coziness lodged itself between the high-powered government district and the wealthy Eiffel Tower and Invalides areas, I'll never know. This is a neighborhood of wide, tree-lined boulevards, stately apartment buildings, and lots of Americans. The American Church, American Library, American University, and many of my readers call this area home.

Become a local at a rue Cler café for breakfast or join the afternoon crowd for *une bière pression* (a draft beer). On rue Cler you can eat and browse your way through a street full of tart shops, delis, cheeseries, and colorful outdoor produce stalls. For an after-dinner cruise on the Seine, it's just a short walk to the river and the Bâteaux-Mouches (see "Organized Tours of Paris," above).

Your neighborhood **TI** is at the Eiffel Tower (May–Sept daily 11:00–18:00, tel. 01 45 51 22 15). The Métro station (École Militaire) and a **post office** are at the end of rue Cler—on avenue de la Motte Piquet, and there's a handy SNCF office under the *Aérogare* at the Invalides Métro stop, where you can get information, buy tickets, and make seat reservations. The nearest Internet access is at the splashy Toyota **Cybercafé** (79 avenue Champs-Élysées, Mo: George V, tel. 01 56 89 29 79). Taxi stands are on avenue de Tourville at avenue la Motte Piquet (near Métro stop) and on avenue Bosquet at rue St. Dominique. The Banque Populaire (across from Hôtel Leveque) changes money. Rue St. Dominique is the area's boutique-browsing street. The Épicerie de la Tour **grocery** is open until midnight (197 rue de Grenelle).

The **American Church and College** is the community center for Americans living in Paris and should be one of your first stops if you're staying in Paris a while (reception open Mon–Sat 9:00–22:30, Sun 9:00–19:30, 65 quai d'Orsay, tel. 01 40 62 05 00). Pick up copies of the *Free Voice* for a monthly review of Paris entertainment, and *France-U.S.A. Contacts* for information on housing and employment through the community of 30,000 Americans living in Paris. The interdenominational service at 11:00 on Sunday, the coffee hour after church, and the free Sunday concerts (18:00, not every week) are a great way to make some friends and get a taste of émigré life in Paris.

Afternoon *boules* (lawn bowling) on the esplanade des Invalides is a relaxing spectator sport. Look for the dirt area to the upper right as you face the Invalides.

You should try at least one of these helpful **bus routes:** Line #69 runs along rue St. Dominique and serves Les Invalides, Orsay, Louvre, Marais, and Père-Lachaise cemetery. Line #92 runs along avenue Bosquet and serves the Arc de Triomphe and Champs-Élysées in one direction and Montparnasse Tower in the other. Line #87 runs on avenue de la Bourdonnais and serves St. Sulpice, Luxembourg Gardens, and the Sevres-Babylone shopping area. Line #49 runs on boulevard La Tour Maubourg and serves the St. Lazare and Gare du Nord stations.

Sleeping in the Rue Cler Neighborhood
(7th arrondissement, Mo: École Militaire, zip code: 75007)

Rue Cler is the glue that holds this pleasant neighborhood together. From here you can walk to the Eiffel Tower, Napoleon's Tomb, the Seine, and the Orsay and Rodin Museums.

Many of my readers stay in this neighborhood. If you want to disappear in Paris, you'll do it better at the hotels away from the rue Cler, or in the other neighborhoods I list. And if nightlife matters, seriously consider sleeping elsewhere (this area is dead at night). The first seven hotels listed below are within Camembert-smelling distance of rue Cler; the others are within a 5- to 10-minute stroll. Warning: The first two hotels are popular with my readers.

Hôtel Leveque** is ideally located, with an air-conditioned lobby (and ice machine), helpful staff, and a singing maid. It's a big place with well-designed rooms that have ceiling fans, cable TV, hair dryers, direct phone lines, safes, and French modem outlets (S-300F, Db-400–500F, Tb-600F, CC:VMA, breakfast-40F, first breakfast free for readers of this book, 29 rue Cler, tel. 01 47 05 49 15, fax 01 45 50 49 36, www.hotel-leveque.com, e-mail: info@hotelleveque.com).

Hôtel du Champ de Mars**, with charming, pastel rooms and helpful English-speaking owners Françoise and Stephane, is a cozier rue Cler option. The hotel has a Provence-style, small-town feel from top to bottom. Rooms are comfortable and a very good value. Single rooms can work as tiny doubles (Sb-400F, Db-440–470F, Tb-560F, CC:VMA, cable TV, hair dryers, 30 meters off rue Cler at 7 rue de Champ de Mars, tel. 01 45 51 52 30, fax 01 45 51 64 36, www.hotel-du-champ-de-mars.com, e-mail: stg@club-internet.fr).

Hôtel Cadran*** charges too much for its fine location and cozy lobby. Rooms are tight and narrow but air-conditioned (Sb or Db-900–980F, 10 rue de Champs de Mars, tel. 01 40 62 67 00, fax 01 40 62 67 13, www.cadranhotel.com).

Hôtel Relais Bosquet*** is modern, spacious, and a bit upscale, with snazzy, comfortable rooms and big beds (Sb-600–800F, Db-650–1,000F, most at 850F, more-expensive rooms with air-con, CC:VMA, cable TV, 19 rue de Champ de Mars, tel. 01 47 05 25 45, fax 01 45 55 08 24, www.relaisbosquet.com).

Hôtel Beaugency*** has small but comfortable rooms, a lobby you can stretch out in, and a helpful staff (Sb-680F, Db-730F, Tb-830F, includes buffet breakfast, 21 rue Duvivier, tel. 01 47 05 01 63, fax 01 45 51 04 96).

Hôtel Le Valadon**, on a quiet street one block west of rue Cler, has fairly spacious, tired rooms and uninspired management (Db-510–560F, Tb-660F, CC:VMA, 16 rue Valadon, tel. 01 47 53 89 85, fax 01 44 18 90 56).

Rue Cler Hotels

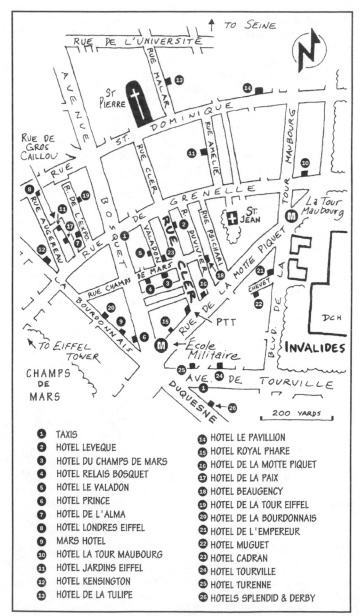

1. TAXIS
2. HOTEL LEVEQUE
3. HOTEL DU CHAMPS DE MARS
4. HOTEL RELAIS BOSQUET
5. HOTEL LE VALADON
6. HOTEL PRINCE
7. HOTEL DE L'ALMA
8. HOTEL LONDRES EIFFEL
9. MARS HOTEL
10. HOTEL LA TOUR MAUBOURG
11. HOTEL JARDINS EIFFEL
12. HOTEL KENSINGTON
13. HOTEL DE LA TULIPE
14. HOTEL LE PAVILLION
15. HOTEL ROYAL PHARE
16. HOTEL DE LA MOTTE PIQUET
17. HOTEL DE LA PAIX
18. HOTEL BEAUGENCY
19. HOTEL DE LA TOUR EIFFEL
20. HOTEL DE LA BOURDONNAIS
21. HOTEL DE L'EMPEREUR
22. HOTEL MUGUET
23. HOTEL CADRAN
24. HOTEL TOURVILLE
25. HOTEL TURENNE
26. HOTELS SPLENDID & DERBY

Hôtel la Motte Piquet**, at the end of rue Cler on a busy street, is pleasant with reasonable rates and a helpful owner (Ss-355F, Sb-375–435F, Ds-400F, Db-420–490F, duplex suites-670–780F, extra bed-100F, CC:VM, 30 avenue de la Motte Piquet, tel. 01 47 05 09 57, fax 01 47 05 74 36).

The following listings are a 5- to 10-minute walk west of rue Cler and are listed in order of proximity.

Hôtel Prince**, just across avenue Bosquet from the École Militaire Métro stop, has fair-value rooms, many overlooking a busy street (Db-470–625F, CC:VMA, 66 avenue Bosquet, tel. 01 47 05 40 90, fax 01 47 53 06 62).

Hôtel le Tourville**** is the most classy and expensive of my Paris listings. This four-star gem is surprisingly intimate and friendly, from its welcoming lobby to its air-conditioned, pastel rooms and vaulted breakfast area (small standard Db-890F, superior Db-1,090F, Db with private terrace-1,350F, extra bed-100F, 16 avenue de Tourville, Mo: École Militaire, tel. 01 47 05 62 62, fax 01 47 05 43 90, e-mail: hotel@tourville.com).

Hôtel de Turenne**, with small air-conditioned rooms, is a good value when it's hot (Sb-370F, Db-440–510F, Tb-600F, extra bed-60F, CC:VM, cable TV, 20 avenue de Tourville, tel. 01 47 05 99 92, fax 01 45 56 06 04, e-mail: hotel.turenne.paris7 @wanadoo.fr).

Hôtel de l'Alma*** is a fair value, with 32 small but pleasant look-alike rooms, all with cable TV and minibar and a tiny lobby (Sb-450F, Db-500F, no triples but a kid's bed can be moved in for free, CC:VMA, includes breakfast, 32 rue de l'Exposition, tel. 01 47 05 45 70, fax 01 45 51 84 47, e-mail: almahotel@minitel.net).

Hôtel Londres Eiffel*** may have rooms when others don't. The helpful staff takes good care of its guests and offers small but thoughtfully appointed rooms and cozy public spaces (Sb-545F, Db-645F, Tb-825F, extra bed-70F, CC:VMA, use handy bus #69 or the RER Alma stop, 1 rue Augerau, tel. 01 45 51 63 02, fax 01 47 05 28 96, www.Londres-Eiffel.com).

Mars Hôtel** is a formal Parisian place, with spacious rooms, thin walls, reasonable rates, and a beam-me-up-Jacques, coffin-sized elevator. Front rooms are noisier but have views of the Eiffel Tower (large Sb-350F, Db-410F, Twin/b-510F, CC: VM, 117 avenue de la Bourdonnais, tel. 01 47 05 42 30, fax 01 47 05 45 91).

Hôtel de la Bourdonnais***, more famous for its highly respected restaurant, is a superb three-star hotel. This perfectly Parisian place mixes Old World elegance with top-notch service, spacious rooms, and pleasant public spaces (Sb-690F, Db-790F, Tb-850F, Qb-910F, Qb suite-1,500F, CC:VMA, cable TV, 111 avenue de la Bourdonnais, tel. 01 47 05 45 42, fax 01 45 55 75 54, e-mail: otlbourd@clubinternet.fr).

Hôtel Kensington** has warmly decorated rooms at a fair

value, but a cold staff (Sb-325F, Db-410–510F, extra bed-80F, CC:VMA, 79 avenue de la Bourdonnais, tel. 01 47 05 74 00, fax 01 47 05 25 81, www.hotel-kensington.com).

Hôtel de la Tulipe** is a unique place two blocks from rue Cler toward the river, with artistically decorated rooms (each one different) surrounding a wood-beamed lounge and a peaceful, leafy courtyard (Sb-570F, Db-680F, extra bed-150F, no elevator, cable TV, 33 rue Malar, tel. 01 45 51 67 21, fax 01 47 53 96 37, www .hoteldelatulipe.com).

The next four listings are within two blocks of the intersection of avenue de la Motte Piquet and Les Invalides. Use Métro stop La Tour Maubourg.

Hôtel Les Jardins Eiffel*** merits its three stars with professional service, a spacious lobby, outdoor patio, and comfortable, air-conditioned rooms—some with private balconies. Ask for a room *avec petit balcon* (Sb-600–840F, Db-700–1,000F, extra bed-135F, CC:VMA, parking-110F/day, 8 rue Amelie, tel. 01 47 05 46 21, fax 01 45 55 28 08, e-mail: Eiffel@unimedia.fr).

Hôtel La Tour Maubourg*** feels like a slightly faded, elegant manor house with spaciously comfortable Old World rooms. It overlooks a cheery green lawn and a busy street, within sight of Napoleon's tomb (Sb-700F, Db-800–900F, suites for up to 4 people-1,100–1,800F, prices reduced mid-July–mid-Aug, CC:VM, includes breakfast with freshly squeezed juice, immediately at La Tour Maubourg Métro stop, 150 rue de Grenelle, tel. 01 47 05 16 16, fax 01 47 05 16 14, www .latour-maubourg.fr).

Hôtel de l'Empereur** is a big, modern place with all the comforts (Sb-430F, Db-470–500F, Tb-650F, Qb-750F, CC:VM, 2 rue Chevert, tel. 01 45 55 88 02, fax 01 45 51 88 54).

Hôtel Muguet** is peaceful, overlooked, and very sharp. Here, you get three-star comfort for the price of two; a pleasant owner; quiet, air-conditioned rooms; and a small garden courtyard (Sb-560F, Db-600F, Tb-780F, CC:VMA, 11 rue Chevert, tel. 01 47 05 05 93, fax 01 45 50 25 37, www.hotelmuguet.com).

These places are lesser values but, in this fine area, acceptable last choices: **Derby Eiffel Hôtel***** (Db-750F–900F, CC:VMA, air-con, 5 avenue Duquesne, tel. 01 47 05 12 05, fax 01 47 05 43 43, www.derbyeiffelhotel.com); **Hôtel Splendid***** (Db-790–930F, 29 avenue Tourville, tel. 01 45 51 24 77, fax 01 44 18 94 60, e-mail: splendid@club-internet.fr); **Hôtel de la Tour Eiffel**** (Sb-370F, Db-420F, Tb-520F, CC:VMA, 17 rue de l'Exposition, tel. 01 47 05 14 75, fax 01 47 53 99 46, Muriel SE); the quiet but tired **Hôtel le Pavillon**** (has unrealized potential and a small courtyard; Db-460F, family suites-575F, 54 rue St. Dominique, tel. 01 45 51 42 87, fax 01 45 51 32 79, e-mail: PatrickPavillon@aol.com); **Hôtel Royal Phare****

(Db-390–460F, CC:VMA, facing École Militaire Métro stop,
40 avenue de la Motte Piquet, tel. 01 47 05 57 30, fax 01 45
51 64 41); the simple, quiet **Hôtel de la Paix** (S-180F, Ds-330F,
Db-350F, Tb-480F, no elevator, 19 rue du Gros-Caillou, tel.
01 45 51 86 17, fax 01 45 55 93 28); and the basic, overpriced
Hôtel la Serre* (Db-500F, has superb location on rue Cler but
generates readers' complaints for its rude staff and bizarre hotel
practices—you can't see room in advance and no refunds are
given, 24 rue Cler, across from Hôtel Leveque, Mo: Ecole
Militaire, tel. 01 47 05 52 33, fax 01 40 62 95 66).

Marais Orientation

Those interested in a more Soho-Greenwich Village locale should
make the Marais their Parisian home. The Marais is a more
happening area than rue Cler, with great access to many museums:
Picasso, Carnavalet, Jewish History, and Pompidou Center. It's
narrow, medieval Paris at its finest, where elegant stone mansions
sit side by side with trendy bars, antique shops, and slick boutiques. Only 15 years ago it was a forgotten Parisian backwater,
but now the Marais is one of Paris' most popular residential and
shopping areas.

The nearest **TIs** are in the Louvre and Gare de Lyon
(arrival level, daily 8:00–20:00, tel. 01 43 43 33 24). The **Banque
de France** changes money, offering good rates and sometimes
long lines (Mon–Fri 9:00–11:45, 13:30–15:30, at the corner
where rue St. Antoine hits place de la Bastille). Most banks and
other services are on the main drag, rue de Rivoli/St. Antoine.
You'll find one **taxi stand** on the north side of rue St. Antoine,
where it meets rue Castex, and another on the south side of St.
Antoine, in front of the St. Paul church.

The new Bastille opera house, Promenade Plantée Park,
place des Vosges (Paris' oldest square), and the Jewish Quarter
(rue des Rosiers) are all nearby. Be sure to stroll into place
des Vosges after dark. The massive budget **department store** is
BHV, next to Hôtel de Ville. Marais **post offices** are on rue
Castex and on the corner of rues Pavée and Francs Bourgeois.
The handiest **Internet cafés** are the Café du Hamman (4 rue
des Rosiers) and the Quick Cybercafé (66 rue de Rivoli, tel.
01 48 87 78 43, Mo. Chatelet).

Helpful **bus routes**: Line #69 on rue St. Antoine takes you
to the Louvre, Orsay, Rodin, and Napoleon's Tomb and ends
at the Eiffel Tower. Line #86 runs down boulevard Henri IV,
crossing Île St. Louis and serving the Latin Quarter along boulevard St. Germain. Line #96 runs on rues Turenne and Francois
Miron and serves the Louvre and boulevard St. Germain (near
Luxembourg Gardens). Line #65 serves the train stations Austerlitz, Est, and Nord from place de la Bastille.

Sleeping in the Marais Neighborhood
(4th arrondissement, Mo: St. Paul or Bastille, zip code: 75004)

The Marais runs from the Pompidou Center to the Bastille (a 15-min walk), with most hotels located a few blocks north of the main east-west drag, rue de Rivoli/St. Antoine. It's about 15 minutes on foot from any hotel in this area to Notre-Dame, Île St. Louis, and the Latin Quarter. Strolling home (day or night) from Notre-Dame along the Île St. Louis is a marvelous plus of this area.

The St. Paul Métro stop puts you right in the heart of the Marais, while the Hôtel de Ville stop serves its western end and the Bastille stop serves its eastern limit.

Hôtel Castex** is a clean, well-run, and cheery place—a great value with comfortable rooms, many stairs, and a good location on a relatively quiet street. Reserve by phone and leave your credit-card number (Sb-310F, Db-360–380F, Tb-480F, CC:VM, no elevator, just off place de la Bastille and rue St. Antoine, 5 rue Castex, Mo: Bastille, tel. 01 42 72 31 52, fax 01 42 72 57 91, e-mail: info@castexhotel.com). The owners have another good-value hotel two Métro stops away in a less appealing location that often has rooms when others don't: **Hôtel de la Republique**** (Sb-350F, Db-400F, cable TV, 31 rue Albert Thomas, 75010 Paris, Mo: Republique, tel. 01 42 39 19 03, fax 01 42 39 22 66, www.republique.com).

Grand Hôtel Jeanne d'Arc**, a warm, welcoming place with thoughtfully appointed rooms and cozy public spaces, is ideally located for connoisseurs of the Marais. Rooms on the street can be noisy until the bars close. Sixth-floor rooms have a view and corner rooms are wonderfully bright in the City of Light. Reserve this place way ahead (small Db-320F, Db-435–500F, Tb-550F, family friendly Qb-620F, extra bed-75F, CC:VM, 3 rue Jarente, Mo: St. Paul, tel. 01 48 87 62 11, fax 01 48 87 37 31).

Hôtel Bastille Speria*** a short block off the Bastille, feels family-run while offering serious, business-type service. Its spacious lobby and 45 rooms are modern, cheery, and pastel. It's English-language friendly, from the *Herald Tribune*s in the lobby to the history of the Bastille posted in the elevator (Sb-540–580F, Db-600–720F, Tb-830F, extra bed-110F, CC:VMA, 1 rue de la Bastille, Mo: Bastille, tel. 01 42 72 04 01, fax 01 42 72 56 38, e-mail: speria@micronet.fr).

Hôtel Lyon-Mulhouse**, on a busy street just off place de la Bastille, is a good value, with pleasant, modern rooms and helpful owners (Sb-345–435F, Db-370–540F, Tb-545–575F, Qb-600–640F, CC:VM, 8 boulevard Beaumarchais, tel. 01 47 00 91 50, fax 01 47 00 06 31, e-mail: hotelyonmulhouse@wanadoo.fr).

Marais Hotels

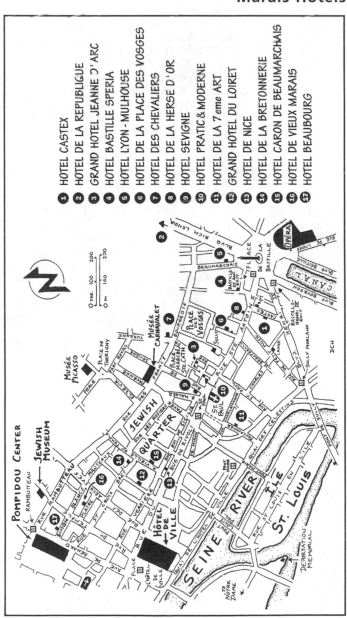

1. HOTEL CASTEX
2. HOTEL DE LA REPUBLIQUE
3. GRAND HOTEL JEANNE D'ARC
4. HOTEL BASTILLE SPERIA
5. HOTEL LYON - MULHOUSE
6. HOTEL DE LA PLACE DES VOSGES
7. HOTEL DES CHEVALIERS
8. HOTEL DE LA HERSE D'OR
9. HOTEL SEVIGNE
10. HOTEL PRATIC & MODERNE
11. HOTEL DE LA 7eme ART
12. GRAND HOTEL DU LOIRET
13. HOTEL DE NICE
14. HOTEL DE LA BRETONNERIE
15. HOTEL CARON DE BEAUMARCHAIS
16. HOTEL DE VIEUX MARAIS
17. HOTEL BEAUBOURG

Hôtel de la Place des Vosges**, quasi-classy with a linoleum/antique feel, is ideally located on a quiet street (Sb-495F, Db-660–690F, CC:VMA, elevator begins on 2nd floor, just off elegant place des Vosges and just as snooty, 12 rue de Biraque, Mo: St. Paul, tel. 01 42 72 60 46, fax 01 42 72 02 64, e-mail: hotel.place.des.vosges@gofornet.com).

Hôtel des Chevaliers***, one block northwest of place des Vosges, offers small, pleasant, and comfortable rooms, with modern comforts from hair dryers to cable TV. Rooms off the street are quiet (Db-660–850F, CC:VMA, skip overpriced breakfast, 30 rue de Turenne, Mo: St. Paul, tel. 01 42 72 73 47, fax 01 42 72 54 10).

Hôtel de la Herse D'Or is industrial-strength, three-coats-of-paint simple, with a good location, tortured floor plan, and hard-to-beat prices for its relatively comfortable rooms (S-180F, D-220F, Db-310F, extra bed-50F, showers-10F, no elevator, 20 rue St. Antoine, Mo: Bastille, tel. 01 48 87 84 09, fax 01 48 87 94 01).

Hôtel Sévigné** provides two-star comfort at fair prices with the cheapest breakfast in Paris—20F (Sb-360F, Db-380–400F, Tb-512F, CC:VM, 2 rue Malher, Mo: St. Paul, tel. 01 42 72 76 17, fax 01 42 78 68 26).

Hôtel Pratic*'s greatest plus is its location on a great people-friendly square. Its pricey rooms are modern (single rooms are tiny) and stairs are many (St-250F, Dt-280F, Ds-390F, Db-460F, no elevator, 9 rue d'Ormesson, Mo: St. Paul, tel. 01 48 87 80 47, fax 01 48 87 40 04).

The bare-bones and dumpy **Hôtel Moderne**, next to Hôtel Pratic, might be better than a youth hostel if you need privacy. The only thing *moderne* about it is the name, which is illegible on the broken sign (S-170F, D-190F, Db-340F, 3 rue Caron, Mo: St. Paul, tel. 01 48 87 97 05).

Hôtel de 7ème Art**, two blocks south of rue St. Antoine, is a relaxed, Hollywood-nostalgia place, run by young, friendly, hip Marais types, with a full-service café/bar and Charlie Chaplin murals. Most rooms are average, but the few large double rooms at 690F are very nice (Sb-300F, Db-430–570F, large Db-690F, extra bed-100F, CC:VMA, 20 rue St. Paul, Mo: St. Paul, tel. 01 44 54 85 00, fax 01 42 77 69 10).

MIJE Youth Hostels: The *Maison Internationale de la Jeunesse des Étudiants* (MIJE) runs three classy old residences clustered a few blocks south of rue St. Antoine. Each offers simple, clean, single-sex, one- to four-bed rooms for families and travelers under the age of 30 (exceptions are made for families). Prices are per person; you can pay more to have your own room or be roomed with as many as three others (Sb-225F, Db-175F, Tb-155F, Qb-145F; includes breakfast but not towels—which you can get from a machine; required membership card-15F extra/person;

rooms locked from 12:00–15:00 and at 01:00). **MIJE Fourcy** (cheap dinners, 6 rue de Fourcy, just south of rue Rivoli), **MIJE Fauconnier** (11 rue Fauconnier), and the best, **MIJE Maubisson** (12 rue des Barres), share the same contact information (tel. 01 42 74 23 45, fax 01 40 27 81 64, www.mije.com) and Métro stop (St. Paul). Reservations are accepted.

The remaining hotels are farther west, and much closer to the Pompidou Center than to the Bastille.

Hôtel de Nice** is a cozy "Marie Antoinette does tie-dye" place with lots of thoughtful touches on the Marais' busy main drag. Twin rooms, which cost the same as doubles, are roomier but on the street side—with effective double-paned windows (Sb-380F, Db-550F, Tb-680F, CC:VM, 42 bis rue de Rivoli, Mo: Hôtel de Ville, tel. 01 42 78 55 29, fax 01 42 78 36 07).

Hôtel de la Bretonnerie***, three blocks north and east of the Hôtel de Ville, is a fine Marais splurge. It has elegant décor; tastefully decorated and spacious rooms with an antique, open-beam coziness; and an efficient, helpful staff (standard Db-660F, Db with character-830F, the standard Db has enough character for me, family-friendly suites-1,050F, CC:VMA, between rue du Vielle du Temple and rue des Archives at 22 rue Sainte Croix de la Bretonnerie, Mo: Hôtel de Ville, tel. 01 48 87 77 63, fax 01 42 77 26 78, www.laBretonnerie.com).

Grand Hôtel du Loiret**, just north of rue de Rivoli, is a fair-enough value. It has laid-back management and is popular with American students (S-190F, Sb-270–350F, D-230F, Db-310–410F, Tb-515F, Qb-600F, CC:VMA, 8 rue des Garçons Mauvais, Mo: Hôtel de Ville, tel. 01 48 87 77 00, fax 01 48 04 96 56, e-mail: HOTELLOIRET@aol.com).

Hôtel Caron de Beaumarchais***, an 18th-century Marais manor house, charges top prices for its precious, comfort-able, and air-conditioned rooms (Db-790–870F, CC:VMA, 12 rue Vielle du Temple, Mo: Hôtel de Ville, tel. 01 42 72 34 12, fax 01 42 72 34 63).

Hôtel de Vieux Marais**, tucked away on a quiet street two blocks east of the Pompidou Center, offers spotless and fairly spacious rooms with air-conditioning, pleasing decor, and we-try-harder owners. Make sure to greet Leeloo, the hotel hound (Sb-600–660F, Db-695–720F, extra bed-150F, CC:VM, cable TV, just off rue des Archives at 8 rue du Platre, Mo: Rambuteau/Hôtel de Ville, tel. 01 42 78 47 22, fax 01 42 78 34 32).

Hôtel Beaubourg***, is an excellent three-star value within spitting distance of the Pompidou Center on a small street. The comfortable rooms are wood-beam cozy and public spaces are warm and pleasant (Db-520–590F, Db with private terrace-690F, CC:VM, 11 rue Simon Lefranc, Mo: Rambuteau, tel. 01 42 74 34 24, fax 01 42 78 68 11, e-mail: htlbeaubourg@hotellerie.net).

Contrescarpe Orientation

This lively, colorful neighborhood is like Montmartre without all the tourists. It's just south of the Latin Quarter, encompassing the area between the Luxembourg Gardens and rue Monge.

The nearest **TI** is at the Louvre Museum. The **post office** (PTT) is between rue Mouffetard and rue Monge at 10 rue de l'Épée du Bois. Place Monge hosts a colorful **outdoor market** on Wednesday, Friday, and Sunday until 13:00. The **street market** at the bottom of rue Mouffetard bustles daily except Monday (Tue–Sat 8:00–12:00, 15:30–19:00, Sun 8:00–12:00, 5 blocks south of place Contrescarpe). The lively place Contrescarpe hops in the afternoon and evening until the wee hours. **Bus #47** runs along rue Monge north to Notre-Dame, the Pompidou Center, and Gare du Nord.

The flowery Jardin des Plantes park is just east and the sublime Luxembourg Gardens are just west. Both are ideal for afternoon walks, picnics, and naps. The doorway at 49 rue Monge leads to a hidden Roman arena (Arènes de Lutèce). Today, *boules* players occupy the stage while couples cuddle on the seats. Admire the Panthéon from the outside (it's not worth paying to go in), and go into the exquisitely beautiful St. Étienne-du-Mont church.

Sleeping in the Contrescarpe Neighborhood
(5th arrondissement, Mo: place Monge, zip code: 75005)

Hotels here are a 20-minute walk from Notre-Dame, Île de la Cité, and Île St. Louis, and a 5- to 10-minute walk from the Luxembourg Gardens and the grand boulevards St. Germain and St. Michel. Fewer tourists sleep in Contrescarpe, and I find the hotel values generally better than in most other neighborhoods. Most hotels listed are on or very near rue Mouffetard, the spine of this area, running from the perfectly Parisian place Contrescarpe south to rue Bazelles. Two thousand years ago, rue Mouffetard was the principal Roman road south to Italy. Today this small, meandering street has a split personality. The lower part thrives in the daytime as a pedestrian market street. The upper part sleeps during the day, but comes alive after dark, teeming with bars, restaurants, and nightlife. These hotels are listed in order of proximity to the Seine and Notre-Dame.

The low-energy, no-frills **Hôtel du Commerce** is run by Monsieur Mattuzzi, who must be a pirate gone good. This 300-year-old place (with vinyl that looks it) is a great rock-bottom deal and as safe as any dive next to a police station can be. In the morning, the landlady will knock and chirp, "*Restez-vous?*"—Are you staying tonight? (S-135F, D-155F, Ds-175F, Ts-225F, Qs-290F, showers-15F, no elevator, takes no reservations, call at 10:0 and monsieur will say "*oui*" or "*non*," 14 rue de La Montagne Ste. Geneviève, Mo: Maubert-Mutualité, tel. 01 43 54 89 69).

Hôtel Central* is unpretentious, with a charming locatior

Contrescarpe Hotels

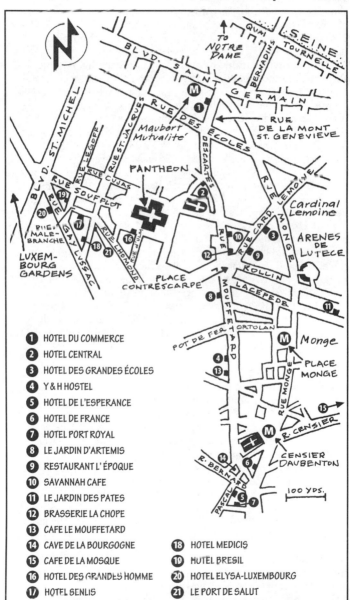

1. HOTEL DU COMMERCE
2. HOTEL CENTRAL
3. HOTEL DES GRANDES ÉCOLES
4. Y & H HOSTEL
5. HOTEL DE L'ESPERANCE
6. HOTEL DE FRANCE
7. HOTEL PORT ROYAL
8. LE JARDIN D'ARTEMIS
9. RESTAURANT L'ÉPOQUE
10. SAVANNAH CAFE
11. LE JARDIN DES PATES
12. BRASSERIE LA CHOPE
13. CAFE LE MOUFFETARD
14. CAVE DE LA BOURGOGNE
15. CAFE DE LA MOSQUE
16. HOTEL DES GRANDES HOMME
17. HOTEL SENLIS
18. HOTEL MEDICIS
19. HOTEL BRESIL
20. HOTEL ELYSA-LUXEMBOURG
21. LE PORT DE SALUT

a steep and slippery castlelike stairway, simple rooms (all with showers, though toilets are down the hall), so-so beds, and plenty of smiles. It's a fine budget value (Ss-165–213F, Ds-240–276F, no elevator, 6 rue Descartes, Mo: Cardinal Lemoine, tel. 01 46 33 57 93).

Hôtel des Grandes Écoles*** is simply idyllic. A short alley leads to three buildings that protect a flowering garden courtyard, preserving a tranquility rare in a city this size. Rooms are spacious and comfortable with large beds. This romantic place is deservedly popular, so call up to four months in advance (Db-555–720F, extra bed-100F, 75 rue de Cardinal Lemoine, Mo: Cardinal Lemoine, tel. 01 43 26 79 23, fax 01 43 25 28 15, www.hotel-grandes-ecoles.com, mellow Marie SE).

The next five hotels lie between the Panthéon and Luxembourg Gardens and a five-minute walk from the rue Mouffetard. For these listings, the RER stop Luxembourg is closer than the nearest Métro stop, Maubert Mutualité.

At **Hôtel des Grandes Hommes*****, spacious, wood-beamed rooms stare across the street at the Panthéon and offer all the comforts you'd expect for the price, including air-conditioning, cable TV, and mini-bar. Some rooms have terraces (Db-850F, suite-1,100F, CC:VM, 17 place du Pantheon, tel. 01 46 34 19 60, fax 01 43 26 67 32, e-mail: henri4@hotellerie.net).

Hôtel Senlis** hides quietly two blocks from the Luxembourg Gardens with simple but comfortable rooms, all with beamed ceilings and TV (Sb-420F, Db-450–530F, Tb-530–580F, Qb-680F, CC:VMA, 7 rue Malebranche, tel. 01 43 29 93 10, fax 01 43 29 00 24).

Hôtel Brésil** lies one block from Luxembourg Gardens and offers unimaginative but comfortable, modern rooms at reasonable rates (Sb-375F, Db-400–500F, CC:VM, 10 rue le Goff, tel. 01 43 54 76 11, fax 01 46 33 45 78).

Hôtel Medicis is as cheap, stripped-down, and basic as it gets with a helpful owner and great location (S-100F, D-190–200F, 214 rue St. Jacques, tel. 01 43 54 14 66).

Hôtel Elysa-Luxembourg*** sits on a busy street at the Luxembourg Gardens and charges top franc for its air-conditioned, impressively decorated rooms (Sb-680F, Db-800F, Tb-900F, CC:VMA, 6 rue Gay Lussac, tel. 01 43 25 31 74, fax 01 46 34 56 27).

The hotels listed below lie on or at the bottom of the rue Mouffetard and are the farthest from the Seine. They may have rooms when others don't.

Y&H Hostel offers a great location, easygoing English-speaking management, Internet access, kitchen facilities, and basic but acceptable hostel-like conditions (beds in 4-bed rooms-117F, beds in double rooms-137F, sheets-15F, rooms closed 11:00–16:00 but reception stays open, 02:00 curfew, reservations

must be paid in advance, 80 rue Mouffetard, Mo: Cardinal
Lemoine, tel. 01 45 35 09 53, fax 01 47 07 22 24, e-mail: smile
@youngandhappy.fr).

Hôtel de l'Esperance**, located at the bottom of rue Mouffetard, gives you nearly three stars for the price of two. It's quiet, pink,
fluffy, and comfortable, with thoughtfully appointed rooms complete
with canopy beds, hair dryers, cable TV, and a flamboyant owner
(Sb-440F, Db-450–550F, small Tb-600F, CC:VM, 15 rue Pascal,
Mo: Censier-Daubenton, tel. 01 47 07 10 99, fax 01 43 37 56 19).

Hôtel de France**, set on a busy street, has fine, modern
rooms and hardworking, helpful owners (Jean and Christine).
The best and quietest rooms are *sur le cour* (on the courtyard),
though streetside rooms are fine (Sb-390F, Db-435–455F,
CC:VM, 108 rue Monge, Mo: Censier-Daubenton, tel. 01 47 07
19 04, fax 01 43 36 62 34, e-mail: hotel.de.fce@wanadoo.fr).

Hôtel Port Royal* is well run (by the same family for 66
years), with a small, pleasant courtyard and incredibly clean,
comfortable rooms at fair prices. Ask for a room off the street
(S-210–260F, D-260F, Db-405F, no CC, climb stairs from rue
Pascal to 8 boulevard de Port Royal, Mo: Gobelins, tel. 01 43 31
70 06, fax 01 43 31 33 67).

Sleeping near Paris, in Versailles

For a laid-back alternative to Paris within easy reach of the big city
by RER train (5/hrly, 30 min), Versailles can be a good overnight
stop—with easy, safe parking and reasonably priced hotels (see map
on page 61).

Hôtel Le Cheval Rouge**, built in 1676 as Louis XIV's
stables, now houses tourists. It's a block behind place du Marché in
a quaint corner of town on a large, quiet courtyard with free, safe
parking and simple but adequate rooms (Ds-300F, Db-360–410F,
extra bed-90F for 1 person, 120F for 2, CC:VMA, cable TV, 18
rue Andre Chenier, tel. 01 39 50 03 03, fax 01 39 50 61 27).

Ibis Versailles**, a slick business-class place, offers all the
comfort with none of the character (Db-425F, cheaper weekend
rates available but can't be reserved ahead, CC:VMA, across from
RER station, 4 avenue du General de Gaulle, tel. 01 39 53 03 30,
fax 01 39 50 06 31, e-mail: accorhotel.com).

Hôtel du Palais, facing the RER station, has cheap and
handy beds; ask for a quiet room off the street. It's a pink and
funky place—dumpy enough to lack even one star but proud
enough to put candy on the beds (D-180F, Ds-250F, Db-250–
280F, extra person-70F, miles of stairs, 6 place Lyautey,
tel. 01 39 50 39 29, fax 01 39 50 80 41).

Hôtel d'Angleterre** is a tranquil old place with comfortable and spacious rooms. Park nearby in the palace lot
Db-350–450F, extra bed-100F, CC:VMA, cable TV, mini-bar,

just below palace to the right as you exit, 2 rue de Fontenay, tel. 01 39 51 43 50, fax 01 39 51 45 63).

Eating in Paris

Paris is France's wine and cuisine melting pot. While it lacks a style of its own (only French onion soup is truly Parisian), it draws from the best of France. Paris could hold a gourmet's Olympics and import nothing.

Picnic or go to bakeries for quick take-out lunches, or stop at a café for a lunch salad or *plat du jour*, but linger longer over dinner. You can eat well, restaurant style, for 100F to 150F. Your hotel can usually recommend nearby restaurants in the 80F to 100F range. Remember, cafés are happy to serve a *plat du jour* (garnished plate of the day, about 70F) or a chef-like salad (60F) day or night. Famous places are often overpriced, overcrowded, and overrated. Find a quiet neighborhood and wander, or follow a local recommendation. Restaurants open for dinner around 19:00, and small local favorites get crowded after 21:00.

To save piles of francs, review the budget eating tips in this book's introduction and consider dinner picnics (great take-out dishes available at *charcuteries*). My recommendations are centered around the same three great neighborhoods listed in "Sleeping," above; you can come home exhausted after a busy day of sight-seeing and have a good selection of restaurants right around the corner. And evening is a fine time to explore any of these delight-ful neighborhoods even if you're sleeping elsewhere.

Restaurants

The Parisian eating scene is kept at a rolling boil. Entire books (and lives) are dedicated to the subject. If you are traveling outside of Paris, save your splurges for the countryside, where you'll enjoy regional cooking for less money. I've listed places that conveniently fit a busy sightseeing schedule and places near recommended hotels. If you'd like to visit a district specifically to eat, consider the many romantic restaurants that line the cozy Île St. Louis' main street and the colorful, touristy-but-fun string of eateries along rue Mouffetard behind the Panthéon (in the Contrescarpe neighborhood). Beware: Many restaurants close Sunday and Monday.

Cafeterias and Picnics

Many Parisian department stores have huge supermarkets hiding in the basement and top-floor cafeterias offering not really cheap but low-risk, low-stress, what-you-see-is-what-you-get meals.

For lunch and dinner picnics, you'll find handy little groceries (*épiceries*) and delis (*charcuteries*) all over town but rarely near famous sights. Good picnic fixings include roasted chicken, drinkable yogurt, fresh bakery goods, melons, and exotic pâtés and cheeses.

Great take-out deli-type foods like gourmet salads and quiches abound. *Boulangeries* make good, cheap mini-quiches and sandwiches. While wine is taboo in public places in the United States, it's *pas de problème* in France.

Romantic Picnic Spots: My favorite dinner-picnic places are the pedestrian bridge (Pont des Arts) across from the Louvre, with unmatched views and plentiful benches; the Champ de Mars park under the Eiffel Tower; and the western tip of Île St. Louis, overlooking Île de la Cité. Bring your own dinner feast and watch the riverboats or the Eiffel Tower light up the city for you. The Palais Royal (across the street from the Louvre) is a good spot for a peaceful, royal picnic, as is the little triangular Henry IV Park on the west tip of Île de la Cité. For lunch picnics with great people watching, try the Pompidou Center (by the *Homage to Stravinsky* fountain), the elegant place des Vosges (closes at dusk), the gardens at the Rodin Museum, and Luxembourg Gardens.

Eating in the Rue Cler Neighborhood

Restaurants: The rue Cler neighborhood isn't famous for its restaurants. That's why I enjoy eating here. Several small family-run places serve great dinner *menus* for 100F and *plats du jour* for 60F to 80F. My first two recommendations are easygoing cafés, ideal if what you want is a light dinner (good dinner salads) or more substantial but simple meals.

Café du Marché, with the best seats, coffee, and prices on rue Cler, serves hearty salads and good 60F *plats du jour* for lunch or dinner to a trendy, mainly French crowd. Arrive before 19:30 or wait at the bar. A chalkboard listing the plates of the day—each a meal—will momentarily be hung in front of you (at the corner of rue Cler and rue Champ de Mars). You'll find the same menu and prices with better (but smoky) indoor seating at their other restaurant, **Le Comptoir du Septième**, at the École Militaire Métro stop (39 avenue de la Motte Piquet, tel. 01 45 55 90 20).

Café le Bosquet's friendly owner Jean Francois will make you feel welcome at his classic Parisian brasserie. Come here for a bowl of French onion soup, a salad, or a three-course set *menu* (98F *menu*, many choices, 46 avenue Bosquet, tel. 01 45 51 38 13).

Leo le Lion, run by Mimi for 20 years, is an easygoing place. A warm, charming souvenir of old Paris, it's popular with locals. The 115F *menu* comes with a first course that could feed two for an entire meal (but no splitting) and a fully garnished main course (closed Sun, 23 rue Duvivier, tel. 01 45 51 41 77).

Vegetarians will appreciate the Mediterranean cuisine at **7ème Sud** (closed Sun, at the corner of rue de Grenelle and rue Duvivier).

Closer to Invalides, the friendly **Le Bistrot du 7ème** opens its cozy interior onto a broad sidewalk and serves a decent 98F

menu with many choices (open daily, 56 boulevard Latour-
Maubourg, tel. 01 45 51 93 08). **La Bressanne** is a country-warm
place with a good 130F *menu* (16 avenue de la Motte Piquet, tel.
01 47 05 98 37). The tiny **Au Petit Tonneau** is a totally Parisian
experience, where the owner/chef prepares everything herself
(open daily, 20 rue Surcouf, tel. 01 47 05 09 10).

   Thoumieux, the neighborhood's classy, traditional Parisian
brasserie, is deservedly popular (skippable 82F but fine 160F *menu*,
complete *à la carte*, 79 rue St. Dominique, tel. 01 47 05 49 75).

   For a special dinner, survey the handful of fine places that line
rue de l'Exposition one block west of avenue Bosquet between rue
St. Dominique and rue de Grenelle: **Restaurant La Serre**, at #29,
has fun ambience, usually great food, but an unpredictable staff
(*plats* 50–70F, daily from 19:00, often a wait after 21:00, good
onion soup and duck specialties, tel. 01 45 55 20 96, Marie-Alice
and intense Philippe speak English). **Le P'tit Troquet**, across the
street at #28, is delightfully Parisian, popular with locals, and ideal
for a last-night splurge—allow 160F per person for dinner (closed
Sun–Mon, tel. 01 47 05 80 39). The quieter **La Maison de
Cosima** at #20 offers refined, creative French cuisine and excellent 100F and 160F *menus* that include a vegetarian option (closed
Sun, tel. 01 45 51 37 71, run by friendly Helene). The softly lit
tables and red velvet chairs of **Auberge du Champ de Mars**, at
#18, draw a romantic crowd (no inexpensive wines, closed Mon).
For top *à la carte*–only cuisine, locals reserve early for the charmingly situated **La Fontaine de Mars** (allow 250F per person with
wine, 129 rue St. Dominique, tel. 01 47 05 46 44). Just off rue de
Grenelle, the friendly and unpretentious **La Varanque** is a good
budget bet, with 60F *plats* and an 80F *menu* (27 rue Augereau,
tel. 01 47 05 51 22).

   Ambassade du Sud-Ouest, a wine and food boutique/
restaurant, specializes in southwestern French cuisine such as *daubes
de canard* (duck meatballs) and cassoulet (46 avenue de la Bourdonnais, tel. 01 45 55 59 59). **L'Ami de Jean** is a lively place to sample
Basque cuisine (closed Sun, 27 rue Malar, tel. 01 47 05 86 89).

   Picnicking: Rue Cler is a moveable feast that gives "fast food"
a good name. The entire street is clogged with connoisseurs of
good eating. Only the health-food store goes unnoticed. A festival
of food, the street is lined with people whose lives seem to be
devoted to their specialty: stacking polished produce, rotisserie
chicken, crepes, or cheese squares.

   For a magical picnic dinner at the Eiffel Tower, assemble it in
no fewer than five shops on rue Cler and lounge on the best grass
in Paris (the police don't mind after dusk), with the dogs, Frisbees,
a floodlit tower, and a cool breeze in the Parc du Champ de Mars.

   The **crepe stand** next to Café du Marché does a wonderful
top-end dinner crepe for 25F. An Asian deli, **Traiteur Asie** (many

Rue Cler Restaurants

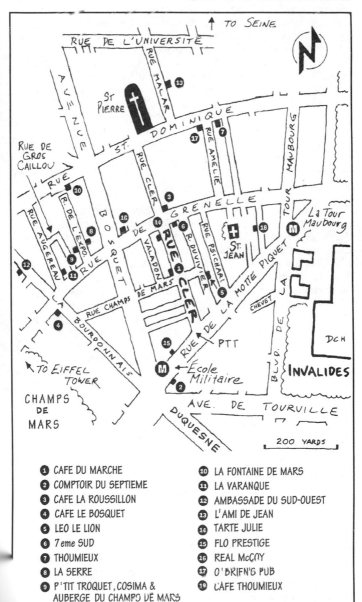

1. CAFE DU MARCHE
2. COMPTOIR DU SEPTIEME
3. CAFE LA ROUSSILLON
4. CAFE LE BOSQUET
5. LEO LE LION
6. 7eme SUD
7. THOUMIEUX
8. LA SERRE
9. P'TIT TROQUET, COSIMA & AUBERGE DU CHAMPS DE MARS
10. LA FONTAINE DE MARS
11. LA VARANQUE
12. AMBASSADE DU SUD-OUEST
13. L'AMI DE JEAN
14. TARTE JULIE
15. FLO PRESTIGE
16. REAL McCOY
17. O'BRIEN'S PUB
18. CAFE THOUMIEUX

in the area, one across from Hôtel Leveque), has tasty low-stress, low-price take-out treats. Its tables offer the cheapest place to sit, eat, and enjoy the rue Cler ambience. For quiche, cheese pie, or a pear/chocolate tart, try **Tarte Julie's** (takeout or stools, 28 rue Cler). The elegant **Flo Prestige** *charcuterie* (at the École Militaire Métro stop) is open until 23:00 and offers mouthwatering meals to go. **Real McCoy** is a little shop selling American food and sandwiches (194 rue de Grenelle). A good, small, late-night grocery is at 197 rue de Grenelle.

The bakery (*boulangerie*) on the corner of rue Cler and rue de Champ de Mars is the place for a fresh baguette, sandwich, tiny quiche, or *pain au chocolat*, but the almond croissants at the *boulangerie* on rue de Grenelle at rue Cler make my day. The bakery at 112 rue St. Dominique is in a league by itself and worth the detour, with classic decor and tables to enjoy your *café au lait* and croissant.

Cafés and Bars: If you want to linger over coffee or a drink at a sidewalk café, try **Café du Marché** (see above), **Petite Brasserie PTT** (local workers eat here, opposite 53 rue Cler), or **Café le Bosquet** (46 avenue Bosquet, tel. 01 45 51 38 13). **Café La Roussillon**, peopled and decorated belle epoque, also offers a quintessential café experience (at the corner of rue de Grenelle and rue Cler). **Le Sancerre** wine bar/café is wood-beam warm and ideal for a light lunch or dinner, or just a glass of wine after a long day of sightseeing. The owner's cheeks are the same color as his wine (open until 21:30, great omelets, 22 avenue Rapp, tel. 01 45 51 75 91). **Maison Altmayer** is a hole-in-the-wall place for a quiet drink (9:00–19:30, next to Hôtel Eiffel Rive Gauche, 6 rue du Gros Caillou). Cafés like this originated (and this one still functions) as a place where locals enjoyed a drink while their heating wood, coal, or gas was prepared for delivery.

Nightlife: This sleepy neighborhood is not the place for night owls, but there are four notable exceptions: **Café du Marché** and its brother, **Le Comptoir du Septième** (both listed above), hop with a Franco-American crowd until about midnight. **O'Brien's Pub** is a relaxed, Parisian rendition of an Irish pub (77 St. Dominique). **Café Thoumieux** is a sophisticated place with big-screen sports and a trendy young crowd (4 rue de la Comete, Mo: Latour Maubourg).

Eating in the Marais Neighborhood

The windows of the Marais are filled with munching sophisticates and crowd-pleasing eateries. And with Île St. Louis a short walk away (see below), those sleeping in the Marais have a great selection of good-value restaurants.

You'll find several good places at place du Marché Ste.

Catherine, a tiny square just off rue St. Antoine between the
St. Paul Métro stop and place des Vosges. **Le Marais Ste.
Catherine** is a good value (110F *menu*, daily from 19:00, nonsmoking, extra seating in candlelit cellar, 5 rue Caron, tel. 01 42
72 39 94), but if it's warm, you may prefer the outdoor tables at
Le Marché (130F *menu*, 2 place Marché Ste. Catherine, tel. 01 42
77 34 88). Just off the square, **L'Auberge de Jarente** offers a
well-respected cuisine with Basque specialities (120F *menu*, closed
Sun–Mon, 7 rue Jarente, tel. 01 42 77 49 35).

Dinners under the candlelit arches of place des Vosges are *très*
romantic. **Nectarine**, at #16, serves salads, quiches, and reasonable
plats du jour daily and nightly (no CC), while **Ma Bourgogne** is
where locals go for a splurge (open daily, reserve dinner ahead,
no CC, at northwest corner, tel. 01 42 78 44 64).

For a fast, cheap change of pace, eat at (or take out from)
the Chinese/Japanese **Delice House**. Two can split 200 grams
of chicken curry (or whatever, 30F) and rice (20F). There's lots of
seating, with pitchers of water at the ground-floor tables and a
roomier upstairs (open until 21:00, 81 rue St. Antoine).

The **Crêperie** at 6 rue Castex serves a 60F all-crepe *menu*
(closed Sun–Mon), and the cozy restaurant **de la Poste** (13 rue
Castex) offers 60F *plats du jour* (closed Sun). **La Bastoche**'s warm
ambience and reasonable 90F *menu* make it a popular place (7 rue
St. Antoine, tel. 01 48 04 74 34). Across the street, **Le Paradis de
Fruit** serves salads and organic foods to a young local crowd (on
small square at rues Tournelle and St. Antoine). **Gaspard de le
Nuit** is a cozy step up with a fine 152F *menu* (6 rue des Tournelles,
tel. 01 42 77 90 53).

Near Hôtel du 7ème Art, try the romantic and traditional
L'Excuse for a worthwhile splurge (190F *menu*, closed Sun,
call ahead, 14 rue Charles V, tel. 01 42 77 98 97). Across the
street, **L'Énoteca** (wine bar) has lively and reasonable Italian
cuisine in a relaxed, open setting (closed Sun, 20 rue St. Paul,
tel. 01 42 78 91 44).

Wine lovers shouldn't miss the superb Burgundy wines and
exquisite, though limited, menu selection at **Au Bourguignon du
Marais** (closed Sat–Sun, call by 19:00 to reserve, 52 rue Francois
Miron, tel. 01 48 87 15 40).

Vegetarians will appreciate the excellent cuisine at the
popular **Picolo Teatro** (closed Mon, 6 rue des Ecouffes, tel.
01 42 72 17 79) and **L'As du Falafel**, serving the best falafel on
rue Rosier at #34.

Picnicking: Picnic at the peaceful place des Vosges (closes
at dusk). Hobos stretch their francs at the supermarket in the
basement of the **Monoprix** department store (close to place des
Vosges on rue St. Antoine), and connoisseurs prefer the gourmet
take-out places all along rue St. Antoine, such as **Flo Prestige**

Marais Restaurants

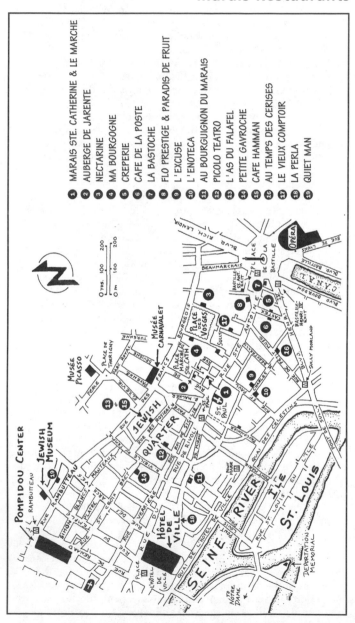

1. MARAIS STE. CATHERINE & LE MARCHE
2. AUBERGE DE JARENTE
3. NECTARINE
4. MA BOURGOGNE
5. CREPERIE
6. CAFE DE LA POSTE
7. LA BASTOCHE
8. FLO PRESTIGE & PARADIS DE FRUIT
9. L'EXCUSE
10. L'ENOTECA
11. AU BOURGUIGNON DU MARAIS
12. PICOLO TEATRO
13. L'AS DU FALAFEL
14. PETITE GAVROCHE
15. CAFE HAMMAN
16. AU TEMPS DES CERISES
17. LE VIEUX COMPTOIR
18. LA PERLA
19. QUIET MAN

(open until 23:00, on the tiny square where rue Tournelle and
rue St. Antoine meet). A few small grocery shops are open until
23:00 on rue St. Antoine (near intersection with rue Castex). An
open-air market, held Sunday morning, is just off place de la
Bastille on boulevard Richard Lenoir.

For a cheap breakfast, try the tiny *boulangerie/pâtisserie*
where the hotels buy their croissants (coffee machine-3F, baby
quiches-10F, *pain au chocolat*-5F, 1 block off place de la Bastille,
corner of rue St. Antoine and rue de Lesdiguieres).

Cafés and Bars: The trendiest cafés and bars are clustered on
rues Vielle du Temple, Archives, and Ste. Croix de la Bretonniere
(open generally until 02:00), and are popular with gay men. The
très local wine bar at **Au Temps des Cerises** is amiably run and a
welcoming, if smoky, place (around the corner from Hôtel Castex,
rue du Petit Musc and rue de Cerisaie).

Nightlife: Le Vieux Comptoir is tiny, lively, and not too hip
(just off place des Vosges at 8 rue Biraque). **La Perla** is trendy and
full of Parisian yuppies in search of the perfect margarita (26 rue
Francois Miron). **The Quiet Man** is a traditional Irish pub with
happy hour from 16:00 to 20:00 (5 rue des Haudriettes).

Eating in the Contrescarpe Neighborhood

The rue Mouffetard and rue du Pot-de-Fer are lined with inexpensive, lively, and forgettable restaurants (see map on page
83). Study the many *menus*, compare crowds, then dive in. **Le
Jardin d'Artemis** is one of the better values on rue Mouffetard
at #34 (89F menu). **Restaurant l'Époque**, a fine neighborhood
restaurant, has excellent *menus* at 78F and 118F (a block off place
Contrescarpe at 81 rue Cardinal Lemoine, tel. 01 46 34 15 84).
Savannah Café's creative Mediterranean cuisine attracts a loyal,
artsy crowd (27 rue Descartes, tel. 01 43 29 45 77). **Le Jardin des
Pates** is popular with vegetarians, serving pastas and salads at
fair prices (near Jardins des Plantes, 4 rue Lacepede, tel. 01 43
31 50 71). **Le Port de Salut**, one block from the Panthéon,
has ambience and inexpensive *menus* (closed Sun–Mon, 163
bis rue St. Jacques, tel. 01 46 33 63 21).

Cafés: Brasserie La Chope, a classic Parisian brasserie
right on place Contrescarpe, is popular until the wee hours.
Sit indoors or outdoors for good people watching. **Café Le
Mouffetard** is in the thick of the street-market hustle and
bustle (at the corner of rue Mouffetard and rue de l'Arbalete).
The outdoor tables at **Cave de la Bourgogne** are picture-perfect
(at the bottom of rue Mouffetard, on rue Razelles). At **Café de la
Mosque** you'll feel like you've been beamed to Morocco. In this
purely Arab café, order a mint tea, pour in the sugar, and enjoy
the authentic interior and peaceful outdoor terrace (behind
mosque, 2 rue Daubenton).

Eating on Île St. Louis

Cruise the island's main street for a variety of good options, from cozy *crêperies* to romantic restaurants. Sample Paris' best sorbet and ice cream at any place advertising *les glaces Berthillon*; the original Berthillon shop is at 31 rue St. Louis en l'Île.

All listings below are on rue St. Louis en l'Île and are listed starting at the end of the island closest to the Île de la Cité. **Café Med**, at #73, serves inexpensive salads, crepes, and lighter *menus* in a cheery setting. **La Castafiore**, at #51-53, serves fine Italian dishes in a cozy atmosphere (160F *menu*). Farther down lie two fine romantic splurges: **Le Tastevin** (150F and 220F *menus*, #46, tel. 01 43 54 17 31) and, next door, **Au Gourmet de l'Isle** (150F and 185F *menus*, closed Mon–Tue).

For a crazy, touristy, cellar atmosphere and hearty, fun food, feast at **La Taverne du Sergeant Recruiter**. The "Sergeant Recruiter" used to get young Parisians drunk and stuffed here, then sign them into the army. It's all-you-can-eat, including wine and service, for 190F (daily from 19:00, #41, tel. 01 43 54 75 42). There's a near-food-fight clone next door at **Nos Ancêtres Les Gaulois** ("Our Ancestors the Gauls," 190F *menu*, daily from 19:00, tel. 01 46 33 66 07).

Elegant Dining on the Seine

La Plage Parisienne is a nearly dress-up riverfront place popular with locals, serving elegant, healthy meals at good prices (Port de Javel-Haut, Mo: Javel, tel. 01 40 59 41 00).

Transportation Connections—Paris

Paris is Europe's rail hub, with six major train stations, each serving different regions: Gare de l'Est (east-bound trains), Gare du Nord (northern France and Europe), Gare St. Lazare (northwestern France), Gare d'Austerlitz (southwest France and Europe), Gare du Lyon (southeastern France and Italy), and Gare Montparnasse (northwestern France and TGV service to France's southwest). Any train station can give you schedule information, make reservations, and sell tickets for any destination. Buying ickets is handier from an SNCF neighborhood office (e.g., Louvre, Invalides, Orsay, Versailles, airports) or at your neighborhood travel agency—worth their small fee (SNCF signs in their window indicate they sell train tickets). For schedule information, call 08 36 35 35 35 (3F/min, English sometimes available).

Gare du Nord: Serves northern France and several international destinations. To **Brussels** (10/day, 1.5 hrs), **Bruges** (3/day, 2.5 hrs), **Amsterdam** (10/day, 4 hrs), **Copenhagen** (3/day, 16 hrs), **Koblenz** on the Rhine (3/day, 7 hrs), **London** via Eurostar Chunnel (12/day, 3 hrs, France tel. 08 36 35 35 39, U.S. tel. 800/EUROSTAR, www.raileurope.com, www.eurostar.co.uk).

Gare de l'Est: Serves eastern France and points east. To **Colmar** (6/day, 5.5 hrs, transfer in Strasbourg or Mulhouse), **Strasbourg** (10/day, 4.5 hrs), **Reims** (8/day, 2 hrs), **Verdun** (5/day, 3 hrs), **Munich** (4/day, 8.5 hrs), **Vienna** (3/day, 13 hrs), **Zurich** (4/day, 6 hrs), **Prague** (2/day, 15 hrs).

Gare Montparnasse: Serves Lower Normandy and Brittany and offers TGV service to Loire Valley and southwestern France. To **Chartres** (10/day, 1 hr), **Mont St. Michel** (2/day, 4.5 hrs, via Rennes), **Dinan** (7/day, 3 hrs, via Rennes and Dol), **Bordeaux** (14/day, 3.5 hrs), **Sarlat** (5/day, 6 hrs, transfer in Bordeaux), **Toulouse** (7/day, 5 hrs, possible transfer in Bordeaux), **Albi** (6.5 hrs, via Toulouse), **Carcassonne** (6.5 hrs, via Toulouse), **Tours** (14/day, 1 hr).

Gare du Lyon: Offers TGV and regular service to southeastern France, Italy, and other international destinations. To **Beaune** (8/day, 2.5 hrs), **Dijon** (13/day, 1.5 hrs), **Chamonix** (3/day, 9 hrs, transfer in Lyon and St. Gervais, 1 direct night train), **Annecy** (8/day, 4–7 hrs), **Lyon** (16/day, 2.5 hrs), **Avignon** (10/day, 4 hrs), **Arles** (10/day, 5 hrs), **Nice** (8/day, 7 hrs), **Venice** (5/day, 11 hrs), **Rome** (3/day, 15 hrs), **Bern** (5/day, 5 hrs).

Gare St. Lazare: Serves Upper Normandy. To **Giverny** (train to Vernon, 5/day, 45 min; then bus or taxi 10 min to Giverny), **Rouen** (15/day, 75 min), **Honfleur** (6/day, 3 hrs, via Lisieux then bus), **Bayeux** (9/day, 2.5 hrs), **Caen** (12/day, 2 hrs).

Gare d'Austerlitz: Provides non-TGV service to the Loire Valley, southwestern France, and Iberia. To **Amboise** (8/day, 2.5 hrs), **Cahors** (5/day, 7 hrs), **Barcelona** (3/day, 13 hrs), **Madrid** (5/day, 16 hrs), **Lisbon** (1/day, 24 hrs).

Buses: Long-distance buses provide cheaper, if less comfortable and flexible, transportation to major European cities. The main bus station in Paris is Gare Routière du Paris-Gallieni (avenue du General de Gaulle, in suburb of Bagnolet, Mo: Gallieni, tel. 01 49 72 51 51). Eurolines buses depart from here.

Charles de Gaulle Airport

Paris' primary airport has three main terminals: T-1, T-2, and T-9. (Air France uses T-2; charters dominate T-9.) Terminals are connected every few minutes by a free *navette* (bus), and the RER (Paris subway) stops at T-1 and T-2 terminals. There is no bag storage at the airport.

Those flying to or from the United States will probably use T-1. Here you'll find an American Express cash machine, an automatic bill changer (at baggage claim 30), and an exchange window (at baggage claim 18). A bank (with lousy rates) and an ATM are near gate 16. At the Meeting Point, you'll find the TI, which has free maps and information (daily 7:00–22:00), and Relais H, which sells *télécartes* (phone cards). Car-rental offices are on the arrival level from gates 10 to 22; the SNCF (train) office is at gate 22. For flight information, call 01 48 62 22 80.

Transportation between Charles de Gaulle Airport and Paris: There are plenty of choices. Three efficient public transportation routes, taxis, and airport shuttle vans link the airport's T-1 and T-2 terminals with central Paris. At T-1 (where most will land), the free *navette* (bus) runs between gate 36, the lower level (take elevator down to floor 2, walk outside, cross street, and catch green bus), and the **RER Roissy Rail** station, where a train zips you into Paris' subway system in 30 minutes (51F, stops at Gare du Nord, Chatelet, St. Michel, and Luxembourg Gardens). The **Roissy Bus** runs every 15 minutes between gate 30 and the old Opéra Garnier (stop is on rue Scribe, in front of American Express), costs 48F (use automatic ticket machine), and takes 40 minutes, but can be jammed. The **Air France Bus** leaves every 15 minutes from gate 34 and serves the Arc de Triomphe and Porte Maillot in about 40 minutes for 60F, and the Montparnasse Tower in 60 minutes for 75F (from any of these stops you can reach your hotel by taxi). For most people, the RER Roissy Rail works best. A **taxi** ride with luggage costs about 230F; a taxi stand is at gate 16. The **Disneyland Express bus** departs from gate 32. (The RER Roissy Rail, Roissy Bus, and Air France bus described above serve the T-2 terminal as efficiently and economically as T-1.)

For a stress-free trip between either of Paris' airports and downtown, consider an airport shuttle minivan, ideal for single travelers or families of four or more. Reserve from home and they'll meet you at the airport. Consider **Airport Shuttle** (allow 150F for 1 person, 89F per person for 2, cheaper for larger groups and kids, plan on 30-min wait if you ask them to pick you up at airport, tel. 01 45 38 55 72, fax 01 43 21 35 67, www.paris-anglo .com/clients/ashuttle.html, e-mail: ashuttle@club-internet.fr) or **Paris Airport Services** (tel. 01 49 62 78 78, fax 01 49 62 78 79, www.magic.fr/pas, e-mail: pas@magic.fr).

Sleeping at or near Charles de Gaulle Airport: Those with early flights can sleep in T-1 at **Cocoon** (60 cabins, Sb-250F, Db-300F, CC:VM, TV, take elevator down to "boutique level" or walk down from departure level, tel. 01 48 62 06 16, fax 01 48 62 56 97). You get 16 hours of silence buried under the check-in level. **Hôtel Ibis****, at the Roissy Rail station, offers more-normal accommodations (Db-420F, CC:VMA, free shuttle bus to either terminal takes 2 min, tel. 01 49 19 19 19, fax 01 49 19 19 21), as does the similarly priced **Novotel***** (CC:VMA, tel. 01 49 19 27 27, fax 01 49 19 27 99).

Orly Airport

This airport feels small. Orly has two terminals: Sud and Ouest. International flights arrive at Sud. After exiting Terminal Sud's baggage claim (near gate H), you'll be greeted by signs directing you to city transportation, car rental, and so on. Turn left to enter the main terminal area and you'll find exchange offices with bad rates, an ATM machine, the ADP (a quasi-tourist office that offers free city maps and basic sightseeing information, open until 23:00), and an SNCF French rail desk (closes at 18:00, sells train tickets and even Eurailpasses, next to ADP). Downstairs is a sandwich bar, WCs, a bank (same bad rates), a newsstand (buy a *télécarte* phone card), and a post office (great rates for cash or American Express traveler's checks). Car-rental offices are located in the parking lot in front of the terminal. For flight information on any airline serving Orly, call 01 49 75 15 15.

Transportation between Paris and Orly Airport: There are three efficient public-transportation routes, taxis, and a couple of airport shuttle services linking Orly and central Paris. The **Air France bus** (outside gate G) runs to Paris' Invalides Métro stop (45F, 5/hrly, 30 min) and is best for those staying in or near the rue Cler neighborhood (at Paris' Invalides terminal, take Métro 2 stops to École Militaire to reach recommended hotels). The **Jetbus #285** (outside gate F, 28F, 4/hrly) is the quickest way to the Paris subway and the best way to the recommended hotels in the Marais and Contrescarpe neighborhoods (take Jetbus to Villejuif Métro stop, buy a carnet of 10 Métro tickets, then take the Métro to the Sully Morland stop for the Marais area, or the Cardinal Lemoine stop for the Contrescarpe area). The **Orlybus** (outside gate H, 35F, 4/hr) takes you to the Denfert-Rochereau RER-B line and the Métro, offering subway access to central Paris. The **Orlyval trains** are overpriced (57F). **Taxis** are to the far right (gate M) as you leave the terminal. Allow 170F for a taxi into central Paris.

Airport shuttle minivans are ideal for single travelers or families of four or more (see "Charles de Gaulle Airport," above; from Orly, figure about 120F for 1 person, 80F per person for 2, less for larger groups and kids).

Sleeping near Orly Airport: The only reasonable airport hotel is the **Hôtel Ibis**** (Db-420F, CC:VMA, tel. 01 46 87 33 50, fax 01 46 87 29 92). The **Hilton***** offers more comfort for more money (Db-680F, tel. 01 45 12 45 12, fax 01 45 12 45 00). Both offer a free shuttle service to the terminal.

NORMANDY

These lands of green, rolling hills are broken up by apple orchards, dramatic coastlines, half-timbered homes, and thatched roofs. Parisians call Normandy "the 21st *arrondissement*." It's their escape—the nearest beach. The British call this area close enough for a weekend away.

Viking Norsemen settled here in the ninth century, giving Normandy its name. William the Conqueror invaded England from Normandy in the 11th century. To see his victory commemorated in a remarkable tapestry, weave Bayeux into your trip. In Rouen, France's all-time inspirational leader, Jeanne d'Arc (Joan of Arc), was convicted of heresy and burned at the stake by the English, against whom she had rallied France during the Hundred Years' War.

The rugged, rainy coast of Normandy harbors tiny fishing villages like little Honfleur, which today has more charm than fish. The cliff-hanger coast, two hours south of Honfleur, was the scene of a WWII battle that changed the course of history. South of the D-Day beaches, on the border of Brittany, is the almost surreal island abbey of Mont St. Michel, rising serene and majestic, oblivious to its tides of tourists.

Planning Your Time
Honfleur, the D-Day beaches, and Mont St. Michel each merit an overnight stop. Visit Giverny and Rouen between Paris and Honfleur, see the Caen Battle of Normandy museum/memorial between Honfleur and the D-Day beaches, and arrive late in the day or very early at Mont St. Michel. Dinan, only 40 minutes from Mont St. Michel (1 hr by train), offers an enchanting introduction to Brittany. Some enjoy Mont St. Michel as a day trip from Dinan.

Normandy

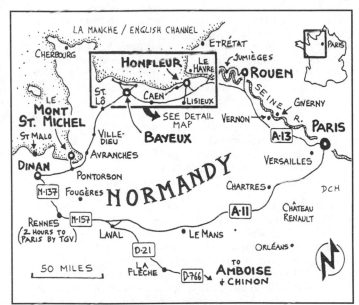

Getting around Normandy

Trains serve Rouen, Caen, Bayeux, Mont St. Michel, and Dinan, with good service from Paris but less service between these sights (e.g., there are only 2 trains/day between Rouen and Bayeux and 2 trains/day between Bayeux and Pontorson, near Mont St. Michel). Plan ahead and you'll do fine. Buses connect Giverny with Rouen or Paris (via Vernon), Honfleur with Paris (via Lisieux), Bayeux (via Caen or Lisieux) with Rouen (via Le Havre), and Arromanches with Bayeux. Sundays have little if any bus service.

Cuisine Scene—Normandy

Known as the land of the four Cs (Calvados, Camembert, cider, and *crème*), Normandy specializes in cream sauces, organ meats (kidneys, sweetbreads, and tripe—"the gizzard salads" are great), and seafood (*fruits de mer*). Dairy products are big here. Local cheeses are Camembert (mild to very strong), Brillat-Savarin (buttery), Livarot (spicy and pungent), Pavé d'Auge (spicy and tangy), and Pont l'Evéque (earthy flavor). Normandy is famous for its powerful Calvados apple brandy, Benedictine brandy (made by local monks), and three kinds of alcoholic apple ciders (*cidre* can be *doux*—sweet, *brut*—dry, or *bouche*—sparkling and the strongest). Look also for Poiret, a tasty pear cider.

ROUEN

This 2,000-year-old city of 100,000 people mixes dazzling Gothic architecture, soaring half-timbered houses, and contemporary bustle like no other in France. Medieval Rouen was France's second largest city with 40,000 residents (only Paris had more) and walked a political tightrope between England and France for centuries. It was an English base during the Hundred Years' War. William the Conqueror lived here 900 years ago; 300 years later, Joan of Arc was burned here.

Tourist Information: The TI faces the cathedral. Pick up their map highlighting a walking tour (in French only), information on Rouen's museums, and a brochure on the Route of the Ancient Abbeys—described below (May–Sept Mon–Sat 9:00–19:00, Sun 9:00–12:30, 14:30–18:00; Sept–April Mon–Sat 9:00–18:00, Sun 10:00–15:00, tel. 02 32 08 32 40, www.mairie-rouen.com).

Arrival in Rouen

By Train: Rue Jeanne d'Arc cuts down from Rouen's station (24-hr lockers available) through the town center to the Seine River. Walk from the station down rue Jeanne d'Arc to rue du Gros Horloge, the medieval center's pedestrian mall that connects the Old Market and Jeanne d'Arc church (to the right) with the cathedral and TI (to the left). To go to the start of the Rouen walking tour (described below), turn right on rue du Gros Horloge (you'll see the sweeping roof of the modern Église Jeanne d' Arc). Rouen's new subway whisks you from the train station to the Palais de la Justice in one stop (8F), one block above the rue du Gros Horloge.

By Car: Follow signs to *centre-ville* (city center) and *rive droite* (right bank) and park along the river (metered until 19:00) or in one of many underground lots (near the cathedral is best). If you get turned around, aim for the cathedral spires.

Walking Tour of Rouen

For a quick dose of Rouen's Gothic and half-timbered wonders, begin at the Jeanne d'Arc church and follow the route described below (most route sights close 12:00–14:00). The ruins of the old St. Sauveur church near the entry to the Jeanne d'Arc church make a good seat and starting point. Sit here.

▲**Église Jeanne d'Arc**—This modern church is a tribute to Jeanne d'Arc. Nineteen-year-old Jeanne was burned at the stake on this square in 1431.

The church, completed in 1979, feels Scandinavian inside and out—reminding us again of Normandy's Nordic roots. Pick up an English pamphlet describing the church (closed 12:30–14:00, public WC 30 meters from church doors). The colorful outdoor market behind the church closes at 12:30.

Rouen

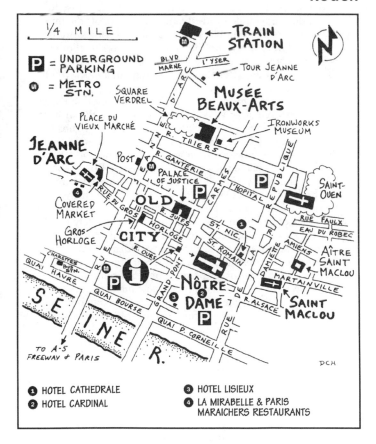

1/4 MILE

P = UNDERGROUND PARKING

Ⓜ = METRO STN.

TRAIN STATION

BLVD MARNE   L'YSER

TOUR JEANNE D'ARC

SQUARE VERDREL

MUSÉE BEAUX-ARTS

PLACE DU VIEUX MARCHÉ

IRONWORKS MUSEUM

JEANNE D'ARC

Post

R. THIERS

R. GANTERIE

PALACE OF JUSTICE

SAINT-OUEN

❹

COVERED MARKET

RUE DU GROS

OLD

R. JUIFS

HORLOGE

L'HOPITAL

CARMES

REPUBLIQUE

GROS HORLOGE

CITY

R. OURS

St. NIC.

St. ROMAIN

❶

RUE FAULX

EAU DU ROBEC

AMIENS

AÎTRE SAINT MACLOU

CHARETTES BUS STN.

QUAI HAVRE

❶

GRAND PONT

NÔTRE DAME

❷

DAMIETTE

MARTAINVILLE

SAINT MACLOU

QUAI BOURSE

❸

R. ALSACE

SEINE R.

QUAI P. CORNEILLE

TO A-13 FREEWAY & PARIS

DCH

❶ HOTEL CATHEDRALE
❷ HOTEL CARDINAL
❸ HOTEL LISIEUX
❹ LA MIRABELLE & PARIS MARAICHERS RESTAURANTS

Now turn around. With the town's lacy Gothic skyline and half-timbered buildings solidly on vertical hold, it's hard to imagine the town devastated by World War II bombs. Its restoration attests to the French commitment to their people-friendly city centers (rather than to suburban sprawl).

The striking **half-timbered houses** (14th–19th centuries) that line Rouen's streets remind us that there's more oak than stone in this region. Cantilevered floors were standard until about 1520. These top-heavy designs made sense because city land was limited, property taxes were based on ground-floor square footage, and the cantilevering minimized unsupported spans on upper floors. Rouen's historic wealth was due largely to its location as the last bridge across the Seine before the Atlantic and its inland river port.

Rue du Gros Horloge—This has been Rouen's main pedestrian and shopping street since Roman times. It links the Église Jeanne d'Arc and the Cathédrale Notre Dame and shows off the impressive Renaissance (1528) public clock, le Gros Horloge. Admire the clock and sculpture in the arch from below. The 10F climb to the top is good only for the exercise (often closed).

Take the first left after the old clock and in a block you'll see the...

Palace of Justice—This impressive Flamboyant Gothic Palace was largely restored after WWII bombing, though the western facade remains littered with pockmarks from German guns. Returning to rue du Gros Horloge, turn left and continue to the rue du Bec, where a plaque up on your left commemorates the assassination in Texas of the explorer (and native Rouen son), Cavelier de la Salle, who gave Louisiana to France. Continue to...

▲▲**Cathédrale Notre Dame**—Grab a seat on the shady benches on the right in the square. This is the church Monet painted at various times of day from an apartment he rented solely for this purpose opposite the cathedral (one example is in Rouen's Musée des Beaux Arts, 4 others are at the Musée d'Orsay in Paris). This soaring exterior is considered one of France's most beautiful, a fine example of the last overripe stage of Gothic architecture called *"flamboyant"*—flamelike. Notice how many statues are missing from niches in the facade. The ugly concrete buildings across from the cathedral are a fine example of function over form. Enter the cathedral and make a marvel-at-the-Gothic circuit inside, stopping halfway down the nave on the right to see photos showing the severe WWII bomb damage. You'll find helpful English explanations in small plaques near the side chapels. This cathedral is far lighter than it should be; only a few original stained-glass windows—behind the altar—survived the bombing.

Leave the cathedral via the left (northern) transept. Enjoy the Gothic facade behind you as you exit and then turn right to rue St. Romain. This fine old medieval lane leads a few blocks to the St. Maclou Church. A plaque on your right (under the ruined Gothic arch) identifies the site of an old chapel, where Joan of Arc was sentenced to death—and where she was proclaimed innocent 25 years later. Take a look down rue des Chanoines (next left) for a half-timbered fantasy. Rue St. Romain leads to the...

St. Maclou Church—Study the unique bowed facade. Inside, walk to the end of the choir and look back at the stained glass framed by the suspended crucifix.

Leaving the church, turn right and right (giving the boys on the corner a wide berth) and wander past a fine wall of half-timbered buildings fronting rue Martainville. Within a block a passageway on the left leads to...

Aître St. Maclou—Wander into this half-timbered courtyard.

Sit at the well in the center. Notice the ghoulish carvings lurking around you. This cemetery for 14th-century plague victims is now an art school. Peek in on the young artists. Examples of their art are in the new exhibition rooms near the entrance. A black cat watches you leave the courtyard.

Return right onto the rue Martainville and stroll toward the leaning towers. Take a right on rue Damiette, passing half-timbered antique shops that lead to Rouen's third fine Gothic church, St. Ouen. A thousand-year-old Danish rune stone stands by the church door, reminding locals of their Nordic heritage. The park behind this church is perfect for a picnic. In front of St. Ouen, rue Hôpital takes you back to rue Jeanne d'Arc and the station or your car.

Sights—Rouen
(All sights are closed Tuesdays.)
Musée des Beaux Arts—This crowd-free, well-organized museum beautifully displays paintings from all periods, including works by Caravaggio, Rubens, Veronese, Steen, Géricault, Ingres, Delacroix, and the Impressionists. Don't miss Monet's painting of Rouen's cathedral and the room dedicated to Gericault. Pick up the museum plan at the ticket desk. Key rooms have excellent English descriptions on small, portable boards and clever foldaway stools (20F, Wed–Mon 10:00–18:00, some rooms close 12:30–13:30, closed Tue, 3 blocks below station, 26 bis rue Jean Lecanuet).
Museum of Ironworks (Musée le Seq des Tournelles)—This surprisingly interesting museum located in a defunct Gothic church contains nothing but iron objects from over 1,500 years ago. Locks, keys, tools, even coffee grinders—virtually anything made out of iron is on display, (15F, Wed–Mon 10:00–12:00, 14:00–18:00, closed Tue, no English explanations, behind Musée des Beaux Arts, 2 rue Jacques Villon).
La Tour de Jeanne d'Arc—Originally eight towers such as this formed the medieval fortifications of Rouen. Joan was kept here before being burned at the stake on place du Vieux Marche—where the church of Joan of Arc now stands. This tower is only worth seeing from the outside (note the moat). Only the second floor has English explanations and there's no view from the top (10F, rue du Donjon, between Musée des Beaux Arts and train station).

Sights—Near Rouen
The Route of Ancient Abbeys (La Route des Anciennes Abbayes)—The route is punctuated with abbeys, apple trees, Seine River views, and pastoral scenery. Drivers follow the D-982 west of Rouen. By bus, take #30, which follows the route of ancient abbeys (4/day, none Sun, 50 min one-way to Jumièges, depart from Rouen's bus station at 25 rue des Charrettes, tel. 02 35 52 92 00).

Stop to admire the Romanesque church at the **Abbey of St.**

Georges de Boscherville but skip the 25F abbey grounds. The romantically ruined abbey at **Jumièges** is worth visiting (follow the river on D-65 from Duclair for a more scenic approach). Founded in 654, it was destroyed by Vikings only to be rebuilt by William the Conqueror (21F, daily mid-April–mid-Sept, 9:30–19:00, mid-Sept–mid-April 9:30–13:00, 14:30–17:30, helpful English handout). The Auberges des Ruines across the street makes a good lunch stop. Cross the Seine between Jumièges and Honfleur on the 10F car ferry at Duclair, or on one of three suspension bridges. The 35F it costs to cross the Pont de Normandie (bridge between Rouen and Honfleur) isn't worth it.

Sleeping and Eating in Rouen
(6.50F = about $1, country code: 33, zip code: 75000)
Sleep Code: **S** = Single, **D** = Double/Twin, **T** = Triple, **Q** = Quad, **b** = bathroom, **t** = toilet only, **s** = shower only, **CC** = Credit Card (**Visa**, **M**asterCard, **A**mex), **SE** = Speaks English, **NSE** = No English, * = Hotel rating (0–4 stars).

All of these hotels are within two blocks of the cathedral; directions are given from the cathedral. The first two hotels are equally good.

The ideally situated and welcoming **Hôtel Cardinal**** is a great value. All of its spotless and comfortable rooms look right onto the cathedral, and a few have private balconies (Sb-265–360F, Db-305–415F, extra bed-55F, CC:VM, elevator, to the right of the cathedral as you face it, 1 place de la Cathedrale, tel. 02 35 70 24 42, fax 02 35 89 75 14).

The central **Hôtel de la Cathédrale**** welcomes you with a flowery, umbrella-filled courtyard; a cozy, wood-beamed breakfast room; and decent rooms (S-235F, Sb-265–315F, D-280F, Db-315–375F, elevator, outside left transept of the cathedral, 12 rue St. Romain, tel. 02 35 71 57 95, fax 02 35 70 15 54, www.hotel-de-la-cathedrale.com, friendly Nathalie SE).

Hôtel de Lisieux** is welcoming, with spacious, colorful rooms and good prices (Db-265–360F, Tb-365F, CC:VM, Internet access for guests, 2 blocks from river below cathedral, 4 rue de Savonnerie, tel. 02 35 71 87 73, fax 02 35 89 31 52, e-mail: lisieux@hotel-rouen.com).

Two of Rouen's best moderately priced seafood restaurants are both on the place du Vieux Marché across from the church of Joan of Arc: **La Mirabelle** (tel. 02 35 71 58 21) and the cheaper **Paris Maraichers** (tel. 02 35 71 57 73). You'll also find many inexpensive alternatives between the St. Maclou and St. Ouen churches.

Transportation Connections—Rouen
Rouen is well served by trains from Paris, through Amiens to other points north, and through Caen to other destinations west and south.

By train to: **Paris**' Gare St. Lazare (nearly hrly, 75 min), **Bayeux** (3/day, 3 hrs, transfer in Caen), **Mont St. Michel** (3/day, 4 hrs, via Caen and Pontorson, short bus ride from Pontorson to Mont St. Michel or taxi, see "Transportation Connections – Mont St. Michel," below).

By train and bus to: **Honfleur** (5/day, 1.5 hrs, train to Le Havre then bus over Pont de Normandie to Honfleur—Le Havre's bus station is 1 block from train station, turn left out of station and cross big boulevard; or in 2 hrs via Lisieux—train from Rouen to Lisieux then bus to Honfleur).

HONFLEUR

Honfleur (ohn-flur) actually feels as picturesque as it looks. Gazing at its cozy harbor, surrounded by skinny, soaring houses, it's easy to overlook the historic importance of this port. For over a thousand years sailors have enjoyed Honfleur's ideal location, where the Seine meets the English Channel. William the Conqueror received supplies shipped from Honfleur, and Samuel de Champlain sailed from here in 1608, discovering the St. Lawrence Waterway and Quebec City. Honfleur was also a favorite of 19th-century Impressionists: Monet, Dufy, and Boudin all painted here. Honfleur escaped the bombs of World War II.

Today's Honfleur, long eclipsed by the gargantuan port of Le Havre just across the Seine, happily uses its past as a bar stool and sits on it. All of Honfleur's interesting streets and activities are packed together within a few minutes' walk of the old port (Vieux Bassin).

Honfleur is low on sights but high on ambience and art galleries. Snoop around the streets behind place Berthelot and Église Ste. Catherine for some of Normandy's oldest half-timbered homes.

Tourist Information: The TI is in left end of the flashy glass public library (*Mediathèque*) on Quai Lepaulmier, two blocks from the Vieux Bassin toward Le Havre. Pick up the handy town map and information on Normandy (Easter–Oct Mon–Sat 9:00–12:30, 14:00–18:30, no midday closing in summer, Sun 10:00–13:00; Nov–Easter Mon–Sat 9:00–12:00, 14:00–17:30, closed Sun, tel. 02 31 89 23 30, www.ville-honfleur.com).

Arrival in Honfleur

By Bus: Arriving from Lisieux or Deauville, the first stop in Honfleur (Albert Sorel) is closer to hotels (walk down rue de la République to the harbor). The other stop is north of the port at the bus station (*gare routière*) and has a useful information counter (see "Transportation Connections," below). Walk up rue des Fosses with Hotel Moderne on your left to reach the center.

By Car: Follow "*centre-ville*" signs and park as close to the old port (Vieux Bassin) as possible. Parking is tight in Honfleur. A pay

Honfleur

❶ HOTEL DAUPHIN	❽ BAR DE LA SALLE DES FETES ROOMS
❷ HOTEL DES LOGES	❾ MADAME BELLEGARDE ROOMS
❸ HOTEL DES CASCADES	❿ LA TORTUE RESTAURANT
❹ HOTEL LE CHEVAL BLANC	⓫ AU PETIT MAREYEUR RESTAURANT
❺ HOTEL LE CHAT	⓬ AUBERGE DU VIEUX CLOCHER
❻ HOTEL ABSINTHE	⓭ LA CIDRERIE BAR
❼ HOTEL DE LA TOUR	⓮ PERROQUET VERT & L'ALBATROSS BARS

lot is across from the TI (10F/3 hrs, 20F/day). Inquire at your
hotel where you can park for free.

Sights—Honfleur
▲▲Église Ste. Catherine—As I stepped inside this church my
first thought was, "If you could turn it over it would float." This
unusual church was built in the 15th century—logically, in this
ship-building town—by naval architects (replacing a ruined stone
church). Rough-hewn wood beams give it a feel-good warmth you

don't find in stone churches. In the last months of World War II, a bomb fell through the roof but didn't explode. The exterior is a wonderful conglomeration of wood-shingle, brick, and half-timbered construction.

The church's bell tower was built across the square to lighten the load on the roof of the wooden church and to minimize fire hazards. (Tower and church open 9:00–18:30 in summer, otherwise 9.00–12:00, 14:00–18:00.) The church is free. In the tower, the room that has a few church artifacts is not worth the 10F.

▲**Eugène Boudin Museum**—This pleasant, airy museum houses a variety of early Impressionist paintings by artists you may not recognize. Look for scenes of Honfleur and nearby Deauville. Norman costumes are on the second floor (26F, mid-March–Sept Wed–Mon 10:00–12:00, 14:00–18:00, Oct–mid-March 10:00–12:00, 14:30–17:30, closed Tue all year, elevator, rue de l'Homme de Bois).

Maisons Satie Museum—Located in composer Erik Satie's birth home and interesting only for his fans, this museum has rooms with modern-art interpretations of his compositions (30F, daily 10:30–18:00, until 19:00 in summer, free English audioguide, 67 boulevard Charles V).

Museums of Old Honfleur—Two museums combine to paint a picture of what daily life has been like in Honfleur since the Middle Ages. The **Musée de la Marine**, located in an old church right on the Vieux Bassin near the TI, offers an interesting collection of ship models and marine paraphernalia. The **Musée d'Ethnographie et d'Art Populaire**, located in the old prison (which you'll pass through) behind Musée de la Marine, re-creates typical rooms, cramming them with objects of daily life from various eras (ask for English explanation, 25F for both or 15F each, Tue–Sun 10:00–12:00, 14:00–18:00).

Boat Excursions—Boats to the Pont de Normandie (see below) depart from in front of Hotel Cheval Blanc (40F-adult, 30F-child, Easter–Nov, 50 min, tel. 02 31 89 21 10). The 30-minute excursions on Honfleur's harbor on the *Calypso* are less interesting (25F).

Côte de Grace Walk—For good exercise and a bird's-eye view over Honfleur and the Pont de Normandie, take the short, steep walk up to the Côte de Grace viewpoint (from Église Ste. Catherine, walk past Hotel Dauphin and up rue Brûlée, turn right on rue Eugene Boudin, then turn left at the top and climb la Rampe de Mont Joli; best early in the morning or at sunset).

Saturday Morning Farmers' Market—The area around the Église Ste. Catherine is transformed into a colorful market each Saturday morning from 9:00 to 12:30.

▲**Normandie Bridge**—The 2.1-kilometer-long Pont de Normandie is the longest cable-stayed bridge in the world (until a Japanese bridge, which will beat it by 40 meters, is completed). This is a key piece of a super-freeway that links the Atlantic ports from Belgium to Spain (35F to take car across). View the bridge from Honfleur (better from an excursion boat or above the town on the Côte de Grace; best when floodlit) or visit the free Exhibition Hall (under tollbooth on Le Havre side, daily 8:00–19:00). The Seine finishes its winding 500-mile journey here. From its source it drops only 1,500 feet. It flows so slowly that in certain places a stiff breeze can send it flowing upstream.

Sleeping in Honfleur
(6.50F = about $1, country code: 33, zip code: 14600)
Honfleur is busy on weekends and holidays and in the summer. English is widely spoken. Off-season rates plunge; the lower room rates listed below are for off-season (generally Oct–May).

A modern launderette (Lavomatique) is a block to the right and behind the TI (daily 7:00–20:00, 4 rue Notre Dame).

Hôtel Dauphin** is a solid and central midrange bet, with a family feel, a homey lounge/breakfast room, an Escher-esque floor plan, many stairs, and very comfortable rooms—some with open-beam ceilings (Db-300–400F, Tb-460–660F, pay-as-you-go breakfast upgrades include cereal-5F, yogurt-5F, fruit-5F, and freshly squeezed juice-12F, CC:VMA, cable TV, all rooms theoretically smoke-free, a stone's throw from church at 10 place Berthelot, SE, tel. 02 31 89 15 53, fax 02 31 89 92 06, e-mail: hotel.dudauphin @wanadoo.fr).

Hôtel des Loges**, next to the Dauphin, is tranquil and very sharp, with many tastefully renovated rooms and pleasant common areas (Db-335–415F, Tb-350F, CC:VM, 18 rue Brûlée, tel. 02 31 89 38 26).

Hôtel des Cascades*, tired but comfortable, is well located a block north of the harbor. It has a tangled-fishnet floor plan and laid-back management (Db-200–300F, third person-50F more, dinner required on summer weekends, CC:VMA, facing rue Montpensier at 17 place Thiers, tel. 02 31 89 05 83, fax 02 31 89 32 13, Melanie SE).

Hôtel Le Cheval Blanc*** is a good three-star splurge right on the water, with port views from every room and a rare (in this town) elevator. It's a big, half-timbered place with no restaurant (Sb-440–510F, Db-460–1,100F, most Db-530F and 640F, includes breakfast, CC:VM, cancel with less than a week's notice and lose 250F—otherwise deposit returned at year's end, 2 quai de Passagers, tel. 02 31 81 65 00, fax 02 31 89 52 80, e-mail: lecheval .blanc@wanadoo.fr).

Hôtel Le Chat*** offers spaciousness, wood beams, and faded-elegant rooms in a historic, ivy-covered stone building across from the Ste. Catherine church (Db-410–510F, CC:VMA, cable TV, bar, restaurant, place Ste. Catherine, tel. 02 31 14 49 49, fax 02 31 89 28 61, e-mail: hotel.lechat@honfleur.com).

Hôtel Absinthe*** is a small, flawlessly restored hotel with seven very comfortable rooms behind the restaurant le Bistro du Port. Jacuzzi tubs, tasteful, wood-beamed décor, and a cozy lounge with fireplace make this a good splurge (Db-750F, Db suite-1,350F, extra bed-150F, CC:VM; if no receptionist, keys available in restaurant Absinthe across the alley, 1 rue de la Ville, tel. 02 31 89 23 23, fax 02 31 89 53 60, www.absinthe.fr).

Hôtel de la Tour** is a modern, no-brainer hotel with easy, free parking and spacious, cookie-cutter rooms (Sb-290–470F, Db-350–470F, loft family rooms-500–650F, CC:VMA, cable TV, mini-bars, elevator, near the bus terminal and TI at 3 Quai de la Tour, tel. 02 31 89 21 22, fax 02 31 89 53 51, www.hoteldelatour.com).

Chambres d'hôte offer a good option here (the TI has a long list), though most are at least 1.5 kilometers from the center of Honfleur. The following two are a short walk from the center.

Bargain rooms are tucked above the *très* local **Bar de la Salle des Fêtes**, where French is spoken with a shy smile by Monsieur and Madame Leguyon (D-160F, nifty studio with kitchenette-200–250F, place Albert Sorel, at bus stop Albert Sorel, 300 meters from harbor out rue de la République, tel. 02 31 89 19 69 or 06 13 31 22 03).

Gentle **Madame Bellegarde** offers comfortable rooms in her pleasant home (Db-180F, a family-friendly Tb with kitchenette and great bathroom view-300F, 10-min uphill walk from TI, 3 blocks up from the St. Leonard church in nontouristy part of Honfleur, 54 rue St. Leonard, look for sign in window, tel. 02 31 89 06 52).

Eating in Honfleur

Eat seafood here. It's a tough choice between the hard-to-resist waterfront tables of the many look-alike places lining the Vieux Bassin (a walk along the port is mandatory after dark) and those with more solid reputations on small side streets.

Several good restaurants line rue de l'Homme de Bois, like the unpretentious **La Tortue** (100F/140F *menus*, closed Mon–Tue off-season, 36 rue de l'Homme de Bois, tel. 02 31 89 04 93). Better still, enjoy Honfleur's best affordable seafood in the *charmant* **Au Petit Mareyeur** (125F *menu*, closed Mon–Tue, reservations necessary, 4 place Hamelin, tel. 02 31 98 84 23). The classy and intimate **Auberge du Vieux Clocher** will tempt any romantic (125/170F *menu*, closed Sun and Wed except in summer, reserve ahead, 9 rue de l'Homme de Bois, tel. 02 31 89 12 06). Near the bottom of the street, **La Cidrerie** is a cozy cider bar with fresh crepes, Calvados, and ambience (closed Tue–Wed, 26 place Hamelin).

Nightlife in Honfleur centers on the old port. Two bar/cafés sit 50 meters apart on the tall-skinny-building side of the port and divide Honfleur's after-hours clientele by age: the **Perroquet Vert** is decidedly over-40s, while **l'Abatross** is clearly Generation X.

Transportation Connections—Honfleur

Buses connect Honfleur with Le Havre, Caen, Deauville, and Lisieux, where you'll catch a train to other points. While train and bus service is usually coordinated, ask at Honfleur's helpful bus station for the best connection for your trip (Mon–Fri 9:00–12:15, 14:30–17:30, Sat 9:15–12:15, closed Sun, tel. 02 31 89 28 41). Railpass holders will save money by connecting though the nearest city, as bus fares increase with distance.

By bus and train to: Bayeux (5/day, 2.5 hrs, bus to Lisieux or quicker via Caen, then train to Bayeux), **Rouen** (5/day, 90 min, bus over the Pont de Normandie to Le Havre, train to Rouen, or in 2 hrs via Lisieux), **Paris'** Gare St. Lazare (5/day, 3 hrs; bus to Lisieux or Deauville, train to Paris; buses from Honfleur meet most Paris trains).

BAYEUX

Only 10 kilometers miles from the D-Day beaches, Bayeux was the first city liberated after the landing and makes an ideal base for visiting the area's sights. Even without its famous tapestry and proximity to the D-Day beaches, Bayeux would be worth a visit for its pleasant *centre-ville* and awe-inspiring cathedral.

Navigating in Bayeux is a breeze on foot or by car. Look for the cathedral spires and follow the signs to *centre-ville* or *tapisserie* to reach the city center (from the train station it's a 15- to 20-min walk or a 30F taxi to any of the recommended hotels). Market days are Wednesday (on pedestrian rue St. Jean) and Saturday (bigger, on place St. Patrice). Both end at noon.

Tourist Information: From the friendly TI on the bridge (Pont St. Jean), pick up a town map, the excellent "D-Day Landings and the Battle of Normandy" brochure, bus schedules, and regional information (June–mid-Sept Mon–Sat 9:00–19:00, Sun 9:30–12:00, 14:30–18:00; mid-Sept–May daily 9:00–12:00, 14:00–18:00, Internet access, on Pont St. Jean leading to pedestrian street rue St. Jean).

Bike Rental: Monsieur Roue rents bikes for 90F per day (boulevard W. Churchill, tel. 02 31 92 27 75).

Bayeux History—The Battle of Hastings

The most memorable date of the Middle Ages is probably 1066 because of this pivotal battle. England's King Edward was about to die without an heir, and the question was who would succeed him: Harold, an English noble, or William, the Duke of Normandy? Harold was captured during a battle in Normandy. To gain his freedom he promised William that, when the ailing King Edward died, he would allow William to ascend the throne. Shortly after that oath was taken, Harold was back in England, Edward died, and Harold grabbed the throne. William, known as William the

Bastard, invaded England to claim the throne he figured was rightfully his. Harold met him in southern England at the town of Hastings, where their forces fought a fierce 14-hour battle. Harold was killed, and his Saxon forces were routed. William—now "the Conqueror"—marched on London to claim his throne, becoming King of England as well as Duke of Normandy. The advent of a Norman king of England muddied the political waters, setting in motion 400 years of conflict between England and France not to be resolved until the end of the Hundred Years' War in 1453.

The Norman Conquest of England brought England into the European mainstream. The Normans established a strong central English government. They brought with them the Romanesque style of architecture (e.g., the Tower of London and Durham Cathedral) that the English call "Norman." Historians speculate that had William not succeeded, England would have remained on the fringe of Europe (like Scandinavia), and French culture (and language) would have prevailed in the New World.

Sights—Bayeux

Note that the 40F ticket for the Bayeux Tapestry gets you into the Baron Gerard Museum and Hotel du Doyon (listed below) but not the WWII museum.

▲▲▲Bayeux Tapestry—Actually woolen embroidery on linen cloth, this document—precious to historians—is a 70-meter cartoon telling the story of William the Conqueror's rise from Duke of Normandy to King of England and his victory over Harold at the Battle of Hastings. Long and skinny, it was designed to hang from the nave of Bayeux's cathedral.

Your visit has three parts (explaining the basic story of the battle three times—which was about right for me): First you'll walk through a "mood-setting images on sails" room into a room with a replica of the tapestry with extensive explanations. You'll then continue to a room designed to set the cultural scene for the battle. Next, a 15-minute AV show in the cinema up one flight gives a relaxing dramatization of the event. Finally you'll get to the real McCoy. It's worth the 5F (have exact change) and the wait for the headphones, which give a top-notch, fast-moving, 20-minute scene-by-scene narration complete with period music. If you lose your place you'll find subtitles in Latin. Remember, this is a piece of Norman propaganda—the English (the bad guys, referred to as *les goddamns*, after a phrase the French kept hearing them say) are shown with mustaches and long hair; the French (*les good guys*) are clean-cut and clean-shaven (40F, mid-March–mid-Oct daily 9:00–18:30, mid-Oct–mid March daily 9:00–12:30, 14:00–18:00, tel. 02 31 92 05 48). Arrive by 9:00 or late in the day to avoid crowds. When buying your ticket, get the English film show times. If you're rushed and the cinema schedule doesn't match

Bayeux

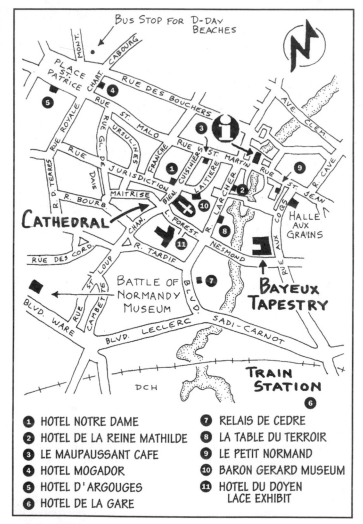

Bus Stop for D-Day Beaches

CATHEDRAL

BAYEUX TAPESTRY

BATTLE OF NORMANDY MUSEUM

HALLE AUX GRAINS

TRAIN STATION

1. HOTEL NOTRE DAME
2. HOTEL DE LA REINE MATHILDE
3. LE MAUPAUSSANT CAFE
4. HOTEL MOGADOR
5. HOTEL D'ARGOUGES
6. HOTEL DE LA GARE
7. RELAIS DE CEDRE
8. LA TABLE DU TERROIR
9. LE PETIT NORMAND
10. BARON GERARD MUSEUM
11. HOTEL DU DOYEN LACE EXHIBIT

yours, skip the film. If you have time, see the film first, exit the way you entered, and backtrack to see the replica (don't follow everyone else; cinemagoers pile into the tapestry room with a crowd).

▲▲**Bayeux Cathedral**—This massive building towers over Bayeux. Walk inside. The view of the nave from the top of the

steps is as good as Gothic gets. Historians believe the tapestry
originally hung here. Imagine it proudly circling the congregation,
draped around the nave from the mini-arches just below the big
and bright upper windows of the clerestory. The nave's huge,
round lower arches are Romanesque (11th century) and decorated
with the same zigzag pattern that characterizes this "Norman"
art in England. But this nave is much brighter because of the later
Gothic windows of the top half of the nave. The finest example
of 13th-century "Norman" Gothic is in the choir (the fancy area
behind the central altar). For maximum 1066 atmosphere, step
into the crypt (below the central altar). Study the frescoed angels
and the ornately carved 11th-century capitals decorated with
Roman-style acanthus leaves and gray meanies (free, daily 9:00–
18:00). The cathedral is beautifully illuminated after dark.
Baron Gerard Museum—This museum, located outside the cathedral's left transept, houses a collection of porcelain and lace and a
modest painting gallery (free with ticket to tapestry, daily 10:00–
12:30, 14:00–18:00, in summer until 19:00 with no midday closing).
Hôtel du Doyen—Watch lace workers design and make intricate
lace as they did in the 1600s and see examples of their finest works
over the years (free with ticket to tapestry, located outside the
cathedral's right transept, same hours as Baron Gerard Museum).
Bayeux Memorial Museum/Battle of Normandy—This
museum provides a good overview of the Battle of Normandy and
features tanks, jeeps, uniforms, and countless informative displays
(33F, May–mid-Sept daily 9:30–18:30, mid-Sept–April closes
12:30–14:00, on Bayeux's ring road, 20 min on foot from center).

Sleeping in Bayeux
(6.50F = about $1, country code: 33, zip code: 14400)
Hotels are a good value here. Also see "Sleeping in and near
Arromanches," below.
  Hôtel Notre Dame*, right across from the cathedral, has
spacious, frumpy rooms with wall-to-ceiling carpeting (ask for a
room with a view of the cathedral) and assumes you'll dine in its
reasonable restaurant (you'll probably be quoted prices including
dinner). Hustling Annick will take care of your every need (D-
180F, Db-270F, Tb-360F, Qb-465F, CC:VMA, 44 rue des
Cuisiniers, tel. 02 31 92 87 24, fax 02 31 92 67 11).
  Hôtel de Reine Mathilde**, one block from the cathedral
on the street just below it, has modern and comfortable rooms
(Db-290F, Tb-370–425F, CC:VM, 23 rue Larcher, tel. 02 31 92
08 13, fax 02 31 92 09 93).
  Le Maupassant Café is dead-center and offers 10 immaculate and modern rooms over a café at bargain rates (S-160F,
D/Db-200F, Tb-300F, Qb-360F, 19 rue St Martin, tel. 02 31
92 28 53, fax 02 31 02 35 40).

The next two hotels are a 15-minute walk from the TI
up rue St. Martin.

Hôtel Mogador** is a solid two-star bet with friendly Monsieur Mencaroni at the helm. Choose between cozy wood-beamed
rooms on the busy square or immaculate, comfortable rooms off
the street (Sb-230F, Db-260–290F, Tb-340F, CC:VMA, easy
parking, 20 rue Alain Chartier/Place St. Patrice, tel. 02 31 92 24 58,
fax 02 31 92 24 85, SE).

For three-plus-star comfort at two-star prices, stay at the
impeccable **Hôtel d'Argouges****. Every room is wood-beam
cozy and meticulously cared for. Named for its builder, Lord
d'Argouges, this tranquil retreat has a château-like feel and a
lovely private garden. Just off the huge place St. Patrice, look for
an archway with a brown sign (Db-390–480F, several fantastic
family suites-560–700F, extra bed-80F, private parking, CC:VMA,
21 rue St. Patrice, tel. 02 31 92 88 86, fax 02 31 92 69 16, e-mail:
dargouges@aol.com).

Desperate train travelers can bed down in the basic, unwel-
coming **Hôtel de la Gare's*** simple rooms (S-95F, D-105F, Db-
215F, T-145F, Tb-310F, Q-205–285F, tel. 02 31 92 10 70).

The four rooms at the Addams Family-esque mansion,
Relais de Cédre, are palatial and managed by formal owners
(Db-200–250F, 10 min from station, turn left down big boulevard,
1 block off the road, next to tour bus park at 1 boulevard Sadi-
Carnot, tel. 02 31 21 98 07, NSE).

Eating in Bayeux

Bayeux's old city centers around the pedestrian rue St. Jean,
which is lined with *crêperies*, cafés, and the best *charcuterie* in
town (salads and quiches to go, across from Hotel Churchill).
For a traditional meal on monastic plank-tables, try **La Table
du Terroir** (good salads, *menus* from 99F, 42 rue St. Jean, tel.
02 31 92 05 53). The restaurants at **Hôtel Notre Dame** (95F
menu, see "Sleeping," above) and **Le Petit Normand** (*menus*
start at 80F, 35 rue Larcher) merit their fine reputations.

Transportation Connections—Bayeux

By train to: Paris' St. Lazare (8/day, 2.5 hrs), **Amboise** (6/day,
4 hrs, transfers in Caen and Tours or Paris Montparnasse and
Tours), **Rouen** (3/day, 3 hrs, transfer in Caen), **Honfleur** (5/day,
2.5 hrs; train to Lisieux or Caen, then bus to Honfleur; trip is
quicker via Caen), **Mont St. Michel** (2–3 trains/day, 2 hrs to
Pontorson, with a convenient late-afternoon departure; from
Pontorson bus to Mont St. Michel—Mon–Sat 4/day, Sun 2/day,
15 min—or find others to share a taxi-80F, 110F after 19:00 and
on weekends, tel. 02 33 60 26 89).

By bus to the D-Day beaches: Bus Vert serves the area

(about 15F one-way to the beaches). Line #74 leaves Bayeux (St. Patrice stop) about 12:00 for Arromanches and returns 90 minutes later. Line #70 has a 12:00 trip that serves the American cemetery and returns 75 minutes later (confirm schedule, particularly for Wed; catch the bus at Bayeux train station or place St. Patrice—a 15-min walk up rue St. Martin from the center, veer right through the square to bus shelters).

D-DAY BEACHES

Along the 120 kilometers of Atlantic coast north of Bayeux (from Sainte Marie du Mont to Ouistreham) you'll find museums, monuments, cemeteries, and battle remains left in tribute to the courage of the WWII British, Canadian, and American armies, who successfully carried out the largest military operation in history. It was on these beautiful beaches, at the crack of dawn, June 6, 1944, that the Allies finally gained a foothold in France and Nazi Europe began to crumble.

> *"The first twenty-four hours of the invasion will be decisive . . . the fate of Germany depends on the outcome . . . for the Allies, as well as Germany, it will be the longest day."*
> —Field Marshall Erwin Rommel to his aide,
> April 22, 1944. From *The Longest Day*.

Getting around the D-Day Beaches

On Your Own: A car is ideal, particularly for three or more persons (the Bayeux TI lists rental agencies), though biking can work for some (rent a bike in Bayeux at M. Roue's shop for 90F/day, boulevard W. Churchill, tel. 02 31 92 27 75). Buses connect Bayeux and Arromanches (see "Transportation Connections— Bayeux," above) to allow you to see the most impressive D-Day (*Jour J* in French) sights.

By Taxi: Figure 95F one way from Bayeux to Arromanches and 150F from Bayeux to the American cemetery. Ask about "waiting rates" (tel. 02 31 92 92 40).

By Tour: Several companies offer good full- and half-day excursions to the D-Day beaches from Bayeux. These are not guided tours; you get an English-speaking driver and transportation between key sights (for fully guided tours of the beaches, see Caen's Battle of Normandy Museum, below). **Bus Fly Excursions** offers four-hour tours (200F, includes Pointe du Hoc, American cemetery, Longues-sur-Mer, and Arromanches); they also offer day trips to Mont St. Michel for about 350F (tel. 02 31 22 00 08 or 02 33 39 23 52, fax 02 31 92 35 10, e-mail: info@busfly.com). **Victory Tours** offers similar tours for less (half day-170F, full day 300F, tel. 02 31 51 98 14, www.victory-tours.com). Book these tours in advance.

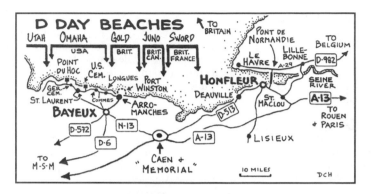

Sights—D-Day Beaches

Most museums will slightly reduce your entry fee if you have a full-price ticket from another museum.

▲▲▲**Caen's Battle of Normandy Museum (le Memorial)**— Caen, the modern capital of lower Normandy, has the best World War II museum in France. Officially named the Memorial for Peace (*le Memorial*), its intent is to put the Battle of Normandy in a broader context. Your visit has four parts: the lead-up to World War II, the actual Battle of Normandy, the video presentations, and the ongoing fight for peace.

The museum is brilliant. Begin with a downward spiral stroll, tracing (almost psychoanalyzing) the path of Europe from World War I to the rise of fascism to World War II.

The lower level gives a thorough look at how World War II was fought—from General de Gaulle's London radio broadcasts to Hitler's early missiles to wartime fashion.

You then see a series of three powerful movies (15 min each, for all languages, the cycle starts every 20 min—a clock at the end of the lower-level exhibits lets you plan your time). Ninety percent of the incredible D-Day footage is real, with a bit taken from the movie *The Longest Day*.

The memorial then takes you beyond World War II to the Gallery of Nobel Prizes. This is a celebration of the courageous work of people such as Andrei Sakharov, Elie Wiesel, and Desmond Tutu, who understand that peace is more than an absence of war.

The finale is a walk through the U.S. Armed Forces Memorial Garden. I was a bit bothered by the mindless laughing of lighthearted children unable to appreciate their blessings. Then I read on the pavement, "From the heart of our land flows the blood of our youth, given to you in the name of freedom." And their laughter made me happy.

Cost and Hours: 74F (free for World War II veterans, 68F for other veterans, free admission and nursery for kids under 10).

The museum is open daily usually from 9:00 to 19:00 (until 20:00 mid-July–Aug, closes at 18:00 Nov–Feb, ticket office closes 75 minutes before museum). Allow 2.5 hours to visit, including an hour for the videos (tel. 02 31 06 06 44— as in June 6, 1944, fax 02 31 06 06 70; www.unicaen.fr/memorial).

Tours: The museum runs minivan guided tours of the D-Day beaches. Tours include entry to the Caen's Battle of Normandy Museum (half-day tours: 340F, 9:00–14:00, includes Longues-sur-Mer, Pegasus Bridge, Arromanches, Courseulles, and Douvres; full-day tours: 480F, 9:00–18:00, adds the American and German cemeteries, St. Mere l'Eglise, and lunch; contact the Caen Museum to reserve and pay in advance, CC:VM).

Getting to Museum: It's on the ring road (*peripherique*) in Caen (sortie #6, at Université, look for signs to *le Memorial*). By train, it's two hours from Paris (14/day) or 15 minutes from Bayeux (10/day); take bus #17-Memorial from Caen's train station (exit right out of the station, 2nd shelter, buses every 15 min, or taxi-60F one-way).

▲▲▲**Arromanches (Musée du Débarquement)**—The first-ever prefab harbor was created by the British in this town. Churchill's brainchild, it was named Port Winston. Walk along the seafront promenade and imagine 18 old ships and 115 football field–size cement blocks (called Mulberries) being towed across the English Channel and sunk right here to create an 11-kilometer-long breakwater and harbor for landing 54,000 vehicles and 500,000 troops in six days. You can still see remains of the temporary harbor and visit the beachfront museum, where this incredible undertaking is re-created with models, maps, mementos, and two short audiovisual shows—ask for English (35F, May–Aug daily 9:00–19:00, April and Sept 9:00–18:00, Oct–Dec and Feb–March 9:00–12:30, 13:30–17:00, closed Jan, tel. 02 31 22 34 31).

Walk to the top of the bluff behind the museum for the view (10F to park if you drive) and ponder how, from this makeshift harbor, the liberation of Europe commenced. Skip the 360-degree screen showing *The Price of Freedom* (too loud, no coherent story, 24F, 2 showings/hrly). For more on Arromanches, see "Sleeping," below.

Longues Sur Mer—Several German bunkers, guns intact, are left guarding against seaborne attacks on the city of Arromanches (the 30F booklet is helpful, skip the 26F tour). Walk to the observation post for a great view over the channel (located between Arromanches and Port en Bessin; turn right at signal in Longues sur Mer). You can drive right down the water by continuing down the small road past the parking lot.

▲▲▲**American Cemetery at St. Laurent**—On a bluff just above Omaha Beach, the 9,400 brilliant white-marble crosses and Stars of David glow in memory of Americans who gave their lives to

free Europe on the beaches below, where fighting was particularly intense. Notice the names and home states inscribed on the crosses. Behind the monument, surrounded by roses, are the names of 1,557 missing or unidentified soldiers. France has given the United States free permanent use of this 172-acre site. It is immaculately maintained by the American Battle Monuments Commission. Pick up the handout in the small office as you enter. The trail to the beach below is open from 9:00 to 18:00, off-season until 17:00 unless wild boars (*sangliers*) are prowling about.
German Military Cemetery—For an opportunity to ponder German losses, drop by this somber, thought-provoking resting place of 21,000 German soldiers. While the American cemetery is the focus of American visitors, visitors here speak in hushed German. The site is glum, with two graves per simple marker and dark crosses that huddle together in groups of five. It's just south of Point du Hoc (right off N-13 in the village of La Cambe, 22 km west of Bayeux; follow signs to *Cimetiére Allemand*).
▲▲Pointe du Hoc—During the D-Day invasion, 225 U.S. rangers attempted a castle-style assault of the German-occupied cliffs by using grappling hooks and ladders borrowed from London fire departments. Only 90 survived. German bunkers and bomb craters remain as they were found (20 min by car west of American cemetery in St. Laurent, just past Vierville-sur-Mer). There's a museum dedicated to the rangers in nearby Grandcamp-Maisy.

Sleeping in Arromanches and on the D-Day Beaches
(6.50F = about $1, country code: 33)
To feel the pulse of World War II, sleep near the beach. The small town of Arromanches, ground zero for the D-Day invasion, is mesmerizing if you can ignore the trinket shops. Get up on the cliffs or walk on the beach. The **TI** is across the parking lot from the museum on rue Colonel Rene Michel (daily 10:00–12:00, 14:00–18:00, no midday closing in summer, tel. 02 31 21 47 56, www.arromanches.com). The population of tiny Arromanches just reached 500 persons (about the same as on June 6, 1944). There's a supermarket (above the town by the parking lot), a post office, and an ATM near the museum. For Arromanche's only taxi, dial 06 07 83 44 48.

Light-hearted **Pappagall Hôtel d'Arromanches**** is a great value, with smartly appointed rooms, a fun bar, and cheery restaurant (Db-260–310F, skip the half-pension, 2 rue Colonel Rene Michel, 14117 Arromanches, tel. 02 31 22 36 26, fax 02 31 22 23 29). **Hôtel de la Marine****, run by an indifferent management, offers beach views from most of its comfy rooms (some squishy beds) and from its elegant restaurant (Db-310–410F, Tb-400–480F, family rooms-560–760F, CC:VMA, restaurant *menus* from 100F, quai du Canada, tel. 02 31 22 34 19, fax 02 31 22 98 80, e-mail: mcverdier@caramail.com). For evening fun, try the bar at **Pappagall Hôtel d'Arromanches** or **Pub Marie Celeste**, right around the corner on rue de la Poste.

Sleeping near Arromanches
(6.50F = about $1, country code: 33)

Chambres d'hôte are everywhere along the coast (the TIs in Bayeux and Arromanches have long lists). It's worth the effort to find **Andre and Madeleine Sebires'** working farmhouse with four homey and cheap rooms and a pleasant garden. It's in tiny Ryes (between Bayeux and Arromanches) at the Ferme du Clos Neuf—look for the faded *chambres* signs. If the Sebires prove too elusive, call from Ryes and they'll come get you (Sb-180F, Db-200F, Tb-250F, includes breakfast, zip code: 14400, tel. 02 31 22 32 34, NSE).

Or consider the almost mystical **Château du Bosq** in Commes. Seven kilometers from Bayeux, this *très* rustic, 700-year-old château comes with turrets, a water-filled moat, and minimally decorated rooms. It's quiet: no TV, no phones, no noise, no kidding (D-190F, Db-300–400F, Tb-450F, between Arromanches and American cemetery, 14520 Commes, tel. 02 31 92 52 77, fax 02 31 92 26 71).

MONT ST. MICHEL
The distant silhouette of this Gothic island-abbey sends the tired sightseer's spirits soaring. Mont St. Michel, which through the ages has been among the top four pilgrimage sites in Christendom, is one of those rare places that looks as enchanting in reality as it does in dreams. While it floats like a mirage on the horizon, it does show up on film.

The causeway, built in 1878, stopped the water from flowing around the island, which in turn contributed to the filling in of the bay around Mont St. Michel—so it's no longer an island. A new bridge is being planned (construction to begin in 2002) that will allow the water to circulate and turn Mont St. Michel into an island again.

Orientation
Mont St. Michel is connected by a three-kilometer causeway to the mainland and surrounded by a sandy mud flat. Your visit features a one-street village that winds up to the fortified abbey. Between 10:00 and 16:00, tourists trample the dreamscape (try to remember that this street was just as jammed with earnest pilgrims 800 years ago). A ramble on the ramparts offers mud-flat views and an escape from the tourist zone. The only worthwhile entry is the abbey itself, at the summit of the island.

Daytime Mont St. Michel is a touristic gauntlet—worth a

stop, but a short one will do. The tourist tide recedes late each afternoon. During nonsummer nights, the island is abbey-quiet, the illumination, beautiful. Poets prefer evenings here.

It helps to arrive late and depart early. The abbey interior (which isn't an essential visit anyway) will likely be open until midnight from May through September when the new lighting scheme is finished (off-season until 22:00). If you're spending the night, consider bringing a dinner picnic (see "Eating," below); there are no grocery shops on the island but there's a handy tourist *supermarché* at the mainland end of the causeway (8:30–20:00).

Tourist Information: The overwhelmed TI (and WC) is to your left as you enter Mont St. Michel's gates. They have *chambres d'hôte* listings, English tour times for the abbey, bus schedules, and the tide table, "Horaires des Marées," which is essential if you explore outside Mont St. Michel (daily 9:00–19:00 in summer, off-season 9:00–12:30, 14:00–18:00, tel. 02 33 60 14 30). A post office (PTT) and ATM are 50 meters beyond the TI.

Tides: The tides here (which rise 17 meters) are the largest and most dangerous in Europe. During a flood tide the ocean rushes in at 20 kilometers per hour. In medieval times the tides clocked in "at the speed of a galloping horse." Even today the undertow can sweep a slow horse (or tourist) away. High tides (*grandes marées*) lap against the tourist-office door (where you'll find tide hours posted).

Parking: Very high tides rise to the edge of the causeway— leaving the causeway open but any cars parked below it under water. Safe parking is available at the foot of Mont St. Michel (15F); you will be instructed where to park under high-tide conditions. There's plenty of parking, provided you arrive off-season or early or late in high season. Make a note of your parking sector and plan on a 15-minute walk to the island from your car.

Sights—Mont St. Michel

The Village below the Abbey—Mont St. Michel's main street of shops and hotels leads to the abbey. With only 30 full-time residents, the village lives solely for tourists. After the TI, check the tide warnings posted on the wall and admire the huge doors you're walking through. Before the drawbridge, on your left, poke through the door of Restaurant Le Mère Poulard, where a virtual theater-kitchen in action shows the colorful making of the traditional omelet. Don't spend 150F for this edible tourist trap. But watch the show as old-time-costumed cooks beat omelets, daddy, eight to the bar.

As you pass through the old drawbridge, Mont St. Michel welcomes you with the most touristy street this side of Tijuana (remember those pilgrims). You can trudge through the crowds uphill past several gimmicky museums to the abbey (all island hotel receptions are located on this street). Or better, climb the

first steps after the drawbridge on your right and then turn right
or left at the top; the ramparts lead all the way up and up to the
abbey in either direction (quieter if you turn right). Public WCs
are next to the TI, halfway up, and at the abbey entrance.

▲▲▲**Abbey of Mont St. Michel**—Mont St. Michel has been an
important pilgrimage center since A.D. 708, when the Archangel
Michael told the bishop of Avranches to "build here and build
high." With uncanny foresight he reassured the bishop, "If you
build it... they will come." Today's abbey is built on the remains
of a Romanesque church, which was built on the remains of a
Carolingian church. Saint Michael, whose gilded statue decorates
the top of the spire, was the patron saint of many French kings,
making this a favored sight for French royalty through the ages.
As you enter, imagine the headaches and hassles the monks ran
into while building it. They had to ferry the granite from across
the bay (then deeper and without the causeway) and make the
same hike you just did—with more luggage.

The visit is a one-way route through fine—but barren—
Gothic rooms. You'll explore the impressive church, delicate cloisters, and refectory (where the monks ate in austere silence) and
then climb down into the dark, damp Romanesque foundations. A
highlight is the giant tread-wheel, which six workers would power
hamster-style to haul two-ton loads of stones and supplies from
the landing below. This was used right up until the 19th century.

Those who go through without a live tour or audioguide find
no English explanations posted—but then, there's not a lot to
explain (40F entry, mid-May–mid-Sept daily 9:00–18:30, spring
and fall 9:30–17:00, closes at 16:00 in winter, ticket office closes
1 hr earlier.) Buy your ticket to the abbey and keep climbing.
Allow 20 minutes to climb at a relaxed, steady pace from the TI.

You'll better appreciate the abbey by renting an audioguide
(25F, 35F for 2) or taking a 75-minute English-language tour (free,
tip requested, 4–6 tours/day, first tour usually at 10:00, last at 17:00,
confirm tour times at TI, meet at top terrace in front of church,
groups can be large). For some, the tours make a short story long.

When you leave the abbey, make a hard right at the bottom
of the steps (just past the WCs) to see more of the village and
avoid crowds.

▲▲**Stroll around Mont St. Michel**—To resurrect that Mont
St. Michel dreamscape and evade all those tacky tourist stalls,
walk out on the mudflats around the island. At low tide it's reasonably dry and a great memory. This can be extremely dangerous,
so be sure to double-check the tides. Remember the scene from
the Bayeux tapestry where Harold rescues Normans from the
quicksand? It happened somewhere in this bay. You may notice
groups hiking in from the muddy horizon. Attempting this without a local guide is reckless.

▲▲▲**Evening on Mont St. Michel**—After dark the island is magically floodlit. Views from the ramparts are sublime. You must exit the island and walk out on the causeway a few hundred yards to best appreciate this magical place. A sound and light show is planned for 2001; ask at the TI.

German Military Cemetery (Cimetière Militaire Allemand)—Located five kilometers from Mont St. Michel near tiny Huisnes-sur-Mer, this somber but thoughtfully presented cemetery/mortuary houses the remains of 12,000 German soldiers and offers insight into their lives with letters they sent home (English translations). From the lookout, there are sensational views over Mont St. Michel.

Sleeping on or near Mont St. Michel
(6.50F = about $1, country code: 33, zip code: 50116)
Sleeping on the island, inside the walls, is the best way to experience Mont St. Michel, though drivers should consider the *chambres d'hôtes* listed below. On the island, most hotels are tired and impersonal and some pad their profits by requiring guests to buy dinner from their restaurant. Several are closed from November until Easter. Because most visitors only day-trip here, you should be able to find a room at almost any time of the year. Still, reserve ahead if possible.

On Mont St. Michel: These hotels are listed in order of altitude (the first are lowest on the island and closest to parking).

Hôtel les Terrasses Poulard***, 50 meters after the TI, has the most polished and priciest rooms on the island (Db-500–950F, CC:VMA, tel. 02 33 60 14 09 fax 02 33 60 37 31). The impersonal **Hôtel du Guesclin**** offers good, clean rooms at competitive rates (Db-280–470F, Tb-550F, tel. 02 33 60 14 10, fax 02 33 60 45 81). **Hôtel Croix Blanche***** needs a face-lift but has a few loft triples and some good-view doubles (Sb-490F, Db-500–550F, Tb/Qb-700–900F, CC:VM, tel. 02 33 60 14 04, fax 02 33 48 59 82, e-mail: hotel.croix-blanche@gofornet.com). **Le Mouton Blanc** has decent, generally cozier rooms (Db-400F, Tb/Qb-470–600F, CC:VMA, tel. 02 33 60 14 08, fax 02 33 60 05 62). The comfortable rooms offered at the **Restaurant le St. Michel** across from Le Mouton Blanc are the best value on the island (Db-250–350F, no dinner requirements but a good restaurant, tel. & fax 02 33 60 14 37, Patricia, Philippe, and Freddo SE). The rooms at **Vielle Auberge**, owned by a moody woman, are among the next best for the price but don't let her talk you into more room than you need (Db-360F, Db with view-420F, Db with view and terrace-670F, CC:V, tel. 02 33 60 14 34, fax 02 33 70 87 04).

On the Mainland: Modern hotels gather at the mainland end of the causeway offering soulless but cheaper rooms with easy parking and a cheesy Coney Island feel. The friendly **Hôtel de la Digue***** is the best and most convenient. Most rooms are spacious and cushy (ask for a room with private terrace on the

riverside: *chambre avec petit balcon sur la Couesnan*). You can dine
with a partial view of Mont St. Michel at their well-respected
restaurant (small Db-350F, spacious Db-470F, Tb-510F,
Qb-520–580F, CC:VMA, tel. 02 33 60 14 02, fax 02 33 60 37 59,
e-mail: hotel-de-la-digue@wanadoo.fr). **Motel Vert**** may
have rooms when others don't (Db-250–400F, tel. 02 33 09 33,
fax 02 33 68 22 09).

Chambres d'Hôte

Simply great values, these places are in the village of Ardevon,
a few minutes' drive from the island toward Avranches. Charming Madame Brault's stone farmhouse, **La Jacotière**, is closest
(walkable to the causeway), with six immaculate, modern rooms
and great views of Mont St. Michel from her picnic-perfect
garden (Db-220F, extra bed-60F, tel. 02 33 60 22 94, fax
02 33 60 20 48, SE). About 1.5 kilometers down the road
you'll find the equally charming **Madame Audienne**'s rustic
stone farmhouse with five simple rooms, four of which have
views of Mont St. Michel (Sb-150F, Db-200F, Tb-250F, includes breakfast, relaxing garden, tel. 02 33 60 23 56, daughter
Estelle speaks a little English).

Train travelers may prefer sleeping in dismal Pontorson, a
15-minute drive from Mont St. Michel (zip code, 51170). **Hôtel
Vauban****, across from the train station, is quiet and comfortable
(D-200F, Db-250–320F, Tb-340F, 2 boulevard Clemenceau, tel.
02 33 60 03 83, fax 02 33 60 35 48). The easygoing **Hôtel de
l'Arrivee** has good, dirt-cheap rooms (D-99–120F, Ds-160–250F,
14 rue Docteur Tizon, tel & fax 02 33 60 01 57).

Eating on Mont St. Michel

Puffy omelets (*omelette Montoise*) are the island's specialty. Also
look for mussels and seafood platters, locally raised lamb (fed on
the saltwater grass), and Muscadet wine (dry, cheap, and white).
I let Patricia and Phillipe cook for me at the light-hearted and
reasonable **Le St. Michel** (good omelets and mussels, tel. 02 33
60 14 37), across from Hôtel le Mouton Blanc. **Hôtel de la
Digue** offers more refined cuisine on the mainland at the foot of
the causeway (expensive wine list, see "Sleeping," above). The
tourist *supermarché*, near Hôtel de la Digue, has what you need for
a romantic picnic (open 8:30–20:00), though you can buy sandwiches and drinks to go on the island. Picnic in the small park
below the abbey (to the left as you look up at the abbey).

ransportation Connections—
ont St. Michel

e nearest train station is in Pontorson, 15 minutes away from
t St. Michel by bus (4/day Mon–Fri, 2/day Sun). A taxi ride

from Pontorson to Mont St. Michel (or vice-versa) will cost about 80F, 110F after 19:00 and on weekends; look for others to share a cab (tel. 02 33 60 26 89). Or you can rent a bike at the Pontorson train station to get to Mont St. Michel.

By train from Pontorson to: Paris (4/day, 4 hrs via Rennes or Caen), **Bayeux** (2/day, 2 hrs), **Dinan** (2–3/day, 1 hr via Dol), **Amboise** (4/day, 7 hrs, via Caen and Tours' main station; or 8 hrs via St. Pierre des Corps, Paris Montparnasse, and Rennes).

By bus from Mont St. Michel to: St. Malo (2/day, 75 min direct), **Rennes** (2/day, morning and evening, 70 min, Couriers Bretons bus, tel. 02 99 19 70 70; at Rennes you can catch trains to Paris).

Sights near Normandy—Brittany

The Couesenan River marks the border between Normandy and Brittany. It hits the sea just west of Mont St. Michel, leaving the island barely in Normandy. The peninsula of Brittany is rugged, with an isolated interior, a well-discovered coast, and strong Celtic ties. This region of independent-minded locals is linguistically and culturally quite different from Normandy and, for that matter, the rest of France. The coastal route from Mont St. Michel through the oyster-famous town of Cancale (good lunch stop), on to the Pointe du Grouin (good hiking), and on to St. Malo gives a good introduction to this province.

DINAN

If you have time for only one stop in Brittany, do Dinan. This perfectly preserved ancient city is conveniently located and offers Brittany's best medieval center (1 hour from Mont St. Michel). Dinan feels real.

Orientation

Tourist Information: Pick up a map at the TI, two blocks off place Du Guesclin on rue de l'Horloge (June–Sept 9:00–19:00, Oct–May 9:00–12:00, 14:00–18:00, skip overpriced tourist magazine, tel. 02 96 39 75 40).

Arrival in Dinan: To get to the center from the train station (no lockers), either take a minibus (2/hrly) or a 30-minute walk (left out of station up rue Deroyer, right on rue Thiers, then cross huge place Duclos-Pinot and walk up rue Marchix). This city is confusing for drivers; follow *centre-ville* signs to the station. From there, take the streets (listed above as the walking route for people arriving by train) to reach the massive place du Guesclin (free parking except July–Sept).

Markets: Thursday is market day until 12:30 on place du Guesclin. Wednesday is flea-market day on place St. Saveur.

Sights—Dinan
Self-Guided Walking Tour—Start at the TI. Walk down rue de l'Horloge to the lookout tower, Tour de l'Horloge (16F, 160 steps, fantastic views, April–Sept 10:00–18:00, Oct–March 14.00–18:00), then continue down rue de l'Horloge and turn left into Dinan's historic commercial center, the place des Merciers. The half-timbered arcaded buildings are Dinan's oldest. They date from the time when property taxes were based on the square footage of your ground floor. To provide shelter from both the taxes and the rain, owners built out their first floors. Turn right where the square ends and then rappel partway down rue Jerzual (for *crêperies*, boutiques, and stiff knees). Crossing under the medieval gate (Porte Jerzual), turn right and climb to the only accessible section of the ramparts. Enjoy the view and then double back down the ramparts. From here, you have two choices, depending on your stamina:

If you're feeling fit, continue down to the old port (where the town was founded). Then, for a breath of Brittany, cross the old bridge, turn right, and follow the river trail 30 minutes to the pristine little village of Lehon, where you'll find a café/*crêperie*.

But if your legs disagree, skip the old port. Jog right after exiting the gate of the ramparts above the Porte Jerzual and take the first left uphill to the Jardins Anglais (English Gardens). Survey Dinan's port and the Rance valley. Then peek inside the very Breton Basilique St. Sauveur (bordering the park, English handout inside).

Château de Dinan—The Donjon (keep) and nearby walls are all that's left of Dinan's once massive castle. Skip it (no English explanations)—the view from the top is not worth the climb.

Rail Museum (Musée du Rail)—This museum, located at the train station, is fun for model railroaders with an impressive display of model trains and related paraphernalia (25F, June–Sept only, 14:00–18:00).

Sleeping and Eating in Dinan
(6.50F = about $1, country code: 33, zip code: 22100)
Hôtel La Tour de l'Horloge** is dead-center and ideal. This 18th-century manor house has cozy, comfortable rooms (Db-270–350F, Tb-420F, Qb-505F, TV, mini-bars, 5 rue de la Chaux, tel. 02 96 39 96 92, fax 02 96 85 06 99, SE). **Hôtel Du Théâtre** is Dinan's bargain with no stars but clean and cheery rooms over a small café opposite the TI (S-90F, D-120F, Db-210F, 2 rue Ste. Claire, tel. 02 96 39 06 91). **Hôtel de France****, facing the train station, provides good rooms at fair rates over a pleasant café (Sb-255F, Db-285F, Tb-365F, Qb-400F, 7 place du Novembre 11, tel. 02 96 39 33 56, fax 02 96 39 08 96).

Other worthwhile hotels: **Hôtel les Grandes Tours** (S-190F,

Sb-280F, D-210F, Db-300F, Tb-340F, Qb-460F, parking-30F, CC:VM, 6 rue du Château, tel. 02 96 85 16 20, fax 02 96 85 16 04) and **Hôtel de la Duchesse Anne*** (Ss-180F, Sb-220F, Db-260F, 18 place du Guesclin, tel. 02 96 39 09 43, fax 02 96 87 57 26). For dinner try any of the cozy *crêperies* in the old city. If you're not in the mood for crepes, try my favorite restaurant, **Le St. Louis**, just around the corner from Hôtel les Grandes Tours. Flames from the fireplace flicker on wood beams and white tablecloths (100F *menu*, great salad bar and desserts, closed Wed except in summer, 9 rue de Lehon, tel. 02 96 39 89 50). If you need more dining elegance, **La Fleur de Sel** has it (*menus* from 125F, just off place du Guesclin at 7 rue Ste. Claire, tel. 02 96 85 15 14).

St. Malo and Fougères
▲**St. Malo**—Come here to experience *the* Breton beach resort. Stroll high up on the impressive ramparts that circle the entire old city, eat seafood, walk as far out on the beaches as the tides allow, then return to Dinan for the night. An easy day trip, St. Malo is a 45-minute drive or a one-hour bus or train ride from Mont St. Michel or Dinan.
▲**Fougères**—This very Breton city is a delightful stop for drivers traveling between the Loire châteaus and Mont St. Michel. Fougères has one of Europe's largest medieval castles, a fine city center, and a panoramic park viewpoint (from St. Leonard church in the Jardin Public). Try one of the café/*crêperies* near the castle, such as the tempting Crêperie des Remparts, one block uphill from the castle. (Crepes, called *galettes* in Brittany, are the local fare.) Pick up a city map and castle description in English at the castle entrance. The interior is grass and walls.

THE LOIRE

Named for France's longest river, the Loire Valley is carpeted with fertile fields, crisscrossed by rivers, and studded with hundreds of châteaus in all shapes and sizes. The medieval castles are here because the Loire was strategically important during the Hundred Years' War. The Renaissance palaces replaced medieval castles when the Loire became fashionable among the hunt-crazy Parisian rich and royalty during that age.

The valley of a thousand châteaus is also the home to many good wines (look for "Dégustation" signs). Vouvray and Chinon, 20 minutes west of Tours, both have many proud and hospitable family wineries.

This region is famous for fanciful nighttime performances called sound-and-light shows (*son et lumière*). Many châteaus host these after-dark events, recreating life in their heyday with actors and music or by offering laser-light shows and mood music while you tour the château on your own (50–80F). The shows are usually of mild interest, in French only, and not worth a long detour. They don't begin until nightfall, which means a late night for summer travelers. Local TIs have schedules.

Planning Your Time

Use Amboise or Chenonceau as a home base for touring the famous châteaus northeast of Tours: Chenonceau, Chambord, Chaumont-sur-Loire, and Cheverny. Use Chinon as your home base to visit the châteaus west of Tours: Chinon, Azay le Rideau, Langeais, and Villandry.

A day and a half is sufficient to sample the best châteaus. Consider this plan: Visit Chenonceau early, when crowds are smaller; spend your midday at Chambord; and enjoy Cheverny late (the hunting dogs are fed at 17:00). Château-philes can then move to Chinon and tour its castle, Azay le Rideau, Villandry's gardens, and Langeais.

If arriving by car, try to see one château on your way in (e.g., Chambord if arriving from the north, Langeais from the west, or Azay le Rideau from the south). If arriving by train from Paris, consider the bus excursion to Chambord and Cheverny from Blois (see "Getting Around the Loire Valley," below) or go directly to Amboise and try to visit Le Clos Lucé that afternoon.

Don't go overboard on château-hopping. Two châteaus, possibly three (if you're a big person), make up the recommended daily dosage. Famous châteaus are least crowded early, at lunchtime, and late. Most open around 9:00 and close between 18:00 and 19:00. During the off-season many close from noon to 14:00 and at 17:00.

The lazy plan for those with low energy, no car, and no money for a day minivan tour is to catch the once-per-day Amboise-Chenonceau bus (from near the Amboise TI at 10:54, giving you 90 min at the château and departing the château at 12:40). Spend the afternoon enjoying Amboise, its château, and Leonardo's place.

Getting around the Loire Valley

By Train: With easy access from Amboise, Tours is the key to château transport for hard-core train travelers. The châteaus of Chenonceau, Langeais, Chinon, and Azay le Rideau have train and/or bus service from Tours' main station (although Chenonceau is easiest by bus or bike from Amboise). In Tours, there are two important train stations and a bus station with service to several châteaus; the main train station is called Tours SNCF, and the TGV station is St. Pierre des Corps. Check the schedules carefully, as service is sparse on some lines.

By Bus: An ideal bus plan for touring Chambord and Cheverny (daily service May–Sept only) is to take the train to Blois (20 min from Amboise), then the excursion bus from Blois' station to these châteaus (65F includes bus fare and reduced château entries; departs Blois station at 9:10, returns at 13:10; or departs Blois at 13:20, returns at 18:00). Call the Blois TI for details (April–Oct Mon–Sat 9:00–19:00, Sun 10:00–19:00, Nov–March Mon–Sat only 9:00–12:00 and 14:00–18:00, tel. 02 54 90 41 41).

By Minibus Tour: Pascal Accolay runs Acco-Dispo, a small and personal minibus company with excellent all-day château tours from Amboise (or other area villages, including Tours; ideal for those day-tripping from Paris whom he'll meet at the station). Tour costs vary with itinerary; figure 140F to 180F for a half day and 240F to 280F for all day. English is the primary language. While you'll get a fun and enthusiastic running commentary on the road covering each château's background as well as the

The Loire Valley

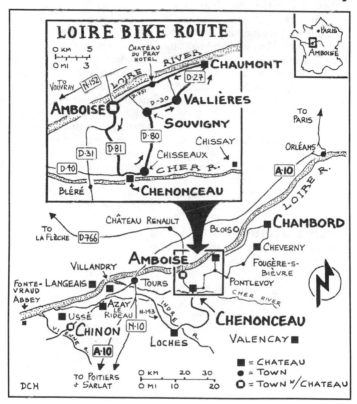

region's contemporary scene, you're on your own at each château (you pay the admission fee). All-day tours depart about 8:30, afternoon tours depart about 12:50. Both return to Amboise around 18:30. Several itinerary options are available; most include Chenonceau. Groups range from two to eight château-hoppers (18 rue des Vallées in Amboise, tours go daily, free hotel pickups, reserve by tel. 06 82 00 64 51, fax 02 47 23 15 73, www.accodispo-tours.com).

By Taxi: A taxi from Amboise to Chenonceau costs about 100F. Your hotel can call one for you. The meter doesn't start until you do.

By Rental Car: In Amboise, consider **Avis** (600F/day unlimted mileage and all insurance, across from Amboise TI, tel. 02 47 57 1 54, fax 02 47 23 22 47) or the cheaper **Garage Jourdain** (280F/ y, 100 kilometers free, 1.5F per kilometer over 100, 1.5 kilometers wnriver from TI at 105 route de Tours, tel. 02 47 57 17 92, fax 02 47 57 77 50). Both close Monday through Friday from noon to 14:00 and at 18:00, at 17:00 on Saturday, and all day Sunday.

By Bike: Cycling options are endless in this region where the elevation gain is generally manageable (still, many find even the shortest rides exhausting and too time-consuming). Amboise, Blois, and Chinon make the best bike bases. From Amboise allow an hour to Chenonceau (warning: the first 3 kilometers are uphill). Only the most fit and serious bikers can ride to Chaumont in 90 minutes and connect Amboise, Chenonceau, and Chaumont with an all-day 60-kilometer pedal (see "Loire Valley" map in this chapter for details). From Blois by bike to Chambord is a manageable 75-minute, one-way ride, but adding Cheverny makes a grueling, full-day, 50-kilometer round-trip. Most can do the pleasant bike ride from Chinon to Ussé (big hill when leaving Chinon), and some will find the energy to continue to Langeais. Only those in top shape will enjoy continuing on to Villandry (see "Chinon," below). Call the Blois TI for bike-rental information (tel. 02 54 90 41 41).

Cuisine Scene—Loire Valley

Here in "the garden of France," anything from the earth is bound to be good. Loire Valley rivers produce fresh trout (*truite*), salmon (*saumon*), and smelt (*éperlau*), which is often served fried (*friture*). *Rillettes*, a stringy pile of cooked, then whipped pork, makes for a cheap, mouthwatering sandwich spread (use lots of mustard and add a baby pickle, called a *cornichon*). The area's fine goat cheeses include Crottin de Chavignol (*crottin* means horse dung, which is what this cheese, when aged, resembles), Saint-Maure Fermier (soft and creamy), and Selles-sur-Cher (mild). For dessert try a mouthwatering *tarte Tatin* (upside-down caramel-apple tart). The best and most expensive white wines are the Sancerres and Pouilly-Fumés. Less expensive but still tasty are Tourraine Sauvignons and the sweeter Vouvrays. The better reds come from Chinon and Bourgeuil.

AMBOISE

Straddling the widest part of the Loire, Amboise slumbers in the shadow of its château. Leonardo da Vinci retired here . . . just one more fine idea. With or without a car, Amboise is an ideal small-town home base for exploring the best of château country. A castle has overlooked the Loire from Amboise since Roman times. As the royal residence of François I, the town wielded far more importance than you'd imagine from a lazy walk down the pleasant pedestrian-only commercial zone at the base of the palace.

Amboise (pop. 11,000) covers both sides of the Loire and an island in the middle. The station is on the north side of the river, but everything else of interest is on the south (château) side, including the information-packed TI on the riverbank.

Tourist Information: The TI is on quai du Général de

Amboise

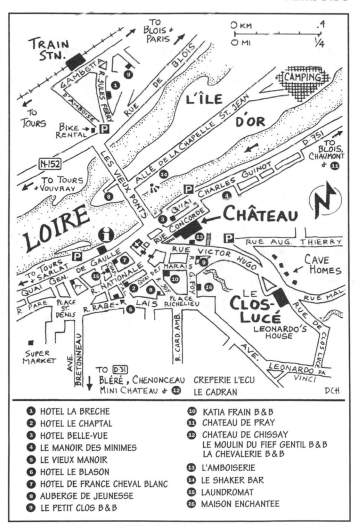

1 HOTEL LA BRECHE
2 HOTEL LE CHAPTAL
3 HOTEL BELLE-VUE
4 LE MANOIR DES MINIMES
5 LE VIEUX MANOIR
6 HOTEL LE BLASON
7 HOTEL DE FRANCE CHEVAL BLANC
8 AUBERGE DE JEUNESSE
9 LE PETIT CLOS B&B

10 KATIA FRAIN B&B
11 CHATEAU DE PRAY
12 CHATEAU DE CHISSAY
   LE MOULIN DU FIEF GENTIL B&B
   LA CHEVALERIE B&B
13 L'AMBOISERIE
14 LE SHAKER BAR
15 LAUNDROMAT
16 MAISON ENCHANTEE

Gaulle in the round building. Their Amboise city map shows restaurants, hotels, and château information, including the time and place of English-language sound and-light shows. Look also for the photo album of regional *chambres d'hôte* (Mon–Sat 9.00–19.00, Sun 10:00–12:00, 15:00–18:00, tel. 02 47 57 09 28, www.amboise-valloire.com).

Arrival in Amboise

By Train: Amboise's train station, with a post office and taxi stand, is birds-chirping peaceful (tel. 02 47 23 18 23). Turn left out of the station, make a quick right, and walk down rue de Nazelles five minutes to the bridge that leads you over the Loire and into town. Within three blocks of the station are a recommended hotel, B&B, and bike-rental shop.

By Car: Drivers set their sights on the flag-festooned château capping the hill. Most recommended accommodations and restaurants cluster just downriver of the château. Street parking near your hotel should be easy.

Helpful Hints

The Michelin Green Guide to the Loire provides a good historical and architectural background on the region and each château (sold for about 70F—40 percent off the U.S. price—at all tourist shops).

Bike Rental: Rent a bike for about 70F per half day and 90F per full day (leave your passport or a photocopy of it). Two reliable places are **Locacycle** (daily 9:00–19:00, near TI at 2 rue Jean-Jacques Rousseau, tel. 02 47 57 00 28, English spoken) and **Cycles Richard**, with better bikes (Mon–Sat, closed 12:00–14:00, on train-station side of river, just past bridge at 2 rue de Nazelles, tel. 02 47 57 01 79, no English spoken).

Laundromat: The handy coin-op Lav'centre is a block from the rue Chaptal toward the château on 9 allée du Sergent Turpin (daily 7:00–21:00, Oct–May until 20:00, 22F to wash, bring four 10F coins to wash and dry a big load, detergent-2F, change machine, figure 90 min). The door locks at closing time; leave beforehand or you'll trigger the alarm system.

Sights—Amboise

▲**Château d'Amboise**—This one-time royal residence was used in the Middle Ages to greet royal pilgrims en route from Paris to Spain's Santiago de Compostela. Leonardo da Vinci is said to have designed the château's vaulted spiral staircases. Pick up the fine free English-tour flier as you enter. The lacy, petite chapel (first stop) is flamboyant Gothic, with two fireplaces "to comfort the king" and a plaque "evoking the final resting place" of Leonardo. Where he's actually buried no one seems to know. Continue into and through the well-furnished château—which, while much larger in the 15th century, feels plenty big. Your last stop is the horsemen's tower, a brick ramp—climbing 40 meters in five spirals—designed to accommodate a mounted soldier in a hurry (40F, March–Oct daily 9:00–18:00, until 19:30 in summer, off-season closes 12:00–14:00 and at 17:00, tel. 02 47 57 00 98).

▲▲**Le Clos Lucé**—This "House of Light" is the plush palace

where Leonardo spent his last three years. France's Renaissance
king François I set Leonardo up just so he could enjoy his intel-
lectual company. There's a touching sketch in Leonardo's bedroom of François comforting his genius pal on his deathbed.
The house thoughtfully re-creates (with adequate English
descriptions) the everyday atmosphere Leonardo enjoyed as he
pursued his passions to the very end. Of all the palaces I've seen
on the Loire, I'd live here. The ground floor is filled with
sketches recording the storm patterns of Leonardo's brain and
models of his remarkable inventions (built by IBM according
to his notes). It's hard to imagine that this Roman candle of
creativity died nearly 500 years ago. There are plans to translate
the French-only video (39F, April–Sept daily 10:00–18:00, until
19:00 in summer, Oct–March 10:00–17:00, located a pleasant
10-min walk from downtown Amboise—you'll pass interesting
troglodyte homes on your left).
Caveau des Vignerons—Under Amboise's château across from
l'Épicerie restaurant, this small cave offers free tastings of regional
wines, cheeses, and foie gras (April–Sept 10:00–19:00).
La Maison Enchantée—Push the buttons and watch dolls dance
in 25 different settings (adult-35F, child-25F, May–Sept Tue–Sun
10:00–18:00, summers until 19:00, Oct and April 10:00–12:00,
14:00–17:00, Nov–March 14:00–17:00, walk down rue de la Tour
from château to 7 rue du General Foy, tel. 02 47 23 24 50).
Mini Château—This five-acre park on the edge of Amboise
shows all the Loire châteaus in 1:25-scale models, forested with
600 bonsai trees and laced together by a model TGV train (adults-
65F, kids ages 4–16-45F, April–Sept daily 10:00–18:00, 9:00–19:00
in summer, off-season closes at 17:00, tel. 02 47 23 44 44).
Château d'Amboise Sound-and-Light—This is one of the
region's best shows, but unfortunately it's entirely in French.
Volunteer locals revive the French Renaissance with costumes,
jugglers, and impressive light displays (adults-75F, kids ages
6–14-35F, Wed and Sat evenings in summer, bring your sweater,
details at the TI).

Sleeping in Amboise
(6.50F = about $1, country code: 33, zip code: 37400)
Sleep Code: **S** = Single, **D** = Double/Twin, **T** = Triple, **Q** = Quad,
b = bathroom, **t** = toilet only, **s** = shower only, **CC** = Credit
Card (Visa, MasterCard, Amex), **SE** = Speaks English, **NSE** = No
English, * = French hotel rating system (0–4 stars).
      Amboise is busy in the summer, but there are lots of hotels
and *chambres d'hôte* (CH) in and around the city. Many hotels
require half pension. The TI has photo albums of local hotels and
CHs and will reserve either. Except for the first hotel and the first
CH, all listings are right in the old town center.

Hotels

Hôtel La Brèche** is a refuge run by a "we try harder" family and has spotless, comfortable rooms and a peaceful garden café (with Ping-Pong and two new ducks). It's 10 minutes from the city center and 100 meters from the train station. Many rooms overlook the garden; those on the street are generally larger and the room off the garden is family-perfect. Half-pension is required in the summer, and it gets you a prize-winning dinner for an extra 80F per person—I spring 20F more for the *menu du terroir* (S/D-165F, Sb/Db-295F, Tb-325F, Qb-355F, a few good family rooms, CC:VM, 26 rue Jules Ferry, tel. 02 47 57 00 79, fax 02 47 57 65 49, Pierre SE, mother Annick NSE).

Hôtel Le Chaptal** is basic, cheap, and central. This place is *très* frumpy, with birds in the lobby and decent rooms—quieter off the street—but marginal beds (Db-210–225F, Tb-255F, Qb-295F, CC:VM, 13 rue de Chaptal, tel. 02 47 57 14 46, fax 02 47 57 67 83, NSE). In summer they request you dine in their cheery, inexpensive dining room.

Hôtel Belle-Vue*** overlooks the river where the bridge hits the town. This hotel has spacious public rooms and effective double-paned windows. Half of its pleasant rooms overlook the château, and four rooms come with huge, shared terraces (Sb-270F, Db-310–360F, Tb-360–420F, Qb-460F, CC:VM, elevator, 12 quai Charles-Guinot, tel. 02 47 57 02 26, fax 02 47 30 51 23).

Le Manoir des Minimes****, a renovated 17th-century mansion, feels overdone with precious furniture but works for those seeking luxury in Amboise. Rooms are modern and large (Db-600–700F, deluxe Db-830F, 3–4 person suites-1,200–1,400F, extra bed-150F, 3 blocks upriver from the bridge at 34 quai Charles Guinot, tel. 02 47 30 40 40, fax 02 47 30 40 77, e-mail: manoir-les-minimes@wanadoo.fr).

Le Vieux Manoir is a better, high-end splurge. American ex-pat Gloria Bellnap has completely restored this secluded but central manor home with attention to detail that Martha Stewart would appreciate. The stunning breakfast room opens to immaculate gardens, the public spaces are American-cozy, and the six bedrooms would make an antique collector drool (rooms $110–150, no CC, pay in francs or U.S. dollars, check or cash, 13 rue Rabelais, tel. & fax 02 47 30 41 27, www.le-vieux-manoir.com).

Hôtel Le Blason**, with a friendly staff, is a half-timbered old building sitting on a square five blocks off the river with small, bright, and modern rooms on a noisy street (Sb-270F, Db-300F, Tb-360F, CC:VMA, cable TV, quieter rooms in back, easy parking, 11 place Richelieu, tel. 02 47 23 22 41, fax 02 47 57 56 18, e-mail: leblason@wanadoo.fr, Danielle SE). The well-respected restaurant deserves every one of its plaques (*menus* for 95F, 165F, and 250F).

Hôtel de France Cheval Blanc[A] rents simple, spotless, and comfortable rooms across from the TI at fair rates (D-160F, Db-195-265F, T-200F, Tb-265-315F, CC:VM, no elevator, TV, 6 quai du General de Gaulle, tel. 02 47 57 02 44, fax 02 47 57 69 54). *Rue* (street) rooms have double-paned windows but some traffic noise seeps in. *Cour* (courtyard) rooms are quieter.

Auberge de Jeunesse is a friendly hostel and a great value (dorm bed-52F, 2- to 6-bed rooms, sheets-17F, first-night fee-10F, reception open 15:00-20:00, ideally located on western tip of island, Centre Charles Péguy, tel. 02 47 57 06 36, fax 02 47 23 15 80).

Chambres d'Hôte in Amboise

The Amboise TI has a long list of private rooms. In summer, if possible, call a day in advance to reserve a room.

Le Petit Clos has three cheery, cottage-type ground-floor rooms on a quiet, picnic-perfect private garden. Charming Madame Roullet speaks a leetle English (Db-350F, family room for up to 5 people-700F, includes big, farm-fresh breakfast with homemade everything, easy parking, 3 blocks from station, turn left out of station and follow tracks to 7 rue Balzac, tel. 02 47 57 43 52).

Katia Frain may be the most engaging person in Amboise. Her comfortable *chambres* in a historic building on a busy road are a good value, but stuffy when it's warm out. Katia and her husband teach music and welcome you to relax in their artsy garden (Sb-190F, Db-280F, big Tb-360F, extra person-80F, includes breakfast, 14 quai des Marais, tel. 02 47 30 46 51, SE).

Sleeping near Amboise

Also see "Sleeping in Chenonceau," below.

Château Hôtels: You'll feel a hint of the original medieval fortified castle behind the Renaissance elegance of the 750-year-old **Château de Pray****. The dining room is splendid (250–305F *menus*), the pool is below. The hotel is only a few minutes upriver from Amboise, toward Chaumont on the D-751 (Db-500–900F, Tb-700–1,300F, Qb-850–1,500F, CC:VMA, 37400 Amboise, tel. 02 47 57 23 67, fax 02 47 57 32 50, e-mail: chateau.depray @wanadoo.fr).

Château de Chissay**, just beyond the village of Chenonceaux, offers a noble experience. Perched above a valley in a private park, this story book 15th-century château was home to two French kings. Now it's home to a large swimming pool, regal rooms, a peaceful courtyard, and professional service (Sb-400F, Db-500–980F, suites 1,220–1,550F, rooms with valley views are more costly but worth it, CC:VM, no elevator, toward Montrichard, 41400 Chissay, tel. 02 54 32 32 01, fax 02 54 32 43 80, e-mail: chateau-chissay@wanado.fr).

Chambres d'Hôte: For a "Peter Mayle does the Loire"

experience 15 minutes from Amboise and Chenonceau, sleep at Roger and Ann's beautifully renovated 16th-century mill house, **Le Moulin du Fief Gentil**, where you get four acres and a back-yard pond (fishing possible), smartly decorated rooms, and a splen-did common living room. If Ann is cooking, splurge for dinner (Db-450–500F, dinner-180F/person, 37150 Bléré, tel. 02 47 30 32 51, fax 02 47 57 95 72, www.fiefgentil.fr.fm, e-mail: fiefgentil @wanadoo.fr). It's located on the edge of the pleasant town of Bléré (from Bléré follow signs toward Luzille).

Closer to Amboise, the bargain *chambres* at **La Chevalerie** are family-friendly in every way—total seclusion in a farm setting, a swing set, a tiny fishing pond, common kitchens, and connect-ing rooms wrapped in a warm reception (Db-240F, Tb-320F, Qb-400F, 37150 La Croix en Touraine, from Amboise take D-31 toward Bléré and look for the sign on your left after about 4 kilometers, tel. 02 47 57 83 64).

Eating in Amboise

Reasonable local eateries abound in Amboise. **Crêperie L'Ecu** is a good spot to sample French crêpes (closed Mon, indoor/outdoor seating, 7 rue Corneille, just off pedestrian street). **Le Cadran** is a low-cost, low-stress place for pizza and grilled foods (14 rue Nationale, tel. 02 47 30 53 60). **Hôtel Le Blason** offers fine cui-sine in a pleasant setting at affordable prices (see "Hotels," above). In any weather **La Brèche's** cozy restaurant with outdoor terrace is a good value (see "Hotels," above). At the base of the château, **L'Amboiserie** offers fine value and a friendly staff (7 rue Victor Hugo, tel. 02 47 39 50 40). For an after-dinner walk, cross the bridge to the island for a floodlit view of the château. The bar **Le Shaker** offers scenic cocktails and outdoor tables with late-night château views (on island to the right as you cross from château). Or consider making the short drive to Chenonceau for dinner with Laurent and Sophie at **Hôtel La Roseraie** (see "Sleeping and Eating in Chenonceau," below).

Transportation Connections—Amboise

Twelve 15-minute trains per day link Amboise to the regional train hub of St. Pierre des Corps (suburban Tours). From there you'll find reasonable connections to distant points (including the TGV to Paris Montparnasse, about hrly, 1 hr). The fastest way to many points, even in the south, may be back through Paris.

By train to: Sarlat (4/day, 6 hrs, via St. Pierre des Corps then TGV to Libourne or Bordeaux St. Jean, then scenic train through Bordeaux vineyards to Sarlat), **Limoges** (near Oradour-sur-Glane, 4/day, 4 hrs, then tricky connection by bus to Oradour-sur-Glane), **Mont St. Michel** (4/day, 7 hrs, via Tours SNCF, Caen, and Pontorson; or 8 hrs via Tours' St. Pierre des Corps, Paris

Montparnasse, and Rennes), **Bayeux** (6/day, 4 hrs via Tours SNCF
and Caen, or via Paris Montparnasse and Caen), **Paris** (12/day,
90 min, via St. Pierre de Corps/TGV to Paris' Gare Montparnasse; or by local train, 8/day, 2 hrs, direct from Amboise to Paris'
Gare d'Austerlitz).

Châteaus Northeast of Tours
Either Amboise (above) or Chenonceau (below) make a good
home base for exploring these châteaus.
▲▲▲**Chenonceau** (shuh-non-so)—The toast of the Loire, this
15th-century Renaissance palace arches gracefully over the Cher
River. One look and you know it was designed by women: The
original builder's wife designed the part of the château that parallels
the river; Diane de Poitiers, mistress of Henry II, added an arched
bridge across the river. She enjoyed her lovely retreat until Henry
died (pierced in a jousting tournament on rue St. Antoine in Paris'
Marais) and his vengeful wife, Catherine de Médici, unceremoni-
ously kicked her out (and into the château of Chaumont). Catherine
added the three-story structure on Diane's bridge. She died before
completing her vision of a matching château on the far side of the
river but not before turning Chenonceau into the local aristocracy's
place to see and be seen. This castle marked the border between
free and Nazi France in World War II. Dramatic prisoner swaps
took place here. Chenonceau is self-tourable (pick up the English
translation), with piped-in classical music and glorious gardens (50F,
skip the 10F Musée de Cires—wax museum, mid-March–mid-Sept
daily 9:00–19:00, early closing off-season, tel. 02 47 23 90 07).
    There are three trains per day from Tours and one bus per day
from Amboise (departs Amboise at 10:54, departs Chenonceau at
12:40, allowing 90-min visit of château). To beat the crowds, arrive
at 8:45 or after 17:30 and plan on a 15-minute walk from the parking lot to the château. The TI is on the road from Amboise as you
enter the village.
    Sleeping and Eating in Chenonceau: If you prefer a quiet
village, set up in sleepy little Chenonceau (zip code: 37150).
Hostel du Roy** is a steal, with more comfortable rooms in the
annex, and good rooms in the main building, a quiet garden
courtyard, and a simple restaurant (S-130F, Sb-220F, D-130F,
Db-225–260F, Tb/Qb-260–310F, CC:VMA, 9 rue Dr. Bretonneau, 5-min walk to château, tel. 02 47 23 90 17, fax 02 47 23 89
81). **Hôtel La Roseraie***** is simply ideal. While English-speaking Laurent and Sophie spoil you, their delightfully decorated,
country-elegant rooms will enchant you (Db-290–550F, a few
grand family rooms-480–750F, CC:VMA, free parking, heated
pool, rental bikes, and a wood-beamed dining room where I dress
up and splurge for a great dinner—100F/135F/180F *menus*,
located dead center on the main drag at 7 rue Dr. Bretonneau,

hard-to-read sign, tel. 02 47 23 90 09, fax 02 47 23 91 59,
www.charminghotel.com). **Relais Chenonceau*****, across
from Hôtel La Roseraie, is a fair value with smaller but cozy,
wood-finished rooms (Db-290–400F, Tb-400–460F, Qb-480F,
tel. 02 47 23 98 11, fax 02 47 23 84 07, www.chenonceaux.com).
Au Gateau de Breton is a friendly, reasonable, and good restaurant for lunch or dinner (16 rue Dr. Bretonneau, tel. 02 47 23
90 14, closed Tue–Wed).

▲▲▲**Chambord** (sham-bor)—More like a city than a château,
this place is enormous. Surrounded by Europe's largest enclosed
forest park, packed with wild deer and boar, it was first built as a
rustic hunting lodge for bored Blois counts. François I, using
1,800 workmen over 15 years, made a few modest additions and
created this "weekend retreat" (you'll find his signature salaman-
der everywhere). Highlights are the huge double-spiral staircase
designed by Leonardo da Vinci, second-floor vaulted ceilings,
enormous towers on all corners, a pincushion roof of spires and
chimneys, and a 100-foot lantern supported by flying buttresses.
To see what happens when you put 365 fireplaces in your house,
wander through the forest of spires on the rooftop (fine views).
Only 80 of its 440 rooms are open to the public—and that's
plenty. Focus on the well-furnished first floor (ground level and
second floors have bare rooms featuring "the hunt"). The brochure is useless. For more information, rent the 25F audioguide
(second earphone-10F) or call ahead for the occasional free tours
given in English. Because most rooms are unfurnished, less information is essential, and for some, seeing it from the outside is
enough (40F, April–Sept daily 9:30–18:15, until 19:15 in summer,
off season closes at 17:15, tel. 02 54 50 40 00). During summer
nights, evening visits to the château are accompanied by music
and mood lighting (80F, 21:30–24:00). Also look for horse-riding
demonstrations (40F, daily June–Sept, mid-morning).

Chambord's TI, next to the souvenir shops, knows where
to rent bikes (30F/hr, 55F/half day, 70F/day) and has a list of
chambres d'hôte. One daily 40-minute bus connects Chambord
with Blois' train station on weekdays, but the Blois excursion bus
is better (65F, departs Blois at 9:10 and 13:20; for more info, see
"Getting around the Loire Valley," above).

Sleeping in Chambord: To wake up with Chambord out
your window, **Hôtel du Grand St-Michel**** comes with Old
World hunting-lodge charm, an elegant dining room (*menus* for
100F, 135F), and a chance to roam the château grounds after the
peasants are run out (Db-300, big Db with view of château-450F,
worth the extra cost, extra person-70F, CC:VM, 41250 Chambord, tel. 02 54 20 31 31, fax 02 54 20 36 40).

▲▲**Chaumont-sur-Loire** (show-mon-sur-lwahr) **and the Festival
of Gardens**—Chaumont's first priority was defense; a castle has

been here since the 900s (you'll appreciate its strategic location on the long climb up). Today's château offers an asymmetrical mix of Gothic and Renaissance architecture, well-furnished rooms, and good views (English handout available). Built mostly in the 15th and 16th centuries, this place was force swapped by Catherine de Médici for Diane de Poitier's Chenonceau, so you'll see tidbits about both women inside. Louis XVI, Marie-Antoinette, Voltaire, and Benjamin Franklin each spent time here. Notice the chest in room 7—it weighs over 1,000 pounds—and the exquisite floor tiles in room 9. Back outside, the fancy royal horse houses (*écuries*) are worthwhile for first-timers. From mid-June to mid-October, the Festival des Jardins—Festival of Gardens—is a gardener's dream (you'll find it across the small footbridge). The superb displays vary each year according to theme (château entry-32F, 45F with stables, add 20F for Festival of Gardens, château open March–Sept daily 9:30–18:00, off-season 10:00–16:30, tel. 02 54 20 98 03).

▲▲▲**Cheverny** (sheh-vayr-nee)—The most lavish furnishings of all the Loire châteaus decorate this very stately hunting palace. Those who complain that the Loire châteaus have stark and barren interiors missed Cheverny. This château was built in 1634, and it's been in the same family for nearly seven centuries. Family pride shows in its flawless preservation and intimate feel. The viscount's family still lives on the third floor—you'll see some family photos. Cheverny was spared by the French Revolution; the owners were popular then, as today, even among the village farmers. Barking dogs remind visitors that the viscount still loves to hunt. The kennel (200 meters in front of the château) is especially interesting at dinnertime when the 70 hounds are fed (17:00 April–Nov, 15:00 Dec–March). The dogs—half English foxhound and half French bloodhound or Poitevin—are fed by trainers who know each dog by name (they all look the same to me). But if a dog misbehaves, it gets an immediate cold bath. The trophy room next door bristles with 2,000 stag antlers (35F, pick up the English self-guided tour brochure at the château, not where you buy your ticket; June–mid-Sept daily 9:15–18:30, mid-Sept–May daily 9:30–12:00, 14:15–17:00, tel. 02 54 79 96 29).

Cheverny village, in front of the château, has a small grocery and a few cafés. The town is easy to reach from Blois by excursion bus (see "Getting around the Loire Valley," above).

Fougeres sur Bievre (foo-zher soor bee-eh-vruh)—This medieval castle is worth a look even if you don't go inside. Located a few minutes from Cheverny on the way to Chenonceau and Amboise, it's right in the village (constructed for defense, not hunting) and was built over the small river (unlimited water supply during sieges). It has been completely renovated, and while there are no furnishings, you'll see models of castle-construction techniques, contemplate the impressive roof structure, gaze through loop holes, stand over drop holes in the main tower (hot oil anyone?), and ponder two medieval latrines demonstrating how little toilet technology has changed in 800 years. Posters throughout (French only) describe modern renovation techniques (25F, April–Sept daily 9:30–12:00, 14:00–18:00, Oct–March closes at 16:30, helpful English handout).

Loches and Valancay (lohsh, vah-lahn-say)—The overlooked town of Loches, located about 30 minutes south of Amboise, would be my choice for the best Loire base if it were more central. This pretty town sits on the serene Indre River and offers an appealing mix of medieval monuments, stroll-worthy streets, and fewer tourists. The castle dominates the skyline and is worth a short visit (good views, sound-and-light shows in summer). **Hôtel George Sand***** is on the river with a good restaurant and comfortable rooms (Db-280–600F, 39 rue Quintefol, tel. 02 47 59 39 74, fax 02 47 91 55 75). The nearby Renaissance château of **Valancay** is a massive, lavishly furnished structure with echoes of Talleyrand (Napoleon's prime minister), lovely gardens, and many summer events such as fencing demonstrations (35F, daily 9:30–18:00, until 19:30 in summer, audioguide available, tel. 02 54 00 10 66).

CHINON

This pleasing town straddles the Vienne River and hides its ancient cobbles under a historic castle. Chinon (shee-non) is best known today for its popular red wines (tasting opportunities abound), but for us it makes the best home base for seeing the sights west of Tours: Azay le Rideau, Villandry, Langeais, Ussè, and the Abbey of Fontevraud.

Tourist Information: The TI has bike rentals, *chambres d'hôte* listings, wine-tasting details, and a handy, English-language, self-guided tour of the town (May–Sept daily 9:00–19:00, Oct–April Mon–Sat 10:00–12:00, 14:00–18:00, in village center on place Hofhein, tel. 02 47 93 17 85).

Bike Rental: Rent bikes at Agnes Sorel Hotel, (helpful owners suggest routes, 4 quai Pasteur, tel. 02 47 93 04 37).

Sights—Chinon

▲▲**Château de Chinon**—Don't underestimate this crumbled castle, especially if you're looking for a stark medieval comparison to those of the lavish hunting-lodge variety. This was Henry II and Eleanor of Aquitaine's favorite residence in France. Here, Joan of Arc first tried to encourage Charles VII to take the throne in 1429. It's a steep walk up from the town of Chinon, but the views are sensational. What remains of this 12th-century castle is well presented in English by tour-on-your-own pamphlets or live tours (6/day in summer, 4/day in winter, free with ticket, call for hours). Start in the "exposition room" with a short, automated history of the château (every other show presented in English) and end at the impressive *donjon* (keep) housing a three-floor museum about Joan of Arc. Press English buttons at the end of each room for a good history. Enjoy the stunning views from the top (29F, mid-March–Oct daily 9:00–18:00, until 19:00 in summer, Nov–mid-March 9:00–12:00, 14:00–17:00, tel. 02 47 93 13 45).

Sleeping and Eating in Chinon
(6.50F = about $1, country code: 33, zip code: 37500)
Hotels are a good value in Chinon. If you sleep here, walk out to the river after dark for a floodlit view of the castle walls.

Hôtel Diderot**, a fine 18th-century manor house on the eastern edge of town, offers comfortable and appealing rooms surrounding a peaceful courtyard. Ground-floor rooms on the courtyard are a bit dark but have private patios. There are a few good family rooms (Sb-260–330F, Db-310–410F, extra bed-80F, CC:VMA, 4 rue Buffon, tel. 02 47 93 18 87, fax 02 47 93 37 10, friendly Rachel speaks enough English).

Hôtel Agnes Sorel is intimate and cozy with helpful owners and six traditionally furnished rooms (Db-200–450F, rental bikes, 4 Quai Pasteur, across river on western end of town, tel. 02 47 03 37, fax 02 47 93 06 37).

Hôtel le Jeanne d'Arc, with clean linoleum rooms above a café, is this town's budget value with no stars, no fluff, lots of stairs, and an owner with an attitude. (Sb-180F, Db-200–220F, 11 rue Voltaire, tel. 02 47 93 02 85, fax 02 47 98 43 72).

Eating: The **Crêperie du Grand Carroi** makes great crepes at reasonable prices (just off pedestrian rue Voltaire at 30 rue du Grand Carroi, closed Tue). **Les Années 30** is my favorite restaurant in town (115F *menus*, 78 rue Voltaire, tel. 02 47 93 37 18). Still, if you have a car, consider driving 15 minutes to Villandry and dining at the farmhouse, **Étape Gourmande**, which serves regional specialties at fair prices (12:00–15:00, 19:30–21:30, Domaine de la Giraudiere, 1 kilometer from château toward Druye, call to reserve, tel. 02 47 50 08 60).

Châteaus West of Tours
Chinon makes the best home base for visiting these châteaus.
▲**Azay le Rideau** (ah-zay luh ree-doh)—Most famous for its romantic reflecting-pond setting, Azay le Rideau features glorious gardens and a skippable interior (35F, imaginative 60F sound-and-light show, daily April–Oct 9:30–18:00, until 19:00 in summer, Nov–March closes 12:30–14:00 and at 17:30, tel. 02 47 45 42 04). The pleasant town center is worth a stroll. **Hôtel Biencourt**** is 'deal and near the château (Ds-220F, Db-280–340F, extra bed-0F, CC:VM, at 7 rue de Balzac, 37190 Azay le Rideau, tel. 02 ⁷ 45 20 75, fax 02 47 45 91 73).

▲▲**Langeais** (lahn-zhay)—This epitome of a medieval castle, complete with a moat, a drawbridge, lavish defenses, and turrets, is elegantly furnished and has English descriptions in each room. Langeais, which provides a good feudal contrast to the other, more playful châteaus, is the area's fourth-most-interesting castle after Chenonceau, Chambord, and Cheverny (40F, April–Oct daily 9:00–18:30, until 21:00 in summer, Nov–March closes 12:00–14:00 and at 17:00, tel. 02 47 96 72 60, frequent train service from Tours).

▲**Villandry** (vee-lahn-dree)—This otherwise mediocre castle has elaborate geometric gardens and a fine *Four Seasons of Villandry* slide show. Skip its interior. Come here for the Loire's most complete gardens and don't miss the overlook behind the château, above the gardens (45F, 33F for gardens, Easter–Sept daily 9:00–18:00, Oct–Easter closes at 17:00, tel. 02 47 50 02 09).

Ussè (oos-seh)—This château, famous as the "*Sleeping Beauty* castle," is worth a quick photo stop for its fairy-tale turrets and gardens, but don't bother touring it. The best view, with reflections and a golden-slipper picnic spot, is from just across the bridge.

▲**Abbaye de Fontevraud** (fohn-tuh-vroh)—Located 15 minutes west of Chinon, this well-presented 12th-century abbey housed nuns and monks and was run by powerful women. The tombs of Henry II, Eleanor of Aquitaine, and Richard the Lionhearted are in the austerely beautiful church. Don't miss the one-of-a-kind medieval kitchen (32F, 5 tours/day in English, otherwise take the informative handout and tour it alone, daily June–Sept 9:30–19:00, Oct–May 9:30–12:00, 14:00–17:00, tel. 02 41 51 71 41).

DORDOGNE

The Dordogne River Valley is a dreamy blend of natural and man-made beauty. Hundreds of fortified castles line the sublime Dordogne, a testament to its strategic importance in the Middle Ages. During the brutal Hundred Years' War, this river separated Britain and France. Today the sleepy Dordogne carries more tourists than goods and struggles to manage its popularity with British and Dutch tourists.

The joys of the region include rock-sculpted villages, fertile farms surrounding I-could-retire-there cottages, film-gobbling vistas, lazy canoe rides, and a local cuisine worth loosening your belt for. The Dordogne's most thrilling sights are its caves decorated with prehistoric artwork. The cave of Font-de-Gaume has the greatest ancient (15,000 years old) cave paintings still open to the public.

To explore this beautiful river valley, sleep in or near Beynac if you have a car and in Sarlat if you don't. If you're visiting in summer, prepare for warm, humid days and consider splurging for a rare air-conditioned room.

Planning Your Time

You'll need a minimum of a day and a half to explore this magnificent region. Your sightseeing obligations are prehistoric cave art, the Dordogne River Valley and its villages and castles, and the well-restored town of Sarlat. The Dordogne riverfront villages offer exciting canoe trips and a break from your sightseeing duties. Call well in advance to reserve a ticket to the cave art at Grotte de Font-de-Gaume or ask your hotel for help.

A good (and exhausting) driving day might go something like this: Morning and lunch in Sarlat, 13:00–Cave tour, 15:00– Two-hour canoe trip, 17:30–Tour Beynac castle with river view,

19:00–Walk behind the castle to the goose farm, 20:30–Dine. This also works well with a cave tour as the first or last stop of the day. For part or most of a second day, explore the twisting alleys in Beynac and La Roque Gageac, tour the castle at Castlenaud, and consider visiting the Lascaux II cave. With a third day and a car, head upriver to explore Rocamadour, Gouffre de Padirac, and villages such as Carennac.

A good day for train travelers based in Sarlat: Morning train to Les Eyzies, see Font-de-Gaume caves, taxi back to Sarlat and arrange an afternoon canoe trip (pick-up possible in Sarlat) or hire a taxi for an all- or part-day excursion (see "Getting around the Dordogne," below).

As you drive in or out the day before or after (connecting the Dordogne with the Loire and Carcassonne), break the long drives with stops in Oradour-sur-Glane (to the north) and Cahors/Albi (to the south). With good preparation, train travelers can manage these stops as well (see "Transportation Connections—Sarlat," below).

Getting around the Dordogne

This region is a joy with a car but tough without. You could rent a car or a bike (in Sarlat, Les Eyzies, or Beynac), hire an all-day taxi service (see below), or get to Beynac and toss your itinerary into the Dordogne.

By Bike or Moped: Bikers find the Dordogne scenic but awfully hilly, with crowded roads. Consider a moped, if you dare. Rent bikes and mopeds in Sarlat and bikes only in Beynac (see below for each). A scenic Dordogne Valley loop ride is described in "Sights—Along the Dordogne Valley," below.

By Train: Train service is sparse. Trains run from Sarlat almost to the Font-de-Gaume caves in Les Eyzies (transfer in Le Buisson), but leave you in Les Eyzies for five hours. Consider a train to Les Eyzies (good early-morning connection in Le Buisson) and a taxi home, or use your time in Les Eyzies to see its museum or rent a bike and ride five kilometers to Abri du Cap-Blanc (rent bikes at Les Eyzies TI, tel. 05 53 06 97 05, fax 05 53 06 90 79).

Car Rental in Sarlat: Try Europcar (le Pontet, place de la Lattre de Tassigny, tel. 05 53 30 30 40, fax 05 53 31 10 39) or Budget (Centre Commercial du Pontet, tel. 05 53 28 10 21, fax 05 53 28 10 92).

By Taxi: These taxis offer customized taxi tours (split the cost with up to 6 travelers, find partners at your hotel, figure 600–700F/half day, 1,300F/day, call and compare): **Allo Sarlat Taxi**, tel. 06 86 54 08 69; or **Allo Taxi Phillipe**, tel. 06 08 57 30 10 (English spoken). For taxi service from Sarlat to Beynac or La Roque-Gageac, allow 90F (130F at night); from Sarlat to Les Eyzies allow 150F (230F at night and on Sun).

Cuisine Scene—Dordogne River Valley

Gourmets flock to this area for its geese, ducks, and wild mushrooms. The geese produce (involuntarily) the region's famous foie gras (they're force-fed, denied exercise, and slaughtered for their livers). Foie gras tastes like butter and costs like gold. The duck specialty is *confit de canard* (duck meat preserved in its own fat—sounds terrible but tastes great). *Pommes Sarladaise* are mouthwatering, thinly sliced potatoes fried in duck fat and commonly served with *confit de canard*. Wild truffles are dirty black mushrooms that farmers traditionally locate with sniffing pigs and then charge a fortune for (3,000F per kilo, $250 per pound). Native cheeses are Cabécou (a silver-dollar-sized, pungent, nutty-flavored goat cheese) and Echourgnac (made by local Trappist monks). You'll find walnuts (*noix*) in salads, cakes, and liqueurs. Wines to sample are Bergerac (red and white) and Cahors (a full-bodied red). The *vin de noix* is a sweet walnut liqueur.

Dordogne Market Days

Market day is a major event in this cuisine-rich area and should be high among your priorities. Try to visit at least one of these markets (they end at 12:00).

Sunday:	St. Cyprien (8 kilometers west of Beynac)
Monday:	Les Eyzies (Grotte de Font-de-Gaume is here)
Tuesday:	Cenac (canoe float begins here)
Wednesday:	Sarlat
Thursday:	Domme
Friday:	Le Buisson (transfer point to Les Eyzies), Souillac (transfer point to Cahors, Carcassonne)
Saturday:	Sarlat, Cahors

SARLAT

Sarlat (sar-lah) is a pedestrian-friendly banquet of a town scenically set amid forested hills. The old city overflows with historical monuments and, in the summer, tourists. Sarlat is just the right size: large enough to have a theater with four screens and small enough so that everything is an easy stroll from the town center. One-time capital of Périgord and current capital of foie gras, Sarlat has been a haven for writers and artists throughout the centuries and remains so today. Geese hate Sarlat.

Orientation

Sarlat is a museum city: no blockbuster sights, just a seductive tangle of cobblestone alleys peppered with medieval and Renaissance buildings and foie gras stores. Rue de la République slices like an arrow through the circular old town. Sarlat's smaller half has no important sights but many quiet lanes. Get lost. Parking is a headache, particularly on market days. Try along avenue

Sarlat

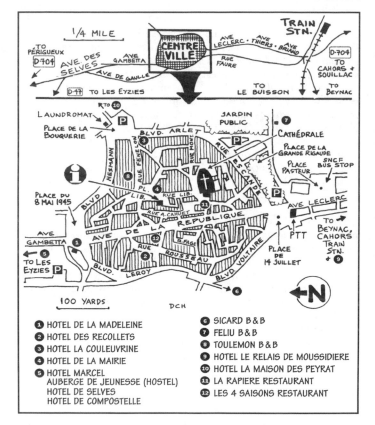

1 HOTEL DE LA MADELEINE
2 HOTEL DES RECOLLETS
3 HOTEL LA COULEUVRINE
4 HOTEL DE LA MAIRIE
5 HOTEL MARCEL
  AUBERGE DE JEUNESSE (HOSTEL)
  HOTEL DE SELVES
  HOTEL DE COMPOSTELLE

6 SICARD B & B
7 FELIU B & B
8 TOULEMON B & B
9 HOTEL LE RELAIS DE MOUSSIDIERE
10 HOTEL LA MAISON DES PEYRAT
11 LA RAPIERE RESTAURANT
12 LES 4 SAISONS RESTAURANT

Gambetta on the north end of town, but be careful not to park
on a market street on Tuesday or Friday nights.

Tourist Information: The overrun English-speaking TI,
in the center on place de la Liberté, has free maps of the city and
region, *chambres d'hôte* listings, and the useful "Guide Pratique"
booklet, which lists bus and train schedules as well as car, bike,
and canoe rentals (July–Sept Mon–Sat 9:00–20:00, Sun 10:00–
12:00, 14:00–18:00; Oct–June Mon–Sat 9:00–12:00, 14:00–18:00,
tel. 05 53 31 45 45). Ask about occasional English walking tours
(25F, 90 min, meet at the TI).

Laundromats: One of the two launderettes (both open
daily 9:00–22:00) is across from the recommended Hôtel Coule-
verine (self-serve or leave and pick up); the other is at 74 avenue
de Selves, near the recommended Hôtel de Selves.

Bike Rental: Rent mopeds or mountain bikes at Peugeot Cycles (36 avenue Thiers, tel. 05 53 28 51 87, fax 05 53 28 50 08).

Sights—Sarlat

▲▲**Stroll through Sarlat**—The well-done three-panel "City of Sarlat" brochure (26F, on sale at many shops and the TI) describes a good walking tour of the city. Start by exploring the musty cathedral. Exit out the right transept. Snoop around through a few quiet courtyards and then turn left, making your way toward the rear of the cathedral. Climb up the steps to that medieval space capsule called the Lanterne des Morts (Lantern of the Dead). Big shots were buried here in the Middle Ages. Exit right (with your back to the lantern). Turn right and climb to the top of this lane for a good look back over Sarlat and then meander back down to the place de la Liberté, ground-zero for market days. Save time to prowl the quiet side of town (the other side of the rue de la République). An automobile museum is just west of the old town (rue Thiers).

▲**Open-Air Markets**—Outdoor markets thrive on Wednesday morning and all day Saturday. Saturday's market is best in the morning (produce and food vendors leave at noon) and seems to swallow the entire town. The best market after Sarlat's is in St. Cyprien on Sunday.

Sleeping in Sarlat

(6.50F = about $1, country code: 33, zip code: 24200)
Sleep Code: **S** = Single, **D** = Double/Twin, **T** = Triple, **Q** = Quad, **b** = bathroom, **t** = toilet only, **s** = shower only, **CC** = Credit Card (**Visa**, MasterCard, Amex), **SE** = Speaks English, **NSE** = No English, * = French hotel rating system (0–4 stars).

Even with summer crowds (which create some impatient hoteliers), Sarlat is the train traveler's best home base. In July and August many hotels require half-pension. These hotels are listed in about the order you would find them, starting at the upper, north end of the city on the rue de Selves. The first four hotels are in the town center.

Hôtel de la Madeleine*** is a grand place with Old World lounges, hotelesque service, and cavernous, polished rooms (Sb-370–445F, Db-410–510F, Tb-575F, Qb-660F, garage parking-35F, CC:VMA, elevator, air-con, at north end of ring road at 1 place de la Petite Rigaudie, tel. 05 53 59 10 41, fax 05 53 31 03 62, e-mail: hotel.madeleine@wanadoo.fr, SE).

Hôtel des Recollets** is popular and offers modern comfort under heavy stone arches, with smartly decorated rooms, big beds, and a mellow courtyard on Sarlat's quiet side, three blocks down from Hotel Madeleine (Db-260–370F, Tb-370F, Qb-70F, obligatory breakfast-35F, no half-pension, CC:VM,

4 rue Jean-Jacques Rousseau, tel. 05 53 31 36 00, fax 05 53 30 32 62, e-mail: otelrecol@aol.com, Christophe SE).

Hôtel La Couleuvrine** has stiff management but plenty of medieval character in its well-appointed rooms. Families enjoy *les châmbres famille*s (Db-300–390F, Tb-370F–420F, Qb-430–470F, CC:VMA, elevator, on ring road at 1 place de la Bouquerie, tel. 05 53 59 27 80, fax 05 53 31 26 83). Half-pension is encouraged at busy periods and in summer (fine cuisine in an elegant restaurant, about 600F for 2).

Hôtel de la Mairie** is friendly and basic, with big rooms and a central location (Ds-220F, Db-260–290F, Ts-270–330F, Qb-420F, CC:VM, on place de la Liberté, check in at the café, tel. & fax 05 53 59 05 71, SE).

The next four listings are a five-minute walk down Avenue Gambetta from Hôtel de la Madeleine.

Hôtel Marcel* is a simple souvenir of old Sarlat with a dark, wood-beamed lobby and flowery wallpaper (Db-250–310F, 50 rue de Selves, tel. 05 53 59 21 98, fax 05 53 30 27 77). A few blocks farther, the poorly marked **Auberge de Jeunesse** (hostel) is a very basic, do-it-yourself place (bunks-50F, sheets-16F, opens at 18:00, no curfew, small kitchen, 77 rue de Selves, call ahead for a bed, tel. 05 53 59 47 59 or 05 53 30 21 27). Closer to the center, **Hôtel de Selves***** is sleek and modern, with pastel decor surrounding a swimming pool and quiet garden (Sb-370–520F, Db-430–600F, CC:VMA, elevator, cable TV, air-con, 93 avenue de Selves, tel. 05 53 31 50 00, fax 05 53 31 23 52, www.selves-sarlat.com). Across the street, the less snazzy **Hôtel de Compostelle**** has modern rooms and a few good family suites (Db-300–340F, Tb/Qb-470F, CC:VMA, elevator, 64 avenue de Selves, tel. 05 53 59 08 53, fax 05 53 30 31 65).

Chambres d'Hôtes in Sarlat

The charming **Sicards** rent three fine rooms on the southeastern edge of the old town, a five-minute walk below the ring road (Sb-180F, Db-190–210F, Tb-230F, Le Pignol, rue Louis Arlet, tel. 05 53 59 14 28). **Madame Feliu's** three rooms, just off the ring road below the park, are more central but less homey (Db-220–260F, tel. 05 53 59 03 21). The **Toulemons** offer comfortable and well-furnished rooms in their 17th-century home a few blocks from the TI (Db-200–260F, look for big steps leading from northeast corner of place de la Liberté, 4 rue Magnanat, tel. 05 53 31 26 60 or 06 08 67 76 90).

Sleeping near Sarlat

Many golden stone hotels surround Sarlat for those preferring to be close yet rural (with easy parking). **Hôtel le Relais de Moussidiere***** has a gorgeous setting with a small lake, restaurant (*menus* from 175F), and cushy rooms (Db-560–800F, CC:VM, tel. 05 53 28 28 74, fax 05 53 28 25 11, in Moussidiere Basse, just south of Sarlat on road to Bergerac). **Hôtel La Maison des Peyrat**** is a fine alternative with a pool and lower prices (Db-260–530F, *menus* from 110F, 1.5 kilometers east of Sarlat, Le Lac de la Plane, tel. 05 53 59 00 32, fax 05 53 28 56 56).

Eating in Sarlat
Sarlat is packed with moderately priced restaurants, most of which serve local specialties. **La Rapière**, opposite the cathedral, provides wood-beam coziness and fine regional cuisine (*menus* from 110F, daily June–Sept, off-season closed Sun, tel. 05 53 59 03 13). On the quieter side, just off rue de la République, **Les 4 Saisons** offers a good 100F *menu* (daily June–Sept, closed Wed off-season, 2 Côte de Toulouse, tel. 05 53 29 48 59). Drivers can go to Beynac or La Roque-Gageac for a beautiful setting and excellent value (see below).

Transportation Connections—Sarlat
Sarlat's TI has schedules. Soulliac and Perigueux are the train hubs for points within the greater region. For all destinations below you can go via Libourne/Bordeaux St. Jean or Souillac (the bus connecting Souillac and Sarlat is covered by railpass). I've listed the fastest path in each case. Sarlat train info: tel. 05 53 59 00 21.

By train to: Paris (4/day, 6 hrs, via Libourne or Bordeaux St. Jean, then TGV), **Amboise** (4/day, 6 hrs, via scenic train to Bordeaux/Libourne, then TGV to St. Pierre des Corps, then local train to Amboise), **Oradour-sur-Glane** (difficult, 3/day, 3–4 hrs via bus to Souillac, train to Limoges and bus to Oradour; return to Limoges to continue to Amboise), **Cahors** (4/day, 2–3 hrs, SNCF bus to Souillac, then train to Cahors), **Albi** or **Carcassonne** (6/day, 6 hrs, bus to Souillac then train with transfer in Toulouse, or train to Bordeaux and Toulouse in same time).

To Beynac: Beynac is accessible only by taxi (95F) or bike, though the folks at Hôtel du Château will pick you up at the Sarlat station for no charge if you reserve ahead (see "Sleeping in Beynac," below).

BEYNAC
The cliff-hanging village of Beynac (bay-nak) sees far fewer tourists than its big brother, Sarlat, and feels more welcoming. You'll have the Dordogne River at your doorstep and a perfectly preserved medieval village winding like a sepia film set from the beach to the hill-capping castle above. The floodlit village is always open for evening strollers.

The **TI** is at the village riverside parking lot (April–Sept daily 9:30–12:30, 14:30–18:00, closed Sun off-season, tel. and

Heart of the Dordogne

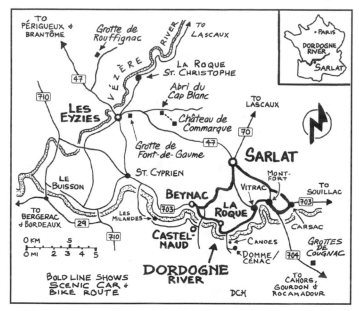

fax 05 53 29 43 08, www.perigord.tm.fr), along with the post
office (with ATM) and a grocery.

Beynac's scenic cafés are right on the river below the TI and
high above, near the castle entry. Park at pay lots on the river, way
up at the castle (follow signs to Château de Beynac), or halfway
between. A pleasant trail follows the river toward Castlenaud
(begins across from Hôtel Bonnet), with great views back toward
Beynac, a good restaurant (see "Eating," below), and, for able
route finders, a healthy hike to Castlenaud (1 hr). Rent bikes at
Canoe Copeyre, below the TI (60F/half day, 90F/day, tel. 05 53
28 95 01, fax 05 53 31 24 22).

Sights—Beynac
▲Château de Beynac—This cliff-clinging castle soars 500 feet
above the Dordogne River. During the Hundred Years' War, the
castle of Beynac housed the French, while the British headquarters
was across the river at Castelnaud. From the condition of the
castles, it looks like France won. The sparsely furnished castle is
most interesting for the valley views. Tour it on your own from
12:15 to 13:45; otherwise you must go with a free French-speaking
guide. Pick up the English translation (40F, mid-March–mid-Nov,
tours 10:00–18:00, in summer last visit is 18:00, tel. 05 53 29 50 40).

River Cruise Trips—Boats leave from Beynac's parking lot and give a mildly interesting, but relaxed 50-minute cruise of the Dordogne with English explanations (35F, about every 30 min from 10:00–18:00, Easter–Oct, tel. 05 53 28 51 15).

Sleeping in Beynac
(6.50F = about $1, country code: 33, zip code: 24220)
Those with a car should sleep in or near Beynac. With hotel pickup services, taxis, and bike-rental possibilities, even those without a car may find Beynac worth the trouble. The tiny Beynac TI posts a listing on its door of all accommodations with prices and current availability. Leave nothing in your car at night; the riverfront lot is a thief's dream.

Hôtel Bonnet**, on the eastern edge of town, offers quasi-classy Old World comfort, river views (which come with noise) from many of its rooms, a peaceful backyard garden, and a well-respected restaurant (Db-300–460F, Tb-350F–380F, CC:VMA, tel. 05 53 29 50 01, fax 05 53 29 83 74).

Hôtel du Château** is dead center with many amenities, including a pool, bar, and terrace café, but feels run-down. The rooms need attention and those on the river are loud—ask for one in the back or skip it (Db-260–330F, extra person-60F, CC:VM, tel. 05 53 29 50 13, fax 05 53 28 53 05, www.perigord.com/spih). Next door, the Hostellerie Malleville restaurant offers quieter, cozier rooms in an annex up the street at their **Hôtel Pontet**** (Db-240–360F, CC:VMA, includes use of pool at their other hotel in nearby Vézac, check in at Hostellerie Malleville, tel. 05 53 29 50 06, fax 05 53 28 28 52).

For truly basic and nearly clean rooms with a romantic view of the river, hike up to **Hôtel de la Poste*** run by gregarious Madame Montestier and her mother-in-law. Relaxed cleaning standards, no TVs, no credit cards, fax…what's that?, but a cool garden and pleasant sitting room (D-175F, Db-215–250F, Tb/Qb-315F, walk a short distance past Hôtel du Château and then turn right up pedestrian street 75 meters, tel. 05 53 29 50 22, NSE).

Chambres Residence Versailles sits high above with castle views and five immaculate rooms, laundry facilities, a quiet garden, and best of all, welcoming Madame Fleury (Db-300F, includes English breakfast, Route du Château, tel. 05 53 29 35 06). Take the small road behind Hôtel Bonnet up 800 meters, turn right at the *atelier menuisier* (woodworkers' workshop) and go 100 meters.

Sleeping near Beynac
Chambres d'Hôtes: In Bezenac, five kilometers from Beynac toward St. Cyprien, friendly British ex-pats **Doug and Jenny Cree** have three spacious rooms (big bathrooms) with valley views and a pleasant terrace over the river (Db-210F, tel. 05 53 59 32 69,

e-mail: cree@perigord.com). Drive into the village, pass the church, and veer left at the top. The Crees are the first house after the small *mairie* (town hall).

Hôtels: For motel-like comfort, drive two kilometers east from Beynac to Vézac and try either the more polished **Relais des 5 Châteaux**** (Db-270–300F, CC:VM, good restaurant, nice pool, tel. 05 53 30 30 72, fax 05 53 31 19 39) or the quieter and kid-friendly **Hôtel l'Oustal**, with a pool, Ping-Pong, volleyball, and grass to burn (Db-300–340F, Tb-350F, Qb-400F, CC:VMA, 24220 Vézac, tel. 05 53 29 54 21, fax 05 53 28 28 52).

Eating in and near Beynac

You'll dine well in air-conditioned comfort at **Hôtel du Château** and, for a bit more, under the wood beams of **Hôtel Bonnet** (see "Sleeping," above, for both). **Taverne des Remparts** is a good value (across from castle, CC:VM, tel. 05 53 29 57 76, Jerome SE). I can't imagine leaving Beynac without relaxing at their view-perfect café, best at night (try the *salade gourmande* for lunch). I also enjoy walking along the river toward Castelnaud, to the reasonable **Auberge du Point de Vue** (open daily in summer, otherwise closed Tue, turn left at rail bridge and follow the road, great views of Beynac, tel. 05 53 30 49 90). Beynac also offers a dreamy dinner-picnic site. Walk up the hill (easier said), pass the château, continue out of the village, and turn right at the cemetery.

In nearby La Roque-Gageac, the restaurant **Hôtel Belle Étoile** serves top regional cuisine in elegant surroundings (*menus* from 125F, reserve ahead, tel. 05 53 29 51 44).

Sights—Cro-Magnon Caves in the Dordogne Region

There are four caves in this region with original cave paintings that tourists can still admire: the top-quality Grotte de Font-de-Gaume (tours in English offered only in summer), the immense Grotte de Rouffignac, the less spectacular but friendly Grotte de Cougnac (some tours in English), and the well-organized and impressive Grotte de Peche Merle (some English tours; listed under "Sights—Southeast of the Dordogne, Lot River," below). Whatever caves you visit, dress warmly, even if it's hot outside.

The first four cave sights—Grotte de Font-de-Gaume, Grotte de Rouffignac, Roque St. Cristophe, and Abri du Cap-Blanc—are within a 20-minute drive of Les Eyzies. The last two sights—Lascaux and Grotte de Cougnac—are a 30-minute drive from Sarlat (in opposite directions).

Les Eyzies—The town of Les Eyzies-de-Tayac is the touristic hub of this cluster of historic caves, castles, and rivers. Except for its interesting museum of prehistory (22F, Wed–Mon 9:30–12:00, 14:00–18:00, summers 9:30–19:00, closed Tue

The Dordogne Region

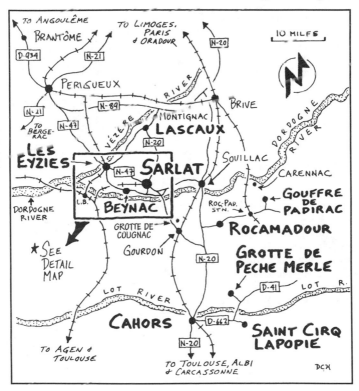

and at 17:00 Nov–March) next to the big statue of Mr. Cro-Magnon, there's little reason to stop here. The **TI** rents bikes (daily 10:00–12:00, 14:00–18:00, summer 9:00–18:00, tel. 05 53 06 97 05, fax 05 53 06 90 79).

Sleeping near Les Eyzies: Just a few minutes by car from Les Eyzies, this simple 14-room farm at **Ferme Veyret** is as friendly as it gets. You'll be expected to dine here, and you'd be a fool not to, as dinner includes everything from *apéritif* to *digestif*, with five courses in between and wine throughout (Db-265F per person, includes breakfast and dinner, pool, on route to Abri du Cap-Blanc, look for yellow signs, 24620 Les Eyzies de Tayac, tel. 05 53 29 68 44, fax 05 53 31 58 28).

▲▲▲**Grotte de Font-de-Gaume**—Even if you're not a connois-seur of Cro-Magnon art, you'll dig this cave. It's the last cave in Europe with prehistoric (polychrome) painting still open to the public, and its turnstile days are numbered. On a carefully guided and controlled 100-meter walk, you'll see about 20 red and black bison—often in elegant motion—painted with a moving sensitivity. Your guide—with a laser pointer and great reverence—will trace the faded outline of the bison and explain how, 15,000 years ago, cave dwellers used local minerals and the rock's natural contour to give the paintings dimension. The paintings were discovered by the village schoolteacher in 1901. Now, since heavy-breathing tourist hordes damage the art by raising and lowering the temperature and humidity levels, tickets are limited to 200 a day.

Visits are by appointment only. Reserve in advance by phone; your hotel can make the call. Summertime spots are booked two weeks in advance. Even off-season, it's smart to call ahead and get a time. Request an English tour (usually summers only) and arrive 30 minutes early or lose your spot. You'll find it interesting even in French but ask for the English brochure and read through the books in the gift shop before you go (35F, Thu–Tue 9:00–12:00, 14:00–17:30, closed Wed and at 17:00 Nov–Feb, no photography or large bags, tel. 05 53 06 86 00). Drivers who can't get a spot here (or who want to see completely different caves) should try the caves at Rouffignac (see below) or aim for the more remote Grotte de Peche Merle, an hour east of Cahors (see "Sights—Southeast of the Dordogne," below).

▲▲**Grotte de Rouffignac**—This is the second-best cave in the area after Font-de-Gaume. Dress warmly; the visit lasts 70 minutes and extends one kilometer into the hillside. In this extensive cave, a French-speaking guide escorts you on a small train, stopping to point out engravings of mammoths (done with wood sticks—many of those vertical lines are prehistoric bear-claw scratches) and brilliant black paintings of rhinos, bison, horses, mammoths, and reindeer. The most interesting stop is at the end as you descend the train into a vault of ceiling paintings (notice the original level of the floor through the end of this cave; the artists had to crawl to this place and draw while lying on their backs). The horse is amazing. The helpful guides make time to answer questions in English but lead the tour in French (36F, daily 10:00–11:30, 14:00–17:30, opens at 9:00 in summer, closed Nov–March, no reservations, tours leave about every 30 min, best strategy is to arrive before opening time and take the first tour—afternoons are busier, and the summertime 14:00 lineup can be ugly, tel. 05 53 05 41 71). It's well signed from the route between Les Eyzies and Perigueux; allow 20 minutes from Les Eyzies.

Roque St. Christophe—These extensive, cliff-hugging ledges and caves (no paintings) were inhabited from 55,000 years ago to the Middle Ages. They'll pique your interest through their sheer size, multiple levels, and stunning setting. Visits are allowed only with a French-speaking guide. Get the English handout and lag behind the group (35F, daily March–Oct 10:00–18:00, Nov–Feb 11:00–17:00, 8 kilometers north of Les Eyzies on D-706).

▲**Abri du Cap-Blanc**—In this prehistoric cave (just up the road from Font-de-Gaume), early artists used the rock's natural contours to add dimension to their sculpture. The small museum, with English explanations, will prepare you, and the handy English handout will guide you. Look for places where the artists smoothed or roughed the surfaces to add depth. In this single stone room, your French-speaking guide will spend 30 minutes explaining 14,000-year-old carvings. Impressive as these carvings are, their subtle majesty bypasses some. Free tours leave on the half hour (31F, Wed–Mon 9:30–19:00 in summer, off-season 10:00–12:00, 14:00–18:00, closed on Tue and Nov–April, tel. 05 53 29 21 74). The sight is well signed, three kilometers after Grotte de Font-de-Gaume on the road to Sarlat.

▲▲**Lascaux**—The region's most famous cave paintings are at Lascaux, 22 kilometers north of Sarlat and Les Eyzies. In the interest of preservation, these caves are closed to tourists. But the adjacent Lascaux II copy caves are impressive in everything but authenticity. At Lascaux II, the reindeer, horses, and bulls of Lascaux I are painstakingly reproduced by top artists using the same dyes, tools, and techniques their predecessors did 15,000 years ago. Anyone into caveman art will appreciate the thoughtful explanations. It's worth working your schedule around English tour times (50F, July–Aug daily 9:30–19:00, Sept–June Tue–Sun 10:00–12:00, 14:00–17:30; call ahead for English tour times, 5 tours/day in summer, on demand in off-season; in July and August tickets are sold only at Montignac TI, caves 2.5 kilometers south of Montignac, tel. 05 53 51 95 03). The nearby **Hôtel Château de Fleunie***** offers regal 15th-century château accommodations, a pool, and a restaurant (Db-360–800F, *menus* from 135F, CC:VM, 24570 Condat sur Vezere, tel. 05 53 51 32 74, fax 05 53 50 58 98, www.la.fleunie.com).

▲**Grotte de Cougnac**—Thirty kilometers south of Sarlat near Gourdon in Payrignac, this less-touristy cave offers stalagmites and a more intimate look at Cro-Magnon cave art (32F, daily 9:00–18:00 in summer, otherwise 9:30–11:00, 14:00–17:00, 70-min tours, some in English, call ahead, tel. 05 65 41 47 54).

Sights—Along the Dordogne River

▲▲▲**Dordogne Valley Scenic Loop Ride or Drive**—The most scenic stretch of the Dordogne lies between Carsac and Beynac. From Sarlat, follow signs toward Cahors and Carsac and then veer right to the Église de Carsac (visit this tiny Romanesque church if it's open). From Carsac, follow the river via Montfort, La Roque-Gageac, and Beynac. The town of Domme, snuggling a hilltop in the distance, is overrun. Bikers, note that the round-trip from Sarlat totals about 45 kilometers (28 miles). Less-ambitious bikers will find the 30-kilometer (18-mile) loop ride from Sarlat to La Roque-Gageac to Beynac and back to Sarlat sufficient. This trip works just as well from Beynac.

Foie Gras in the Making—You can witness (evenings only) the force-feeding of geese (*la gavage*) at many places. Look for *gavage* signs but beware: You are expected to buy and locals know that Americans are squeamish. Friendly Madame Gauthier's farm offers a peek at the *gavage* and is down the road behind the Château de Beynac (park right there or walk 10 min from the château away from river through parking lot—you'll see the signs, demonstrations 18:00–19:30, tel. 05 53 29 51 45).

▲▲**Castelnaud**—Château de Beynac's crumbling rival looks a little less mighty, but the inside packs a medieval punch. Several rooms display weaponry and artifacts from the Hundred Years' War. The courtyard comes with a 46-meter-deep well (drop a pebble) and an entertaining video showing catapults, which litter the grounds, in action. The rampart views are as unbeatable as the siege tools outside the walls are formidable. Borrow the English explanations from the ticket lady for the room-by-room story (38F, May–Sept daily 10:00–19:00, 9:00–20:00 in summer, Oct–April 10:00–18:00, closes at lunch and at 17:00 Dec–Feb, from the river it's a steep hike through a pleasant peasant village, the car park is closer, tel. 05 53 31 30 00). You can stop here halfway through your canoe trip or take a one-hour hike from Beynac along a difficult-to-follow riverside path (it hugs the river as it passes though campgrounds and farms).

▲▲▲**Dordogne Canoe Trips**—For a refreshing break from the car or train, explore the riverside castles and villages of the Dordogne by canoe. Several outfits rent plastic two-person canoes (and 1-person kayaks) and will pick you up at an agreed-upon spot. If Beynac is home, make sure the outfit allows you to get out in Beynac. For 130F, two can paddle the best two-hour stretch from Cénac to Beynac (includes shuttle, call ahead to arrange if you don't have a car, in summer the usual pick-up time in Beynac is 9:00). In Cénac, look for **Dordogne Randonées** (coming from Sarlat or Beynac, take the first left after crossing the bridge to Cénac, tel. 05 53 28 22 01, e-mail: randodordogne@wanadoo.fr). In La Roque-Gageac, **Canoe-Dordogne** rents canoes for the pleasant two-hour float to Château Milandes (140F, tel. 05 53 29 58 50). While you need to be in decent shape for the longer trips, it's OK if you're a complete novice—the only whitewater you'll encounter will be your partner frothing at the views. You'll get a life vest and, for a few extra francs, a watertight bucket. Beach your boat wherever you want to take a break. The best two stops are the village of La Roque-Gageac and the castle at Castelnaud.

▲**La Roque-Gageac**—La Roque (the rock), as the locals call this village, is sculpted into the cliffs rising from the Dordogne River (small TI in parking lot, open summers 10:00–12:00, 14:00–18:00). La Roque was once a thriving port, exporting Limousin oak to Bordeaux for wine barrels. Find the old ramp leading down to the river. Look for markers showing the water levels of three floods and ask someone about the occasional rock avalanches from above. For views, wander up the narrow tangle of backstreets that seem to disappear into the cliffs. The sky-high Fort Troglodyte is a good energy burner but offers little more than views (25F, get English explanation, open 10:00–19:00). For a small splurge, enjoy a romantic dinner and, better yet, stay overnight at the reasonable **Hôtel Belle Étoile****. It has classic decor, a cozy bar, river views from most rooms, some squishy beds, and a great restaurant (Db-300–350F, Tb/Qb-350–450F, no half-pension requirement, 24250 La Roque-Gageac, tel. 05 53 29 51 44, fax 05 53 29 45 63). **Hôtel Gardette**** has well-kept rooms at good rates and is right above the main village parking lot (Ds-200F, Db-250–300F, CC:VM, 24250 La Roque-Gageac, tel. 05 53 29 51 58, fax 05 53 28 38 73).

Sights—North of the Dordogne (near Limoges)

▲▲▲**Oradour-sur-Glane**—Located two hours north of Sarlat and 25 kilometers west of Limoges, this is one of the most powerful sights in France. French schoolchildren know this town well. Most make a pilgrimage here. "La Ville Martyr," as it is known, was machine-gunned and burned on June 10, 1944, by Nazi troops. The Nazis were either seeking revenge for the killing of one of their officers (by French resistance fighters in a neighboring village) or simply terrorizing the populace in preparation for the upcoming Allied invasion (this was four days after D-Day). With cool, German attention to detail, the Nazis methodically rounded up the entire population of 642 townspeople. The women and children were herded into the town church, where they were tear-gassed and machine-gunned. Plaques mark the place where the town's men were grouped and executed. The town was then set on fire, its victims left under a blanket of ashes. Today the ghost town, left untouched for 50 years, greets every pilgrim who enters with only one English word: Remember.

The new **underground museum** at the entry provides a helpful introduction (30F, daily 9:00–19:00, closes at 18:00 Nov–April). Hushed visitors walk the length of Oradour's main street, past gutted, charred buildings in the shade of lush trees, to the underground memorial on the market square (rusted toys, broken crucifixes, town mementos under glass). Visit the cemetery where most lives ended on June 10, 1944, and finish with the church with its bullet-pocked altar (free, daily, long hours, helpful 10F English booklet).

Public transport here is a challenge. Four daily buses connect Limoges with Oradour in 20 minutes (10-min walk to bus stop from train station to place Winston Churchill). Consider a taxi. Limoges is a stop on an alternative train route between Amboise and Sarlat.

Mortemart—With a car and extra time, visit this nontouristy village (15 min northwest of Oradour on D-675). You'll find a medieval market hall, a few cafés, and a sweet château (good picnic benches behind). **Hôtel Relais**** offers five rooms over a well-respected restaurant (Db-250–300F, Tb-330F, CC:VM, *menus* from 100F, 87330 Mortemart, tel. 05 55 68 12 09).

Sights—Southeast of the Dordogne

Some find this remote, less-visited section of the Dordogne even more beautiful than the area around Sarlat. Follow the Dordogne upriver east from Souillac to explore the *charmant* villages of Martel, Carennac, Bretenoux, and the impressively situated château de Castelnau-Bretenoux. Just below are the Tom Sawyer–like Grottes de Padirac and the cliff-hanging Rocamadour.

▲**Rocamadour**—One hour east of Sarlat, this historic pilgrimage town's dramatic rock-face setting and medieval charm can be trampled by daily hordes of tourists. Those who arrive late and spend the night enjoy fewer crowds and a floodlit fantasy. Learn the legend of St. Amadour, climb the steps to the various churches in la Cité Medievale, and remember that in the Middle Ages, religious pilgrims outnumbered those tourists you're irritated with. Eight hundred years ago this was an important stop on the famous pilgrimage route to Santiago de Compostella in Spain. There are two **TIs**: a small office is in La Cité Medievale; the main TI is above the medieval town in l'Hospitalet (daily 10:00–12:30, 14:00–18:00, summer 10:00–20:00, tel. 05 65 33 22 00). Trains (transfer in Brive-la-Gaillarde) leave you five kilometers from the village (hire a taxi, rent a bike from the station, hitch, or hike).

Sleeping in and near Rocamadour: Hôtel Sainte Marie**, in the Cité Medievale, is comfortable enough and welcoming (D-180F, Db-260F, tel. 05 65 33 63 07, fax 05 65 33 69 08). Or sleep peacefully eight kilometers from Rocamadour in the very comfy *chambre d'hôte* **Moulin de Fresquet** (Db-400F, 46500 Gramat, tel. & fax 05 65 38 70 60, cellular 06 08 85 09 21, SE).

Idyllic little Carennac also makes a good home base for this area. Stay in the simple, friendly **Hôtel des Touristes*** (Db-250F, tel. 05 65 10 94 31, fax 05 65 39 79 85) or the more cushy **Hôtel Fenelon**** (Db-290–360F, Tb-370–420F, CC:VM, pool, tel. 05 65 10 96 46, fax 05 65 10 94 86).

▲▲**Gouffre de Padirac**—Ten kilometers from Rocamadour is a fascinating cave (lots of stalagmites but no cave art). Follow the 90-minute French-language tour through this huge system of caverns. You'll ride elevators, hike along a buried stream, and even take a subterranean boat ride (48F, April–Oct daily 9:00–12:00, 14:00–18:00; longer hours, crowds, and delays in summer; closed off-season; day trips organized from Rocamadour TI; Gouffre de Padirac TI tel. 05 65 33 47 17). The nearest train station is in Rocamadour.

Lot River and Cahors—Ninety minutes south of the Dordogne, the lesser-known Lot River meanders through one of France's most beautiful valleys. The prehistoric cave paintings at Grotte of Peche Merle, the fortified bridge at Cahors (Pont Valentré), and the rock-top village of St. Cirq Lapopie are remarkable sights in this valley—each within a half hour of the others. These sights are worthwhile for drivers connecting the Dordogne with Albi or Carcassonne or as a long day trip from Sarlat. Without a car, skip 'em.

▲**Pont Valentré at Cahors**—One of Europe's finest medieval monuments, this fortified bridge was built in 1308 to keep the English out of Cahors. It worked. Learn the story of the devil on the center tower. The steep trail on the non-city side leads to great views (keep climbing, avoid branch trails, be careful if trail is wet). Just past the city-side end of the bridge is Le Cèdre, a wine shop/café/souvenir stand with delightful owners. Taste Cahors' black wine and foie gras (duck is cheaper than goose and just as tasty).

▲▲**Grotte de Peche Merle**—About 30 minutes east of Cahors, this cave with prehistoric paintings rivals the better-known ones at Grotte de Font-de-Gaume. The cave is filled with stalactites and stalagmites. I liked the mud-preserved Cro-Magnon footprint. Call to reserve a time (English spoken). Start at the museum with a film subtitled in English. Then descend to the caves. If you can't join an English tour, ask for the English translation booklet. In summer, arrive by 9:30 or reserve a spot in summer (44F, 38F during off-season, Easter–Oct daily 9:30–12:00, 13:30–17:00, closes earlier off-season, tel. 05 65 31 27 05, fax 05 65 31 20 47).

▲**St. Cirq Lapopie**—Suspended high above the Lot River, this is one of southern France's most spectacularly situated hill towns. Be careful of summer crowds. Wander the rambling footpaths and stay for lunch. You'll find ideal picnic perches and several reasonable restaurants. Sleep at **Auberge du Sombral**** (Db-350–400F, Tb-450F, good 100F *menu*, CC:VM, tel. 05 65 31 26 08, fax 05 65 30 26 37).

LANGUEDOC

From the 10th to the 13th centuries, this powerful and independent region ruled an area reaching from the Rhône River to the Pyrénées. The Albigensian (Cathar) Crusades started here in 1208 and ultimately led to Languedoc's demise and incorporation into the state of France. The word *languedoc* comes from the language its people spoke at that time: *Langue d'oc* ("language of Oc," *Oc* for the way they said "yes") was the dialect of southern France, *langue d'oil*, was the dialect of northern France (where *oil*, later to become *oui*, was the way of saying "yes"). As Languedoc's power faded, so did its language.

The Moors, Charlemagne, and the Spanish have all called this home. You'll see, hear, and feel the strong Spanish influence on this dry, hilly region. I'm lumping Albi in with the Languedoc region, though locals don't think of it as true Languedoc.

Planning Your Time

Key sights in this region are Albi, Carcassonne, Minerve, the Cathar castle ruins, and Collioure. Albi makes a good day or overnight stop between the Dordogne region and Carcassonne. Plan your arrival at Carcassonne carefully: Arrive late in the afternoon, spend the night, and leave by noon the next day and you'll miss the daytrippers. Collioure is your Mediterranean beach town vacation-from-your-vacation. You'll need wheels of your own and a good map to find the Cathar castle ruins and Minerve. If you're driving, the most exciting Cathar castles—Peyrepertuse and Queribus—work well as stops between Carcassonne and Collioure. No matter what transport you use, Languedoc is a logical stop between the Dordogne and Provence or on the way to Barcelona, which is just over the border.

Languedoc

Getting around Languedoc

Albi, Carcassonne, and Collioure are a snap by train, but a car is
essential for seeing the remote sights in this area. You can rent a
car near the train stations in Albi or Carcassonne or in downtown
Collioure. Buy the local Michelin map #83. The roads can be tiny
and the traffic very slow. East of Montauban, the D-115 from
Bruniquel (along the l'Averyon River then south to Cordes) is
simply sublime, and the D-964 south of Bruniquel to Gaillac is a
scenic route to Albi.

Cuisine Scene—Languedoc

Hearty peasant cooking and full-bodied red wines are Languedoc's
tasty trademarks. Be adventurous. *Cassoulet,* an old Roman con-
coction of goose, duck, pork, mutton, sausage, and white beans, is
the main-course specialty. You'll also see *cargolade,* a stew of snail,
lamb, and sausage. Local cheeses are Roquefort and Pelardon (a
nutty-tasting goat cheese). Corbières, Minervois, and Côtes du

Roussillon are the area's good-value red wines. The locals distill a fine brandy, Armagnac, that tastes just like cognac and costs less.

The Cathars

The Cathars, a heretical group of Christians who grew in numbers under a tolerant rule in Languedoc from the 11th through the 13th centuries, saw life as a battle between good (the spiritual) and bad (the material). They considered material things evil and of the devil. While others called them "Cathars" (from the Greek word for "pure") or "Albigenses" (for their main city, Albi), they called themselves simply "friends of God." Cathars focused on the teachings of St. John and recognized only baptism as a sacrament. Because they believed in reincarnation, they were vegetarians.

Travelers encounter the Cathars in their Languedoc sightseeing because of the Albigensian Crusades (1209–1240s). The king of France wanted to consolidate his grip on southern France. The pope needed to make a strong point that the only acceptable Christianity was Roman-style. Both found self-serving reasons to wage a genocidal war against these people—who never amounted to more than 10 percent of the local population and who coexisted happily with their non-Cathar neighbors. After a terrible generation of torture and mass burnings, the Cathars were wiped out. The last Cathar was burnt in 1321.

Today tourists find haunting castle ruins (once Cathar strongholds) high in the Pyrénées and eat hearty *salade Cathar*.

ALBI

Those coming to see the basilica and the Toulouse-Lautrec Museum will be pleasantly surprised by Albi's enchanting redbricked and half-timbered city center sitting above the beautiful Tarn River. The Albigensian Crusades were born here, as was Toulouse-Lautrec. The visitor's Albi (TI, Toulouse-Lautrec Museum, and cobbled pedestrian zone) clusters around its fortress basilica. Consider spending a night.

Tourist Information: Albi's information-packed TI is between the basilica and the Toulouse-Lautrec Museum (July–Aug Mon–Sat 9:00–19:30, Sept–June Mon–Sat 9:00–12:00, 14:00–18:00, Sun all year 10:30–12:30, 15:30–17:30, tel. 05 63 49 48 80).

Arrival in Albi

By Train: From the station, take a left onto avenue Marechal Joffre and then another left on avenue General de Gaulle, cross place Laperouse keeping left of the gardens, then follow the signs to *cathédrale* and to Albi's old city.

By Car: Follow signs to "*centre-ville*" and "*cathédrale*" and park in front of the cathedral.

Sights—Albi

Pick up a map of the city center at the TI (get the purple *circuit poupre* walking tour in English) and follow its suggested walking tour, reading the English information posted at key points along the way. On this walk you'll see...

▲▲▲**Basilique Ste. Cécile**—This 13th-century fortress/basilica was the nail in the Albigensian coffin. Both the imposing exterior and the stunning interior of this cathedral drive home the message of the Catholic (read "universal") Church. The extravagant porch looks like the afterthought it was. The interior is an explosion of colors and geometric shapes framing a vivid *Last Judgment*. Even with the gaping hole that was cut from it to make room for a newer pipe organ, the *Last Judgment* makes its point in a way that would stick with any medieval worshiper (June–Sept 8:30–18:45, Oct–May closes 12:00–14:30 and at 18:30). The choir is worth the small admission, and the Sound and Light Show—*Son et Lumière Spectacle*, offered in summer, is worth staying up for (30F, 22:00, ask at TI).

▲▲**Musée Toulouse-Lautrec**—The Palais de la Berbie (once the fortified home of the archbishop) has the world's best collection of Lautrec's paintings, posters, and sketches. The artist, crippled from youth and therefore on the fringe of society, had an affinity for people who didn't quite fit in. He painted the dregs of Parisian society because that was his world. His famous Parisian-nightlife posters are here. The top floor houses a skippable collection of contemporary art (25F, April–May daily 10:00–12:00, 14:00–18:00; July–Aug daily 9:00–18:00; Oct–March Wed–Mon 10:00–12:00, 14:00–17:00; tel. 05 63 49 48 70). The gardens below have fine views.

Église St. Salvy and Cloître—This is an OK church with fine cloisters. Delicate arches surround an enclosed courtyard, providing a peaceful interlude from the shoppers that fill the pedestrian streets (open all day).

Market Hall—This quiet Art Nouveau market is good for picnic gathering and people watching (Tue–Sun until 13:00, closed Mon, 2 blocks from the basilica).

Sights—Near Albi

Cordes sur Ciel—Hill-town lovers won't be able to resist this brilliantly situated and well-preserved medieval marvel just 25 kilometers north of Albi. Cordes, once an important Cathar base, is now too busy in the summer, but quieter off-season. It's a long, steep walk up from the lower parking lots. Trains get you as far as Cordes-Vindrac, where a taxi-bus will shuttle you five kilometers to Cordes (25F, tel. 05 63 56 14 80). The TI is in the center (tel. 05 63 56 00 52).

Gorges du Tarn—Adventure lovers can canoe, hike, or drive the stunning Tarn River gorge by heading east of Albi to Millau, then following the gorge all the way to St. Enimie. Roads are slow but spectacular. The best base for canoeing is in tiny La Malene. Stay in the simple but fine **Auberge de l'Emarcadere** (Db-250F, Tb-300F, tel. 04 66 48 51 03, fax 04 66 48 58 94).

Sleeping and Eating in Albi
(6.50F = about $1, country code: 33, zip code: 81000)
Sleep Code: **S** = Single, **D** = Double/Twin, **T** = Triple, **Q** = Quad, **b** = bathroom, **t** = toilet only, **s** = shower only, **CC** = Credit Card (Visa, MasterCard, Amex), **SE** = Speaks English, **NSE** = No English, * = French hotel rating system (0–4 stars).

Hôtel St. Clair**, offering steep stairs and fine rooms, is decorated with a loving touch (Db-255–315F, Tb-360–420F, CC:VM, easy parking, 20-min walk from station, 2 blocks from cathedral in pedestrian zone on rue St. Clair, tel. 05 63 54 25 66, fax 05 63 47 27 58). **Le Vieil Alby Hôtel****, located in the heart of Albi's pedestrian area, has good rooms and a worthwhile restaurant (Sb-255–320F, Db-290–350F, Tb-370F, garage-45F, 25 rue Toulouse-Lautrec, tel. 05 63 54 14 69, fax 05 63 54 96 75). **Hôtel Laperouse**** has a pool and is a good value (Db-260–300F, 21 place Laperouse, tel. 05 63 54 69 22, fax 05 63 38 03 69).

Albi is filled with inexpensive restaurants whose specialty is organ meats. Rue Toulouse-Lautrec (2 blocks from Hôtel St. Clair) is home to many good places. **Le Vieil Alby** at #25 is traditional and tasty. For a real treat, find **Le Robinson**, where Lices Georges Pompidou meets the river. A path leads down to the river to this vine-strewn paradise (reasonable *menus*, 142 rue Eurand Branly, tel. 03 63 46 15 69).

Transportation Connections—Albi
You'll connect to just about any destination through Toulouse.

By train to: Toulouse (12/day, 75 min; no trains 14:00–17:00 from Toulouse or 18:45–21:00 from Albi), **Carcassonne** (12/day, 2.5 hrs, transfer in Toulouse), **Sarlat** (6/day, 6 hrs; train to Toulouse, then either transfer to Souillac and catch bus to Sarlat or train to Bordeaux St. Jean and take scenic train to Sarlat), **Paris** (7.5 hrs via Toulouse, then TGV).

CARCASSONNE
Medieval Carcassonne is a 13th-century world of towers, turrets, and cobblestone alleys. It's a walled city and Camelot's castle rolled into one, frosted with too many tourists. At 10:00 the salespeople stand at the doors of their main-street shops, their gauntlet of tacky temptations poised and ready for their daily ration of customers. A quieter Carcassonne rattles in the early morning or evening breeze. Enjoy the town early or late by spending the night. If you're here between June and September and are sensitive to

Carcassonne Overview

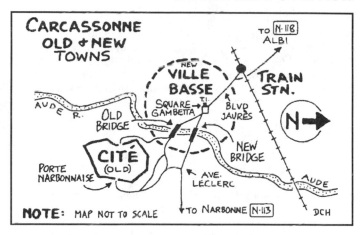

crowds, consider sleeping in nearby Caunes-Minervois (see "Sleep-ing near Carcassonne" below).

Locals like to believe that Carcassonne got its name this way: 1,200 years ago Charlemagne stood before this fortress/town (then called La Cité) with his troops and besieged it for several years. A cunning townsperson named Madame Carcas saved the town. Just as food was running out, she fed the last bits of grain to the last pig and tossed him over the wall. Splat. Charlemagne's bored and frustrated forces, amazed that the town still had enough food to throw fat party pigs over the wall, decided they would never succeed in starving the people out. They ended the siege and the city was saved. Madame Carcas *sonne*-d (sounded) the long-awaited victory bells, and La Cité had a new name: Carcas-sonne. Histor-ians, however, suspect that Carcassonne is a Frenchified version of the town's original name (Carcas).

From Rick's journal on his first visit to Carcassonne: "Before me lives Carcassonne, the perfect medieval city. Like a fish that everyone thought was extinct, somehow Europe's greatest Roman-esque fortress city has survived the centuries. I was supposed to be gone yesterday, but here I sit imprisoned by choice—curled in a cranny on top of the wall. The wind blows away the sounds of today, and my imagination 'medievals' me. The moat is one foot over and 100 feet down. Small plants and moss upholster my throne."

Orientation

Contemporary Carcassonne is neatly divided into two cities: the magnificent Cité (medieval city) and the lively *ville basse* (modern downtown).

Tourist Information: Carcassonne has two TIs, one in the Cité and one in the *ville basse*. The handy Cité TI is just to your right as you enter the main gate called Narbonnaise (July–Sept daily 9:00–19:00, Oct–June 9:00–13:00, 14:00–18:00). The TI in the *ville basse* is on place Gambetta, near the huge French flags, at 15 boulevard Camille Pelletan (Mon–Sat 9:00–12:15, 14:00–18:30, closed Sun, tel. 04 68 10 24 30 or 04 68 25 68 81). Pick up the map of La Cité with English explanations, get English tour times for Château Comtal, and ask about festivals.

Arrival in Carcassonne

By Train: The train station is located in the *ville basse*. A shuttle bus signed "La Cité" connects the station with La Cité except on Sunday and during winter months (2/hrly, 5F, pay driver, in the winter take bus #2 or #8 to place Gambetta, as close as you can get). Or you can walk 30 minutes across Canal du Midi, across the traffic circle, and up the pedestrian street to the heart of the *ville basse*. From there a left on rue de Verdun takes you to place Gambetta and across Pont Vieux to La Cité. Figure 55F for a taxi to La Cité from the train station.

By Car: Following signs to La Cité, you'll come to a large parking lot (20F) and a drawbridge (Porte Narbonnaise) at the walled city's entrance. If staying inside the walls, show your reservation (verbal assurances won't do) and park free in the outside lot then drive into the city after 18:00. Theft is common—leave nothing in your car at night.

Sights—Carcassonne

▲▲▲**Medieval Wall Walk**—La Cité is a medieval fortress first constructed during the time of the Roman Empire. It was completely reconstructed in 1844 as part of a program to restore France's important monuments. Walk much of the outer wall (no charge; in town, follow signs to *lices*). The higher inner walls are mostly inaccessible, except for those in Château Comtal. Savor every step and view.

▲**Carcassonne Terre d'Histoire**—A busy medieval fair fills up most of the first three weeks of August. Don't miss the jousting tournament (*spectacle équestre*), usually at 18:00.

▲▲▲**Walk to Pont Vieux**—For the best view back onto the floodlit city, hike down to the old bridge. As you exit the Narbonnaise Gate, go left on rue Nadaud to rue Gustave and then turn left onto rue Trivalle. Ask, "*Où est le Pont Vieux?*" (oo ay luh pohn vee-uh). Return via the back-door entry to La Cité near Basilique St. Nazaire.

▲**Basilique St. Nazaire**—Enter this church and slowly walk down the aisle. Enjoy the colors of the 14th-century stained glass sparkling all around you and find the delicately vaulted Gothic

Carcassonne

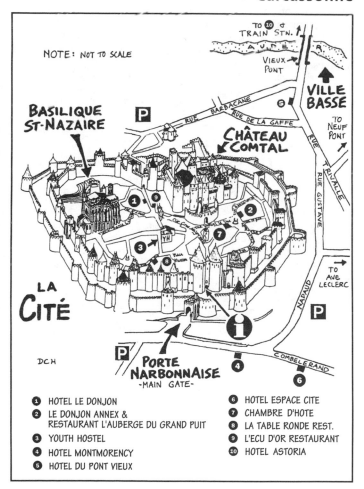

NOTE: NOT TO SCALE

TO 10 &
TRAIN STN.

L'AUDE R.

VIEUX
PONT

VILLE
BASSE

BASILIQUE
ST-NAZAIRE

P

RUE BARBACANE

RUE DE LA GAFFE

CHÂTEAU
COMTAL

TO
NEUF
PONT

RUE TREVALLE

RUE GUSTAVE

❶

❾

❷

❼

❸

YH

❽

LA
CITÉ

TO
AVE
LECLERC

NAPAUD

P

DCH

P

PORTE
NARBONNAISE
-MAIN GATE-

❹

COMBELERAND

❻

❶ HOTEL LE DONJON	❻ HOTEL ESPACE CITE
❷ LE DONJON ANNEX &	❼ CHAMBRE D'HOTE
RESTAURANT L'AUBERGE DU GRAND PUIT	❽ LA TABLE RONDE REST.
❸ YOUTH HOSTEL	❾ L'ECU D'OR RESTAURANT
❹ HOTEL MONTMORENCY	❿ HOTEL ASTORIA
❺ HOTEL DU PONT VIEUX	

ceiling behind the altar. This is one of the best examples of Gothic architecture in southern France.

Château Comtal—Carcassonne's third layer of defense was originally built in 1125 but was completely redesigned in later reconstructions. Peek into the inner courtyard and admire the towers, but skip the French tour (no English translation) and ask about English tours (free with admission, generally 2–4/day May–Sept; château entry-35F, June–Sept daily 9:00–19:00, Oct–May 9:30–12:30, 14:00–18:00).

Wine Cooperative (Cellier des Vignerons)—Stop in to sample a fine selection of local wines. You are expected to buy a bottle if you taste, but it's cheap (rue du Grand Puits).
Canal du Midi—Completed in 1681, this sleepy, 250-kilometer canal connects France's Mediterranean and Atlantic coasts. Before railways, Canal du Midi was jammed with commercial traffic. Today it's busy with pleasure craft. Look for the slow-moving hotel barges strewn with tanned and well-fed vacationers. The towpath that spans the length of the canal makes for ideal biking. The canal runs right in front of the train station in Carcassonne.

Sleeping in Carcassonne
(6.50F = about $1, country code: 33, zip code: 11000)

Sleeping in Carcassonne's La Cité
Sleep in or near the old walls. In the summer, when La Cité is jammed with tourists, consider sleeping in quieter Caunes-Minervois (see "Sleeping near Carcassonne," below). Three hotels and a great hostel offer rooms inside the walls. Except for the mid-July-to-mid-August peak, there are plenty of rooms.

Best Western's **Hôtel Le Donjon***** offers small, pricey, but well-appointed rooms, a comfortable lobby, and a great location inside the walls (Db-420–550F, Tb-430–610F, CC:VMA, tel. 04 68 11 23 00, fax 04 68 25 06 60, e-mail: hotel.donjon .best.western@wanadoo.fr).

Best Western also owns the **Hôtel des Remparts**. Right by the castle, it has a 12th-century staircase leading to modern rooms (same rates as Le Donjon, CC:VM, 5 place de Grand Puits, to book rooms at des Remparts, call or drop by the Hôtel Le Donjon, above).

The *chambre d'hôte* across from Hôtel des Remparts (inquire in small boutique) rents two huge apartment-like rooms that could sleep five and have a kitchenette and private terrace (Db-320F, Tb-350F, Qb-420F, family deals, stocked fridge and self-serve breakfast included, tel. & fax 04 68 25 16 67).

The **Auberge de Jeunesse** (youth hostel) is clean and well-run, with an outdoor garden courtyard, a self-service kitchen, a TV room, a bar, video games, and a welcoming ambience. If you ever wanted to bunk down in a hostel, do it here. Only July is tight. Nonmembers pay 20F extra (bed with breakfast-74F, sheet-17F, 2 doubles, a few quads, otherwise 6 to a room, open all day, closes at 01:00, rue de Vicomte Trencavel, tel. 04 68 25 23 16, fax 04 68 71 14 84).

Sleeping near La Cité
Hôtel Montmorency**, 100 meters from La Cité's drawbridge, is a Santa Fe–style place sporting new owners and a pool with a

fortress view (Db-300–450F, Tb-450F, Qb-550F, CC:VMA, free parking, 2 rue Camille St. Saens, tel. 04 68 11 96 70, fax 04 68 11 96 79, www.lemontmorency.com, e-mail: le.montmorency @wanadoo.fr).

Hôtel Espace Cité**, two blocks downhill from Hôtel Montmorency, is sterile and modern but handy for drivers (Db-300F, Tb-350F, Qb-400F, small rooms, CC:VMA, 132 rue Trivalle, tel. 04 68 25 24 24, fax 04 68 25 17 17).

Hôtel du Pont Vieux** is a 10-minute downhill walk from La Cité and offers spacious rooms around a garden courtyard with a view-top terrace and a third-floor three-person suite (#19) that opens out onto a private terrace with a five-star view of La Cité (Db-260–350F, Tb-380–450F, Qb-450–500F, CC:VM, garage parking-30F, 32 rue Trivalle, tel. 04 68 25 24 99, fax 04 68 47 62 71, e-mail: hoteldupontvieux@minitel.net, friendly, Canadian owner Serge).

Train travelers will appreciate the spotless, reasonable **Hôtel Astoria*** (S-110F, D-130F, Db-250F, Ts-190–210F, Tb-240F, Qb-300F, Internet access, near station at 18 rue Tourtel, tel. 04 68 25 31 38, fax 04 68 71 34 14, e-mail: hotelastoria@wanadoo.fr).

Sleeping near Carcassonne

To avoid the crowds and experience unspoiled Languedoc, sleep 15 minutes from Carcassonne in the unspoiled wine village of Caunes-Minervois (zip code: 11600). The next two places sit side by side in the heart of the village with owners eager to help you explore their region. Ex-pat Americans Terry and Lois Link take good care of you at **L'Ancienne Boulangerie** (D-225F, Db-350F, extra bed-100F, includes breakfast, tel. 04 68 78 01 32, e-mail: ancienneboulangerie@compuserve.com). **Hôtel d'Alibert****, a wonderful Old World place, is run by Frederic with relaxed panache (large Db-250–350F, Tb-300–400F, tel. 04 68 78 00 54). Don't skip a meal in his terrific restaurant (closed Sun–Mon). Closer to Carcassonne, British Diana and Chris of **la Ferme de la Suzette** welcome English-speaking travelers in their country stone farmhouse with five antiqued rooms and the possibility of a home-cooked dinner (Db-335–400F, dinner with wine-150F, take D-142 5 kilometers south of Carcassonne to Cazilhac, then look carefully for the D-56, take D-56 toward Villefloure, farmhouse is just before town, 11570 Villefloure, tel. 04 68 79 81 32, fax 04 68 79 65 99).

Eating in La Cité

Other than in the touristy joints lining the main drag, prices nd quality seem about the same everywhere. Dine with Jacques rel at **L'Auberge du Grand Puits** (cheap, hearty *salade Cathar* d cassoulet, place des Grands Puits, tel. 04 68 71 27 88).

above-average cassoulet, try **La Table Ronde** (80F *menu*,

30 rue du Plô, tel. 04 68 47 38 21). For a bit more money, enjoy the fine regional cuisine in an elegant setting at l'Écu d'Or (*menus* from 135F, tel. 04 68 25 49 03), across from Hôtel Donjon.

Picnics can be gathered at the small *alimentation* (grocery) on the main drag (generally open until 20:30). For your beggar's banquet, picnic on the city walls. For fast, cheap, hot food, look for places on the main drag with quiche and pizza to go.

Transportation Connections—Carcassonne
By train to: Sarlat (6/day, 6 hrs, transfer probable in Toulouse and certain at Bordeaux's St. Jean station; or via Souillac, then bus from Souillac), **Arles** (8/day, 3 hrs, a few are direct, but most require a transfer in Narbonne), **Nice** (6/day, 6.5 hrs, a few are direct, most transfer in Narbonne and/or Marseille), **Paris**' Gare Montparnasse (8/day, a few direct in 10 hrs or in 6.5 hrs by TGV via Toulouse, additional transfer possible in Bordeaux), **Toulouse** (hrly, 1 hr), **Barcelona** (3/day, 5 hrs, transfer in Narbonne and Port Bou, the border town).

Sights—Languedoc
These sights are worth a visit only if you're driving. Peyrepertuse and Queribus make ideal stops between Carcassonne and Collioure (allow 2 hours from Carcassonne on narrow, winding roads).

▲▲▲**Châteaus of Hautes Corbières**—Two hours south of Carcassonne toward the boring little country of Andorra, in the scenic foothills of the Pyrénées, lies a series of surreal, mountain-capping castle ruins. The Maginot Line of the 13th century, these sky-high castles were strategically located between France and the Spanish kingdom of Roussillon. As you can see by flipping through the picture books in Carcassonne tourist shops, these castles' crumpled ruins are an impressive contrast to the restored walls of Carcassonne. Bring a good map (lots of tiny roads) and sturdy walking shoes—prepare for a climb.

The most spectacular is the château of **Peyrepertuse**. The ruins seem to grow right out of a narrow splinter of cliff. The views are so sensational you can almost reach out and touch Spain. Let your imagination soar, but watch your step as you try to reconstruct this eagle's nest (25F, 9:00–sunset May–Sept, 10:00–sunset Oct–April, tel. 04 68 45 40 55).

Nearby, **Queribus** is also impressive and is famous as the last Cathar castle to fall. It was left useless when the border between France and Spain was moved (in 1659) farther south into the high Pyrénées (25F).

▲**Châteaus of Lastours**—Ten miles north of Carcassonne (forget public transportation), these five side-by-side ruined hillto~ castles offer drivers the most accessible look at the region's Cath~ castles and an ideal picnic site. From Carcassonne follow signs

to Conques and then Lastours. In Lastours follow signs to the Bellevedere for a panorama overlooking the five castles. The small fee also allows you to hike up to the castles (park back down the hill). It's long and steep but worthwhile if it's not too hot.
Minerve—A onetime Cathar hideout, Minerve is remarkably situated in the middle of a deep canyon that provided a natural defense. Strong as it was, it didn't keep out the pope's army. The entire village was destroyed and all residents were killed during the Albigensian Crusades. An interesting path leads down to the river and around the village from the higher end. Minerve has two pleasant cafés, one hotel, a compelling museum of prehistory—and not much more. Stay here and melt into southern France. Sleep and eat at the friendly and cozy **Relais Chantovent** (Sb-190F, Db-235–270F, Tb-270F, Qb-300F, ask for the new rooms, CC:VM, Minerve: 34210, tel. 04 68 91 14 18, fax 04 68 91 81 99). People travel great distances to dine at their moderately priced restaurant (closed Sun–Mon), so reserve early.

Minerve, between Carcassonne and Beziers, is 15 kilometers northeast of Olonzac (40 min by car from Carcassonne) and makes a good stop between Provence and Carcassonne. In the mood for wine tasting? The friendly (and French-only) Remaury family offers a good selection and an exquisite setting from which to sample the local product. Just over the hill from Minerve toward Carcassonne and past Azillanet, you'll see the signs to their **Domaine de Pech d'Andre** (tel. 04 68 91 22 66, NSE).

COLLIOURE

Collioure, while surrounded by less-appealing resorts, is blessed with an ideal climate (the temperature has not dropped below 55 degrees in three years) and a romantic setting. By Mediterranean standards this seaside village should be overrun—it has everything. Like an ice-cream shop, Collioure offers 31 flavors of pastel houses and six petite, scooped-out, and pebbled beaches sprinkled lightly with beachgoers. This sweet scene, capped by a winking lighthouse, sits under a once-mighty castle in the shade of the Pyrénées.

Come here to unwind and do nothing. Even with its crowds of French vacationers in peak season, Collioure is what many are looking for when heading to the Riviera—a sunny, peaceful vacation from their vacation.

Tourist Information: The TI is behind the main beachfront cafés at 5 place du 18 Juin (Mon–Sat 9:00–19:00, Sun 10:00–12:00, 15:00–18:00 in summer only; otherwise Mon–Fri 9:30–12:00, 14:00–18:00, tel. 04 68 82 15 47, www.little-france.com/collioure).

Laundromat: Laverie 3L will do your laundry while you do your relaxing (daily 9:00–19:00 in summer, otherwise daily 00–12:00, 15:00–18:00, 1 block up from post office at 28 rue la Republique, tel. 04 68 98 04 17).

Car Rental: Rent a car at Garage Renault, opposite the Laundromat on rue de la Republique (tel. 04 68 82 08 34).
Taxi: Tel. 04 68 82 05 30.

Arrival in Collioure
By Train: Walk out of the station, turn right, and follow the road down until you see Hôtel Fregate (hotels are listed from this point).
By Car: Follow Collioure, "centre-ville" signs. Look for a parking spot on the street or, if you have no luck, follow Gare SNCF signs (pay lot at the train station until you find better). Ask your hotel for parking suggestions and take everything out of the car.

Sights—Collioure
Check your ambition at the station. Enjoy a slow coffee, snuggle into the pebble-sand beach, and lose yourself in the old city's narrow, hilly streets. The 800-year-old **Château Royal** (great ramparts and views, a mildly interesting exhibit on the local history, and contemporary art exhibits) and the waterfront **Notre Dame des Anges** church are worth exploring. On walls along the waterfront, the **Chemin de Fauvism** (path of fauvism) displays copies of Derain's and Matisse's works inspired by Collioure (TI has details).

Consider renting a paddleboat or taking a **Promenade sur Mer** motorboat or sailboat excursion (1 or 3 hours, the longer trip is better, all boats depart from breakwater near château). The TI has information on hikes into the hills (the ruined castle of St. Elme, 1.5 kilometers in 1 hour straight up, offers the best views) and a list of wine shops offering relaxed tastings of the locally produced sweet Banyuls and Collioure reds and rosés (**Les Caves du Roussillon** offer a great selection and good prices at 9 avenue General de Gaulle). Evenings are best in Collioure— inspect every foot of the waterfront you can find. As the sky darkens, yellow lamps reflect warm pastels and deep blues.

Sights—Near Collioure
For drivers, the picturesque villages of Castelnou (fine 10th-century castle) and Ceret (interesting modern-art museum) make an easy day trip (allow 50 min by car to Castelnou). The 40-minute coastal drive via the Col de Banyuls into Spain is beautiful and well worth the countless curves, even if you don't venture past the border. Train travelers can make a day trip to Spain, to either Barcelona (3.5 hrs one-way) or, closer, Figueres and its Dalí museum (get schedules at the station).

Sleeping in Collioure
(6.50F = about $1, country code: 33, zip code: 66190)
You have two good choices for hotel location: tucked behind the castle in the old city (closer to train station) or in a quieter area

Collioure

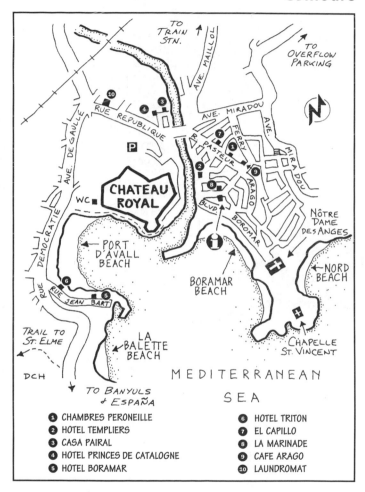

1 CHAMBRES PERONEILLE
2 HOTEL TEMPLIERS
3 CASA PAIRAL
4 HOTEL PRINCES DE CATALOGNE
5 HOTEL BORAMAR

6 HOTEL TRITON
7 EL CAPILLO
8 LA MARINADE
9 CAFE ARAGO
10 LAUNDROMAT

across the bay, with views of the old city (10-min walk from castle). The first four hotels are in the old city; directions are given from the big Hôtel Fregate, at the entrance to the old city.

The cheapest rooms in the old city are the simple, clean, and comfortable rooms at Monsieur and Madame Peroneille's **Chambres** on the pedestrian street two blocks past Hôtel Fregate at 20 rue Pasteur (Ds-230F, Db-270F, Tb-380F, Qb-400F, rooms in main building are pricier but infinitely better than those in annex, to see rooftop terrace, tel. 04 68 82 15 31, fax 04 68 82 35 94).

The artsy and eternally hip **Hôtel Templiers****, one block from Hôtel Fregate, has a complacent staff but rents delightfully decorated rooms, some with views (Db-320–400F, 12 avenue l'Amiraute, tel. 04 68 98 31 10, fax 04 68 98 01 24, e-mail: info @hotel-templiers.com). Opposite Hôtel Fregate, Collioure's best splurge is the Mediterranean-elegant **Casa Pairal*****, with a cozy lounge and fine air-conditioned rooms around a garden courtyard and pool (small Db-390–440F, pleasant Db-510–580F, big Db-570–790F, Tb-850–990F, extra bed-130F, garage-40F, CC:VMA, impasse Palmiers, tel. 04 68 82 05 81, fax 04 68 82 52 10, e-mail: roussillhotel@wanadoo.fr, SE).

For American style and efficiency, try **Princes de Cata-logne's***** spacious, comfortable, and air-conditioned rooms (Db-380–420F, Tb/Qb-550–700F, next to Casa Pairal, rue des Palmiers, tel. 04 68 98 30 00, fax 04 68 98 30 31).

On the view side of the bay, your best bet is the **Hôtel Boramar****. Get a room with a terrace facing the sea or sleep elsewhere (no view Db-260F, Db with view-320F, Tb with view-360F, rue Jean Bart, tel. 04 68 82 07 06). Next door, the neon-pink **Hôtel Triton**** is impersonal but has acceptable rooms at fair rates, many with fine views (Ds-190F, Db-260–300F, verify prices first, rue Jean Bart, tel. 04 68 98 39 39, fax 04 68 82 11 32).

Eating in Collioure

In the old city, **El Capillo** is a good value (2 rue Pasteur) and **La Marinade** is better for seafood (120F *menu*, near TI at 14 place du 18 Juin, tel. 04 68 82 09 76). For a lively, local, and smoky tapas-bar experience, find **La Cave Arago** (18 rue Pasteur, open Thu–Sun, tourists tolerated). I love buying something to go (*à emporter*) and finding a romantic spot to eat somewhere on the water.

Transportation Connections—Collioure

By train to: Carcassonne (8/day, a few direct in 2 hrs, via Narbonne in 2.5 hrs), **Paris** (1/day direct to Gare d'Austerlitz, 10 hrs; or, even better, transfer at Narbonne and Toulouse to TGV and zip into Gare Montparnasse, 7 hrs), **Barcelona** (5/day, 3.5 hrs), **Avignon/Arles** (12/day, 3 hrs, transfer in Narbonne). The train station ticket office closes at 17:45 (tel. 04 68 82 05 89). Consider handy night trains to Paris, key Italy destinations, and Geneva.

PROVENCE

This magnificent region is shaped like a giant wedge of quiche. From its sunburnt crust fanning out along the Mediterranean coast from Nîmes to Nice, it stretches north along the Rhône Valley to Orange. The Romans were here in force and left many ruins— some of the best anywhere. Seven popes, great artists like van Gogh, Cézanne, and Picasso, and author Peter Mayle all enjoyed their years in Provence. The region offers a splendid recipe of arid climate (but brutal winds known as the *mistral*), captivating cities, exciting hill towns, dramatic scenery, and oceans of vineyards.

Explore the ghost town of ancient Les Baux and France's greatest Roman ruin, Pont du Gard. Spend your starry, starry nights where van Gogh did, in Arles. Uncover its Roman past then find the linger-longer squares and café corners that inspired Vincent. Youthful but classy Avignon bustles in the shadow of its brooding popes' palace. It's a short hop from Arles or Avignon into the splendid scenery and villages of the Côtes du Rhône and Luberon regions that make Provence so popular today.

Planning Your Time
Make Arles or Avignon your sightseeing base (hotels are a far better value in Arles). Italophiles prefer Arles, while poodles pick Avignon. To measure the pulse of Provence, spend at least one night in a smaller town. Vaison la Romaine is ideal for those heading to/from the north, and Isle sur la Sorgue is centrally located between Avignon, the wine route, and the Luberon (all described below). Everything is accessible by public transit. You'll want a full day for sightseeing in Arles (ideally on Wed or Sat, when the morning market rages), a half day for Avignon, and a day or two for the villages and sights in the countryside.

Provence

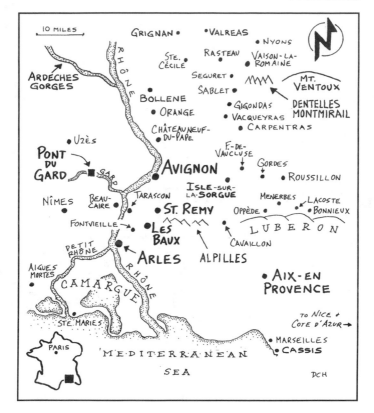

Getting around Provence

By Car: The yellow Michelin map to this region is essential for drivers. Avignon is a headache for drivers; Arles is easier. Park only in well-watched spaces and leave nothing in your car. For some of Provence's most scenic drives, follow my day-trip routes (see "Villages of the Côtes du Rhône" and "Hill Towns of the Luberon," below). If you're heading north from Provence, consider a three-hour detour through the spectacular Ardeches Gorges: Exit the A-6 autoroute at Bollene and follow the villages of Pont St. Esprit, Vallon Pont d'Arc (which offers all-day canoe-kayak floats through gorges), Privas, and Aubenas, then head back to the autoroute. Adorable Balazuc, a village north of the gorges, makes a fine stop.

By Bus or Train: Public transit is good between cities and marginal to small towns: Frequent trains link Avignon, Arles, and Nîmes (about 30 min between each), and buses connect smaller towns. Les Baux is accessible by bus from Arles. Pont du Gard, St. Rémy, Vaison la Romaine, and some Côtes du Rhône villages are all accessible by bus from Avignon. While a tour of the villages of Luberon is possible only by car or bus excursion from Avignon, nearby Isle sur la Sorgue is an easy hop by train from Avignon. The TIs in Arles and Avignon have information on bus excursions to regional sights that are hard to reach *sans* car (120F/half day, 200F/full day).

Cuisine Scene—Provence

The almost extravagant use of garlic, olive oil, herbs, and tomatoes makes Provence's cuisine France's liveliest. To sample it, order anything *à la Provençale*. Among the area's spicy specialties are *ratatouille* (a thick mixture of vegetables in an herb flavored tomato sauce), *brandade* (a salt cod, garlic, and cream mousse), *aioli* (a garlicky mayonnaise often served atop fresh vegetables), *tapenade* (a paste of puréed olives, capers, anchovies, herbs, and sometimes tuna), *soupe au pistou* (vegetable soup with basil, garlic, and cheese), and *soupe à l'ail* (garlic soup). Look also for *riz Camarguaise* (rice from the Camargue) and *taureau* (bull meat). Banon (wrapped in chestnut leaves) and Picodon (nutty taste) are the native cheeses. Provence also produces some of France's great wines at relatively reasonable prices. Look for Gigondas, Sablet, Côtes du Rhône, and Côte de Provence. If you like rosé, try the Tavel. This is the place to splurge for a bottle of Châteauneuf-du-Pape.

Provence Market Days

Provençal market days offer France's most colorful and tantalizing outdoor shopping. The best markets are Tuesday in Vaison la Romaine, Wednesday in St. Rémy, Thursday in Nyons, Saturday in Arles, and, best of all, Sunday in Isle sur la Sorgue. Crowds and parking problems abound at these popular events—arrive by 9:00 or, better, sleep in the town the night before.

Monday:	Cadenet (near Vaison la Romaine)
Tuesday:	Vaison la Romaine, Tarascon, Gordes
Wednesday:	St. Rémy, Arles, Violes (near Vaison la Romaine)
Thursday:	Nyons, Beaucaire, Vacqueyras, Isle sur la Sorgue
Friday:	Remoulins (Pont du Gard), Bonnieux Châteauneuf-du-Pape
Saturday:	Arles, Oppède, Valreas
Sunday:	Isle sur la Sorgue, Uzès, Coustelet

ARLES

By helping Julius Caesar defeat Marseille, Arles ea- nod and was made an important port city. With t the Rhône, Arles was a key stop on the Roman r

Spain, the Via Domitia. After reigning as a political center of the early Christian church (the seat of an archbishopric for centuries) and thriving as a trading city on and off until the 18th century, Arles all but disappeared from the map. Van Gogh settled here a hundred years ago, but left only memories. American bombers destroyed much of Arles in World War II, but today Arles thrives again. This compact city is alive with great Roman ruins, an eclectic assortment of museums, made-for-ice-cream pedestrian zones, and squares that play hide-and-seek with visitors.

Tourist Information: The TI at the train station is open only in summer (June–Sept 9:00–13:00, 14:00–18:00, closed Sun). The main TI is on the ring-road esplanade Charles de Gaulle (daily 9:00–18:40, in winter Mon–Sat 9:00–18:45, Sun 9:00–13:00, tel. 04 90 18 41 20). Pick up the good city map, the "Arles et Vincent Van Gogh" walking tour brochure (5F), the free *Guide Pratique*, and information on the Camargue Wildlife area. Ask about bullfights and bus excursions to regional sights.

Arrival in Arles

By Train and Bus: Both stations are next to each other on the river and a 10-minute walk from the center. Lockers are available at the train station. Get the bus schedule to Les Baux at the bus station (tel. 04 90 49 38 01). To reach the old town, walk to the river and turn left.

By Car: Follow signs to *centre-ville*, then follow signs toward the *gare SNCF* (train station). You'll come to a huge roundabout (place Lamartine) with a Monoprix department store to the right. Park along the city wall or in nearby lots (6F/hr, or 17F for 4 hrs; pay attention to no-parking signs on Wed and Sat until 13:00). Theft is a big problem. From place Lamartine, walk into the city through the two stumpy towers.

elpful Hints

ermarket: Place Lamartine has a big, handy Monoprix super-
et/department store (Mon–Sat 8:30–19:25, closed Sun).
anks: Several banks on place de la République across from
phime change money.
ndromats: One is at 12 rue Portagnel (daily 7:00–21:00).
nearby at 6 rue Cavalarie, near place Voltaire (daily
later once you're in), has a confusing central-com-
20F for wash (push machine number on top row),
nutes of dryer (push dryer number on 3rd row 5
F for flakes (button #11). Dine at the recom-
n restaurant (across the street, see "Eating in
le you clean.
There are two public pools in Arles. Ask at

Getting around Arles

Arles faces the Mediterranean and turns its back to Paris. Its
spaghetti street plan disorients the first-time visitor. Landmarks
hide in the medieval tangle of narrow, winding streets. Everything
is deceptively close. While Arles sits on the Rhône, it completely
ignores the river. The elevated riverside walk provides a direct
route to the excellent Ancient History Museum, an easy return
to the station, and fertile ground for poorly trained dogs. Hotels
have free city maps, but Arles works best if you simply follow
street-corner signs pointing you toward the sights and hotels of
the town center. Racing cars enjoy Arles' medieval lanes, turning
sidewalks into tightropes and pedestrians into leaping targets.

By Minibus: The free "Starlette" shuttle minibus circles the
town's major sights twice an hour, but does not serve the Ancient
History Museum so isn't very helpful (just wave at the driver and
hop in; Mon–Sat 7:30–19:30, never on Sun).

By Bike: While Vaison la Romaine and Isle sur la Sorgue
make better biking bases (see below), rides to Les Baux (very steep
climb) or into the Camargue work from Arles, providing you're in
great shape (forget it in the wind). The Peugeot store rents bikes
(15 rue du Pont, tel. 04 90 96 03 77), as does the newsstand next
to the main TI (tel. 04 90 96 44 20).

By Taxi: Arles' taxis charge a minimum flat 60F fee.
Nothing in town is worth a taxi ride (figure 110F to Les Baux,
tel. 04 90 96 90 03).

Car Rental: Rent a car at ADA (cheapest, 22 avenue
Stalingrad, tel. 04 90 07 87), Avis (at train station, tel. 04 90
96 82 42), and Europcar (downtown at 15 boulevard Victor
Hugo, tel. 04 90 93 23 24).

Sights—Arles' Museums

There are two monument passes with reduced entries to Arles'
many sights: one that covers all of the sights listed in this section
(65F, sold at each sight), or a 55F pass good for all Roman sights
but not the Arlaten or Reattu museums. Otherwise, it's 20F per
sight and museum (35F apiece for the Ancient History Museum
and the Arlaten folk museum). While any sight is worth a few
minutes, many aren't worth the individual admission. (All sights
except the Ancient History Museum and Arlaten folk museum
open June–mid-Sept 9:00–19:00; April–May and latter
9:00–12:30, 14:00–19:00; Oct–March 10:00–12:30, 1
See listings for the Ancient History Museum and M
below, for their hours.

▲▲▲Ancient History Museum (Musée de L'
Begin your visit of Arles in this superb, air-con
Models and original sculpture (with the help c
handout) re-create the Roman city of Arles,

Arles

EL REGENCE

DE L'AMPHITHEATRE

OU MUSEE

TROPHIME

NDAL

TAN

9 HOTEL TERMINUS ET VAN GOGH

10 L'ARLATAN RESTAURANT

11 LA GIRAUDIERE RESTAURANT

12 L'OLIVIER RESTAURANT

13 LA VITAMINE

14 LA PAILLOTTE RESTAURANT

15 LE CRIQUET RESTAURANT

16 LAUNDROMATS

and culture easier to imagine. Notice what a radical improvement the Roman buildings were over the simple mud-brick homes of pre-Roman peoples. Models of Arles' arena even illustrate the moveable stadium cover, good for shade and rain. While virtually nothing is left of Arles' chariot racecourse, the model shows that it must have rivaled Rome's Circus Maximus. Jewelry, fine metal and glass artifacts, and well-crafted mosaic floors make it clear that Roman Arles was a city of art and culture. The finale is an impressive row of pagan and early Christian sarcophagi (2nd to 5th centuries). In the early days of the Church, Jesus was often portrayed beardless and as the good shepherd—with a lamb over his shoulder.

Built at the site of the chariot racecourse, this museum is a 20-minute walk from Arles along the river. Turn left at the river and follow it to the big modern building just past the new bridge—or take bus #1 (5.20F) from boulevard des Lices and the TI (35F, daily 9:00–19:00 March–Oct, Nov–Feb 10:00–17:00, tel. 04 90 18 88 88).

▲▲▲**Roman Arena (Amphithéâtre)**—Nearly 2,000 years ago, gladiators fought wild animals here to the delight of 20,000 screaming fans—cruel. Today matadors fight wild bulls to the delight of local fans—still cruel. While the ancient third row of arches is long gone, three towers survive from medieval times, when the arena was used as a fortress. In the 1800s it corralled 200 humble homes and functioned as a town within the town. Climb the tower. Walk through the inner corridors of this 440-by-350-foot oval and notice the similarity to modern-day stadium floor plans. And if you don't mind the gore, a bullfight is an exciting show.

Classical Theater (Théâtre Antique)—Precious little survives from this Roman theater, which served as a handy town quarry throughout the Middle Ages. Two lonely Corinthian columns look from the stage out over the audience. The 10,000 mostly modern seats are still used for concerts and festivals. Take a stroll backstage through broken bits of Rome.

Musée Réattu—Highlights of this mildly interesting museum a a fun collection of 70 Picasso drawings (some two-sided and al' done in a flurry of creativity) and a room of Henri Rousseau' Camargue watercolors.

▲**Musée Arlaten**—This cluttered folklore museum, given t by Nobel prize winner Frederic Mistral (see "Place du For below), is filled with interesting odds and ends of Proven The employees wear the native costumes. It's like a faile the-century garage sale—shoes, hats, wigs, old photos. boards, and the beetle-dragon monster. If you're into museum is for you (35F, April–Sept daily 9:00–12.3' Oct–March closes at 17:00).

▲▲**St. Trophime Cloisters and Church**—T' after a third-century bishop of Arles, sports th west portal (main doorway) I've seen anywhe

But first enjoy the place de la République. Sit on the steps opposite the church. The **Egyptian obelisk** used to be the centerpiece of Arles' Roman Circus. Watch the peasants—pilgrims, locals, and street musicians. There's nothing new about this scene. Like a Roman triumphal arch, the church trumpets the promise of Judgment Day. The tympanum is filled with Christian symbolism. Christ sits in majesty, surrounded by symbols of the four evangelists (Matthew—the winged man, Mark—the winged lion, Luke—the ox, and John—the eagle). The Twelve Apostles are lined up below Jesus. Move closer. This is it. Some are saved and others aren't. Notice the condemned—a chain gang on the right bunny-hopping over the fires of hell. For them the tune trumpeted by the three angels on the very top isn't a happy one. Ride the exquisite detail back to a simpler age. In an illiterate medieval world long before the vivid images of our Technicolor time, this message was a neon billboard over this town's square. A chart just inside the church (on the right) helps explain the carvings. On the right side of the nave, a fourth-century early-Christian sarcophagus is used as an altar.

The adjacent **cloisters** are the best in Provence (20F, covered by pass, enter from square, 20 meters to right of church). Enjoy the sculpted capitals of the rounded Romanesque columns (12th century) and the pointed Gothic columns (14th century). The second floor offers only a view of the cloisters from above.

More Sights—Arles

▲▲**Place du Forum**—This café-crammed square is always lively and best at night. Named for the Roman Forum that stood here, only two columns from a second-century temple survive. They are incorporated into the wall of Hôtel Nord Pinus. Van Gogh lounged under these same plane trees—his *Le Café de Nuit* was painted from this square. The bistros on the square, while no place for a fine dinner, put together a good salad, and when you sprinkle the ambience, that's 50F well spent. The guy on the pedestal is Frederic Mistral; in 1904 he received the Nobel Prize for literature. He used his prize money to preserve and display the folk culture of Provence (by founding the Arlaten folk museum) at a time when France was rapidly centralizing.

Wednesday and Saturday Markets—On these days until noon, Arles' ring road erupts into an outdoor market of fish, flowers, produce, and you-name-it (boulevard Emile Combes on Wed, boulevard des Lices on Sat). Join in, buy flowers, try the olives, sample the cheeses, swat a pickpocket. On the first Wednesday of the month it's a grand flea market.

Fondation Van Gogh—A two-star sight for his fans, this small gallery features works by several well-known contemporary artists honoring Vincent through their thought-provoking interpretations. 30F, not covered by monument passes,

April–mid Oct daily 10:00–19:00, mid-Oct–March Tue–Sun 10:00–
12:30, 14:00–17:30, facing Roman arena at #24).
Van Gogh in Arles Self-Guided Walking Tour—The 5F
"Arles et Vincent Van Gogh" brochure (available at TI) describes
several interesting walks through Arles using pavement markers as
guides. By far the most worthwhile walk follows the footsteps of
Vincent van Gogh.
▲▲**Bullfights (Courses Camarguaise)**—Occupy the same seats
fans have been sitting in for nearly 2,000 years and take in one
of Arles' most memorable experiences—a bullfight *à la Provençale*.
Three classes of bullfights take place here. The *course protection* is
for aspiring matadors; it's a daring dodge-bull game of scraping hair
off the angry bull's nose for prize money offered by local businesses
(no blood). The *trophée de l'avenir* is the next class, with amateur
matadors. The *trophée des as excellence* is the real thing à la Spain:
outfits, swords, spikes, and the whole gory shebang (tickets 30–60F;
Easter–Oct Sat, Sun, and holidays; skip the "rodeo" spectacle, tel.
04 90 96 03 70 or ask at TI). There are nearby village bullfights in
small wooden bullrings nearly every weekend (TI has schedule).

Sleeping in Arles
(6.50F = about $1, country code: 33, zip code: 13200)
Sleep Code: **S** = Single, **D** = Double/Twin, **T** = Triple, **Q** = Quad,
b = bathroom, **t** = toilet only, **s** = shower only, **CC** = Credit Card
(**V**isa, **M**asterCard, **A**mex), **SE** = Speaks English, **NSE** = No
English, * = French hotel rating system (0–4 stars).
    Hotels are a great value here though few have elevators. If
you're sweating, get a room with air-conditioning. All except the
last are central.
    Hôtel Régence** sits on the river with immaculate and
comfortable rooms, good beds, safe parking, and easy access to
the train station. Helpful, gentle Sylvie speaks English (Db-200–
300F, Tb-260–360F, Qb-370F, choose river-view or quiet, air-
con courtyard rooms, most with cable TV, CC:VM, from place
Lamartine turn right immediately after passing through towers,
5 rue Marius Jouveau, tel. 04 90 96 39 85, fax 04 90 96 67 64).
    Hôtel Acacias**, next door, was just redone and is owned b
Hôtel Régence (above) The rooms are a bit small but provide
the comforts including cable TV, an elevator, and air-conditio
(Db-300–430F, Tb-455–485F, Qb-510F, CC:VM, 1 rue Mar
Jouveau, tel. 04 90 96 37 88, fax 04 90 96 32 51).
    Hôtel de l'Amphithéâtre**, a boutique hotel, is small,
friendly, and *très* cozy, with thoughtfully decorated, air-con
rooms and a pleasant atrium breakfast room. It's located o
from the arena toward place du Forum (Db-290–420F, T
parking-25F, CC:VMA, 5 rue Diderot, tel. 04 90 96 10
04 90 93 98 69, www.hotelamphitheatre.fr, SE).

Hôtel du Musée** is a quiet, delightful manor-home hideaway with comfortable air-conditioned rooms, a terrific two-tiered courtyard, and an art-gallery lounge. The rooms in the new section are worth the few extra francs. The relaxed Dubreuils speak some English (Sb-240–300F, Db-300–400F, Tb-390–420F, Qb-490F, parking-40F, CC:VMA, follow signs to Musée Réattu, 11 rue de la Grande Prieure, tel. 04 90 93 88 88, fax 04 90 49 98 15).

Hôtel St. Trophime** is another fine place with a grand entry, charming courtyard, broad halls, large rooms, and helpful owners (Db-300–350F, Tb-400F, huge Qb-450F, CC:VM, 16 rue de la Calade, near place de la République, tel. 04 90 96 88 38, fax 04 90 96 92 19).

Hôtel Calendal** should be three stars and is a better value than the Hôtel d'Arlatan (below). It's Provençal chic, with an exquisite outdoor garden, smartly decorated rooms, Internet access, and a seductive ambience (Db-350–480F, Tb-490F, Qb-530F, splurge for a room on the garden, CC:VMA, air-con, strong beds, modern bathrooms, parking-60F, just above the arena on rue Porte de Laure, tel. 04 90 96 11 89, fax 04 90 96 05 84, www .lecalendal.com, SE).

Hôtel d'Arlatan*** is classy yet affordable with a pleasant courtyard, air-conditioned, antique-filled rooms, and stiff staff. In the lobby of this 15th-century building, a glass floor looks down into Roman ruins (Db-500–850F, Db/suites-1,000–1,500F, CC:VMA, elevator, parking-70F, very central, a block off place du Forum at 26 rue du Sauvage, tel. 04 90 93 56 66, fax 04 90 49 68 45, www.hotel-arlatan.fr, SE).

Starving artists can afford these two clean but spartan places: friendly **Hôtel Voltaire*** rents 12 small rooms with great balconies overlooking a caffeine-stained square a block below the arena (D-160F, Ds-180F, Db-200F, 3rd or 4th person-50F each, CC:VM, 1 place Voltaire, tel. 04 90 96 49 18, fax 04 90 96 45 49). **Hôtel La Gallia**, with small but clean rooms, is a steal (Ds-140F, Db-150F, above lively café, 22 rue de l'Hôtel de Ville, tel. 04 90 96 00 63).

Hôtel Terminus et Van Gogh* has bright, cheery rooms cing a busy square at the gate of the old town, a block from the in station. This building appears in the painting of van Gogh's se; the artist's house was bombed in World War II (D-150F no shower available, Ds-185F, Db-225F, CC:VM, 5 place ⁓rtine, tel. & fax 04 90 96 12 32).

⁓ing near Arles

⁓ielle: Many drivers, particularly those with families, ⁓ing up in the peaceful countryside with good access ⁓'s sights. Just 10 minutes from Arles and Les Baux ⁓vignon) lies **Le Domaine de la Forêt**, a restored ⁓th modern apartments for five to six people (kitchen,

2 bedrooms, private terrace). Surrounded by vineyards and rice fields, this retreat offers a pool, swings, and a volleyball court. While most spend a full week, shorter stays are possible off-season (nightly-600F, weekly rental required in summer-3,500F, from Arles take the D-17 toward Fontvieille and look for **Gîtes Ruraux** signs, route de L'Aqueduc Romain, 13990 Fontvielle, tel. 04 90 54 70 25, fax 04 90 54 60 50, e-mail: BERARD.sylvie@wanadoo.fr).

Near Les Baux: Easier for short stays is the welcoming and kid-friendly **Mas de L'Esparou**, with three-star terraced *chambre d'hôte* rooms, a swimming pool, Ping-Pong, and distant views of Les Baux. Monsieur Roux painted the paintings in your room (Db-380F, extra person-100F, a few kilometers north of Maussane on D-5, look for sign, 13520 Les Baux de Provence, tel. & fax 04 90 54 41 32, NSE). If money is no object, the luxurious **Mas de l'Oulive***** is a sumptuous option. Wallow in the huge pool, lovely gardens, and posh common rooms, and gaze at Les Baux just above (Db-620–1,400F, extra bed-160F, on D-78, 13520 Les Baux de Provence, tel. 04 90 54 35 78, fax 04 90 54 44 31, www.masdeloulivie.com).

Eating in Arles

Great atmosphere and mediocre food at fair prices await on place du Forum. Elsewhere, near Hôtel Régence, **L'Arlatan** is unpretentious and friendly and serves a fine meal and great desserts (105F *menu*, opposite Laundromat on rue Cavalarie, closed Wed). Just up the street on the place Voltaire, **La Giraudiere** offers excellent regional cooking (115F *menu*, closed Tue, tel. 04 90 93 27 52). Near Hôtel du Musée, **L'Olivier** is my Arles splurge, offering exquisite *Provençale* cuisine (160F *menu*, 1 bis rue Reattu, reserve ahead, tel. 04 90 49 64 88). Vegetarians love **La Vitamine**'s salads and pastas (closed Sat–Sun, just below place du Forum on 16 rue Dr. Fanton, tel. 04 90 93 77 36). Almost next door, **La Paillotte** specializes in traditional *Provençale* cuisine (95F *menu*, 28 rue Dr. Fanton). **Le Criquet** is cheap, fun, and good (1 block from Hôtel Calendal at 12 Porte de Laure).

Transportation Connections—Arles

By bus to: Les Baux (4/day, 30 min; none on Sun, ideal departure about 8:30 with a return from Les Baux about 11:20 or 12:40, departs Arles bus station and 16 boulevard Clemenceau downtown, service reduced Nov–March, tel. 04 90 49 38 01).

By train to: Paris (2 direct TGVs, 4.5 hrs; otherwise transfer in Avignon, 8/day, 5.5 hrs), **Avignon** (8/day, 20 min, check for afternoon gaps), **Carcassonne** (8/day, 3 hrs, a few direct, most require a painless transfer in Narbonne), **Beaune** (7/day, 5 hrs, transfer in Lyon), **Nice** (8/day, 3.5 hrs, likely transfer in Marseille), **Barcelona** (3/day, 7 hrs, at least 1 transfer), **Italy** (3/day, via Marseille and Nice;

from Arles it's 5 hrs to Ventimiglia on the border, 9 hrs to the
Cinque Terre, 9 hrs to Milan, 11 hrs to Florence, or 13 hrs to
Venice or Rome). Train info: tel. 04 90 96 43 94.

AVIGNON

Famous for its nursery rhyme, medieval bridge, and brooding
Palace of the Popes, contemporary Avignon bustles and prospers
behind its mighty walls. During the 68 years (1309–1377) that
Avignon played Franco Vaticano, it grew from a quiet village
to the thriving city it still is. Today this city combines a huge
student population with a white-collar, sophisticated-city feel.
Street mimes play to international crowds enjoying Avignon's
sprawling cafés and chic boutiques. If you're here any time in
July, save evening time for Avignon's rollicking theater festival
and reserve your hotel early. Clean, polished, and popular
Avignon is more impressive for its outdoor ambience than its
museums and monuments. Come here to see its pope's palace,
then explore its thriving streets and beautiful vistas from the
Parc de Rochers des Doms.

Orientation

The cours Jean Jaurès (which turns into the rue de la République)
leads from the train station to place de l'Horloge and the Palace of
the Popes, splitting Avignon in two. The larger right (southern)
half is where the action is. Climb to the parc de Rochers des
Doms for a fine view, enjoy the people scene on place de l'Horloge, and meander the backstreets (see "Sights—Walking Tour Of
Avignon's Backstreets," below). Avignon's shopping district fills
the traffic-free streets where rue de la République meets place de
l'Horloge (creamy gelato just off place de l'Horloge, where St.
Agricol meets Joseph-Vernet). Walk across Pont Daladier (bridge)
for a great view of Avignon and the Rhône River.

 Tourist Information: The main TI is between the train
station and the old town at 41 cours Jean Juarés (Mon–Fri 9:00–
18:00, Sat–Sun 9:00–13:00, 14:00–17:00, longer hours during the
July festival, tel. 04 32 74 32 74, www.avignon-tourisme.com.fr).
A branch TI is inside the city wall at the entrance to Pont St.
Bénezet (May–Sept only, daily 9:00–18:00). Pick up the handy
Guide Pratique (info on car and bike rental, hotels, and museums)
as well as their Avignon discovery guide, which includes several
good (but tricky to follow) walking tours. The TI offers English-
language walking tours of Avignon (50F, Tue and Thu at 10:00).
They also have regional bus and train schedules to all destinations
described in this chapter and information on bus excursions
to popular regional sights (including the wine route, Luberon,
and Camargue). Note that most of Avignon's sights are closed
on Tuesdays.

Arrival in Avignon

By Train: Walk through the city walls onto the cours Jean Juarés (TI 3 blocks down at #41). The bus station (*gare routière*) and car rentals are 100 meters to the right of the train station, near the IBIS hotel.

By Car: Drivers enter Avignon following "centre-ville" signs. Park along the wall close to Pont St. Bénezet (ruined old bridge) and use that TI. Hotels have advice for smart overnight parking. Leave nothing in your car.

Sights—Avignon

▲**Palace of the Popes (Palais des Papes)**—In 1309 a French pope was elected (Pope Clement V). At the urging of the French king, His Holiness decided he'd had enough of unholy Italy. So he loaded his carts and moved north to peaceful Avignon for a steady rule under a supportive king. The Catholic Church literally bought Avignon, then a two-bit town, and popes resided here until 1403. From 1378 on, there were twin popes, one in Rome and one in Avignon, causing a split in the Catholic Church that wasn't fully resolved until 1417.

The pope's palace is two distinct buildings, one old and one older. Along with lots of big, barren rooms, you'll see frescoes, tapestries, and some beautiful floor tiles. The audiophone self-guided tours do a good job of overcoming the lack of furnishings and give a thorough history lesson while allowing you to tour this vast place at your own pace. Enjoy the view and windswept café at the tower (45–55F, occasional supplements for special exhibits, April–Oct daily 9:00–19:00, until 20:00 in summer, off-season 9:00–17:45, ticket office closes 1 hr earlier, tours in English twice daily March–Oct, call 04 90 27 50 74 to confirm).

▲**Musée du Petit Palais**—This palace superbly displays medieval Italian painting and sculpture. Since the Catholic Church was the patron of the arts, all 350 paintings deal with Christian themes. Visiting this museum before going to the Palace of the Popes gives you a sense of art and life during the Avignon papacy (30F, June–Sept Wed–Mon 10:00–12:00, 14:00–18:00, Oct–May Wed–Mon 9:30–13:00, 14:00–17:30, closed Tue).

▲**Parc de Rochers des Doms and Pont St. Bénezet**—Hike above the Palace of the Popes for a panoramic view over Avignon and the Rhône valley. At the far end, drop down a few steps for a good view of Pont St. Bénezet. This is the famous "sur le Pont d'Avignon," whose construction and location were inspired by a shepherd's religious vision. Imagine a 22-arch, 1,000-meter-long bridge extending across two rivers to that lonely Tower of Philippe the Fair, the bridge's former tollgate, on the distant side, (equally great view from that tower back over Avignon). The island the bridge spanned is now filled with campgrounds. You can pay 15F to walk along a section of the ramparts and do your own jig on the Pont St. Benezet (nice view, otherwise nothing special). The castle on the right, the St. André Fortress, was once another island in the Rhône. Cross Daladier Bridge for the best view of the old bridge and Avignon's skyline.

Fondation Angladon Dubrujeaud—This museum mixes a small but enjoyable collection of art from Post-Impressionists (including Cézanne, van Gogh, Daumier, Degas, and Picasso) with recreated art studios and furnishings from many periods. It's a quiet place with a few superb paintings (30F, Wed–Sun 13:00–18:00, closed Tue, 5 rue Laboureur).

Musée Calvet—This fine-arts museum impressively displays its good collection without any English explanations (30F, Wed–Mon 10:00–12:00, 14:00–18:00, closed Tue, on quieter northern half of Avignon at 65 rue Jospeh Vernet, its antiquities collection is a few blocks away at 27 rue de la République, same hours and ticket).

Walking Tour of Avignon's Backstreets—Use the TI's barely adequate, single-sheet-of-paper city map to navigate and the Avignon Discovery Guide (Strolling the Old Streets tour) to narrate this one-hour walk. Begin at the Agricol Perdiguier Park by the TI and work your way to the triangular place des Corps Saints. Walk up to the rue des Lices, turn right, then turn right again after about five minutes on the rue des Tenturiers, ground-zero in Avignon for all that's hip. Earthy cafés, cheap restaurants, galleries, and a small stream line this atmospheric street. Go as far as the waterwheel then return, crossing back over the rue des Lices. Now angle up rue de la Bonterre to the modern market hall, Les Halles (produce, meats, fish until 12:30). Cross over to the cafés of place Pie, then up rue Gal Leclerc. Make a left on rue Carnot, then veer right on the first street, rue Peyrolle, and continue to place des Chataignes. Work your way around the church of St. Pierre to charming place St. Pierre (recommended restaurant, L'Épicerie, see "Eating," below). Then head back down to place Carnot and enter Avignon's thriving network of pedestrian streets.

Sleeping in Avignon
(6.50F = about $1, country code: 33, zip code: 84000)
Hotel values in Avignon pale in comparison to Arles. These hotels are listed in the order you would pass them from the train station. The first three are a right turn off the cours Jean Jaurés on rue Agricol Perdiguier.

At **Hôtel Splendid***, friendly Madame Prel-Lemoine rents firm beds in good rooms for a fair price near the station (Db-210F–290F, on small park near TI, 17 rue Agricol Perdiguier, tel. 04 90 86 14 46, fax 04 90 85 38 55). Across the street at #18, **Hôtel du Parc**'s tastefully designed rooms with small beds are a good value (D-170–210F, Ds-220–270F, Db-230–290F, tel. 04 90 82 71 55, fax 04 90 85 64 86).

Hôtel Colbert**, one block down, is a simple two-star hotel with air-conditioning and cheap rates (Sb-190–260F, Db-240–340F, Tb-270–370F, 7 rue Agricol Perdiguier, tel. 04 90 86 20 20, fax 04 90 85 97 00).

Hôtel Blauvac** offers cozy rooms with stone walls in an old manor home near the pedestrian zone (Sb-350–400F, Db-380–470F, Tb/Qb-470–550F, CC:VMA, 1 block off rue de la République, 11 rue de La Bancasse, tel. 04 90 86 34 11, fax 04 90 86 27 41).

Hôtel Danieli** is a hello-dolly fluff-ball of a place with good modern rooms needing new carpeting (Db-330–475F, Tb-470–570F, CC:VM, tel. 04 90 86 46 82, fax 04 90 27 09 24).

Hôtel Medieval** is a fine value in an old mansion with friendly owners. Kitchenettes are in all of its unimaginative but comfortable and fairly spacious rooms (Db-250–360F, Tb-390F, extra bed-50F, 5 blocks east of place de l'Horloge, behind Église St. Pierre, 15 rue Petite Saunerie, tel. 04 90 86 11 06, fax 04 90 82 08 64).

For predictable, ultramodern comfort with air-conditioning and a great location, try one of two **Hôtel Mercures***** (Db-550–650F). One is just inside the walls near Pont St. Bénezet (Quartier de la Balance, tel. 04 90 80 93 93, fax 04 90 80 93 94); the other is within spitting distance of the Palace of the Popes and has many rooms with good views (Cité des Papes, 1 rue Jean Vilar, tel. 04 90 80 93 00, fax 04 90 80 93 01, e-mail: H1952 @accor-hotels.com).

You'll find dirt cheap beds across Pont Daladier on the Island (*Île de la*) Barthelasse at the **Auberge Bagatelle's hostel/ campground**, which has a pool, laundry, a cheap café, and campers for neighbors (dorm bed-64F, Ile de la Barthelasse, tel. 04 90 86 30 39).

Eating in Avignon
L'Épicerie, charmingly located on a tiny square a few blocks east of place de l'Horloge, offers a good selection of à la carte items (open daily, 10 place St. Pierre, tel. 04 90 82 74 22). I also like strolling the cafés that line the rue des Tenturiers (see "Sights—Walking Tour of Avignon's Backstreets," above), where you'll find several inexpensive places.

Transportation Connections—Avignon
By train to: Arles (8/day, 20 min), **Orange** (hrly, 15 min), **Nîmes** (hrly, 20 min), **Isle sur la Sorgue** (6/day, 30 min), **Nice** (10/day, 4 hrs; a few direct, most require transfer in Marseille), **Carcassonne** (8/day, 3 hrs, possible transfer in Narbonne), **Lyon** (14/day, 2.5 hrs),

Paris' Gare du Lyon (10 TGVs/day, 4 hrs), **Barcelona** (2/day, 5 hrs, possible transfer in Narbonne; direct night train is convenient).

By bus to Pont du Gard (6/day in summer, 4/day off-season, 40 min): The stop is at Auberge Blanche, a 15-minute walk from Pont du Gard (STD Gard buses, tel. 04 66 29 27 29). Off-season service can leave you stranded for hours. Consider visiting Pont du Gard, continuing on to Nîmes or Uzès (both merit exploration), and returning to Avignon from there. Try these plans: Take the 12:00 bus from Avignon, arriving at Pont du Gard at 12:45. Then take either the 14:45 bus from there to Nîmes, where trains run hourly back to Avignon, or a 16:00 bus (Mon–Fri) on to Uzès, arriving at 16:30, with a return bus to Avignon at 18:30. Make sure you're waiting for the bus on the right side of the road at the Pont du Gard Auberge Blanche stop (ask at the small inn: "*Nîmes? Uzès? Avignon? Par ici?*"). The Avignon TI should have schedules. Service is reduced or non-existent on Sunday and holidays. In Avignon, the bus station (tel. 04 90 82 07 35) is adjacent to the train station.

By bus to other regional destinations: St. Rémy (6/day, 45 min, handy way to visit its Wed market); **Isle sur la Sorgue** (5/day, 45 min); **Vaison la Romaine, Sablet**, and **Seguret** (all 2/day, 75 min); **Gordes** (via Cavaillon, 1/day, very early, 2 hrs, spend the night or taxi back to Cavaillon); **Nyons** (2/day, 2 hrs).

Sights—Provence

A car is a dream come true here. Below I've described key sights and two full-day excursions deep into the countryside (see "Villages of the Côtes du Rhône" and "Hill Towns of the Luberon," below), both better done as overnights. Les Baux and St. Rémy work well by car with the Luberon excursion. Orange ties in tidily with a trip to the Côtes du Rhône villages. The Pont du Gard is on the way to/from Languedoc for drivers. Nondrivers are better off choosing Côtes du Rhône villages over Luberon villages for their rural Provençal experience. However you tour this magnificent area, notice the wind-buffeting rows of bamboo and cypress and how buildings are oriented south, with few or no windows facing north.

▲▲▲**Les Baux**—This rock-top ghost town is worth visiting for the lunar landscape alone. Arrive by 9:00 or after 17:00 to avoid ugly crowds. A 12th-century regional powerhouse with 6,000 fierce residents, Les Baux was razed in 1632 by a paranoid Louis XIII, who was afraid of these troublemaking upstarts. What remains is a reconstructed "live city" of tourist shops and snack stands and the "dead city" ruins carved into, out of, and on top of a 200-meter-high rock. Spend your time in the dead city—best in the morning or early-evening light. Don't miss the slideshow on van Gogh, Gaugin, and Cézanne in the small chapel near the entry. Spend some time in the small museum as you enter (good exhibits) and pick up the English explanations. In the tourist-trampled live city, you'll find shops, some Renaissance homes, and a fine exhibit of paintings by Yves Brayer (20F), who spent his final years here (39F for dead city, includes entry to all the town's sights, Easter–Oct 9:00–19:00, until 20:00 in summer, Nov–Easter 9:30–17:00, pick up the interesting brochure, "A Sense of Place," at TI, tel. 04 90 54 34 39). To best experience the bauxite rock quarries and a great view of Les Baux, go one kilometer up D-27 and sample wines with atmosphere at **Caves de Sarragnan** (until 19:00, tel. 04 90 54 33 58). Nearby, **Cathedrale d'Images** uses 48 projectors showing 3,000 images inside a rock quarry to immerse its visitors in themes from the region (43F, daily 10:00–18:00, just above Les Baux on the D-27). If you're tempted to spend the night, try the enchanting **Hôtel Reine Jeanne****, 50 meters to your right after the main entry to the live city (Db-280–380F, great family suite-550F, ask for a *chambre avec terasse*, CC:VM, good *menus* from 110F, 13520 Les Baux, tel. 04 90 54 32 06, fax 04 90 54 32 33).

Four daily buses serve Les Baux from the Arles bus station (see "Transportation Connections—Arles," above).

St. Rémy—This chic Provençal town is a scenic ride over the hill from Les Baux. Here you'll find a thriving Wednesday market (until 13:00), the sprawling, crumbled ruins of Glanum, and the mental ward where Vincent van Gogh was sent after cutting off his ear.

Glanum—This was a once-thriving Roman city located at the crossroads of two ancient trade routes between Italy and Spain. The setting is beautiful. Walk to the gate and peek in to appreciate its size. The ruins are worth the effort if you haven't been to Pompeii or Ephesus. Get the English handout (35F, April–Sept daily 9:00–12:00, 14:00–19:00, Oct–March 9:30–12:00, 14:00–17:00). Across the street, opposite the entrance, is a Roman arch and tower. The arch marked the entry into Glanum. The tower is a memorial to the grandsons of Emperor Augustus.

Across the street from Glanum is the still-functioning mental hospital that took care of van Gogh: **St Paul de Mausole Monastery** (Clinique St. Paul). Wander into the small chapel and intimate cloisters. Vincent's favorite walks outside the hospital are signposted. Glanum and the Clinique St. Paul are 800 meters from St. Rémy on the road to Les Baux (D-5).

In St. Rémy, sleep dead center at the simple **Hôtel du Cheval Blanc**** (Db-290–310F, CC:VM, streetside rooms are noisy, 6 avenue Fauconnet, tel. 04 90 92 09 28, fax 04 90 92 69 05) or just east of town at the tranquil and comfortable **Canto Cigalo** (Db-290–360F, extra bed-100F, chemin Canto Cigalo, tel. 04 90 92 14 28, fax 04 90 92 24 48, e-mail: hotel.cantocigalo@wanadoo.fr).

▲▲▲**Pont du Gard**—One of Europe's great treats, this perfectly preserved Roman aqueduct was built before the time of Christ. It was the missing link of a 35-mile canal that, by dropping one foot for every 300, supplied 44 million gallons of water to Nîmes daily. Study it up close. There's no mortar—just expertly cut stones. Signs direct you to "panoramas" above the bridge on either side. The best view of the aqueduct is from the cool of the river below, floating flat on your back—bring a swimsuit and sandals for the rocks (always open and free). Consider renting a canoe from Collas to Remoulins, ending at the Pont du Gard (2-hr trip, 185F per 2-person canoe; shuttle to bus stop, car park, or Remoulins included; Collas Canoes, tel. 04 66 22 85 54).

Buses run to Pont du Gard from Nîmes, Uzès, and Avignon. Combine Uzès (see below) and Pont du Gard for an ideal day excursion from Avignon (see "Transportation Connections—Avignon," above). By car, Pont du Gard is an easy 30-minute drive due west of Avignon (follow signs to Nîmes) and 45 minutes northwest of Arles (via Tarascon). Park on the *rive gauche* side (you'll see signs) and leave nothing in your car.

Uzès—An intriguing, less-trampled town near Pont du Gard, Uzès is best seen slowly on foot, with a long coffee break in its mellow main square, the place aux Herbes (not so mellow during the colorful Sunday-morning market). You can tour the round Tour Fenestrelle (all that remains of a 12th-century cathedral) and the palace of the Duché de Uzès (55F, French-only tour, get English handout). Uzès is a short hop west (by bus) of Pont du Gard and is well served by bus from Nîmes (9/day) and Avignon (3/day). Uzès is officially in Languedoc, not Provence.

The Camargue—This is one of the few truly "wild" areas of France, where pink flamingos, wild bulls, and the famous white horses wander freely amid rice fields, lagoons, and mosquitoes. It's a three-star sight for nature lovers and boring for others. The D-37 that follows the Étang du Vaccares has some of the best viewing. The Camargue's biggest town is Aigue Mortes. That means "dead town," and it should stay that way.

▲▲Orange—This most northern town in Provence is notable for its Roman arch and theater. The 20-meter-tall Roman Arc de Triomphe (from 25 B.C., north of city center) honors Julius Caesar's defeat of the Gauls in 49 B.C., but is lightweight compared to its best-preserved Roman theater (*Théâtre Antique*) in existence. Find a seat up high to appreciate the acoustics and contemplate that 2,000 years ago Orange residents enjoyed grand spectacles with high-tech sound and lights affects like thunder, lightning, and rain. A huge awning could be unfurled from that awesome 40-meter-high stage wall to provide shade that you might appreciate right now. It still seats 10,000 (30F, April–Sept 30 daily 9:00–18:30, Oct–March 9:00–12:00, 13:30–17:00; ticket includes entrance to city museum across street, which has more

Roman art; Orange TI tel. 04 90 34 70 88). Trains run hourly
between Avignon and Orange (15 min). From Orange's train station to the old town and theater, it's a 20-minute walk or 10-
minute ride on bus #2. Buses to Vaison la Romaine and other wine
villages depart from the big square, place Pourtoules (turn right
out of the theater and keep right).

Villages of the Côtes du Rhône:
A Loop Trip for Wine and Village Lovers

If you have a car (or a bike, best rented in Vaison la Romaine—
good riding from here unless it's windy) and a fondness for fine
wine or beautiful countryside, take this loop trip through
Provence's Côtes du Rhône wine country. Endless vineyards,
impressive mountains, and old stone villages form the landscape.
While this trip is doable as a day trip by car from Avignon or
Arles, you won't regret a night in one of the villages listed below
(Vaison la Romaine makes the best base—see "Sleeping in Vaison
la Romaine," below—and is ideal if you're heading to or coming
from the north). From Avignon, go to Carpentras and then con-
nect the wine villages of Vacqueyras, Gigondas, Rasteau, Sablet,
Vaison la Romaine, Rasteau, and adorable, if almost too perfect,
Seguret (figure on a 100-kilometer round-trip from Avignon;
2 buses/day from Avignon and Orange follow a similar route).
The tiny, twisty D-90 between Baumes de Venise and Malaucene
is spectacular. This is a hospitable and relaxed wine-tasting region.
Each village seems to have a *Caveau des Vignerons* (wine-maker
cooperative), which are easy places to sample a variety of wines.
Near Rasteau village, at **Le Domaine des Girasols**, friendly
Francoise or John (SE) will take your palate on a tour of some
of the area's best wine. It's well marked and worth a stop, and
while you aren't pressured to buy, their wine is a good value.

　　The less-traveled Dromme region just north of Vaison la
Romaine is ideal if you're continuing to the Alps or if you're here
in July when lavender blooms. It's laced with vineyards (producing
less-expensive yet good wines), lavender fields, and still more post-
card-perfect villages. From Vaison take the loop north to Visan,
Valreas, Taulignan, and Nyons, and then back to Vaison. Pleasant
Nyons is France's olive capital and hosts a massive Thursday-
morning market. Each village is a detour waiting to happen.

Sleeping, Eating, and Wine Tasting
in the Wine Country

For more listings, see "Vaison la Romaine," below.
　　Gigondas: This trendy village, nestled enviably at the base
of the Dentelles de Montmirail mountains, produces some of the
region's best wines. Several good tasting opportunities are on its
small square. Consider **Le Caveau des Vignerons**, with its vast

selection, nifty micro-bottle samples, and a donation-if-you-don't-buy system (daily 10:00–12:00, 14:00–19:00). **L'Oustalet**'s shady wooden tables are the place to savor a slow lunch (tel. 04 90 65 85 30), though **Chez Jacques et Monique Café** has view tables, a salad bar, and *plats du jour*. The info-packed **TI** (on the main square, rue du Portail, tel. 04 90 65 85 46) has a list of area *chambres d'hôtes* and good hikes into the mountains (the blue route takes you on a scenic 3-hr loop from the TI). Don't miss the view from the small church above the village or the spectacular drive past the recommended Hostellerie les Florets to the trailhead for the Col du Cayron (good hike up the dirt road). The comfortable and peaceful **Hostellerie les Florets*****, one kilometer above the village, is the complete refuge and a good value. It's huddled at the foot of the Dentelles de Montmirail peaks, with a huge, shady terrace, thoughtfully appointed rooms, and an exceptional restaurant (Db-460F, Tb-560F, annex rooms are best, *menus* from 140F, 84190 Gigondas, tel. 04 90 65 85 01, fax 04 90 65 83 80).

Sablet: This wine village, while impressive from a distance, has little of interest except scads of good *chambres d'hôtes*. Sablet wines are good (the TI and wine cooperative share space in the town center) and its location is central on the wine route. **Madame Fert's** *chambres* are bird-chirping peaceful with a small pool and common kitchen, garden tables, and a good location close to many hiking trails (Db-350F, includes breakfast, well-signed directions from center, 1 kilometer outside of town, tel. & fax 04 90 46 94 77). Consider hiking to Seguret from here.

Seguret: Flawless little Seguret has a smattering of shops, two cafés, and a natural spring. Come here for vistas and a quiet lunch. The unpretentious **Café des Poternes** and the full-service restaurant **Le Mesclun** are good lunch options. **La Bastide Bleue** is a bright, stone, blue-shutter Provençal with seven good rooms at great prices and a well-respected restaurant (Db-280F, just below Seguret, route de Sablet, tel. & fax 04 90 46 83 43).

Nyons: Hôtel Colombet***, right on Nyons' main square, is a great value with air-conditioning, big, comfy rooms, and a backyard terrace (Db-330–480F, CC:VM, 53 place de la Liberation, tel. 04 75 26 03 66, fax 04 75 26 42 37).

Vaison la Romaine

With bus service from Avignon and Orange, quick access to smaller villages (by car or bike), and vineyards knocking at its door, this thriving town makes a great base for exploring the Côtes du Rhône region. You get two villages for the price of one: Vaison's "modern" lower city is like a mini Arles, with worthwhile Roman ruins, a lone pedestrian street, and too many cars. The medieval hill town is perched above and is car-free, with meandering cobbled lanes, art galleries, cafés, and a ruined castle (good view from its base).

Orientation

The city is split in two by the Ouveze River. The newer city (Ville-Basse) lies on its right bank; the medieval city (Ville-Haute) sits above on the left bank. The impressive Roman bridge connects the two.

Tourist Information: The superb TI is in the newer city, between the Roman ruins at place de Chanoine Sautel. At the TI, get times of English tours of the Roman ruins, ask about festivals and bike rental, and say *bonjour* to charming Valery who has worked here for 15 years (May–Sept Mon–Sat 9:00–12:30 and 14:00–18:45, Sun 9:00–12:00; Oct–April Mon–Sat 9:00–12:30 and 14:00–17:45, closed Sun, tel. 04 90 36 02 11, www.vaison-la-romaine.com).

Arrival in Vaison la Romaine: Walk five minutes down avenue De Gaulle to reach the TI. Drivers park free across from the TI.

Bike Rental: You can rent bikes at Lacombe on avenue Jules Ferry (tel. 04 90 36 03 29).

Sights—Vaison la Romaine

Market Day—The lively Tuesday market (until 12:30) is worth organizing your trip and parking plans around.

Roman Ruins—If you've seen Pompeii, this will seem like small potatoes, but the remains of Vaison's two Roman sights—La Villasse and Puymin—are well-presented and give a good picture of life during the Roman Empire. Gaze up at the medieval city for a visual statement of what happened after the fall of the Empire (English tours available April–Sept, several days/week, usually at 11:00, check with TI, or get informative English handout and do tour on your own). The museum inside the ruins has English explanations (41F, includes both ruins and cloister at cathedral, Notre Dame de Nazareth; daily June–Sept 9:30–18:30, Oct–March 10:00–13:00, 14:30–18:00, Nov–Feb closes at 16:00). If it's summer, ask at the TI about sound-and-light shows at the ruins.

Wine Tasting—Cave la Romaine, a five-minute walk up avenue General de Gaulle from the TI, offers a variety of great-value wines from nearby villages in a pleasant, well-organized tasting room (daily 8:30–13:00, 14:00–19:00, avenue St. Quenin, tel. 04 90 36 55 90).

Sleeping in Vaison la Romaine
(6.50F = about $1, country code: 33, zip code: 84110)

Hotels here are a good value. Those in the medieval town (Ville-Haute) are quieter, cozier, cooler, and a 15-minute walk uphill from the TI (parking available nearby).

Hôtel Burrhus**, easily the best value in the lower city, is right in the thick of things with a huge, shady terrace over the raucous place Montfort (Db-290–330F, extra bed-50F, ask for a 'oom off the square if you want to sleep, tel. 04 90 36 00 11, fax 04 90 36 39 05). Ask about their adjacent and more cushy **Hôtel des Lis***** (Db-290–460F, contact Hôtel Burrhus for reservations and reception). **Le Brin d'Olivier** has a few nice rooms just below the pedestrian street (Db-400–450F, 4 rue du Ventoux tel. 04 90 28 74 79, fax 04 90 36 13 36).

The next two listings are in the Ville-Haute. **Hôtel Beffroi***** is red-tile-and-wood-beamed classy with spacious rooms (some with views), a restaurant, and cozy public spaces (Db-470–660F, C:VM, *menus* from 145F though I enjoy their cheaper garden *menu*, rue de l'Eveche, tel. 04 90 36 04 71, fax 04 90 36 24 78, www.le-beffroi .com). **La Fête en Provence**'s *chambres* sit above a good restaurant and look onto a stone courtyard (Db-300–450F, huge duplex sleeps up to 5 people-700F, CC:VM, place du Vieux Marche, tel. 04 90 36 36 43, fax 04 90 36 21 49).

Château Taulignan's *chambres d'hôte*, with six large rooms, offer a kid-friendly and dreamy setting from which to contemplate this beautiful region. Enjoy the big pool, Ping-Pong, and picnic tables (Db-450–550F, 84110 St. Marcellin, tel. 04 90 28 71 16, fax 04 90 28 75 04, e-mail: chateau@pacwan.fr). It's just five minutes from Vaison's TI; follow Carpentras signs and look for brown *chambres d'hôte* signs just as you leave Vaison.

A few kilometers away, below spectacularly situated Crestet (follow Malaucene from Vaison), **l'Ermitage Chambres** is run by British ex-pats Nick and Nicole, who were born for this business. They have renovated a fine old mansion with three big, simple rooms, firm beds, and a pool with magnificent views (Db-350F, turn right off D-938 at Loupiotte restaurant, 84110 Crestet, tel. 04 90 28 88 29).

Eating in and near Vaison la Romaine

La Bartavelle is the place to savor a slow meal in the lower city (145F *menu*, 12 place sus-Auze). **Le Brin d'Olivier** is also excellent (*menus* from 140F, see "Sleeping," above). The Ville-Haute has a view *crêperie* and a pizzeria with fair prices. I enjoy the cool garden café at **Hôtel Beffroi** (60–70F dinner salads and pastas, views and serenity, rue de l'Eveche). The best view in Provence might well be from the simple **Restaurant Le Panorama** in tiny Crestet, a five-minute drive from Vaison la Romaine (cheap *menus* or simple *à la carte*, absolutely call ahead, tel. 04 90 28 86 62), though the roadside **Restaurant Loupiote** (below Crestet on D-938) is where locals go.

Transportation Connections— Vaison la Romaine

The most central bus stop is at Cave Vinicole. **By bus to: Avignon** (2/day, 90 min), **Orange** (3/day, 45 min). Bus info: tel. 04 90 36 09 90.

NOT QUITE A YEAR IN PROVENCE: THE HILL TOWNS OF LUBERON

The Luberon region, stretching 50 kilometers along a ridge of rugged hills east of Avignon, hides some of France's most appealing and popular hill towns. Bonnieux, Lacoste, Oppède le Vieux, Roussillon, and the very-discovered (and overpriced) Gordes, to mention a few, are quintessential Provençal hill towns.

Those intrigued by Peter Mayle's *A Year in Provence* will enjoy a day joyriding through the region. Mayle's best-selling book describes the ruddy local culture from an Englishman's perspective as he buys an old home, fixes it up, and adopts the region as his new home. This is a great read while you're here.

The Luberon terrain in general (much of which is a French regional natural park) is as appealing as its hill towns. Gnarled vineyards and wind-sculpted trees separate tidy stone structures from abandoned buildings—little more than rock piles—that seem to challenge city slickers to fix them up.

The wind is an integral part of life here. The infamous *mistral*, finishing its long ride in from Siberia, hits like a hammer—hard enough, it's said, to blow the ears off a donkey. Throughout the region you'll see houses designed with windowless walls facing the mistral. Walking from village to village is a popular pastime here—local TIs have trail information.

Planning Your Time

To enjoy the windblown ambience of the Luberon, plan a leisurely day trip visiting three or four of the characteristic towns (impossible *sans* car). Isle sur la Sorgue, located halfway between Avignon and the Luberon, has train service from Avignon (easy day trip) and Nice (via Marseilles transfer) and makes a good biking base.

For the ultimate Luberon experience, hill town connoisseurs should bypass Isle sur la Sorgue and sleep in one of the villages described below. The famous villages are beautiful but attract tourists like flypaper. For a pure and peaceful overnight, sleep in Oppède le Vieux, Goult, or Lacoste, where you'll find *chambres d'hôtes*, but no hotels (see "Sleeping in or near Roussillon," below).

Getting around the Luberon

By Bus: To reach the hill towns such as Roussillon, go to Cavaillon or Apt then taxi (1 bus/day from Avignon to Gordes, 2 buses/day from Cavaillon to Gordes, bus tel. 04 90 71 03 00).

By Train: Arrive in Isle sur la Sorgue from Avignon (6/day, 30 min) or from Nice (4/day, 4 hrs, transfer in Marseille). Isle sur la Sorgue's train station is called l'Isle Fontaine de Vaucluse.

By Car: Town-hop for a day, side tripping from your home base, or visit these villages as a detour en route to the French Riviera. Of course, tumbling in for an hour from the car park, you'll be just another flash-in-the-pan, camera-toting Provence fan. Spend a night and you'll feel more a part of the scene. You need the local Michelin map to follow this scenic loop: Take the N-100 east of Avignon toward Apt and find little Lagnes just after Isle sur la Sorgue. Go through Lagnes, then Cabrieres d'Avignon, Gordes, Goult, and Roussillon.

Luberon

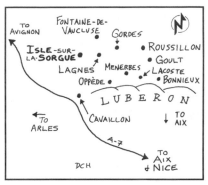

From Roussillon, follow Bonnieux and cross the Roman Pont Julien, then find Lacoste, Menerbes, and, to complete the loop, Oppède le Vieux. I've listed places to sleep and eat in several of these villages (see below).

Isle sur la Sorgue

This sturdy market town, literally, "Island on the Sorgue River," sits within a split in its happy little river. (Do not confuse it with the nearby plain town of Sorgue.) While Isle sur la Sorgue is renowned for its market days, it is otherwise a pleasantly average flat town with no important sights and a steady trickle of tourism. It's quiet at night and dead on Mondays.

With clear water babbling under pedestrian bridges decorated with flower boxes and its old-time carousel always spinning, Isle sur la Sorgue erupts into a market frenzy, with hearty crafts and local produce, each Sunday and Thursday (the Sunday market is more impressive and renowned for its antiques; the Thursday market is more intimate).

Navigate the town by its mossy waterwheels, which, while still turning, power only memories of the town's wool and silk industries. The 12th-century church with a festive Baroque interior seems too big for its town.

Tourist Information: The TI, next door to the church, has a line on rooms in private homes, all of which are outside the town (Tue–Sat 9:00–12:30, 14:00–18:00, Sun 9:00–12:30, closed Mon, tel. 04 90 38 04 78).

Bike/Car Rental: Rent mountain bikes at Plein Air Location, 30 meters in front of the train station (60F/half day, 100F/day, tel. 04 90 38 25 80, cellular 06 83 37 04 90), and cars at Avis at the train station. These places make good biking destinations: Velleron (8 flat kilometers away, it's a tiny version of Isle sur la Sorgue, with waterwheels, fountains, and an evening farmer's market Mon-Sat 18:00–20:00); Lagnes (5 mostly flat kilometers away), it's a pretty, well-restored hill town with views from its ruined château; see "Sleeping near Isle sur la Sorgue," below); and Fontaine de Vaucluse (11 uphill kilometers away, see "Villages of the Luberon," below).

Sleeping in and near Isle sur la Sorgue
(6.50F = about $1, country code: 33, zip code: 84800)
Arrive the night before market day to best experience Isle sur la Sorgue. Drivers may prefer sleeping in a quieter Luberon village listed below. There's a **Laundromat** on l'impasse de la République (open 8:00–20:00).

Hôtel les Nevons**, two blocks from the center (behind the PTT—post office) is motel-modern outside. Inside, however, it seems to do everything right, with comfortable, air-conditioned rooms (a few family suites), a small rooftop pool, Internet access, and eager-to-please owners, Mireille and Jean-Philipe (Db-310–320F, Tb/Qb-480F, easy and secure parking, 205 Chemin des Nevons, tel. 04 90 20 72 00, fax 04 90 20 56 20, www.hotel-les-nevons.com). The bargain beds in town are sufficiently clean and quiet and above a local bar at **Hôtel Le Cours** (D-130F, Db-190F, place Gambetta, tel. 04 90 38 01 18). **Hôtel Le Pescador***, 1.5 kilometers from the center toward Apt on the Sorgue River, is peaceful and reasonable with a good restaurant (Db-210–300F, Le Partage des Eaux, tel. 04 90 38 09 69, fax 04 90 38 27 80). In nearby adorable Lagnes, **Le Grand Jas'** *chambre d'hôte* has a pool and four fine rooms in a beautiful stone farmhouse across from a ruined castle (Db-320–420F, 84800 Lagnes, tel. 04 90 20 25 12, fax 04 90 20 29 17).

Eating in and near Isle sur la Sorgue
Begin any meal with a glass of wine at the cozy **Le Caveau de la Tour de l'Isle**—part wine bar, part wine shop (12 rue de la République). **L'Oustau de l'Isle** is well-suited for a fine dinner (*menus* from 140F, closed Wed–Thu off-season, near post office, 21 avenue des 4 Otages, tel. 04 90 38 54 83). The riverfront cafés, **Café de la Sorgue** and **Café de Bellevue**, offer fair cuisine with maximum ambience. For a true Provençal experience, head three kilometers toward Velleron to **La Villa** and dine poolside. Mama cooks and Jerome serves a limited but flawless *menu* (115F, no CC, reservations necessary, kid-perfect, tel. 04 90 38 25 50).

Roussillon
With all the trendy charm of Santa Fe on a hilltop, this town will cost you at least a roll of film (and 15F for parking). Climb a few minutes from either car park, past the picture-perfect square and under the church to the summit of the town (signs to *castum*), where a dramatic view, complete with a howling *mistral* and an

interesting *table d'orientation*, awaits. Then, back under the church, see how local (or artsy) you can look over a cup of coffee on what must be the most scenic village square in the Luberon. On the south end of town, beyond the upper parking lot, a brilliant ochre canyon (10F)—formerly a quarry—stands ready for those who wish they were in Utah's Bryce Canyon. You could paint the entire town without ever leaving the red and orange corner of your palette. Many do. Thursday is Roussillon's market day.

Sleeping in or near Roussillon
(6.50F = about $1, country code: 33, zip code: 84220)
The **TI**, across from the David restaurant, posts a list of hotels and *chambres d'hôte* (April–Oct Mon–Sat 10:00–12:00, 14:00–18:00, Sun 14:00–18:00, tel. 04 90 05 60 25). Just below the charm, near the north-side lower parking, is the appealing **Hôtel Reves d'Ocres**** with helpful owners (Db-400F, Tb-500F, balcony room-50F extra, CC:VM, air-con, tel. 04 90 05 60 50, fax 04 90 05 79 74). **Madame Cherel** rents simple but clean rooms with firm mattresses and a common view terrace (D-200F, 3 blocks from upper parking lot, between gas station and school, tel. 04 90 05 68 47). Cherel speaks English, is a wealth of regional travel tips, and rents mountain bikes to guests only (100F/day). The *chambre d'hôte* **Les Huguets**, three kilometers from Roussillon on D-108 toward Bonnieux, is friendly and comfortable (Db-280–310F, includes breakfast, les Passiflores, tel. & fax 04 90 05 69 61, friendly Chantal). **Hôtel Les Sables d'Ocre**** is kid-friendly with modern rooms, a big pool, lots of grass, and reasonable rates (Db-320F, Db with garden balcony-420F, Tb-550F, 1.5 kilometers from Roussillon toward Apt, tel. 04 90 05 55 55, fax 04 90 05 55 50).

La Ferme de la Huppe*** hides down in the valley between Roussillon and Gordes and is my Luberon splurge. This country-classy, hacienda-like farmhouse offers all the comfort and then some—a slick pool and restaurant worthy of a long detour (Db-400–750F, extra bed-150F, *menus* from 150F, CC:VM, Route D-156, 84220, Gordes, tel. 04 90 72 12 25, fax 04 90 72 01 83, www.laprovence.com/lahuppe/).

More Luberon Towns
Fontaine de Vaucluse—You'll read and hear a lot about this sublimely located village at the source of the river Sorgue where Petrarch mourned for his love Laura. This beautiful river seems to magically appear from nowhere (the actual source is a murky green water hole) and flows through Fontaine de Vaucluse, past a lineup of cafés, souvenir shops, and enough tourists to make Disney envious. Arrive by 9:00, after 19:00, or skip it.
Gordes—This is the most touristy and trendy town in the Luberon. Parisian big shots love it. Once a virtual ghost town

of derelict buildings, it's now completely fixed up and filled by people who live in a world without calluses. The view as you approach is incredible and merits a detour, though the village has little of interest. The nearby Abbey de Senanque is busy but worth a visit, particularly in July when the lavender blooms.

Oppède le Vieux—This is a windy barnacle of a town with a few boutiques and a dusty main square at the base of a short, ankle-twisting climb to a ruined church and castle. The Luberon views justify the effort. This way-off-the-beaten-path fixer-upper of a village must be how Gordes looked before it became chic. It's ideal for those looking to perish in Provence. The cozy **Restaurant L'Oppidum** rents three classy rooms and dorm beds in a larger room (Db-300F, big room with terrace-400F, dorm bed-130F, place de la Croix, tel. & fax 04 90 76 84 15, NSE).

Lacoste—Slumbering under its ruined castle, tiny, steep, and over-looked Lacoste has great views and a few *chambres*. **Café de Sade** is spotless, simple, and cheap with six rooms and a great little restaurant (D-200F, Db-290F, 1 family room-350F, for dorm beds—75F—bring your own sheet, tel. 04 90 75 82 29, fax 04 90 75 95 68).

Goult—Bigger than its sister hill towns, this surprisingly quiet town seems content away from the tourist path. Wander up the hill to the panorama and windmill. **Patrick Payet** has two rooms in the center above a little restaurant (Db-530F, place de l'Ancienne Mairie, 84220, Goult, tel. & fax 04 90 72 22 35).

THE FRENCH RIVIERA

A hundred years ago, celebrities from London to Moscow flocked here to socialize, gamble, and escape the drab, dreary weather at home. The belle époque is today the tourist craze, as this most sought-after fun-in-the-sun destination now caters to budget travelers. Some of the Continent's most stunning scenery and intriguing museums lie along this strip of land—as do millions of sun-worshiping tourists. This place is crowded. Nice has world-class museums, a grand beachfront promenade, and a seductive old city. Day trips are easy—Monte-Carlo welcomes all with open cash registers, Antibes has a great port and silky-sandy beaches, and the hill towns offer a breezy and photogenic alternative to the beach scene. Evenings on the Riviera, a.k.a. the Côte d'Azur, were made for the promenade and outdoor dining.

Choose a Home Base

I've listed accommodations for three different places: Nice, Antibes, and Villefranche. **Nice** is the region's capital and France's fifth-largest city. With its excellent public transportation to most regional sights, it's probably the most practical base for train travelers. Nice also has a full palate of museums and rock-hard beaches, the best selection of hotels in all price ranges, and lively nightlife. A car is a headache in Nice. Nearby **Antibes** is much smaller (but still lively) with fewer hotels but fine sandy beaches and the Picasso Museum. It has good train service to Nice and Monaco, and is easier for drivers. **Villefranche** is the romantic's choice, with a serene setting and small-town warmth. It has finely ground pebble beaches, good public transport (particularly to Nice and Monaco), and easy parking. Its few hotels leap from simple to sublime, letting Nice handle the middle ground.

Planning Your Time

Most should plan a full day for Nice (a half day *sans* museums) and at least a half day each for Monaco and Antibes. I prefer Monaco at night (sights are closed but crowds are few, consider dinner here) and Antibes during the day (great beaches and Picasso Museum). St. Paul de Vence, Vence, and Eze Village are lower priorities, but offer a scenic, hilly escape from the beach scene.

Getting around the Riviera

Getting around the Côte d'Azur by train or bus is easy (drivers should seriously consider parking their cars and leaving the driving to others). For some of the Riviera's best scenery, follow the coast road between Cannes and Fréjus (when arriving in or leaving the Côte d'Azur) and take the short drive along Moyenne Corniche from Nice to Eze Village.

Nice is perfectly located for exploring the region. Like prostitutes on bar stools, the resort towns of the Riviera await your visit. Monaco, Eze, Villefranche, Antibes, St. Paul, and Cannes are all a 15- to 60-minute bus or train ride apart from each other. The TI (and probably your hotel) has information on minivan excursions from Nice (half day-about 400F, full day-600–700F; Tour Azur is one of many, tel. 04 93 44 88 77, www.tourazur.com).

Bus service can be cheaper and more frequent than rail service—plus it often drops you closer to where you want to be. At Nice's efficient bus station (*gare routière*, on boulevard J. Jaures—see map of Nice; baggage check, Mon–Sat), competing companies vie for your business, offering free return trips (keep your ticket). Get schedules and prices at the helpful information desk in the bus station.

Here's an overview of public transport options to key Riviera destinations from Nice (rt = round-trip, ow = one-way):

Destination	Bus	Train
Monaco	4/hr, 40 min, 20F rt	2/hr, 20 min, 20F ow
Villefranche	4/hr, 15 min, 9F rt	2/hr, 10 min, 9F ow
Antibes	3/hr, 50 min, 25F, ow	2/hr, 25 min, 22F ow
Cannes	way too long	2/hr, 30 min, 32F ow
St. Paul	2/hr, 30 min, 20F, ow	none
Eze Village	every 2 hrs, 25 min, 15F, rt	none

Two bus companies, RCA and Cars Broch, provide service between Nice, Villefranche, and Monaco; RCA's buses run more frequently, (tel. 04 93 85 61 81 for info on both).

Cuisine Scene—Côte d'Azur

The Côte d'Azur (technically a part of Provence) gives Provence's cuisine a Mediterranean flair. Local specialties are *bouillabaisse*

The French Riviera

(the spicy seafood stew-soup that seems worth the cost only for those with a seafood fetish), *bourride* (a creamy fish soup thickened with aioli, a garlic sauce), and *salade niçoise* (nee-swaz; a tasty tomato, potato, olive, anchovy, and tuna salad). You'll also find these tasty bread treats: *pissaladière* (bread dough topped with onions, olives, and anchovies), *fougasse* (a spindly, lacelike bread), *socca* (a thin chickpea crepe), and *pan bagnat* (a bread shell stuffed with tomatoes, anchovies, olives, onions, and tuna). Good Italian cuisine is easy to find and generally a good value. White and rosé Bellet and the rich reds and rosés of Bandol are the local wines.

This is the most difficult region in France to find reliable restaurant listings. Because most visitors come more for the sun than the cuisine, and because the clientele is predominantly international, most restaurants aim for the middle and are hard to distinguish from each other. You'll find relatively few restaurant listings in this book. Look for views and ambience and lower your expectations.

NICE

Nice is a melting pot of thousands of tanning tourists and 400,000 well-tanned residents. You'll share the sand with the chicest of the chic, the cheapest of the cheap, and everyone else in this scramble to be where the mountains meet the water. Nice's spectacular Alps-to-Mediterranean scenery, thriving Old City, eternally entertaining seafront promenade, and fine museums make settling into this city exciting. Nice is nice, but hot and jammed in July and August. Get a room with air-conditioning (*avec climatization*).

Take only a piece of Nice, and leave the rest to the residents. Outside of a few museums, everything you want is within a small area—near the Old City and along the seafront.

Orientation

Tourist Information: Nice has four helpful TIs (terminal 1 at airport; next to train station; on the RN-7 after airport on the right; and near the waterfront at 5 promenade des Anglais). All are open daily from 8:00 to 19:00 and until 20:00 in summer (tel. 04 93 87 07 07 or 04 92 14 48 00). Pick up the excellent free Nice map (which lists all the sights and hours), the museums booklet, and the extensive *Practical Guide to Nice*. TIs make hotel reservations for a small fee.

Arrival in Nice

By Train: Nice has one main station with luggage lockers (Nice-Ville) where all trains stop and you get off. Avoid the suburban stations. The TI is next door to the left as you exit the train station; Avis car rental is to the right. To reach my recommended hotels, turn left out of the station then right on avenue Jean Médecin. To get to the beach and the promenade des Anglais from the station, continue on foot for 20 minutes down avenue Jean Médecin or take bus #12 (stop on Jean Médecin). To get to the Old City and the bus station (*gare routière*), catch bus #5 from avenue Jean Médecin.

By Car: Use the roadside TI just past the airport then park at the lot at Nice Étoile on avenue Jean Médecin (ticket booth is on 3rd floor, about 80F/day, 48F from 20:00–8:00). Most Nice street parking is metered, and garages cost from 60F to 90F per day.

By Plane: Nice's mellow and TI-equipped airport (tel. 04 93 21 30 30) is right on the Mediterranean. The TI and international flights use terminal 1; domestic flights use terminal 2. The airport is about 25 minutes from the city center. There are three **buses** to downtown Nice: the airport shuttle direct to the SNCF train station (23F, 2/hrly until 21:00, drops you near most of my hotel listings—or catch the train to Antibes); bus #23 (9F, 4/hrly, direction: St. Maurice, serves stops between the airport and SNCF station); and the yellow "NICF" bus to the bus station (*gare routière*, 23F, 3/hrly). To get to Villefranche from the airport, go to the bus station (*gare routière*) and transfer to the Villefranche bus (9F, 4/hrly). **Taxis** to Nice will cost about 150F to 175F; to Villefranche pay no more than 280F.

Helpful Hints

Think safety first. Have nothing important on or around your waist, unless it's a moneybelt tucked out of sight (no fanny packs, please), and stick to main streets in old Nice after dark.

The new regional **museum pass**, Carte Musées, is a good deal for those planning to visit three or more museums in the area (80F for 3 consecutive days, 150F for 7 consecutive days, valid at all museums described in this chapter except Foundation Maeght, available at any museum or TI).

The **American Express** office faces the beach at 11 promenade des Anglais (tel. 04 93 16 53 53). For new and used **English-language books** and guidebooks, try The Cat's Whiskers (closed Sun, 26 rue Lamartine, near Hôtel Star). Cycles Arnaud rents mountain **bikes** (4 place Grimaldi, just off avenue Jean Médecin, tel. 04 93 87 88 55). Self-serve **Laundromats** abound in Nice; ask your hotelier and guard your load.

Internet access is easy. Both of these are a block off avenue Jean Médecin: Europolis (13 rue Paul Deroulede, tel. 04 93 88 40 01) and, nearer the station, 3.W.O Internet (32 rue Assalit, tel. 04 93 80 51 12).

Sights—Nice

▲▲**Promenade des Anglais**—There's something for everyone along this seafront circus. Watch the Europeans at play, admire the azure Mediterranean, anchor yourself in a blue chair, and prop your feet up on the made-to-order guardrail. Join the evening parade of tans along the promenade. Start at the pink-domed Hôtel Negresco and, like the belle époque English aristocrats for whom the promenade was built, stroll to the Old City and Castle Hill.

Hôtel Negresco, Nice's finest hotel and a historic monument, offers the city's most costly beds and a free "museum" interior (reasonable attire is necessary to enter). March through the lobby into the exquisite Salon Royal. The tsar's chandelier hangs from an Eiffel-built dome. Read the explanation, check out the room photos, and stroll the circle. On your way out, pop into the Salon Louis XIV.

The next block to your left as you exit has a lush park and the Masséna Museum. The TI is just beyond that. Cross over to the promenade.

Pull up a chair and admire the scene (beautiful after dark). To your right is the airport (built on a landfill) and, on that tip of land way out there, Cap d'Antibes. Until the late 1800s, Antibes and Nice were in different countries; the Italians gave Nice to the

Nice

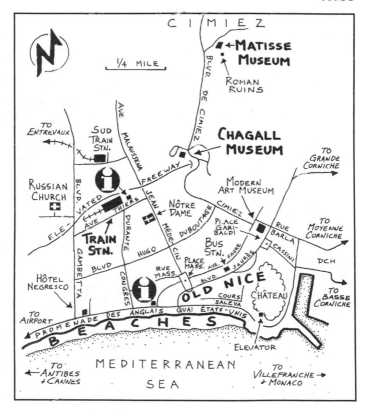

French as thanks for their help during the reunification of Italy in 1870. To the left lies Villefranche (after the second tip of land), Monaco, then Italy. Behind you are the pre-Alps (les Alpes Maritimes), which gather threatening clouds and leave the Côte d'Azur in sunshine over 300 days per year. Get down to that beach.

Beaches—The beaches of Nice are where the jet set relaxes on rocks. After settling into the smooth pebbles, you can play beach volleyball, Ping-Pong, or *boules*; rent paddleboats, jet skis, or windsurfing equipment; explore ways to use your zoom lens as a telescope; or snooze on comfy beach beds with end tables (mattress-60F, mattress and chaise lounge-70F, umbrella-30F). Before heading off in search of sandy beaches, try it on the rocks.

▲▲**Old City (Vieux Nice)**—The thriving Old City is characteristic Nice in the buff. Here Italian and French flavors mix to create a spicy Mediterranean dressing. The modern age drove old Nice into a triangle of spindly streets filling a corner between Castle Hill and the beach. A broad, park-lined boulevard seals it off. The streets, while straight, are anything but predictable. Stealth pigeons fly under tall, pastel, domestic cliffs, while tattoo shops show their work. The Naples-like rue Droite plays host to simple bars, chic art shops, and shady walking; stop by Le Four à Bois bakery (at #38) and watch them make *fougasse*. The fresh pasta shops (which you'll find nowhere else in France) and many *gelaterias* remind us how close Italy is. Cours Saleya, a long broad square, collects people, produce, and flowers like a trough between all this and the sea. Restaurant tables tangle with market stalls and browsers. Dinner here is a treat—not for the cuisine, but for the sea of tables and festive feel. The daily flower and produce market becomes a flea market on Monday. Nearby place Rosetti is more intimate and utterly Italian at night (more average restaurants). Duck into the cathedral St. Reparate for a dose of Italian-Baroque. The fish market on place St. Francois isn't worth the detour.

Castle Hill—Climb or take the elevator up this saddle horn in the otherwise flat city center only for exercise or the view. Walk up rue Rossetti or catch the elevator from the beach side. The 360-degree view of Nice, the Alps foothills, and the Mediterranean is a decent reward, better if it's clear or near sunset. You'll find a waterfall, a playground, and a cemetery, but no castle on Castle Hill.

▲**Russian Cathedral**—Even if you've been to Russia, this Russian Orthodox church, which claims to be the finest outside Russia, is interesting. Its one-room interior is filled with icons and candles. Tsar Nicholas II gave his aristocratic countryfolk—who wintered on the Riviera—this church in 1912. (A few years later, Russian comrades who didn't winter on the Riviera shot him.) Here in the land of olives and anchovies, these proud onion domes seem odd. But so did, I imagine, those old Russians (12F, daily 9:00–12:00, 14:30–18:00, services Sat at 18:00, Sun at 10:00, no shorts, 10-min walk behind station at 17 boulevard du Tsarevitch, tel. 04 93 96 88 02).

Nightlife—Nice's bars play host to a lively late-night scene full of jazz and rock 'n' roll. Most activity focuses on Old Nice, near place Rossetti. If you're out very late, avoid walking alone. Plan on a cover charge or expensive drinks.

Museums—Nice

▲▲**Musée National Marc Chagall**—Even if you're suspicious of modern art, this museum—with the largest collection of Chagall's work anywhere—might appeal to you. After World War II, Chagall returned from the United States to settle in nearby Vence. Between 1954 and 1967 he painted a cycle of 17 large murals designed for and donated to this museum. These paintings, inspired by the books of Genesis, Exodus, and the Song of Songs, make up the "nave," or core, of what Chagall called the "House of Brotherhood."

Each painting is a lighter-than-air collage of images drawing from Chagall's Russian-folk-village youth, his Jewish heritage, Biblical themes, and his feeling that he existed somewhere between heaven and earth. He felt the Bible was a synonym for nature, and color and Biblical themes were key ingredients for understanding God's love for his creation. Chagall's brilliant blues and reds celebrate nature, as do his spiritual and folk themes. Notice the focus on couples. To Chagall, humans loving each other mirrored God's love of creation.

Don't miss the stained-glass windows of the auditorium (enter through the garden), early family photos of the artist, and a room full of Chagall lithographs. The small 20F guidebook begins with an introduction by Chagall (30F, 38F in summer, July–Sept Wed–Mon 10:00–17:40, Oct–June 10:00–16:40, closed Tue, ask about English tours, tel. 04 93 53 87 20). An idyllic café awaits in the garden.

Getting to Chagall and Matisse Museums: The Chagall Museum is a confusing but manageable 15-minute walk from the top of avenue Jean Médecin and the train station; the Matisse Museum (described below) is a 30-minute uphill walk from there. Buses #15 and #17 serve Chagall and Matisse from the Italy side of avenue Jean Médecin (each 6/hrly, 8.5F). Consider walking to Chagall and taking the bus to Matisse.

To walk to the Chagall Museum, get to the train-station end of avenue Jean Médecin and turn right onto rue Raimbaldi along the overpasses, then turn left under the overpasses onto avenue Comboul. Once under the overpass, angle to the right up rue Olivetto to the alley with the big wall on your right. A pedestrian path soon emerges, leading up and up to signs for Chagall and Matisse. The bus to Matisse is on avenue Cimiez, two blocks up from Chagall.

▲**Matisse Museum** (▲▲▲ for his fans)—The art is beautifully displayed in this elegant orange mansion and represents the single largest collection of Matisse paintings. While many (including one of your authors) don't get Matisse, this museum offers a painless introduction to this influential artist whose style was shaped by the southern light and fellow Cote d'Azur artists, Picasso and Renoir. Watch as his style becomes simpler with time. A room on the top floor has models of his famous Chapelle du Rosaire in nearby Vence and illustrates the beauty of his simple design (25F, April–Sept Wed–Mon 10:00–18:00, Oct–March 10:00–17:00, closed Tue, take bus #15 or #17 to Arènes stop, see directions under Chagall Museum listing above, tel. 04 93 81 08 08).

Modern Art Museum—This ultramodern museum features an enjoyable collection of art from the 1960s and 1970s (25F, Wed–Mon 11:00–18:00, Fri evening until 22:00, closed Tue, on promenade des Arts near bus station).

Other Nice Museums—These museums offer decent rainy-day options and are generally open from 10:00 to noon and 14:00 to 18:00 or 19:00. The **Musée des Beaux Arts** (Fine Arts Museum), with 6,000 works from the 17th to 20th centuries, will satisfy your need for a fine-arts fix (25F, at western end of Nice, 3 avenue des Baumettes). The **Musée de la Marine** (Naval Museum) is interesting and relevant (free, in Tour Bellanda at base of Château Hill). The **Musée Masséna** describes Nice's history (25F, facing the beach next to Hôtel Negresco at 65 rue de France, tel. 04 93 88 11 34). The **Musée Archeologique** (Archeological Museum) displays Roman ruins and various objects from the Romans' occupation of this region (25F, by Matisse Museum at 160 avenue des Arenes).

Sleeping in Nice
(6.50F = about $1, country code: 33, zip code: 06000)
Sleep Code: **S** = Single, **D** = Double/Twin, **T** = Triple, **Q** = Quad, **b** = bathroom, **t** = toilet only, **s** = shower only, **CC** = Credit Card (Visa, MasterCard, Amex), **SE** = Speaks English, **NSE** = No English, * = Hotel rating (0–4 stars).

Don't look for charm in Nice. Go for modern and clean with a central location, and in summer, air-conditioning. Reserve early for summer visits. Prices drop from October to April and are the lower of the prices listed. The hotels near the station are overrun, overpriced, and loud. I sleep halfway between the Old City (Vieux Nice) and the train station, near avenue Jean Médecin. Drivers can park under the Nice Étoile shopping center (on avenue Jean Médecin and boulevard Dubouchage).

Hôtel du Petit Louvre* has art-festooned walls, lighthearted owners, and close-to-clean rooms (Ds-225F, Db-250F, Tb-260–300F, CC:VM, payment due on arrival, elevator, 10 rue Emma Tiranty, tel. 04 93 80 15 54, fax 04 93 62 45 08).

Hôtel Clemenceau** is a good value with a homey, family feel and mostly spacious, traditional, and comfortable rooms, some with balconies (S-160–180F, Db-200–310F, Tb-250–360F, Qb-400–520F, kitchenette-50F extra, CC:VMA, 1 block west of avenue Jean Médecin, 3 avenue Clemenceau, tel. 04 93 88 61 19, fax 04 93 16 88 96, daughter Marianne SE).

Hôtel St. Georges**, a block away, is bigger with less personality. It has air-con, a peaceful garden courtyard, and reasonably roomy and comfortable rooms (Db-330–400F, 3-bed Tb-430–500F, CC:VMA, TVs with CNN, elevator, 7 avenue Clemenceau, tel. 04 93 88 79 21, fax 04 93 16 22 85, e-mail: nicefrance.hotelstgeorges @wanadoo.fr).

Hôtel Star**, a few blocks east of avenue Jean Médecin, is immaculate, air-conditioned, comfortable, and a great value. It's run by intense Françoise and mellower Georges (SE). They expect you to respect their high standards, but they are losing patience with

Nice Center Hotels

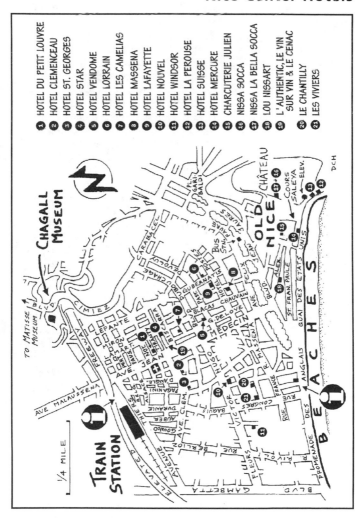

1. HOTEL DU PETIT LOUVRE
2. HOTEL CLEMENCEAU
3. HOTEL ST. GEORGES
4. HOTEL STAR
5. HOTEL VENDOME
6. HOTEL LORRAIN
7. HOTEL LES CAMELIAS
8. HOTEL MASSENA
9. HOTEL LAFAYETTE
10. HOTEL NOUVEL
11. HOTEL WINDSOR
12. HOTEL LA PEROUSE
13. HOTEL SUISSE
14. HOTEL MERCURE
15. CHARCUTERIE JULIEN
16. NISSA SOCCA
17. NISSA LA BELLA SOCCA
18. LOU NISSART
19. L' AUTHENTIC, LE VIN SUR VIN & LE CENAC
20. LE CHANTILLY
21. LES VIVIERS

imperfect behavior. Toe the line and have a superb stay; otherwise, prepare to be chastised (Sb-200–250F, Db-280–350F, Tb-370–450F, CC:VMA, fine beds, beach towels, no elevator, 14 rue Biscarra, reserve by fax or e-mail rather than by phone, tel. 04 93 85 19 03, fax 04 93 13 04 23, e-mail: star-hotel@wanadoo.fr).

Hôtel Vendome*, a manor house, gives you a taste of faded belle époque, pink pastels, and high ceilings. Some rooms are average, but the best have balconies—request *avec balcon*. The most desirable rooms are #105, #102, or any on the fifth floor (Sb-385–485F, Db-485–595F, Tb-505–675F, Qb-575–775F, air-con, off-street parking, 26 rue Pastorelli, tel. 04 93 62 00 77, fax 04 93 13 40 78, e-mail: contact@vendome.hotel-nice.com).

Hôtel Lorrain* is conveniently located near the bus station and Old Nice and is a solid budget option with new, ambitious owners who plan to install air-conditioning and upgrade all rooms (Sb-200F, Db-220–300F, Tb-280–320F, CC:VM, 6 rue Gubernatis, push top buzzer to release door, tel. 04 93 85 42 90, fax 04 93 85 55 54).

Hôtel les Camelias** reminds me of the Old World places I stayed in as a kid traveling with my parents. A well-located, dark, creaky, and floral place burrowed behind a small parking lot and garden, it has linoleum halls, simple rooms (some lumpy beds), and a loyal clientele who give the TV lounge a retirement-home-after-dinner feeling. Some basic rooms have balconies—request a *chambre avec balcon* (S-200F, Ss-250F, Sb-320F, Db-360–420F, Tb-420–500F, includes breakfast, parking-30F, CC:VM, elevator, 3 rue Spitaleri, tel. 04 93 62 15 54, fax 04 93 80 42 96, formal Madame Vimont and her son Jean Claude SE). Guests here gum their 70F four-course dinner—simple, hearty, and stressless.

Hôtel Masséna***, a few blocks from place Massena in a beautiful old building, is a business hotel offering 100 four-star rooms with all the comforts at three-star rates. Rooms are well-appointed and spacious with air-conditioning, mini-bars, and cable TV (Db-560–990F, Tb-950–1,150F, CC:VMA, reserve a parking space ahead-80F, Internet access in lobby, 58 rue Giofreddo, tel. 04 93 85 49 25, fax 04 93 62 43 27, www.hotel-massena-nice.com, SE).

Hôtel Lafayette** looks massive from the outside, but inside it's cozy a good value with air-conditioning and three-star rooms at two-star rates (Db-310–560F, 32 rue de l'Hôtel des Postes, tel. 04 93 85 17 84, fax 04 93 80 47 56).

The next two hotels are several blocks west of avenue Jean Médecin.

Hôtel Nouvel** is a well-run, spotless place set on a broad sidewalk with air-conditioning, modern rooms, and an elevator (Db-450–525F, 19 bis boulevard Victor Hugo, tel. 04 93 87 15 00, fax 04 93 16 00 67, www.nouvel-hotel.com).

Hôtel Windsor*** is a snazzy, airy, garden retreat with many contemporary rooms designed by modern artists. It also has a swimming pool—rare in Nice (Db-570–750F, extra bed-100F, rooms over garden worth the higher price, CC:VMA, sauna-60F, free gym, elevator, 10 blocks west of Jean Medécin and 5 blocks from sea, 11 rue Dalpozzo, tel. 04 93 88 59 35, fax 04 93 88 94 57, e-mail: windsor@webstore.fr, SE).

The next three hotels are on the water, near the Old City (Vieux Nice).

Hôtel La Perouse****, my top Nice splurge, lies under Château Hill a few minutes from Old Nice and is refined in every way, with sumptuous rooms (many with balconies), a beautiful backyard terrace, a glassy pool, and a 100F buffet breakfast that will make you skip lunch (no view Db-750– 1,150F, view Db-1,350–2,000F, extra bed-230F, CC:VMA, 11 quai Rauba-Capeu, tel. 04 93 62 34 63, fax 04 93 62 59 41, www.hroy.com/la-perouse).

Hôtel Suisse*** abuts the far fancier Hôtel la Perouse with great views from balcony rooms over a very busy road to the sea. All rooms have air-conditioning and modern conveniences (quiet, no view Db-420F, great view Db-640F, extra bed-130F, CC:VM, 15 quai Rauba-Capeu, tel. 04 92 17 39 00, fax 04 93 85 30 70).

Hôtel Mercure***, also on the water, is behind Cours Saleya and offers predictable cookie-cutter rooms at great rates considering the location (Db-460–620F, air-con, some balconies and views, 91 quai des États-Unis, tel. 04 93 85 74 19, fax 04 93 13 90 94).

Eating in Nice

Nice's Old City overflows with restaurants in all shapes and sizes. The dinner scene on Cours Saleya is as entertaining as the food is average. It's a fun, festive place to compare tans and new outfits. Comparison shopping is half the fun (I go Italian). **Charcuterie Julien** is a good deli that sells an impressive array of local dishes by weight. Buy 200 grams of your choice plopped into a plastic carton to go (Thu–Tue 11:00–19:30, closed Wed, rue de la Poissonnerie, at Castle Hill end of cours Saleya). **Nissa Socca** café offers good, cheap Italian cuisine in Vieux Nice in a lively atmosphere (opens at 19:00, arrive early, a block off place Rossetti on rue Reparate). If they're full, try the mirror image across the alley, **Nissa la Bella Socca**.

Just below place Masséna, **Lou Nissart** serves good regional specialties to appreciative locals in unair-conditioned rooms (moderate prices, across place Masséna at 1 rue de l'Opéra, tel. 04 93 85 34 49).

Several relaxed places line the broad sidewalk on rue Biscarra, just east of avenue Jean Medécin between #s 16 and 18. They're near most hotels recommended in this book and away from the tourist activity: **L'Authentic**, **Le Vin sur Vin** (wine emphasis), and **Le Cenac** are all reasonable places. **Le Chantilly**, a 10-minute walk west of Jean Medécin, is friendly and serves local specialties at very reasonable prices in air-conditioned comfort (12 rue Grimaldi, tel. 04 93 87 50 08). For authentic Nicoise cuisine (allow 200F for dinner), reserve a table at the cozy **Les Viviers** (5-min walk west of avenue Jean Médécin at 22 rue Alphonse Karr, tel. 04 93 16 00 48; they also run the elegant restaurant next door).

Transportation Connections—Nice

By train to: Arles (8/day, 3.5 hrs, transfer in Marseille), **Paris'** Gare de Lyon (3 direct TGVs/day, 6.5 hrs; 6/day via Marseille then TGV, 8 hrs; 1 direct night train), **Chamonix** (4/day, 10 hrs, transfer in St. Gervais and Lyon, night train available), **Beaune** (7/day, 8 hrs, transfer in Lyon), **Digne/Grenoble** (consider the scenic little trains that run from Nice to Digne then on to Grenoble; see "Travel Notes for La Route de Napoleon" at end of this chapter), **Munich** (2/day, 12 hrs, night train with transfer in Verona), **Interlaken** (1/day, 12 hrs), **Florence** (2/day, 7 hrs, transfer in Pisa and/or Genoa, 1 morning departure, 1 night train), **Milan** (4/day 6 hrs), **Venice** (3/day, 8 hrs, direct night train), **Barcelona** (3/day, 10 hrs, direct night train or day trips with at least 1 transfer). Train info: tel. 04 36 35 35 35.

By plane to: Paris (hrly, 1 hr, about the same price as a train ticket).

VILLEFRANCHE-SUR-MER

Come here for upscale, small-town Mediterranean atmosphere. Villefranche (between Nice and Monte-Carlo, with frequent 15-min buses and trains to both) is quieter and more exotic than Nice. Narrow cobbled streets tumble into the mellow waterfront, a scenic walkway below the castle leads to the hidden port, and luxury yachts glisten in the harbor below. More-or-less sandy beaches and a handful of interesting sights keep visitors just busy enough.

The **TI** is in the park Francois Binon just below the main bus stop (Mon–Sat 9:00–12:00, 14:00–18:30, summers daily 9:00–19:00, a 20-min walk or 45F taxi from train station, tel. 04 93 01 73 68). Pick up the brochure detailing a self-guided walking tour of Villefranche and ask for information on the Rothschild Villa Ephrussi's gardens (49F, a scenic 50-min walk around the bay past train station or 10 min on bus #111).

The stunning interior of the **Chapel of St. Pierre**, decorated by Jean Cocteau, is the town's cultural highlight, but at 12F it's not worth it for many (daily 10:00–12:00, 16:00–20:30, below Hôtel Welcome). **Boat rides** (*promenades en mer*) are offered in the summer below Hôtel Welcome (80F, 2 hrs). Lively *boules* action takes place each evening just below the huge soccer field. Walk beyond the train station for views back to Villefranche and a quieter beach.

Even if you're sleeping elsewhere, consider a beachfront dinner or an ice cream–licking village stroll. The last bus leaves Nice for Villefranche at about 19:45; the last bus from Ville-franche to Nice leaves at about 21:00; and trains run later. Beware of taxi drivers who overcharge—the normal weekday daytime rate to central Nice is about 175F; to the airport, 250F to 280F.

Sleeping in Villefranche-sur-Mer
(6.50F = about $1, country code: 33, zip code: 06230)

There's precious little middle ground here. Hotels are linoleum-floor cheap or million-dollar-view expensive. The lone *chambre d'hôte* offers the only normal mid-range comfort.

If your idea of sightseeing is to enjoy the view from your bedroom deck, the dining room, or the pool, stay at the welcoming **Hôtel La Flore***, where most rooms have unbeatable views (Db-560–820F, Tb-930F, Qb-1,130F, less Nov–March, CC:VMA, no half-pension required but a superb restaurant, smartly designed family rooms, elevator, just off main road high above harbor, 2 blocks from TI toward Nice on boulevard Princess Grace de Monaco, tel. 04 93 76 30 30, fax 04 93 76 99 99, e-mail: Hotel -La-Flore@wanadoo.fr, SE).

Hôtel Welcome* is buried in the heart of the Old City, right on the water, with most rooms overlooking the harbor. You'll pay top dollar for all the comforts in a classy hotel that seems to do everything right and couldn't be better located (Db-600–1,100F, extra person-200F, air-con, cable TV, 1 quai Courbet, tel. 04 93 76 27 62, fax 04 93 76 27 66, www.welcomehotel.com, e-mail: steves@welcomehotel.com, SE). The rooms at both Hôtel La Flore and Hôtel Welcome, while different in cost, are about the same in comfort. La Flore has a pool, Welcome is on the harbor.

The hotelesque **Hôtel Provençal** needs a facelift but offers fine views from well-worn rooms, some with air-conditioning and cable TV (Db-440–600F, Tb-480–560F, extra bed-60F, CC:VMA, skip the no-view rooms, a block from TI at 4 avenue Maréchal Joffre, tel. 04 93 76 53 53, fax 04 93 76 96 00, e-mail: provencal @riviera.fr).

At **Le Home**, Madame Repellin-Villard rents the town's best budget beds in 10 simple rooms around a lovely garden with a welcoming terrace (Db-245F; from main road near TI, walk between cafés Riche and Regence and then climb the steps and turn left, avenue de Grande Bretagne, tel. 04 93 76 79 88).

Hôtel la Darse, a simple hotel sitting in the shadow of its highbrow brothers, offers a low-key alternative right on the water in Villefranche's Port de la Darse (long walk up to the bus stop, 10-min level walk along water to the village center). The rooms are quiet, plain, and not really clean, with linoleum floors and great view balconies on the seaside (easily worth the extra cost). Gentle Madame Guillou speaks English (Db-250–370F, extra person-60F, from TI walk across park then down steps and down avenue General de Gaulle, Port de la Darse, tel. 04 93 01 72 54, fax 04 93 01 84 37).

Hôtel Vauban*, two blocks down from the TI, is a central and basic place with a homey feel and cheery, simple rooms (Db-290–340F, with view-340–440F, 11 avenue General De Gaulle, tel. & fax 04 93 76 62 18).

Eating in Villefranche-sur-Mer

If you want to eat well, spring for dinner at **Hôtel la Flore** (see "Sleeping in Villefranche," above). Or, for a cool view and good-enough food at reasonable prices, try **Restaurant Le Marinières** on the beach below the train station (salads and *à la carte*, open daily, tel. 04 93 01 76 06). The many places on the harbor all look the same to me.

ANTIBES

Antibes is larger than Villefranche but tiny compared to Nice. Come here for sandy beaches, an enjoyable old town, good hiking, and a great Picasso collection. Twenty-five minutes from Nice by train (skip the 50-min bus), Antibes' glamorous port glistens below its fortifications, with luxurious yachts and color-ful fishing boats. Boat lovers are welcome to browse. The Fort Carré that dominates the port was the last fortification before Italy in the 1500s. The festive Old City is charming in a sandy-sophisticated way and sits atop the ruins of the fourth-century-B.C. Greek city of Antipolis. The daily market (*marche Provençal*) under a 19th-century canopy brings out the locals (behind Picasso Museum on cours Masséna, daily until 13:00, closed Mon off-season). Stroll along the sea between the Picasso Museum and place Albert 1er (where boulevard Albert 1er meets the sea). Place Audiberti becomes a flea market on Thursdays and Saturdays (7:00–18:00, in the Old City a block from the port). Good children's play areas are on place des Martyrs de la Resistance (near Hôtel Relais du Postillon, below).

Tourist Information: The Maison de Tourisme has an interesting "Discovering Old Antibes" walking-tour brochure and good city maps (Mon–Sat 9:00–12:30, 14:00–18:30, in summers Mon–Sat 9:00–19:00, Sun 9:00–13:00, downtown at 11 place de Gaulle, tel. 04 92 90 53 00). The Nice TI has Antibes maps; plan ahead.

Arrival in Antibes

By Train: From the train station (lockers available), the port is five minutes straight ahead down avenue de la Liberté. The TI is a 10-minute walk to the right down avenue Soleau; follow "Maison du Tourisme" signs to place de Gaulle. The Old City center lies between the port and avenue Soleau. A free minibus (Minibus Gratuit) circulates around Antibes from the train station and serves place Albert 1er, the Old City, and the port (4/hrly).

By Bus: The bus station is a block from the TI on place Guynemer.

By Car: Follow "Centre Ville, Vieux Port" signs and park near the Old City walls on the port. The first half hour is free. Municipal lots cost about 50F per day.

Sights—Antibes
▲▲**Musée Picasso (Château Grimaldi)**—Sitting serenely where the Old City meets the sea, this museum offers a remarkable collection of Picasso's work—paintings, sketches, and ceramics. Picasso, who lived and worked here in 1946, said if you want to see work from his Antibes period, you'll have to do it in Antibes. You'll understand why Picasso liked working here. Several photos of the artist make this already-intimate museum more so. In his famous *Joie de Vivre* (the museum's highlight), there's a new love in Picasso's life, and he's feelin' groovy (30F, June–Sept Tue–Sun 10:00–18:00, closed Mon and Oct–May 12:00–14:00, tel. 04 92 90 54 20).
Musée d'Histoire et d'Archeologie—Featuring Greek, Roman, and Etruscan odds and ends, this is the only place to get a sense of this city's ancient roots. I liked the 2,000-year-old lead anchors (10F, no English explanations, Tue–Sun 10:00–12:00, 14:00–18:00, closed Mon, on the water between Picasso Museum and place Albert 1er).
Beaches (Plages)—The best beaches stretch between Antibes' port and Cap d'Antibes. All are golden sandy. Plage Salis is busy in summer, but it's manageable and has snack stands every 100 meters and views to the fortified city. The smaller plage de la Gravette at the port remains relatively calm in any season.

Hikes and Day Trips from Antibes
▲**Chapelle et Phare de la Garoupe**—The chapel and lighthouse are a 25-minute uphill climb from the far end of plage Salis (follow Chemin du Calvaire) and offer magnificent views over Juan les Pins, Antibes, the pre-Alps, and Nice. Roads allow car access. The best view is at sunset.
Cap d'Antibes Hike (Sentier Touristique de Tirepoll/Sentier Littoral)—At the end of the mattress-ridden, over-crowded plage de la Garoupe is a well-maintained trail around the Cap d'Antibes. The beautiful trail follows the rocky coast for about three kilometers then heads inland. Take bus #2A from the bus station (*gare routière*) to Hôtel Beau Site (2/hrly, get return times) and walk 10 minutes down to plage de la Garoupe (parking available). The trail begins at the far-right end of the beach. Allow two hours for the loop that ends at the recommended Hôtel Beau Site (see "Sleeping in Antibes," below) and use your Antibes map.
Day Trips—Antibes is halfway between Nice and Cannes (fast train service to both) and close to the artsy pottery and glass-blowing village of Biot, home of the Fernand Léger Museum (frequent buses, ask at TI).

Sleeping in Antibes
(6.50F = about $1, country code: 33, zip code: 06600)
Central pickings are slim here where most hotel owners seem more interested in their restaurants. A **Laundromat** is at 14 rue Thuret.

Hôtel Relais du Postillon**, on a thriving square, offers small, tastefully-designed rooms, accordion bathrooms, and helpful owners who take more pride in their well-respected restaurant (Db-270–470F, extra bed-60F, CC:VM, *menus* from 200F, elevator, 8 rue Championnet, tel. 04 93 34 20 77, fax 04 93 34 61 24, e-mail: postillon@atsat.com, SE).

Hôtel Le Cameo** is a big, rambling, refreshingly unaggressive old place. It faces Antibes' main square above a bar filled with smoky locals. The public areas are dark and disorienting, but its nine *bon petit* rooms are almost huggable (Ss-230F, Ds-280F, Db-350F, Ts-350F, Tb-450F, 5 place Nationale, tel. 04 93 34 24 17, fax 04 93 34 35 80, NSE).

Auberge Provençale*, on the same square, has seven fine rooms, mysterious management, and a popular restaurant (Sb-250–410F, Db-300–460F, Tb-350–510F, Qb-560F, CC:VMA, reception in restaurant, 61 place Nationale, tel. 04 93 34 13 24, fax 04 93 34 89 88). Their loft room, named Celine, is huge. It comes with a royal canopy bed and a dramatic open-timbered ceiling and costs no more than the other rooms.

Hôtel Mediterranee** is Old World simple with quiet rooms around a garden courtyard and noisier rooms on the street (Db-270–370F, Tb-310–420F, Qb-350–460F, CC:VM, 6 avenue Maréchal Reille, tel. 04 93 34 14 84, fax 04 93 34 43 31, NSE).

These next two unique listings are located near place Albert 1er in a classy neighborhood and make most sense for drivers (free and safe private parking). Both require dinner from May to September (you'll probably dine better here than at most Antibes restaurants) and give priority to those who book dinner in other seasons.

Hôtel Ponteil's** gregarious owners offer quick beach access, a garden terrace, and bungalow-style rooms in and around a breezy manor house. They attract a loyal clientele willing to pay their prices (S-315–415F, D-360–400F, Db-400–490F, bunky family deals, includes breakfast, add about 100F per person for dinner, CC:VM, 11 impasse Jean-Mesnier, tel. 04 93 34 67 92, fax 04 93 34 49 47).

A few blocks uphill, **Mas Djoliba***** is a good splurge but a 10-minute walk to the beach. Reserve early for this tranquil, bird-chirping, flowers-everywhere manor house where no two rooms are the same. Enjoy breakfast and dinner by the pool (Db with breakfast and dinner-410–510F per person, several good family rooms, go up avenue Gaston Bourgeois to 29 avenue de Provence, tel. 04 93 34 02 48, fax 04 93 34 05 81, e-mail: info @hotel-pcastel-djoliba.com).

Hôtel Beau Site***, my only listing on Cap d'Antibes and a 10-minute drive from the old city, is a good value if you want to get away to a manor house, but not too far away. The friendly

owners, nice pool, outdoor terrace, easy parking, and pleasant
rooms make it worthwhile (Db-320-680F, CC:VM, 141 boulevard
Kennedy, tel. 04 93 61 53 43, fax 04 93 67 78 16). The hotel is a
10-minute walk down to the crowded plage de la Garoupe and a
nearby hiking trail.

MONACO
Still impressive despite over-development, high prices, and wall-
to-wall daytime tourists, Monaco will disappoint anyone looking
for something below the surface. This glittering two-square-
kilometer country is a tax haven for its miniscule full-time population who pay no income tax, and is the kind of place you visit
once and probably don't need to see again. France surrounds
Monaco on all sides but the Mediterranean and provides Monaco's
currency, telephones (French phone cards work here), electricity,
and water. About the only thing you'll use that's made locally
are its stamps.

Orientation
Monaco (the principality) is best understood when separated
into its three tourist areas: Monaco-Ville, Monte-Carlo, and la
Condamine (a 4th area, Fontvieille, is of no interest to tourists).
Monaco-Ville, dangling on the rock high above, is the oldest
section, housing Prince Rainier's palace and all sights except the
casino; Monte-Carlo is the area around the casino; and La Condamine (the port) divides the two. A brief bus ride on routes #1
or #2 links all areas (10/hrly, 8.50F, or 21F for 4 tickets). It's a
30-minute uphill walk from the port (and train station) to Prince
Rainier's palace, 20 minutes to the casino, and a 50-minute down-
and-up walk between the palace and the casino.
      Tourist Information: There are several TIs, but you
shouldn't need one as sightseeing is straightforward (a map is
helpful). The main TI is near the casino (2 boulevard des
Moulins), but the handiest one for most is in the train station;
pick up a city map (daily 9:00–19:00, tel. 00-377/92 16 61 66).
From June to September, you'll find information kiosks in the
Monaco-Ville parking garage and on the port.
      Telephone Tip: To call Monaco from France, dial 00,
377 (Monaco's country code), and the eight-digit number.
Within Monaco simply dial the eight-digit number.

Arrival in Monaco
By Bus from Nice and Villefranche: Keep your receipt for the
return ride (RCA buses run twice as often as Cars Broch). There
are three stops in Monaco, in order from Nice: In front of a tunnel
at the base of Monaco-Ville (place d'Armes), on the port, and
below the casino (on avenue d'Ostende). The first stop is the best

starting point. To walk up to Monaco-Ville or catch a local bus there (lines #1 or #2), cross the street right in front of the tunnel and turn right with the rock on your right—the bus stop and steps up to Monaco-Ville are in 70 meters. The bus stop back to Nice is across the major road from your arrival point at the light. The last bus leaves Monaco for Nice at about 19:00 (the last train leaves about 23:30).

By Train from Nice: A dazzling new train station provides central access to Monaco. The TI and baggage check are up the escalator at the Italy end of the tracks. To exit the station, follow "sortie la Condamine" signs from the tracks, then "Access Port" signs. The stop for local buses is in front of the station exit. The port is straight ahead, the casino is uphill along the left side of the port, and Monaco-Ville is uphill to the right of the port.

By Car: You'll be directed to parking structures under Monaco-Ville, under the casino, or above at the Jardins Exotique (40F/4 hrs).

Sights—Monaco-Ville

Start with a look at Monaco-Ville. The bus leaves you a five-minute walk to the palace; follow the green signs (good *pan bagna* sandwiches at #8 rue Basse). Find a seat to the right of the palace for a *magnifique* view (particularly at night). This funny little country was born on this rock in 1215 and has managed to stay independent for most of its 800 years. A medieval castle sat where the palace is today, its strategic setting having a lot to do with Monaco's ability to resist attackers. They still **change guards** the old-fashioned way (11:55 daily, fun to watch). As you look back over the port, notice the faded green roof above to the right—it's the famous casino. In the mid-1800s, Prince Charles began an aggressive economic development plan for his tiny, isolated country. He built spas and a casino to lure a growing aristocratic class with leisure time. It worked. Today Monaco has the world's highest per-capita income. The name Monte-Carlo means "Charles' Hill" in Spanish (the Spanish were traditional protectors of Monaco and have 200 guards present today). The famous Grand Prix of Monte-Carlo started in 1929 and still runs right through the streets of the port and around the casino. Walk to the opposite side of the square and more Louis XIV cannon balls. Down below is Monaco's newest area, Fontvieille, where much of its post-WWII growth has gone. Prince Rainier has continued Monaco's economic growth with landfills, flashy ports, new beaches, and the new rail station. Today, thanks to Prince Rainier's efforts, tiny Monaco is a member of the United Nations.

Palace—Automated and uninspired tours (in English) take you through part of the prince's lavish palace in 30 merciful minutes and yet still manage to describe every painting. The rooms are well furnished and impressive, but interesting only if you haven't seen a château lately (June–Sept only 9:30–18:30, closed off-season, 30F, or 40F with the Napoleon collection).

Napoleon Collection—Napoleon occupied Monaco after the French Revolution. This is the prince's private collection of what Napoleon left behind: military medals, swords, guns, letters, and, most interesting, his hat. I found this collection more appealing than the palace (20F, June–Sept 9:30–18:30, Oct–May 10:00–12:30, 14:00–17:00, next to palace entry).

Cathédrale de Monaco—This somber cathedral, built in 1878, is where Princess Grace is buried (near the left transept).

Jardins Botanique—Take in sensational views as you meander back to the bus stop through these immaculately maintained gardens (or pick up a *pan bagna* sandwich in the Old City and picnic here).

Musée de l'Océanographique (Cousteau Aquarium)—This monumental building overhangs the Mediterranean. It was inaugurated in 1910 and is the largest of its kind, thanks to the oceanographic zeal of Prince Albert I. It can be jammed and disappoints some, though kids love it (60F, 30F-children 6–18, CC:VM, daily April–Oct 9:00–19:00, until 20:00 in summer, Nov–March 10:00–18:00, at opposite end of Monaco-Ville from palace, down the steps from Monaco-Ville bus stop).

Monte-Carlo Story—This informative 35-minute film gives a helpful account (English headphones) of Monaco's history and is a comfortable soft-chair break from all that walking (38F, usually on the hour from 11:00–18:00, frequent extra showings for groups that you can join; from the Monte-Carlo side of the Aquarium take the escalator into the parking garage, then take the elevator down and follow the signs).

Leave Monaco-Ville and ride the shuttle bus or stroll down through the pedestrian-pleasant port and up to Monte-Carlo.

Sights—Monte Carlo

▲**Casino**—This is designed to make the wealthy feel comfortable while losing money. Charles Garnier, the same architect who built the Paris Opéra, constructed this casino in 1878 in part to thank the prince for his financial help in completing the Opéra. Count the counts and Rolls Royces in front of Hôtel de Paris. Strut inside the lavish casino (opens at 12:00). Anyone (even in shorts, if it's before 20:00) can get as far as the one-armed bandits and the sumptuous lobby; push the button on the slot machines to claim your winnings and enjoy the marble WCs in the casino lobby. After 20:00 shorts are off-limits anywhere. Only adults 21 and older are allowed to dive deeper and pay 50F for the first rooms, Salons Européens (open at 12:00); or 100F for the glamorous private game rooms where you can rub elbows with high rollers (these rooms open at 15:00, some at 21:00, reasonable attire is required though a tie is not necessary). The scene is great at night and downright James Bond–like in the 100F rooms. The park behind the casino offers a good view of the casino's rear facade and of Monaco-Ville. Entrance is free to all games in the new, plebeian, American-style Loews Casino, adjacent to the old casino. To return to the train station, walk up the parkway in front of the casino, turn left on boulevard des Moulins, right on Impasse de la Fontaine, and left on boulevard Princesse Charlotte.

Sleeping and Eating in Monaco
(6.50F = about $1, country code: 377)
If you must spend the night, try the comfortable **Hôtel de France** (Db-360–420F, in port area, 6 rue de la Turbie, tel. 00-377/93 30 24 64, fax 00-377/92 16 13 34, e-mail: hotel-france@monte-carlo.mc). For a bit less, stay next door at **Hôtel Cosmopolite*** (Db-320–350F, 4 rue de la Turbie, tel. 00-377/93 30 16 95, fax 00-377/93 30 23 05, e-mail: hotel-cosmospolite@monte-carlo.mc). You'll find several affordable restaurants in Monaco-Ville and in the pleasant port (le Condamine) area.

MORE FRENCH RIVIERA TOWNS
Menton—Just a few minutes by train (8/day) from Monte-Carlo or 40 minutes from Nice, beautiful and overlooked Menton is a peaceful and relaxing spa/beach town with a fine beachfront promenade and a sandy-cobbled old town (TI tel. 04 93 57 57 00).
Cannes—Its sister city is Beverly Hills, but its beaches and the beachfront promenade are beautiful.
St. Paul-de-Vence and Vence—If you prefer hill towns to beaches, head for St. Paul and Vence (the same bus from Nice's bus station serves both towns, 20F one-way, 2/hrly, 45 min). Unless you go early, you'll escape only some of the heat and none of the crowds. **St. Paul** is part cozy medieval hill town and part local-artist shopping mall. It's charmingly artsy but gets swamped with tour buses. Meander into St. Paul's quieter streets and wander far to enjoy the panoramic views (TI tel. 04 93 32 86 95).

The prestigious, far-out, and high-priced **Fondation Maeght** art gallery is a steep (uphill) 15-minute walk from St. Paul (get off at second bus stop in St. Paul). If ever modern art could appeal to you, it would be here. Its world-class contemporary-art collection is arranged between pleasant gardens and well-lit rooms (45F, July–Sept daily 10:00–19:00, Oct–June 10:00–12:30, 14:30–18:00, tel. 04 93 32 81 63).

The enjoyable hill town of **Vence** (10 min from St. Paul by bus) disperses St. Paul's crowds over a larger and more engaging city. Vence, which bubbles with work-a-day and tourist activity (no boutique shortage here), once attracted the likes of D. H. Lawrence, Henri Matisse, and Marc Chagall. Catch the daily market (ends at 12:30) and find the small cathedral in the town center, with its Chagall mosaic and moving Chapelle St. Sacrament. The bus stop and Vence TI are on place du Grand Jardin (TI tel. 04 93 58 06 38). Matisse's much-raved-about **Chapelle du Rosaire** may disappoint all but Matisse fans, for whom this is a necessary pilgrimage (1.5 kilometers from Vence toward St. Jeannet; taxi or walk). The yellow-, blue-, and green-filtered sunlight does a cheery dance in stark contrast to the brooding tile sketches (donation, open only Tue and Thu 10:00–11:30, 14:30–17:30; in summer the chapel is also open on Wed and Fri afternoons and on Sat 10:00–11:30, 14:30–17:30; closed Nov–mid-Dec, tel. 04 93 58 03 26). If Vence tempts you to stay, the **Hôtel la Villa Roseraie***** will take good care of you (Db-500–760F, pool, CC:VM, 128 avenue H. Giraud, tel. 04 93 58 02 20, fax 04 93 58 99 31, e-mail: rvilla5536@aol.com). The small and simple **Auberge des Seigneurs**** is cheaper and near the bus stop (Db-370–400F, CC:VM, place du Frene, tel. 04 93 58 04 24, fax 04 93 24 08 01).

Eze Village—Floating high above the sea, Eze Village (don't confuse it with the seafront town of Eze-Bord de la Mer) is a spectacular medieval hill town mixing perfume outlets, upscale boutiques, outrageously priced hotels, steep, cobbled lanes, and jaw-numbing views. About 15 minutes east of Villefranche on the Moyenne Corniche (6 buses/day from Nice, 25 min), Eze Village makes a handy stop between Nice and Monaco. You can drop in on the Fragonard or Gallimard perfume outlets to understand the interesting fabrication process and shop the fragrant collections (both open daily 8:30–18:00, Gallimard breaks for lunch 12:00–14:00). You can also enjoy the charming church (Église Paroissial), but skip the Jardins Exotiques (exotic gardens). For a panoramic view and ideal picnic perch (they say on a clear day you can see Corsica), walk up to the hill town from the parking lot, take a left at the top of the first hill, and walk 20 meters down a dirt path.

Travel Notes on Connecting Nice and the Alps—La Route de Napoleon

After getting bored in his toy Elba empire, Napoleon gathered his entourage, landed on the Riviera, bared his breast, and told his fellow Frenchmen, "Strike me down or follow me." France followed. But just in case, he took the high road, returning to Paris along the route today's holiday-goers call La Route de Napoleon. (Waterloo followed shortly afterward.)

By Car: The scenic route between the Riviera and the Alps is beautiful (from south to north follow Digne, Sisteron, and Grenoble). You'll join the route Napoleon followed when returning from his exile. An assortment of pleasant villages with inexpensive hotels lies on this route, making an overnight easy. Little Entrevaux feels forgotten and still stuck in its medieval shell. Cross the bridge, meet someone friendly, and consider the steep hike up to the citadel (10F). **Hôtel Vauban** provides overnight refuge (tel. 04 93 05 42 40, fax 04 93 05 48 38). Sisteron's Romanesque church alone makes it worth a quick leg stretch. If a night in this area appeals, stay farther north, surrounded by mountains near the tiny hamlet of Clelles at **Hôtel Ferrat****. This family-run mountain hacienda at the base of Mont Aiguille (after which Gibraltar was modeled) is the place to break this long drive. Enjoy your own *boules* court, a swimming pool, and a fine restaurant (Db-280–380F, 38930 Clelles, tel. 04 76 34 42 70, fax 04 76 34 47 47).

By Train: Leave the tourists behind and take the scenic train-bus-train combination (free with railpass) that runs between Nice, Digne, and Grenoble through canyons, along whitewater rivers, between snow-capped peaks, and through many tempting villages. Start with a 9:00 departure on the little Chemins de Fer de Provence train to Digne (4/day, 3 hrs, these trains depart from a different train station about 10 blocks behind Nice's main station, 4 rue Alfred Binet, tel. 04 93 82 10 17). In Digne you can catch a main line to other destinations or, better, the bus (quick transfer, free with railpass) to Veynes (6/day, 90 min) where you can then catch the most scenic two-car train to Grenoble (5/day, 2 hrs). From Grenoble connections are available to many destinations. To do the entire trip from Nice to Grenoble in one day, you must start with the 9:00 departure from Nice (arrives Grenoble about 18:00), but I'd spend the night in one of the tiny villages en route. Clelles has the best hotel, but Sisteron and Entrevaux are also interesting (see "By Car," above).

THE FRENCH ALPS
(ALPES-SAVOIE)

Savoie is the northern and highest tier of the French Alps (the Alpes-Dauphiné lie to the south). In the 11th century, Savoie was a powerful region with borders stretching down to the Riviera and out to the Rhône. Today it is France's mountain-sports capital, with the Alps' highest point, Mont Blanc, as its centerpiece. Savoie, which didn't become part of France until 1860, feels more Swiss than French.

The scenery is spectacular. Serene yet thriving Annecy is a picture-perfect blend of natural and manmade beauty. In Chamonix, it's just you and Madame Nature—there's not a museum or important building in sight. If the weather's right, take Europe's ultimate cable-car ride to the 12,600-foot Aiguille du Midi in Chamonix.

Lyon is the southern gateway to the Alps, easily accessible by train or car. This captivating city is France's most interesting major city after Paris. If you need a city fix, linger in Lyon.

Planning Your Time

Lakefront Annecy is charmingly elegant and enjoyable for an evening. But if you're pressed for time and you've got Alps on your mind, go directly to Chamonix (most trains to Chamonix pass through Annecy, making it a convenient stopover). Here you can skip along high ridges or stroll tranquil river paths. You can zip down the mountain on a wheeled bobsled or rent a mountain bike. Ride the gondolas early (crowds and clouds roll in later in the morning) and save your afternoons for lower altitudes. Plan a minimum of two nights and one day in Chamonix. (If you're driving or training from here to the Riviera, see "La Route de Napoleon" tips at the end of the previous chapter.) Lyon is France's best-kept

The French Alps

urban secret. Strategically situated at the foot of the Alps where the Saone and Rhône Rivers meet, this manageable city merits at least one night and a full day.

Getting around the Alps

Lyon, Annecy, and Chamonix are well connected by trains. Buses run from Chamonix to nearby villages, and the Aiguille du Midi lift takes travelers from Chamonix to Italy over Europe's most scenic border crossing.

Cuisine Scene—Savoie and Lyon

The Savoie offers mountain-country cuisine. Robust and hearty, it shares much with the Swiss. Specialties include *fondue savoyarde* (melted Beaufort and Comté cheeses and local white wine, sometimes with a dash of cognac), *raclette* (chunks of semi-melted cheese

served with potatoes, pickles, sausage, and bread), *tartiflettes* (hearty
scalloped potatoes with melted cheese), *poulet de Bresse* (the best
chicken in France), *morteau* (smoked pork sausage), *gratin savoyarde*
(a potato dish using cream, cheese, and garlic), and fresh fish. Local
cheeses are Morbier (look for a charcoal streak down the middle),
Comté (like Gruyère), Beaufort (aged for two years; hard and
strong), Reblochon (mild and creamy), and Tomme de Savoie
(semi-hard and mild). Evian water comes from Savoie, as does
Chartreuse liqueur. Aprémont and Crépy are two of the area's
surprisingly good white wines. The local beer, Baton de Feu, is
more robust than other French beers.

Lyon is French cuisine at its best. Surprisingly affordable, this is
an intense palate experience—try the *salad lyonnaise* (croutons, ham,
and a poached egg on a bed of lettuce), *andouillettes* (pork sausages),
and *quenelles* (large dumplings, sometimes flavored with fish).

ANNECY

There's something for everyone in this lakefront resort city:
mountain views, flowery cobbled lanes and canals, a château, and
swimming or boating in the crystal-clear lake. Annecy (ahn-see)
is France's answer to Switzerland's Luzern. You may not have the
mountains in your lap as in nearby Chamonix, but the distant
peaks make a beautiful picture with Annecy's lakefront setting.

Tourist Information: The TI is a few blocks from the old
center across from the big grass field in the brown-and-glass
Bonlieu shopping center (daily in summer 9:00–18:30, otherwise
9:00–12:00, 13:45–18:30, 1 rue Jean Jaures, tel. 04 50 45 00 33).
Get a city map and the helpful Annecy Guide with everything a
traveler needs to know.

Arrival in Annecy

By Train: Cross the busy rue de l'Industrie, walk up rue de la
Gare, and turn left after crossing the canal to reach the pedestrian
center and the lake.

By Car: Take the Annecy Nord exit from the autoroute and
follow the green Annecy signs (you don't want Annecy le Vieux),
then follow "centre-ville" and "Tourist Information" signs. Park
at the Hôtel de Ville garage (10F/hr, 112F/24 hrs).

Sights—Annecy

Strolling—Amble along the canals and famous arcaded streets of
this handsome old city. Saunter by the Palais de l'Île, where you'll
find the Museum of Annecy (20F, Wed–Sun 10:00–12:00, 14:00–
18:00, no midday closing June–Sept). Wander deep along the canal
past rue de la Gare and find the Île St. Joseph. The views from the
Château Museum alone make it worth the entry price and climb
(see below). Luscious ice-cream shops line the pedestrian streets

(scout out the impressive display at Glaces l'Arlequin, across from Hôtel du Palais de l'Isle; see "Sleeping in Annecy," below).

Château Museum (Musée-Château d'Annecy)—This mildly interesting museum mixes local folklore, anthropology, natural history, and modern and fine arts with great views over the lake and city (30F, Wed–Sun 10:00–12:00, 14:00–18:00, no midday closing June–Sept).

Boating—Rent a paddleboat (45F/30 min, 60F/hr) and tool around the incredibly clear (and surprisingly warm) lake or let a one-hour cruise do the work for you (61F, 7 departures/day April–Sept, 18/day in summer, Compagnie des Bateaux du Lac Annecy, on the lake behind Hôtel de Ville, tel. 04 50 51 08 40). Get schedules and prices at the TI or at the boat dock right on the lake where the canal meets the old city.

Biking—A scenic bike trail (*piste cyclable*) runs along the west side of the lake. Get details at the TI. The small village of Duingt makes a good destination for serious riders. Little Big Shop rents bikes at 80 rue Carnot (tel. & fax 04 50 67 42 13).

Open-Air Market—A thriving outdoor market occupies most of the old-city center on Tuesday, Friday, and Sunday mornings.

Sleeping in Annecy
(6.50F = about $1, country code: 33, zip code: 74000)
Sleep Code: **S** = Single, **D** = Double/Twin, **T** = Triple, **Q** = Quad, **b** = bathroom, **t** = toilet only, **s** = shower only, **CC** = Credit Card (**V**isa, **M**asterCard, **A**mex), **SE** = Speaks English, **NSE** = No English, * = French hotel rating system (0–4 stars).

This city knows how to be popular, so reserve ahead, particularly in summer. A short but steep walk up the rampe du Château leads to my two favorite places (just below the château, parking available):

Hôtel du Château** has spotless rooms, some with views, and a cool view terrace (Sb-270F, Db-300–340F, Tb-350F, Qb-440F, 16 rampe du Château, tel. 04 50 45 27 66, fax 04 50 52 75 26, www .multimania.com/hotelduchateau). Just above at the **Chambres d'Hôtes**, friendly Anne-Marie and Jean-Paul have created the ultimate urban refuge at their chalet bed-and-breakfast, with a small garden, eight modern yet cozy rooms, and some views and balconies (Db-370–450F, great family rooms-450–530F, open May–Oct, 1 place du Château, tel. 04 50 45 72 28, SE).

The rest of my listings are in the pedestrian-friendly center and tend to be noisier. Right on the canal near the lake, **Hôtel de Savoie**** has a few view rooms (S-150F, D-210F, Db-310–460F, Tb-410–440F, Qb-440–490F, CC:VM, place St. François, tel. 04 50 45 15 45, fax 04 50 45 11 99, e-mail: hotel.savoie@mail.dotcom.fr).

Hôtel du Palais de l'Isle*** is in a romantic location and has ultramodern, air-conditioned rooms with mini-bars

(Db-395–560F, extra bed-100F, 13 rue Perriere, tel. 04 50 45 86 87, fax 04 50 51 87 15, e-mail: palisle@aol.com).

Hôtel Ibis** is a good if sterile last resort, and is well situated on a modern square deep in the old city with tight and tidy rooms (Db-360–410F, extra person-45F, CC:VMA, 12 rue de la Gare, tel. 04 50 45 43 21, fax 04 50 52 81 08, e-mail: HO538 @accor-hotels.com).

Hôtel Splendid*** offers all the comforts (including air-con) on Annecy's busiest street across from the TI and makes an impression with its almost lakefront location, grand façade, and regal entry (Sb-600–710F, Db-670–770F, CC:VMA, 4 quai Eustache Chappuis, tel. 04 50 45 20 00, fax 04 50 45 52 23, e-mail: splenditel@aol.com).

Hôtel Central* is just that, and is a relaxed and basic but good budget bet on a quieter courtyard just off a big pedestrian street (D-180F, Db-240F, T-220F, Tb-280F, 6 bis rue Royale, tel. 04 50 45 05 37).

Hôtel des Alpes**, with spotless, comfortable, and bright rooms, is across from the train station at a busy intersection (Sb-250F, Db-280–350F, CC:VM, 12 rue de la Poste, tel. 04 50 45 04 56, fax 04 50 45 12 38).

Eating in Annecy

Restaurant John specializes in tasty regional cuisine (115F *menu*, at the foot of Rampe du Château, 10 rue Perriere, tel. 04 50 51 36 15). The reasonable **L'Aventure** is nearby and specializes in southwestern France cuisine (closed Wed, 33 rue Ste. Claire, tel. 04 50 45 45 05). **Restaurant Vivaldi** offers reasonably priced Italian food (where the old city meets the lake at 12 Faubourg des Annociades, tel. 04 50 51 08 41). **Auberge du Lyonnais** is well respected and a classy place for regional cuisine (*menus* from 180F, near Hôtel Ibis, see "Sleeping in Annecy," above). **Le Lilas Rose** is a fine place for fondue (passage de l'Évêché).

Transportation Connections—Annecy

By train to: Chamonix (5/day, 2.5 hrs, transfer in St. Gervais), **Beaune** (6/day, 6.5 hrs, transfer in Lyon), **Nice** (8/day, 10 hrs, transfer in Lyon), **Paris**' Gare de Lyon (6 TGVs/day, 4 hrs).

CHAMONIX

Hemmed in by snow-capped peaks, churning with mountain lifts, and crisscrossed with hikes of all levels of difficulty, the resort of Chamonix is France's best base for Alpine exploration. Sophisticated Chamonix is the largest of five villages at the base of Mont Blanc and is served by several mountain lifts. Chamonix's purpose in life has always been to accommodate those coming here with some of Europe's top Alpine thrills—it's busy in the summer and on winter holidays, but peaceful at other times. Chamonix's sister city is Aspen.

Chamonix Valley 3–D

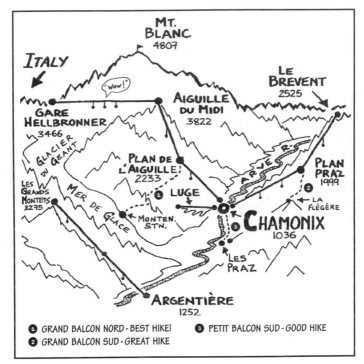

ITALY

MT. BLANC 4807

"Wow!"

LE BREVENT 2525

GARE HELLBRONNER 3466

AIGUILLE DU MIDI 3822

GLACIER DU GEANT

PLAN DE L'AIGUILLE 2233

PLAN PRAZ 1999

LES GRANDS MONTETS 3275

MER DE GLACE

① LUGE

A R V E R S

② LA FLÉGÈRE

MONTEN. STN.

CHAMONIX 1036

③

LES PRAZ

ARGENTIÈRE 1252

① GRAND BALCON NORD - BEST HIKE!   ③ PETIT BALCON SUD - GOOD HIKE
② GRAND BALCON SUD - GREAT HIKE

Planning Your Time

If you have one sunny day, spend it this way: Start with the Aiguille du Midi lift (go as early as you can, reservations possible), take it all the way to Hellbronner (hang around the needle longer if you can't get to Hellbronner), double back to Plan de l'Aiguille, hike to Montenvers (Mer de Glace—snow-level permitting), and train down from there. If the weather disappoints or the snow line's too low, hike the Petit Balcon Sud trail.

Orientation

Eternally white Mont Blanc is Chamonix's western limit; the Aiguilles Rouges mountains form the eastern limit. The frothy Arve River splits Chamonix in two. The small pedestrian zone, just west of the river and rues du Docteur Paccard and Joseph Vallot are Chamonix's main drag. The TI is west of the river, just above the pedestrian zone, while the train station is east of the river.

Tourist Information: Pick up the town and valley map and the 25F hiking map called Carte des Sentiers. Ask for weather

forecasts, hours of lifts, biking information, and help with hotel
reservations (July–Aug daily 8:30–19:30, Sept–June daily 8:30–
12:30, 14:00–19:00, on place de l'Église, next to Hôtel Mont
Blanc, 1 block west of—and above—rue du Docteur Paccard and
pedestrian zone, tel. 04 50 53 00 24, fax 04 50 53 58 90).

Chamonix Quick History

1786—Monsieurs Balmot and Paccard are the first to climb
      Mont Blanc
1818—First ascent of Aiguille du Midi
1860—After a visit by Louis Napoleon, the trickle of
      nature-loving visitors to Chamonix turns to a gush
1924—First winter Olympics held in Chamonix
1955—Aiguille du Midi *téléphérique* opens to tourists
2001—Your visit

Arrival in Chamonix

By Train: Walk straight out of the station (lockers available) and up
avenue Michel Croz. In three blocks you'll hit the center and TI.

By Car: Take the Chamonix Nord turnoff (second exit coming from Annecy) and park in the huge lot adjacent to the large
traffic circle near Hôtel Alpina or at your hotel. Most parking is
metered (5F/hr), though your hotel can direct you to free parking.

Getting around Chamonix

By Lifts: Gondolas (*téléphériques*) climb mountains all along the
valley, but the best two leave from Chamonix (see "Sights—
Chamonix," below). Sightseeing is optimal from the Aiguille du
Midi gondola, but hiking is generally better from the Le Brévent
gondola (less snow and views to Mont Blanc). Those over 59 get a
10 to 20 percent reduction on the area's lifts. Kids ages 4 to 12 ride
for half price. While the lift to Aiguille du Midi stays open year-
round, the *télécabines* to the Panoramic du Mont Blanc in Hellbronner (Italy) are open only from May or June to early October
and in bad weather (call the TI to confirm). Other area lifts are
open from January to mid-April and from July to late October.

By Hiking: If you want detailed information, visit the Office
de la Haute Montagne (Office of the High Mountains, a block
uphill from TI on 3rd floor of building marked "Maison de la
Montagne"). Get up-to-date weather and trail-condition reports
from the English-speaking staff (daily 8:30–12:00, 14:30–18:00, tel.
04 50 23 22 08). For your hike, wear warm clothes and good shoes
and pack sunglasses, sunscreen, rain gear, water, and snacks.

By Bike: The TI has a brochure proposing the best bike rides
and where to rent. The peaceful river valley trail is ideal for bikes
and pedestrians.

By Bus or Train: One road and one rail line lace together

the towns and lifts of the valley. Local buses run twice an hour
from in front of the TI for local destinations.

Sights—Chamonix

▲▲▲**Aiguille du Midi**—This is easily the valley's (and arguably,
Europe's) most spectacular and popular lift. If the weather's
clear, the price doesn't matter. Pile into the *téléphérique* (gondola)
and soar to the tip of a rock needle 12,600 feet above sea level.
Chamonix shrinks as trees fly by, soon replaced by whizzing rocks,
ice, and snow until you reach the top. No matter how sunny it is,
it's cold. The air is thin. People are giddy. Fun things can happen
at Aiguille du Midi if you're not too winded to join the locals in
the halfway-to-heaven tango.

From the top of the lift, cross the bridge and ride the elevator
through the rock to the summit of this pinnacle. Missing the
elevator is a kind of Alpus-Interruptus I'd rather not experience.
The Alps spread before you. In the distance is the bent little
Matterhorn (a tall, shady pyramid behind a broader mountain,
listed on the observation table in French as "Cervin—4,505
meters"). And looming just over there is Mont Blanc, at 15,781
feet, the Alps' highest point. Use the free telescope to spot
mountain climbers; over 2,000 climb this mountain each year.
Dial English and let the info box take you on a visual tour.
Check the temperature next to the elevator. Plan on 32 degrees
Fahrenheit even on a sunny day. Sunglasses are essential.

Explore Europe's tallest lift station. More than 150 meters
of tunnels lead to a cafeteria, a restaurant, a gift shop, and the
icicle-covered gateway to the glacial world. This "ice tunnel"
is where summer skiers and mountain climbers depart. Just
observing is exhilarating. Peek down the icy cliff and ponder
the value of an ice axe.

Next, for your own private glacial dream world, get into
the little red *télécabine* and head south to the Panoramic du Mont
Blanc at Hellbronner Point, the Italian border station. This line
stretches five kilometers with no solid pylon. (It's propped by a
"suspended pylon," a line stretched between two peaks 400 meters
from the Italian end.) In a gondola for four, you'll dangle silently
for 40 minutes as you glide over the glacier to Italy. Hang your
head out the window; explore every corner of your view. From
Hellbronner Point you can continue into Italy (see "Transportation Connections," below), but there's really no point unless
you're traveling that way.

From Aiguille du Midi you can ride all the way back to Chamonix (shame) or get off halfway down at the Plan de l'Aiguille
(great idea). From here you can hike 20 minutes down to the
refuge (40 min back up, great views, reasonable lunches at the
refuge), four hours to the valley floor (long, steep trail—bad idea),

Over the Alps—France to Italy

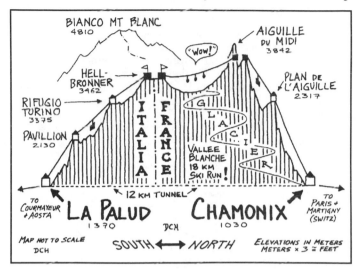

or best of all, the spectacularly scenic, undulating two- to three-hour trail to Montenvers (the Mer de Glace glacier; see Mer de Glace listing and "Hike #1," below). From there you can hike (long, steep trail—another bad idea) or ride the train (60F) back into Chamonix.

To beat the clouds and crowds, ride the lifts (up and down) as early as you can. To beat major delays in August, leave by 7:00. If the weather has been bad and turns good, expect crowds in any season (worse on weekends). If it's clear, don't dillydally. Lift hours are weather dependent, but generally run daily from 7:00 to 17:00 in summer; 8:00 to 16:45 in May, June, and September; and 8:00 to 15:45 in winter. The last *télécabine* departure to Panoramic du Mont Blanc (Hellbronner) is about 14:00. Smart travelers reserve ahead either at the information booth next to the lift (open June–Sept), or by telephone in any season (toll-free tel. 08 36 68 00 67, English spoken). You can reserve up to 10 days in advance and must retrieve your reservation at the lift station at least 30 minutes before your departure. Since you don't pay to reserve, you have nothing to lose by reserving ahead. You can't reserve the *télécabines* to Hellbronner.

Costs: These are approximate ticket costs for summer (slightly less off-season). From Chamonix to: Plan de l'Aiguille—85F round-trip (66F one-way); Aiguille du Midi—200F round-trip (168F one-way, not including parachute); the Panoramic du Mont Blanc at Hellbronner—300F round-trip (228F one-way).

Tickets from Aiguille du Midi to Hellbronner/Panoramic du Mont Blanc are sold at the base or on top (100F or 66F one-way). It's L38,000 (about $22, sold there, many currencies accepted) to drop down into Italy. (Yes, you can bring your luggage.)

Time to allow: Chamonix to Aiguille du Midi—20 minutes one-way, two hours round-trip, three to four hours in peak season; Chamonix to Hellbronner: 90 minutes one-way, three to four hours round-trip, longer in peak season. On busy days, minimize delays by getting your return lift time upon arrival at the top (tel. 04 50 53 30 80).

▲**Mer de Glace (Montenvers)**—From the little station over the tracks from Chamonix's main train station, a two-car cogwheel train (look for the red trains, 79F round-trip, 60F one-way) toots you up to a rapidly moving and dirty glacier called the Mer de Glace (Sea of Ice), and a fantastic view up the white valley (Vallée Blanche) to splintered, snow-capped peaks. The glacier—France's largest, at 10 kilometers long—is impressive from above and below. The **ice caves** are funky—filled with ice sculptures (take the small gondola down, 39F round-trip to the caves, includes entry, or hike down 20 min and pay 18F to enter). If you've already seen a glacier up close, you might skip this one.

From Plan de l'Aiguille, you can **hike** the scenic two- to three-hour trail to Montenvers—see "Hike #1," below (or from Montenvers, you can hike uphill 3–4 hours to Plan de l'Aiguille then catch the Aiguille du Midi lift from there, or go as far as you feel—the views get better and better). It's also possible to hike down to and on the glacier. The trail departs from Bar Panoramique (get details there and allow 2 hrs). For lunch with great views at Montenvers, consider Bar Panoramique (35F sandwiches, better view) or Hôtel Montenvers (better food, big 50F salads and 50F pasta dishes; also has cool rooms—see "Sleeping in Chamonix," below).

▲**Luge**—Here's something for thrill seekers. Ride a chairlift up the mountain and scream down a twisty, banked, concrete slalom course on a wheeled sled. Chamonix has two roughly parallel luge courses. While each course is a kilometer long and about the same speed, one is marked for slower bobsledders, the other for the speed demons. Young or old, hare or tortoise, any fit person can manage a luge. Don't take your hands off your stick. The course is fast and slippery (33F/1 ride, 135F/5 rides, 240F/10 rides, rides can be split with companions, July–Aug daily 10:00–19:30, until 22:30 Tue and Fri, weekends only mid-June and Sept 13:30–18:00, 10-min walk from center, just beyond train station, tel. 04 50 53 08 97.) A kid's play area is next to the luge (entry fee).

▲▲▲*Téléphérique* to Le Brévent—While the Aiguille de Midi offers a more spectacular ride, hiking options are better on this lower side of the valley, with views of the Mont Blanc range to the east and the Aiguilles Rouges peaks to the west.

From Chamonix, walk up the road past the TI and keep going to Le Brévent station. Take the *téléphérique* to Planpraz (57F round-trip, 48F one-way, nice restaurant, great views and hiking, particularly the two-hour hike along the Grand Balcon Sud to La Flégère lift (see "Hike #3," below) or the hike to Lac Cornu. The *téléphérique* continues up to Brévent with more views and hikes, though Planpraz offers plenty for me (82F round-trip, 57F one-way from Chamonix, daily 9:00–17:00, 8:00–18:00 in summer, closed April–mid-June and Nov).

Chamonix-Area Hikes

These hikes give nature lovers of almost any ability in just about any weather a good opportunity to enjoy the valley. The region's hiking map is extremely helpful; pick it up at the TI (25F). Serious hikers should buy the 80F trail booklet (English version) that includes the hiking map. Start early when the weather's generally best and confirm lift closing hours or you'll end up with a long, steep hike down. Bring water, sunscreen, a hat, good hiking shoes, and a raincoat. Trails are rocky and uneven. Take your time, watch your footing, and don't take shortcuts.

▲▲▲**Hike #1: Plan de l'Aiguille to Montenvers (Grand Balcon Nord)**—This is the easiest way to incorporate a two- to three-hour high-country walk into your ride down from the valley's greatest lift and check out a glacier to boot. The well-used trail undulates (dropping 1,500 feet) and is moderately easy providing the snow is melted (get trail details at the Office de la Haute Montagne). From the Aiguille du Midi lift, get off halfway down (Plan de l'Aiguille) and follow signs down to the refuge (reasonable food and drinks). From there follow Montenvers signs for about an hour, then follow the Signal Montenvers sign at the fork (the Montenvers route is shorter but very tricky and less scenic). At this point you'll climb to the best views of the trail. It's a long, incredibly scenic drop to the Mer de Glace (60F train back to Chamonix at the small gondolas). Snow covers this trail generally until June.

▲▲▲**Hike #2: La Flégère to Planpraz (Grand Balcon Sud)**—For a moderately easy and scenic high-country hike, walk 40 minutes along the Arve River or take the Chamonix bus (10-min ride, every 30 min from TI) to the tiny village of Les Praz (get off at lift station). Ride the lift from Les Praz to La Flégère (46F one-way, 58F round-trip, restaurant at La Flégère), drop below the station, then hike the undulating Grand Balcon Sud two and one-half hours back to Chamonix. Take the lift down to Chamonix at Plan Praz (48F one-way, 57F round-trip); skip the steep hike down (of course, this route can be done in reverse).

▲**Hike #3: Petit Balcon Sud**—This two-hour hike parallels the Grand Balcon Sud at a lower elevation and is ideal when snow or

Chamonix Valley

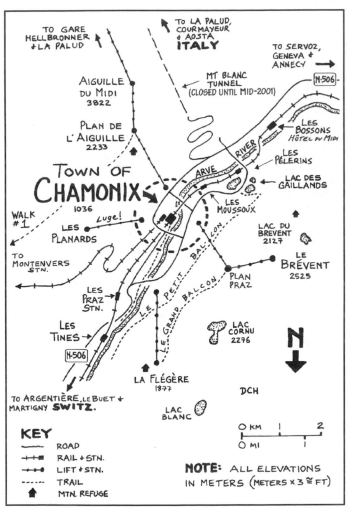

poor weather make the Grand Balcon Sud inaccessible. No lifts are required—just firm thighs to climb to the trail. From Chamonix, walk up to Le Brévent lift station. Follow the asphalt road to the left of the lift leading uphill; it turns into a dirt road that signs mark as the Petit Balcon Sud trail. After about an hour, look for signs down to Les Praz (not La Flégère!). When you reach the road, turn left to explore the village of Les Praz, or

turn right for the bus stop and river trail back to Chamonix.
Return via Chamonix bus or by walking the level Arve River
trail (40 min). This hike works just as well in reverse.

Hike #4: Arve Riverbank Stroll—For an easy forested-valley
stroll, follow the Arve River out of Chamonix toward Les Praz
(path starts across river from Chamonix's Hôtel Alpina). Les
Praz makes a pleasant destination with several cafés and a
charming village green.

Other Good Hiking Destinations—To get away from the
valley and into the backcountry, consider the beautiful trails to Lac
Cornu from the Planpraz station above Chamonix, or to Lac Blanc
from La Flégère above Les Praz. Both are moderately easy, three-
hour round-trip hikes. The Lac Blanc trail is slightly more beautiful and has a great refuge (90 min one-way from La Flégère, take
lift to l'Index to save 30 min of uphill walking). Get details at the
Office de la Haute Montagne.

Sleeping in Chamonix
(6.50F = about $1, country code: 33, zip code: 74400)

Reasonable hotels and dormlike chalets abound. With the helpful
TI, you can find budget accommodations anytime. Mid-July to
mid-August is most difficult when some hotels have five-day-
minimum stay requirements. Prices tumble off-season. If you
want a view of Mont Blanc, ask for *coté Mont Blanc* (coat-ay Mont
Blahn). Summertime travelers should seriously consider a night in
a refuge/hotel high above.

The TI has a list of **Laundromats**. One is off rue Joseph
Vallot, three blocks north of Hôtel Touring at 40 impasse
Primaviere (daily 8:00–20:00), and another is near the Aiguille du
Midi lift at 174 avenue du Aiguille du Midi (daily 9:00–20:00).

Hotels in the City Center

Hôtel de l'Arve** has a slick, modern, Alpine feel, with sharp view
rooms right on the Arve River overlooking Mont Blanc, or cheaper
rooms without the view. Take advantage of the fireplace lounge,
pleasant garden, sauna, and climbing wall (Db-348–572F, extra
person-70F, a few cheaper rooms *sans* bathroom, CC:VMA, elevator, behind huge Hôtel Alpina, 60 impasse des Anémones, tel. 04
50 53 02 31, fax 04 50 53 56 92, http://hotelarve-chamonix.com,
Isabelle and Beatrice SE).

Richemond Hôtel** is dead center and offers Old World
Alpine elegance, spacious lobbies, Ping-Pong, overstuffed chairs,
a private terrace, and generally great rooms (Sh-270–310F, Db-
394–476F, Tb-474–590F, Qb-580F, CC:VMA, 228 rue du
Docteur Paccard, tel. 04 50 53 08 85, fax 04 50 55 91 69, e-mail:
richemond@wanadoo.fr).

Hôtel Au Bon Coin**, a few blocks toward the town center from the Aiguille du Midi lift, is a friendly, traditional-feeling place with great views, private balconies, and thin walls in most of its spotless rooms; the cheaper rooms are wood-panel cozy but lack views (Ds-235F, Db-350–390F, Tb-400F, Qb-500F, usually closed mid-April–June, 80 avenue L'Aiguille du Midi, tel. 04 50 53 15 67, fax 04 50 53 51 51, friendly Julie SE).

Boule de Niege* ("Snowball") hotel is a small, simple, and good central budget option run by a friendly owner who was born in Chamonix. Two rooms share a huge view terrace (Ss-160–220F, Db-210–250F, T-290–350F, Tb-330–390F, 362 rue Joseph Vallot, tel. 04 50 53 04 48, fax 04 50 55 91 09, e-mail: laboule @claranet.fr).

Chamonix's most classy *chambre d'hôte*, **Chalet Beauregard**, a short but steep walk above the TI, is relaxed and peaceful, with a private garden. Five of its seven cushy rooms have balconies with grand views (Sb-250–270F, Db-400–600F, Tb-500–700F, includes breakfast, free parking, may require 5-day minimum in summer, on road to Le Brévent lift, 182 montée La Mollard, tel. & fax 04 50 55 86 30, www.chalet-beauregard.com, Manuel and Laurence SE).

Chalet Ski Station is my cheapest and most basic listing (dorm beds only-65F, showers-5F, reductions on area lifts for clients, great location next to Le Brévent lift, 6 rue des Moussoux, tel. 04 50 53 20 25).

Hôtel la Savoyarde***, a steep but rewarding walk above Chamonix, has views from the outdoor café tables, elegant chalet ambience, and a good restaurant. The rooms are comfy but pricey (Db-690–850F, Tb-850–1,100F, Qb-850–1,350F, CC:VMA, includes breakfast, add 80F per person for dinner, next to Le Brévent lift, 28 rue des Moussoux, tel. 04 50 53 00 77, fax 04 50 55 86 82).

Hôtel Gourmets et Italy*** offers three-star comfort, a cool riverfront terrace, an elevator, and balcony views from many of its tastefully decorated rooms (Db-385–800F, Tb-530–860F, CC:VMA, 2 blocks from casino at 96 rue du Lyret, tel. 04 50 53 01 38, fax 04 50 53 46 74, e-mail: gourmet -chamonix@laposte.fr).

Hôtel Touring**, with basic but cavernous rooms (many with 4 beds), some saggy beds, and a friendly British staff, is good for families (Ds-235–300F, Db-290–370F, add 60F for 3rd person and 100F for 4th, 95 rue Joseph Vallot, tel. 04 50 53 59 18, fax 04 50 53 67 25, e-mail: ngulliford@aol.com). They also run the nearby **Hôtel du Midi****, with a courtyard café and cheap dinners. The Midi often has rooms when other hotels don't (Db-260–320F, small rooms with view, some with balconies, 16 impasse du Génépy, tel. 04 50 53 05 62, same fax and e-mail as Hôtel Touring).

Chamonix Town

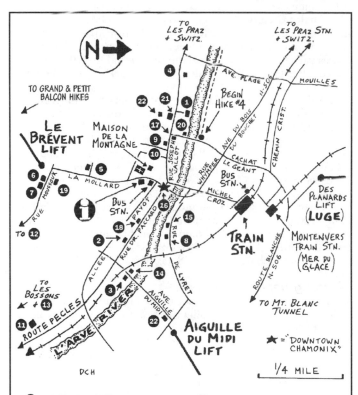

1 HOTEL DE L'ARVE
2 RICHEMOND HOTEL
3 HOTEL AU BON COIN
4 HOTEL BOULE DE NEIGE
5 CHALET BEAUREGARD B & B
6 CHALET SKI STATION
7 HOTEL SAVOYARDE
8 HOTEL GOURMETS ET ITALY
9 HOTEL DU MIDI
10 HOTEL TOURING
11 CHALET CHANTEL
12 AUBERGE DU BOIS PRIN & LA GIRANDOLE B & B
13 HOTEL L'AIGUILLE DU MIDI
14 LA BOCCALATTE
15 CHEZ NOUS RESTAURANT
16 L'ATMOSPHERE REST.
17 BISTROT DES SPORTS
18 LE BIVOUAC
19 LA CABOLEE
20 CODEC GROCERY
21 SUPER U GROCERY
22 LAUNDROMATS

Hotels for Drivers

A few minutes above Chamonix, these are practical only by car.

Chalet Chantel**, which feels more like a bed-and-breakfast inn, is meticulously kept by friendly Peter (British) and Françoise (French). The place is small, homey, and reasonable. The balcony rooms facing Mont Blanc are worth reserving (Db-420–460F, includes breakfast, 391 route des Pecles, tel. 04 50 53 02 54, fax 04 50 53 54 52).

Auberge du Bois Prin****, my only four-star listing, is cheaper than many three-star hotels and has the best views I found. All rooms but one at this 11-room, flowery chalet come with a terrace and cozy ambience. The restaurant is as romantic as its views are impressive (Db-700–820F, T or Qb-780–860F, CC:VMA, sauna, Jacuzzi, *menus* from 180F, well-signed from Le Brévent lift, Les Moussoux, tel. 04 50 53 33 51, fax 04 50 53 48 75, www.boisprin.com).

Chambre d'Hôte la Girandole, just above Auberge du Bois Prin, must be the highest home in Chamonix with three ground-floor rooms, three good bathrooms in the hall, and immense views from the garden (D-350F, includes breakfast, 46 Chemin de la Perserverance, tel. 04 50 53 37 58, fax 04 50 55 81 77).

Sleeping near Chamonix

If Chamonix overwhelms you, spend the night in one of the valley's overlooked lower-profile villages. For the following hotel, accessible to drivers and train travelers, you must reserve ahead.

Three kilometers from Chamonix (toward Annecy), in the village of Les Bossons, lies the best two-star hotel in the valley, **Hôtel l'Aiguille du Midi****. Engaging Madame Farini offers polished service, a parklike setting with beautiful lawns, a swimming pool, tennis court, Jacuzzi, and Ping-Pong, as well as a laundry room and Alpine-comfortable rooms. There's also a restaurant where Chamonix locals go for their big meal (Db-350–460F, add 30 percent each for 3rd and 4th person, half-pension preferred in summer, 160F *menu* or à la carte, easy by train, get off at Les Bossons, tel. 04 50 53 00 65, fax 04 50 55 93 69, www.hotel-aiguilledumidi.com, SE).

Refuges and Refuge-Hotels near Chamonix

Chamonix has the answer for hikers who want to sleep high above but don't want to pack tents, sleeping bags, stoves, or food: refuges and refuge-hotels (open mid-June–mid-Sept, depending on snow levels). For about 70F, sleep on bunks high in the peaceful mountains (no hot water) and let the guardian cook your meals (80–150F for dinner, about 40F for breakfast). Reserve in advance. The refuges at **Lac Blanc** (half pension-270F, great place, tel. 04 50 53 49 14), **Plan de l'Aiguille** (beds-65F, cheap meals, very simple, tel. 06 85 17 31 25), and, for the more adventurous, **Pierre à Berrard** (half-pension 155F, tel. 04 50 54 62 08), are all good and accessible. The Office de la Haute Montagne in Chamonix can explain your options and might help with reservations.

For those preferring the comfort of their own room and hot showers, refuge-hotels are ideal. **Refuge-Hôtel Montenvers**, right at the Montenvers train stop, is wood-everywhere rustic (S-210F, D-290F, T-370F, good showers down the hall, tel. 04 50 53 12 54, fax 04 50 53 98 72; for more information see "Sights—Chamonix, Mer de Glace," above).

Eating in Chamonix

La Boccalatte is an excellent-value restaurant with a lively atmosphere and a large selection of local specialties. It's run by a friendly Alsatian, Thierry (open late, across from Hôtel au Bon Coin, 59 avenue de l'Aiguille du Midi, tel. 04 50 53 52 14). For Savoyarde specialties, you can't beat the alpine-cozy **Chez Nous** (92F *menu*, turn right at casino, 78 rue du Lyret). If you're feeling romantic, reserve a balcony table right on the river at the aptly named **l'Atmosphere** (*menus* from 120F, open daily, next to post office at 123 place Balmat, tel. 04 50 55 97 97). **Bistrot des Sports** is a souvenir of old Chamonix, with wood tables, old photos, good food, and smoky locals (50–100F *menus*, 182 rue Joseph Vallot, tel. 04 50 53 00 46). The cute, cozy, and central **Le Bivouac** serves fine local specialties (across from Patagonia store on rue Paccard, tel. 04 50 53 34 08). **La Cabolée**, next to the Brévent *téléphérique*, is a hip eatery with great omelets and a wonderful view from its outdoor tables.

Picnic assembly: The best grocery is Codec, below Hôtel Alpina. The more central Super U is next to Hôtel Touring at 117 rue Joseph Vallot (Mon–Sat 8:30–19:30, Sun 8:30–12:00) and there's a long-hours grocery a block in front of the train station. The park next to the church is picnic-pretty.

Transportation Connections—Chamonix

Bus and train service to Chamonix is surprisingly good. You'll find helpful bus and train information desks at the train station.

By train to: Annecy (5/day, 2.5 hrs, transfer in St. Gervais); **Beaune** and **Dijon** (3/day, 8 hrs, transfers in St. Gervais and Lyon); **Nice** (4/day, 10 hrs, transfers in St. Gervais and Lyon, night train available); **Arles** (5/day, 8 hrs, transfers in St. Gervais and Lyon); **Paris'** Gare de Lyon (4/day, 7 hrs, longer at night, transfers in St. Gervais and Annecy; take handy night train); **Martigny, Switzerland** (2 hrs, scenic trip); **Geneva** (3/day, 2.5 hrs, quick transfers in St. Gervais, La Roche-sur-Foron, and Annemasse).

By bus: Buses provide service to destinations not served by train and also to some cities that are served by train—but at a lower cost and higher speed. Get information at the bus station (*gare routière*) in the SNCF train station (tel. 04 50 53 01 15).

To Italy: Take the spectacular lift (Chamonoix-Aiguille du Midi-Hellbronner) to Italy, described in "Sights—Chamonix," above. If you prefer a more down-to-earth experience, take the train to Martigny and bus from there to Courmayeur (2/day, 1 hr, Italian side of Aiguille du Midi gondola) and Aosta (2/day, 2 hrs). Once the Mont Blanc tunnel reopens (probably late in 2001), you'll be able to take the bus directly and efficiently from Chamonix to Aosta, Italy (90 min).

Itinerary Options from Chamonix

A Day in French-Speaking Switzerland—There are plenty of tempting Alpine and cultural thrills just an hour or two away in Switzerland. A road-and-train line sneaks you scenically from Chamonix to the Swiss town of Martigny. While train travelers cross without formalities, drivers are charged a one-time 40-SF fee ($24) for a permit to use Swiss Autobahns.

A Little Italy—The remote Valle d'Aosta and its historic capital city of Aosta are a spectacular gondola ride over the Mont Blanc range. The side trip is worthwhile if you'd like to taste Italy (spaghetti, gelato, and cappuccino), enjoy the town's great evening ambience, or look at the ancient ruins in Aosta, often called the "Rome of the North."

From Hellbronner (see "Sights—Chamonix, Aiguille du Midi," above), catch the L38,000 lift down to La Palud and take the bus to Aosta (hrly, change in Courmayeur). Or, if you have exceptional social skills, try to talk a gondola mate with a car in La Palud into a ride down the valley. From Aosta, trains or buses will take you to Milan and the rest of Italy.

LYON

Nestled at the base of the Alps between Burgundy and Provence, overlooked Lyon is one of France's big-city surprises. Its strategic location, straddling the Rhône and Saone Rivers, has made Lyon important since pre-Roman times. After Paris, Lyon is the most historic and culturally important city in France. You get two distinctly different-feeling cities: the *molto* Italian cobbled alleys, Renaissance mansions, and colorful facades of Vieux Lyon; and the more staid but classy, Parisian-feeling shopping streets of Presqu'ile. Lyon makes a handy day visit for train travelers, as many trains pass through Lyon and both stations have baggage lockers.

Orientation

Lyon may be France's second-largest city, but inside it feels manageable. Most sightseeing is near the Saone River and can be done on foot. If you stick to the sights listed below, you won't need more than the funicular to help you get around, though the subway is easy.

Lyon's sights are concentrated in three areas: Fourvière Hill, Vieux Lyon, and the Presqu'ile (the tourist map of Lyon has a helpful enlargement of this area).

Start your day on Fourvière Hill (take the funicular near St. Jean Cathedral in Vieux Lyon to Fourvière) and visit the Gallo-Roman Museum (lunch closing at 11:40), Roman Theater, and Basilique Notre Dame before catching the funicular or walking down to Vieux Lyon. In Vieux Lyon, explore the covered passageways, or *traboules* (see "Sights—Vieux Lyon," below), then finish your day on the Presqu'ile. Note that most of Lyon's important sights close Monday and Tuesday.

Tourist Information: The well-equipped TI is on place Bellecour (Mon–Fri 9:00–18:00, until 17:00 on weekends and in winter, until 19:00 mid-June–mid-Sept, tel. 04 72 77 69 69). The good 5F English map, which has museum information and a good enlargement of central Lyon, is free at your hotel. Pick up the free map of Vieux Lyon, the list of open *traboules*, and a schedule of events and concerts (ask about concerts in the Roman Theater). The TI sells a useful museum pass (1 day-90F, 2 day-160F, 3 day-200F; includes all museums, a day pass on the bus or Métro, and a walking tour of Lyon via live guide or audioguide). The well-done 35F World Heritage Excursions book, sold at the TI, describes excellent self-guided walking tours (Vieux Lyon and Presqu'ile North are best). You can also rent handy audioguides (40F) with good walking tours of Lyon, or take a guided walking tour through the TI (principal language is French, though guides will translate).

Arrival in Lyon

By Train: Two train stations serve Lyon: Perrache and Part-Dieu. Many trains stop at both, and through trains connect the two stations every 10 minutes. Both are well served by Métro, bus, and taxi, and have lockers and baggage-checking services, making Lyon an easy stopover visit for train travelers.

The Perrache station is more central and within a 20-minute walk of place Bellecour (cross place Carnot and walk straight up rue Victor Hugo). Or take the Métro (direction Laurent Bonnevay) two stops to Bellecour and follow "sortie rue République" signs (see "Getting around Lyon," below, for Métro tips).

To get to the city center from the Part-Dieu station, follow sortie Vivier Merle signs to the Métro, take it toward Jean Mace, transfer at Saxe Gambetta, continue riding toward Gare de Vaise, get off at Bellecour, and follow signs for "sortie rue République" (see "Getting around Lyon" for Métro help).

Figure 60F to 80F to taxi from either train station to the hotels listed near place Bellecour.

By Car: The city center is fairly easy to navigate, though you'll encounter traffic on the surrounding freeways. From the freeways, follow signs to "centre-ville" and "Presqu'ile" and then follow "place Bellecour" signs. Park in the lots under place Bellecour or place des Celestins (yellow P means parking lot) or get advice from your hotel (half day-50F, 24 hrs-100F). The TI's map has all public car parks well identified.

Getting around Lyon

Lyon's Métro, with only four lines (A, B, C, and D), is a breeze. While similar to Paris' Métro in many ways (e.g., routes are signed by direction for the last stop on the line), Lyon's Métro is highly automated, cleaner, and less crowded. There are no turnstiles and no obvious ticket windows. Efficient ticket machines (coins only) are located just before the platforms and give change (1 ride-8F, 10 rides-70F). Buy your ticket (firmly push top button for one ticket and then put your coins in), then validate your ticket by punching it in the nearby orange box, and you're in business. Study the wall maps to be sure of your direction; ask a local if you're not certain. Your ticket is good until you complete your one-way trip. Métro tickets can be used on the two funiculars, but you cannot transfer from Métro to funicular with the same ticket.

Sights—Fourvière Hill

▲▲**Gallo-Roman Museum (Musée de la Civilisation Gallo-romaine)**—Constructed in the hillside with views of the Roman Theater, this museum makes Lyon's importance in Roman times clear. Lyon was the military base that Julius Caesar used to conquer Gaul (much of modern-day France). Admire the bronze chariot from the seventh century B.C. and then orient yourself with the model of Roman Lyon. As the museum cascades downhill you'll pass Gallo-Roman artifacts that allow you to piece together life in Lyon during the Roman occupation, including 2,000-year-old lead pipes, a speech by Claudius (translated into English), Roman coins, models of Roman theaters complete with moving stage curtains, and haunting funeral masks (20F, Wed–Sun 9:30–12:00, 14:00–18:00, rooms begin closing 20 min early, helpful English explanations).

Basilique Notre Dame de Fourvière—In the late 1800s, the Bishop of Lyon vowed to build a magnificent tribute to God if the Prussians left his city alone (the same reason and vow that built the Sacré-Coeur in Paris). The whipped-cream exterior is neo-everything, and the interior screams, "overdone," with mosaics. Don't miss the chapel below or the panoramic views from behind the church.

Sights—Vieux Lyon (Old Lyon)

▲*Traboules* (**Covered Passageways**)—Lyon is the Florence of France, offering the best concentration of well-preserved Renaissance buildings in the country. From the 16th to the 19th centuries Lyon was king of Europe's silk industry; at one point it hummed with more than 18,000 looms. The fine buildings of the old center were designed by Italians and financed by the silk industry. Pastel courtyards, beautiful loggias, and delicate arches line the passageways (*traboules*) connecting these buildings. The serpentine *traboules* provided shelter when the silk was being moved from one stage to the next and would provide ideal cover for the French resistance in World War II. Several of Lyon's 315 *traboules* are open to the public (press top button next to streetfront door to release door when entering; push lit buttons to illuminate dark walkways; pull lever sideways at door handle when leaving; please respect residents' peace when wandering through). The TI's map of Vieux Lyon proposes an interesting route connecting some of the most interesting *traboules*, though many are periodically closed. As you wander Vieux Lyon, look for plaques next to doors giving a history of the building and *traboule*. Explore the courtyards at #24 and #26 rue St. Jean, and walk all the way through Lyon's longest *traboule* at #27 rue de Boeuf (push buttons as you go for mood lights).

Cathedral of St. Jean—Stand as far back as you can in the square for the best view. This took 300 years to build and transcends Romanesque and Gothic styles. This cathedral does not soar like northern French cathedrals from the same period (churches in southern France are typically less vertical than those in the north). Inside you'll find a few beautiful stained-glass windows and a remarkable astrological clock with a performance at 12:00, 14:00, 15:00, and 16:00 (Mon–Fri 8:00–12:00, 14:00–19:30, Sat–Sun 14:00–17:00). Check out the ruins predating the cathedral outside the left transept.

Museum of Automatons (Musée des Automates)—A 15-minute walk downriver from the funicular, this seven-room mom-and-pop place displays 250 moving dolls in 20 scenes of international (but mostly French) events, (25F, daily 14:30–18:00, good English handout, 100 rue St. Georges).

Sights—On or near Lyon's Presqu'ile

From the Perrache station to place des Terreaux, the Presqu'ile is Lyon's shopping spine, with thriving pedestrian streets and chic boutiques. Cruise the shops of rue de la République and the *bouchons* (characteristic bistros) of rue Mercière and relax at a café on place des Terreaux. You'll also find these interesting museums:

▲**Musée des Beaux Arts**—Located in a former abbey, this fine-arts museum has an impressive collection ranging from Egyptian

Lyon

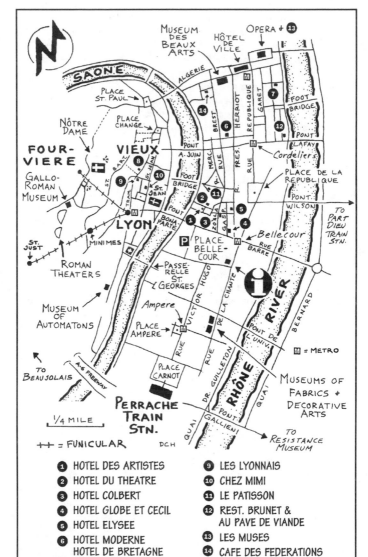

1 HOTEL DES ARTISTES

2 HOTEL DU THEATRE

3 HOTEL COLBERT

4 HOTEL GLOBE ET CECIL

5 HOTEL ELYSEE

6 HOTEL MODERNE
HOTEL DE BRETAGNE

7 HOTEL IRIS

8 LES ADRETS REST. &
LES RETROUVAILLES

9 LES LYONNAIS

10 CHEZ MIMI

11 LE PATISSON

12 REST. BRUNET &
AU PAVE DE VIANDE

13 LES MUSES

14 CAFE DES FEDERATIONS

antiquities to medieval armor to Impressionist paintings. Still, if you're short on time and going to Paris, it's skippable (25F, Wed–Sun 10:30–18:00, closed Mon–Tue, pick up a museum layout on entering, great café-terrace, 20 place des Terreaux, Métro: Hôtel de Ville).

Museums of Fabrics and Decorative Arts (Musées des Tissus et des Arts Decoratifs)—These special-interest museums are well organized and help to understand Lyon's historic importance, but provide no English explanations. The Musée des Tissus is more interesting and takes you on a good tour of Lyon's important silk industry with beautiful displays of silk from Napoleon's Throne room to dresses, hats, and other clothing. The Musée des Arts Decoratifs is a large manor home decorated with period furniture and art objects (30F covers both museums, Tue–Sun 10:00–17:30, Decorative Arts Museum closes 12:00–14:00, closed Mon, 34 rue de la Charite, Métro: Bellecour).

▲Resistance and Deportation Center (Centre d'Histoire de la Resistance et de la Deportation)—Located near Vichy, the capital of the French puppet state, Lyon was the center of French Resistance from 1942 to 1945. This well-organized museum, once used as a Nazi torture chamber, uses headsets, videos, reconstructed rooms, and, it seems, anything they can get their hands on to help you understand how the Resistance came to be and what life was like for its members. English explanations and headsets help, but you need to move slowly with your headset and stand near the remote signal boxes or you'll feel like you're decoding your own enemy messages (25F, Wed–Sun 9:00–17:30, 15-min walk from Perrache station, cross Pont Gallieni and walk 3 blocks to 14 avenue Berthelot; or, easier, take Métro to Jean Mace and walk back 3 blocks toward the river).

Sights—Near Lyon

Beaujolais Wine Country—Virtually knocking on Lyon's door, the beautiful vineyards and villages of the Beaujolais (relaxed tastings) make a pleasant detour for drivers heading north. The most scenic and interesting section lies between Villefranche sur Saone and Macon just west of A-6 on D-68. Beaujolais' most important villages lie on this short route: Chiroubles, Fleurie, and Julienas. Look for "Route de Beaujolais" signs. The route continues north into the Maconnais wine region at the famous village of Pouilly-Fuisse. Lyon's TI has information on afternoon bus excursions to the Beaujolais (200F, includes 2 tastings).

Sleeping in Lyon
(6.50F = about $1, country code: 33, zip code: 69002)
Hotels in Lyon are a steal compared to those in Paris. Weekends are generally discounted as this city still thrives on business travelers

first. Skip the hotels near either train station. All hotels listed below are on the Presqu'ile; the first five are on or near the intimate place des Celestins, two blocks north of place Bellecour (Métro: Bellecour).

Hôtel des Artistes***, ideally located right on place des Celestins, is red velvet plush, comfortable, central, and the best value in its price range (Sb-400–560F, Db-440–600F, CC:VMA, elevator, 8 rue Gaspard-Andre, tel. 04 78 42 04 88, fax 04 78 42 93 76, e-mail: hartiste@clubinternet.fr, SE).

Hôtel du Théâtre**, across the small square from Hôtel des Artistes, is an artsy place with breezy rooms in all sizes and shapes, many wonderfully funky, some with sliver showers. Those overlooking the place Celestins tend to be larger and are worth the extra cost. Expect friendly owners and plenty of stairs (Sb-285–320F, Db-300–360F, extra bed-50F, 10 rue de Savoie, entrance on back side of place des Celestins, tel. 04 78 42 33 32, fax 04 72 40 00 61).

Hôtel Colbert**, just off place des Celestins, is ideal and warmly run by Chantal. Bright, cheery rooms on the street side are larger but come with street noise (Sb-325F, Db-355F, CC: VMA, good buffet breakfast, elevator, TV, 4 rue des Archers, tel. 04 72 56 08 98, fax 04 72 56 08 65).

Hôtel Globe et Cecil*** is the most elegant of my listings and offers refined comfort in a classy setting (Db-670–740F, CC: VMA, 21 rue Gasparin, tel. 04 78 42 58 95, fax 04 72 41 99 06).

Hôtel Élysée** is sharp with small but fine rooms and cheery decor (Sb-290–360F, Db-365–420F, 92 rue Pdt. Edouard Herriot, tel. 04 78 42 03 15, fax 04 78 37 76 49).

These hotels are located closer to place des Terreaux, about 10 to 15 blocks north of place Bellecour.

Hôtel Moderne** is a good value, with pleasant pastel rooms and a cheery lobby, in the heart of the shopping area (Db-330–350F, elevator, 15 rue Dubois, Métro: Cordeliers, tel. 04 78 42 21 83, fax 04 72 41 04 40).

Hôtel de Bretagne* is the best one-star value I could find. It has sincere owners, tight and tidy rooms, and good beds but tired carpeting (Sb-205F, DB-250F, Tb-290F, CC:VMA, 10 rue Dubois, Métro: Cordeliers, tel. 04 78 37 79 33, fax 04 72 77 99 92).

Hôtel Iris**, tucked away near the Opera, is better than the lobby and courtyard suggest. The basic but comfortable rooms are a good value (Sb-210–280F, Db-220–260F, CC:VM, 26 rue de l'Abre Sec, tel. 04 78 39 93 80, fax 04 72 00 89 91).

Eating in Vieux Lyon

With an abundance of excellent restaurants in all price ranges, it's hard to go wrong—unless you order *tripes* (cow stomach) or come on Sunday when almost all restaurants close. Look for these classics: *quenelles* (large dumplings), roasted chicken from Bresse, and *salade lyonnaise* (lettuce, ham, and poached eggs).

Bouchons are small bistros evolving from the days when mama would feed the silk workers. Vieux Lyon has the most *bouchons*, though the rue Merciere on the Presqu'ile offers many good places. Here are a few to get you started (all are closed Sun):

The epicenter of restaurant activity in Vieux Lyon is place Neuve St. Jean—compare the crowds and sift through their menus. **Les Adrets** is cozy and good (115F *menu*, 30 rue de Boeuf, tel. 04 78 38 24 30). At 38 rue de Boeuf, **Les Retrouvailles** offers an excellent 120F *menu*, a charming dining room, and a terrific overall experience. A block south, **Les Lyonnais** is cheaper, lighthearted, and locally popular, with photo portraits of loyal customers lining the walls (95F *menu*, 1 rue Tramssac, tel. 04 78 37 64 82). For a salad or quiche and a glass of wine with great ambience, consider **Chez Mimi**'s small café one block from the cathedral (inside can be smoky, 66 rue St. Jean).

Eating on the Presqu'ile
The classic bistro **la Francotte** is good for a relaxing drink or a meal and is handy to many hotels (closed Sun, 8 place des Celestins). Vegetarians and nondrinkers will appreciate the fair-priced fine cuisine at **Le Patisson** (2 blocks north of place des Celestins at 17 rue du Port du Temple, closed Fri–Sun, tel. 04 72 41 81 71). Near the Opera, these two fine places go unnoticed by tourists: the warmly decorated **Restaurant Brunet** (100F *menu*, 23 rue Claudia, tel. 04 78 37 44 31) and the more formal **Au Pave de Viande** (100F *menu*, 15 rue Claudia, tel. 04 78 37 23 89). If it's a view you want, **Les Muses** is seven floors up the dazzling Opera with a brilliant terrace (open lunch and dinner, take the exterior elevator to floor 7, tel. 04 72 00 45 58). **Café des Federations** is a venerable institution worth a stop for the traditional Lyonnais ambience and good wine selection (150F *menu*, closed Sun and in Aug, 8 rue Major-Martin).

Transportation Connections—Lyon
After Paris, Lyon is France's most important rail hub. Rail travelers will find this gateway to the Alps, Provence, the Riviera, and Burgundy an easy stopover. **By train to: Paris** (20/day, 2 hrs), **Dijon** (14/day, 2 hrs), **Beaune** (9/day, 2 hrs), **Avignon** (14/day, 2.5 hrs), **Nice** (14/day, 6 hrs), **Annecy** (8/day, 90 min), **Venice** (3/day, 10 hrs), **Rome** (3/day, 11 hrs), **Florence** (3/day, 10 hrs), **Geneva** (6/day, 2 hrs), **Barcelona** (2/day, 9 hrs).

Drivers: En route to Provence, consider a three-hour detour through the spectacular Ardeches Gorges, exit the A-6 autoroute at Privas and follow the villages of Aubenas, Vallon Pont d'Arc (offers kayak trips), and Pont St. Esprit.

BURGUNDY

The rolling hills of Burgundy gave birth to superior wine, fine cuisine, and sublime countryside crisscrossed with canals and dotted with tourist-free hill towns. Bucolic Burgundy is the transportation funnel for eastern France and makes a convenient stopover for travelers (car or train), with quick access north to Paris or the Alsace, east to the Alps, and south to Provence. Only a small part of Burgundy is covered by vineyards, but wine making is what they do best. The white cows you see everywhere are Charolais. France's best beef ends up in *boeuf bourguignon*. The Romanesque churches dotting the countryside owe their origins to the once-powerful influence of Burgundy's Abbey of Cluny.

Planning Your Time

Stay in or near Beaune. It's conveniently located for touring the vineyards and countryside. Plan on a half day in Beaune and a half day for the countryside. Ideally, sleep in Beaune Friday night and awake to the sounds of the Saturday market. If you have more time, visit (or sleep in) unspoiled Semur-en-Auxois and tour the awesome Romanesque church in the hill town of Vezelay.

Getting around Burgundy

Trains link Beaune with ease; less-frequent buses cruise the wine route between Dijon, Beaune, and Chalon sur Saone. Bikes and minivan tours get nondrivers from Beaune into the countryside. Buses serve Semur-en-Auxois from Dijon and Montbard.

Cuisine Scene—Burgundy

Considered by many to be France's best, Burgundian cuisine is peasant cooking elevated to an art. Several classic dishes were born

Burgundy

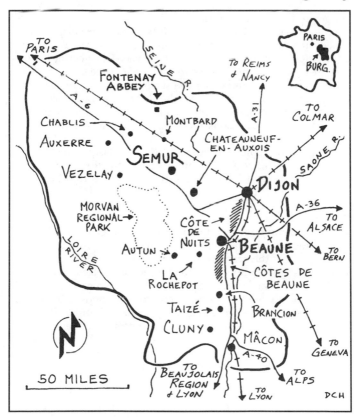

here—escargots *bourguignon* (snails served sizzling hot in garlic butter), *boeuf bourguignon* (beef simmered for hours in red wine with onions and mushrooms), *coq au vin* (chicken stewed in red wine), and *oeufs en meurette* (poached eggs on a large crouton in red wine)—as were the famous Dijon mustards. Look also for *ambon persillé* (cold ham layered in a garlic-parsley gelatin), *pain d'épices* (spice bread), and *gougère* (light, puffy cheese pastries). Native cheeses are Epoisses and Langres (both mushy and great), and my favorite, Montrachet (a tasty goat cheese). *Crème de cassis* (a black currant liqueur) is another Burgundian specialty; look for it in desserts and snazzy drinks (try a *kir*).

    With Bordeaux, Burgundy is why France is famous for wine. From Chablis to the Beaujolais, you'll find it all here—great, fruity reds; dry whites; and crisp rosés. The three key grapes are

Chardonnay (dry, white wines), Pinot Noir (medium-bodied red wines), and Gamay (light, fruity wines like Beaujolais). Every village produces its own distinctive wine—like Chablis and Meursault; road maps read like fine wine lists. If the wine village has a hyphenated name, the latter half of its name often comes from the town's most important vineyard (e.g., Gevery-Chamberin, Ladoix-Serrigny). Look for the "*Dégustation Gratuite*" (free tasting) signs and prepare for serious tasting and steep prices if you're not careful. For more relaxed tastings, head for the hills; the less prestigious Hautes-Côtes (upper slopes) produce some terrific and overlooked wines. Look for village cooperatives or try my suggestions for Beaune tastings (see "Wine Tasting in and near Beaune," below). The least expensive (but still tasty) wines are Bourgogne Ordinaire and Passetoutgrain (both red), and whites from the Macon and Chalon areas. If you like rosé, try Marsannay, considered one of France's best.

BEAUNE

You'll feel comfortable right away in this manageable and fun-loving wine capital, where life centers around the production and consumption of the prestigious, expensive Côte d'Or wines. *Côte d'Or* means "golden hillsides," and they are a spectacle to enjoy in late October as the leaves of the vineyards turn colors.

Beaune is a compact, prosperous little city (pop. 25,000) with a handful of interesting monuments and vineyards on its doorstep. Limit your Beaune ramblings to the town center, contained within its medieval walls and circled by a one-way ring road. All roads and activities converge on the perfectly French place Carnot, as do the Wednesday and Saturday markets.

Tourist Information: The TI, across the street from Hôtel Dieu on place de la Halle, has city maps, a room-finding service, *chambre d'hôte* pamphlets, bus schedules, and information on wine-tasting tours (April–Nov daily 9:00–19:00, summers until 20:00, Dec–March daily 10:00–18:00, from place Carnot walk toward thin spire, tel. 03 80 26 21 30).

Arrival in Beaune

By Train: To reach the city center from the train station (lockers available), walk straight out of the station up avenue du Huit (8) Septembre, cross the busy ring road, and continue up rue du Château.

By Bus: Beaune has no bus station—only several stops in the center. Ask the driver for *le centre ville* (city center)—the Jules Ferry stop is central and closest to the train station.

By Car: Follow "*centre ville*" signs to the ring road. Once on the ring road, turn right at the first signal after the new post office (rue d'Alsace) and park (free) in the place Madeleine.

Helpful Hints
Internet Access: Check your e-mail at Point Diz (open 13:00–21:00, 28 rue de Lorraine).

Best Souvenir Shopping: The **Athenaeum** has a great variety of souvenirs and many books in English (daily 10:00–19:00, across from Hôtel Dieu at 7 rue de l'Hôtel Dieu).

Best Wine Store: Dennis Perret has a fine selection from a variety of producers in all price ranges and a helpful, English-speaking staff (they can chill a white for your dinner picnic). If you've tasted a wine you like elsewhere, they can usually find a less costly bottle with similar qualities (June–Nov Mon–Sat 9:00–19:00, Dec–May closed 12:00–14:00, closed Sun, 40 place Carnot).

Sights—Beaune
▲▲**Hôtel Dieu**—The Hundred Years' War and the Black Death devastated Beaune, leaving more than 90 percent of its population destitute. Nicholas Rolin, Chancellor of Burgundy and a peasant by birth, had to do something for "his people." So, in 1443, he paid to build this flamboyant Flemish/Gothic charity hospital. It was completed in only eight years. Tour it on your own with the helpful English handout. In the St. Louis wing (where patients replaced the winepresses that once occupied this space), you'll find Van der Weyden's dramatic *Last Judgment* polyptych, commissioned by Rolin to give the dying something to ponder. Ask the attendant to let the giant roaming monocle give you a closer look and keep this painting in mind if you see the Isenheim altarpiece in Colmar—they were commissioned for similar reasons with very different results (32F, April–Nov daily 9:00–18:30, Dec–March 9:00–11:30, 14:00–17:30).

▲**Collégiale Notre Dame**—Built in the 12th and 13th centuries, this is a good example of Cluny-style architecture (except for the front porch addition). Enter to see the 15th-century tapestries (behind the altar, drop in a franc for lights), a variety of stained glass, and what's left of frescoes depicting the life of Lazarus (daily 8:30–19:00). To find the Musée du Vin from here, walk 30 steps straight out of the cathedral, turn left down a cobbled alley (rue d'Enfer), keep left, and enter the courtyard of Hôtel des Ducs, today's Musée du Vin, located in the old residence of the dukes of Burgundy.

Musée du Vin—You don't have to like wine to appreciate this folk-wine museum. The history and culture of Burgundy and wine were fermented in the same bottle. At least wander into the court-yard for a look at the duke's palace, antique winepresses (in the barn), and an interesting model of 15th-century Beaune. Inside the museum you'll find a great model of the regions, tools, costumes, and scenes of Burgundian wine history—but no tasting. New English explanations are in each room (25F, ticket good for other Beaune museums, daily 9:30–18:00, closed Tue Dec–Jan).

Beaune

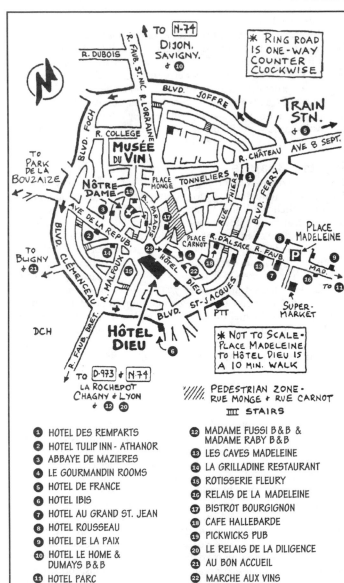

* RING ROAD IS ONE-WAY COUNTER CLOCKWISE

TO N-74
DIJON,
SAVIGNY,
& ⑩

R. DUBOIS

BLVD. JOFFRE

TRAIN STN.
& ⑤

R. FAUB. ST. NIC.
R. LORRAINE

BLVD. FOCH

R. COLLEGE

MUSÉE DU VIN

AVE 8 SEPT.

R. CHÂTEAU

TO PARK DE LA BOUZAIZE

NÔTRE DAME ⑲

PLACE MONGE   TONNELIERS   ①

RUE THIERS

BLVD. FERRY

AVE DE LA REPUB.

③

A. PARADIS

⑰

②

⑭

⑮

R. MALFOUX

BLVD. CLÉMENCEAU

TO BLIGNY
& ㉑

PLACE CARNOT

R. D'ALSACE

⑧   **PLACE MADELEINE**

㉓

HOTEL DIEU

④   ⑱

⑫   ⑬   ⑦

R. FAUB.

P

⑨

⑯

MAD.

TO ⑪

㉒

BLVD. ST-JACQUES

PTT

SUPER-MARKET

DCH

R. FAUB. BRET.

HÔTEL DIEU

⑥

TO D-973 & N-74
LA ROCHEPOT
CHAGNY & LYON
& ⑫ ⑳

* NOT TO SCALE • PLACE MADELEINE TO HÔTEL DIEU IS A 10 MIN. WALK

////// **PEDESTRIAN ZONE - RUE MONGE & RUE CARNOT**

▥ **STAIRS**

① HOTEL DES REMPARTS
② HOTEL TULIP INN - ATHANOR
③ ABBAYE DE MAZIERES
④ LE GOURMANDIN ROOMS
⑤ HOTEL DE FRANCE
⑥ HOTEL IBIS
⑦ HOTEL AU GRAND ST. JEAN
⑧ HOTEL ROUSSEAU
⑨ HOTEL DE LA PAIX
⑩ HOTEL LE HOME & DUMAYS B&B
⑪ HOTEL PARC

⑫ MADAME FUSSI B&B & MADAME RABY B&B
⑬ LES CAVES MADELEINE
⑭ LA GRILLADINE RESTAURANT
⑮ ROTISSERIE FLEURY
⑯ RELAIS DE LA MADELEINE
⑰ BISTROT BOURGIGNON
⑱ CAFE HALLEBARDE
⑲ PICKWICKS PUB
⑳ LE RELAIS DE LA DILIGENCE
㉑ AU BON ACCUEIL
㉒ MARCHE AUX VINS
㉓ TOURIST OFFICE

Parc de la Bouzaise and Vineyards—To get to this peaceful park, walk toward the ring road on avenue de la République, cross it, and follow the stream for three blocks; the park and vineyards are straight ahead. Stroll through the park and then enter the vineyards just beyond, climbing high on dirt paths for the best views.

Wine Tasting in and near Beaune

Countless opportunities exist (for a price) for you to learn the fine points of Burgundy's wine. Many small wine shops offer free tastings (with the expectation that you'll buy) and several large cellars (*caves*) charge an entry fee, allowing you to taste a variety of wines (with less expectation that you'll buy). Most *caves* offer some form of introduction or self-guided tour and are open daily, generally 9:30 to 11:30 and 14:00 to 17:30 (also see "Minibus Tours," below).

Start or end your tour at **Athenaeum**, which is a bookstore (with many titles in English), wine bar, and Burgundian wine chamber of commerce all in one (across from Hôtel Dieu, next to TI). ▲▲▲**Marché aux Vins**—This is Beaune's wine smorgasbord and the best way to sample its impressive wines. You pay 50F for a wine-tasting cup (you keep it) and get 45 minutes to sip. Plunge into the labyrinth of candlelit *caves* dotted with 18 barrels, each offering a new tasting experience. You're on your own. Relax; this is world-class stuff. The $70 reds are upstairs in the chapel, at the end of the tasting. (Hint: Enjoy your taste more by sneaking in a hunk of bread or crackers.) If you grab an empty wine basket at the beginning and at least pretend you're going to buy, the occasional time checker will leave you alone (daily 9:00–12:00, 14:00–18:00, last entry at 17:30, July–Aug 10:00–18:30, tel. 03 80 25 08 20).

More Self-Guided Tours in Beaune—While the Marché aux Vins is the ultimate wine-tasting experience, you may want to sample other cellars. If you have less time for wine, **Caves des Cordeliers** offers good self-guided tours (with English explanations) and six wines to taste for just 20F (6 rue de l'Hôtel Dieu, tel. 03 80 24 53 79). **Cave Patriache Père et Fils** has self-guided tours of Beaune's largest underground cellars, and 13 different wines to sample (50F, includes tasting cup, 7 rue du Collège, tel. 03 80 24 53 78). The TI has a complete list of area vintners for those who want to venture into the countryside; remember, you're expected to buy (also see "The Hautes-Côtes to Châteauneuf-en-Auxois," below for tastings in the less-prestigious, more-relaxed Hautes-Côtes).

Minibus Tours of Vineyards near Beaune—Wine Safari minibus wine-tasting tours offer three two-hour itineraries (190F, tour #2 is best for beginners, departs from TI, call TI for information, tel. 03 80 26 21 30). These tours are well run, in English, and will get you through the countryside and to the wineries you couldn't get into otherwise. Transco buses run from Beaune through all the great wine villages for those who want to explore the wine road on their own (see "Getting around the Beaune Region," below).

Sleeping in Beaune
(6.50F = about $1, country code: 33, zip code: 21200)
Sleep Code: **S** = Single, **D** = Double/Twin, **T** = Triple, **Q** = Quad, **b** = bathroom, **t** = toilet only, **s** = shower only, **CC** = Credit Card (**V**isa, **M**asterCard, **A**mex), **SE** = Speaks English, **NSE** = No English, * = French hotel rating system (0–4 stars).

Hôtel des Remparts*** is classy but affordable, with fine rooms in a manor house complete with beamed ceilings, period furniture, a quiet courtyard, and great family rooms (Db-300–470F, most at 470F, Db suites-650F, Tb-550–590F, Qb-570–770F, CC:VM, cozy attic rooms, parking-45F, between train station and main square, just inside ring road at 48 rue Thiers; tel. 03 80 24 94 94, fax 03 80 24 97 08, e-mail: hotel.des.remparts @wanadoo.fr, SE).

Hôtel Tulip Inn-Athanor*** mixes modern comfort with a touch of old Beaune and is very central (Sb-300–460F, Db-385–560F, most Db-460F, Tb/Qb-770F, CC:VM, elevator, 9 avenue de la République, tel. 03 80 24 09 20, fax 03 80 24 09 15, e-mail: Hotel.Athanor@wanadoo.fr, SE).

Abbaye de Mazieres is ideally located and has 12 quiet, colorful, and spacious rooms in a 15th-century building over a restaurant near the basilica (Db-360–650F, Tb-550–770F, 19 rue Mazieres, tel. 03 80 24 74 64, fax 03 80 22 49 49, if no response contact Hôtel Tulip above).

The **Le Gourmandin** restaurant rents three spacious, comfortable, and air-con rooms right on place Carnot (Db-360F, big Db/Tb or Qb-470F, CC:VM, many stairs, 8 place Carnot, tel. 03 80 24 07 88, fax 03 80 22 27 42).

Train travelers will appreciate the friendly and well-run **Hôtel de France****, across from the train station (Sb-200–250F, Db-280–300F, Tb/Qb-340–360F, easy parking, 35 avenue du Huit Septembre, tel. 03 80 24 10 34, fax 03 80 24 96 78).

Hôtel Ibis**, modern, efficient and comfortable with a pool and pleasant terrace, is located at the ring road and avenue Charles de Gaulle (Sb-330F, Db-350–400F, tel. 03 80 22 75 67, fax 03 80 22 77 17). There's another IBIS closer to the autoroute, but it's less central.

Sleeping on Place Madeleine
These hotels are a few blocks from the city center and train station and offer easy parking.

What **Hôtel au Grand St. Jean**** lacks in character it makes up for in value and location. Like a sprawling motel with ample and safe parking, it's simple, practical, and, with its helpful, English-speaking owner, Monsieur Neaux, plenty French. Color-blind travelers will love the TV lounge (Db-260F, Tb/Qb-320F, CC:VM, on place Madeleine, tel. 03 80 24 12 22, fax 03 80 24 15 43).

Across the square, the no-frills **Hôtel Rousseau** will make you smile, with cheerful and quirky owners, pet birds, and a pleasant enclosed garden. The cheapest rooms are simple but fine; those with showers are like grandma's, though maintenance can be spotty (S-145F, D-190F, Db-300–350F, Tt-255F, Tb-355F, Q-300F, Qb-360F, showers down the hall-20F, includes breakfast, free private parking, 11 place Madeleine, tel. 03 80 22 13 59).

Hôtel de la Paix*, just off place de la Madeleine, is a fine value with tastefully decorated rooms and an owner who cares (Sb-300F, Db-400–450F, loft Tb-550F, Qb-600F, CC:VM, 45 rue du Faubourg Madeleine, tel. 03 80 24 78 08, fax 03 80 24 10 18, SE).

Sleeping near Beaune
Hotels: Hôtel Le Home, with cushy rooms in an old mansion, is an excellent value. It's a kilometer out of town on N-74 toward Dijon. The less-expensive rooms are fine, but the rooms on the parking courtyard (400F) have a nice terrace (Db-330–460F, Tb/Qb-500F, CC:VM, free parking, 138 route de Dijon, tel. 03 80 22 16 43, fax 03 80 24 90 74). Call ahead—it's popular.

Hôtel Parc, three kilometers from Beaune in Levernois, is a delightful vine-covered manor house with fine rooms and a welcoming staff (Db-280–530F, Tb-350–620F, CC:VM, 21200 Levernois, tel. 03 80 24 63 00, fax 03 80 24 21 19).

Chambres d'Hôte: The Côte d'Or has many *chambres d'hôte*; get a pamphlet at the TI and reserve ahead in the summer. Most can be found only in small wine villages, and many are only a short drive from Beaune. In Magny le Villers, the friendly **Dumays** have two attached rooms in a restored farmhouse, ideal for three or more (Ss-185F, Db-235F, Tb-285F, Qb-350F, from Beaune go north on N-74 then west at Ladoix, in Magny look behind church, tel. 03 80 62 91 16). There are scads of *chambres d'hôte* in the cliff-dwelling villages of Baubigny and Orches, just under La Rochepot (zip code for both: 21340). In Baubigny, **Madame Fussi** has four comfortable rooms in a modern home over a sweeping lawn (Db-250F, Tb-300F, tel. & fax 03 80 21 84 66). A few kilometers away in Orches, **Madame Raby** offers one double room and a good family-size room in her newly renovated home with a cute pool and a nice yard (Db-290F, Tb-350F, extra person-50F, 5 maximum, big breakfast, tel. & fax 03 80 21 78 45, e-mail: praby@wanadoo.fr).

Eating in Beaune

For a traditional Burgundian setting, step down to the wine-soaked-cellar atmosphere of the 12th-century **Abbaye de Mazieres** (98F *menu*, closed Tue, see "Sleeping," above). On the place Madeleine, try the relaxed ambience and friendly surroundings of **Les Caves Madeleine** and dine surrounded by shelves of wine (good wines by the glass, reasonable *plats du jour* and *menus*, closed Sun, 8 rue Faubourg Madeleine). For fine traditional Burgundian cuisine (escargot, hot goat-cheese salad, *oeufs en meurette*) at digestible prices, consider **La Grilladine** (75F/105F/135F *menus*, closed Mon, 17 rue Maufoux, tel. 03 80 22 22 36). Or try the nearby **Rotisserie Fleury** (15 place Fleury, tel. 03 80 2 35 50). Beaune's best budget restaurant is **Relais de la Madeleine**, run by the entertaining Monsieur Neaux Problem (44 place Madeleine, tel. 03 80 22 07 47).

Beaune's best wine bar is the relaxed **Bistrot Bourgignon** (costly wines by the glass and a good but limited *menu*, on a pedestrian-only street at 8 rue Monge, closed Sun). Drop by **Café Hallebarde** for a grand selection of draft beer (24 rue d'Alsace); and if you're tired of speaking French, pop into the late-night-lively **Pickwicks Pub** (behind church at 2 rue Notre Dame).

Eating near Beaune

Five minutes away is **Le Relais de la Diligence**, where you can dine surrounded by vineyards and taste the area's best budget Burgundian cuisine with many *menu* options (inexpensive–moderate, closed Tue eve and all day Wed, take N-74 toward Chagny/Chalon and turn left at L'Hôpital Meursault on D-23, tel. 03 80 21 21 32). **Au Bon Accueil** is relaxed and ideal, on a hill above Beaune, with great outdoor tables, a cozy interior, and five-course *menus* for 110F (closed Mon–Wed, leave Beaune's ring road and take Bligny-sur-Ouche turnoff, a few minutes outside Beaune you'll see signs to Au Bon Accueil, tel. 03 80 22 08 80). If you're willing to drive 45 minutes, consider a late afternoon and evening in Châteauneuf-en-Auxois (see "Hautes-Côtes to Châteauneuf-en-Auxois," below).

Transportation Connections—Beaune

By train to: Dijon (9/day, 30 min), **Colmar** (6/day, 4.5 hrs, transfers in Dijon and Besançon), **Arles** (7/day, 5 hrs, transfer in Lyon), **Nice** (7/day, 8 hrs, transfer in Lyon), **Chamonix** (3/day, 8.5 hrs, transfers in Lyon and St. Gervais), **Amboise** (8/day, 9 hrs, transfer in Paris), **Paris**' Gare de Lyon (3 TGVs/day, 2 hrs; otherwise transfer to the TGV in Dijon, 3 hrs).

Getting around the Beaune Region

By Bus: Transco buses run from Beaune through the vineyards and villages south to Chalon-sur-Saône, west to La Rochepot, and north to Dijon. Ask at the TI for schedules and stops or call for information (tel. 03 80 42 11 00).

By Bike: The well-organized, English-speaking, and helpful Bourgogne Randonnées has good bikes, bike racks, maps, and thorough countryside itineraries. They can deliver your bike to your hotel anywhere in France (bikes-20F/hr, 90F/day, Mon–Sat 9:00–12:00, 13:30–19:00, Sun 10:00–12:00, 14:00–17:00, near train station at 7 avenue du Huit Septembre, tel. 03 80 22 06 03, fax 03 80 22 15 58).

Sights—Beaune Region

Bike Routes—Get the local Michelin map and suggestions from Bourgogne Randonnées (see above) and consider the long scenic loop ride through vineyards and over hills to La Rochepot. Take D-17 from Pommard through St. Romain and Orches (it adds time but is more scenic and has fewer cars compared to the D-973). From La Rochepot return to Beaune or continue to St. Aubin and Gamay via D-33 (it runs behind Hôtel Relais du Château in La Rochepot). Follow the tiny road to Puligny-Montrachet and Meursault, and head back to Beaune via D-973 (all day, 35 kilometers round-trip). The D-18 to Savigny-les-Beaune and Pernand Vergelesses is shorter and easier. (Check out Savigny's unusual château.)

▲**Château La Rochepot**—This very Burgundian castle rises above the trees and its village 12 kilometers from Beaune. It's accessible by car, bike (hilly), or infrequent bus. Cross the drawbridge and knock three times with the ancient knocker to enter. This pint-size castle is splendid inside and out. Tour half on your own and the other half with a French guide (get the English explanations, some tours in English). The kitchen will bowl you over. Look for the 15th-century highchair in the dining room. Climb the tower and see the Chinese room, sing chants in the resonant chapel, and make ripples in the well. (Can you spit a bull's-eye? It's 72 meters down!) Don't leave without driving, walking, or pedaling up D-33 a few hundred meters toward St. Aubin (behind Hôtel Relais du Château) for a romantic view (35F, June–Aug Wed–Mon 10:00–18:00, closed Tue, closes 11:30–14:00 and at 16:30 in winter, tel. 03 80 21 71 37).

▲**Brancion and Chapaize**—An hour south of Beaune by car (20 kilometers west of Tournus on D-14) are two churches that owe their existence and architectural design to the nearby once-powerful Cluny Abbey. Brancion's nine-building hamlet floats on a hill with the purest example of Romanesque architecture I've seen—a 12th-century church (with faint frescoes inside), a charming château (climb the tower for views), and a 15th-century market hall. **Auberge du Vieux Brancion** offers fine Burgundian cuisine at fair prices. For a peaceful break, spend a night in one of

Beaune Region

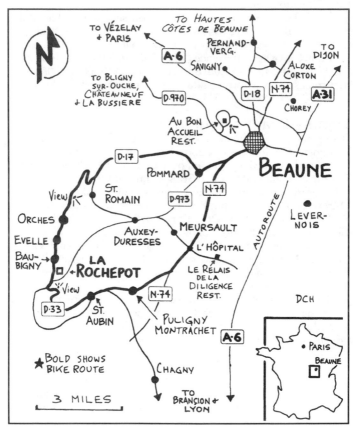

the Auberge's simple, funky-but-cozy rooms (Ds-220F, Db-350F, good family rooms-350–450F, tel. & fax 03 85 51 03 83). A few kilometers closer to Beaune, Chapaize's beautiful church is famous for its 11th-century belfry and its listing interior (English brochure available). Wander around the back for a view of the belfry and check out the friendly café across the street.

Cluny and Taizé—Twenty kilometers southwest of Brancion lies the historic town of Cluny. The center of a rich and powerful monastic movement in the Middle Ages is today a pleasant town with very sparse and crumbled remains of its once-powerful abbey. For a new trend in monasticism, consider visiting the booming Christian community of Taizé (teh-zay), just north of Cluny. Brother Roger and his community welcome visitors who'd like to spend a few days getting close to God through meditation, singing, and simple living. Call or write first if you plan to stay overnight. There are dorm beds only. (Taizé Community, 71250 Cluny, tel. 03 85 50 14 14.)

The Hautes-Côtes to Châteauneuf-en-Auxois

This half-day loop trip takes you through vineyards and pastoral landscapes, along the Burgundy canal, past abbeys, and through medieval villages. (If you're heading to Paris, Châteauneuf-en-Auxois can be done en route or as an overnight stop). It requires a car, the local Michelin map, and navigational patience. From Beaune's ring road, head toward Dijon on N-74. In a few minutes take the Savigny-les-Beaune turnoff then connect Pernand Verge-lesses with the Hautes-Côtes villages of Echevronne, Magny-les Villiers, Villers la Faye, and Marey-les-Fussey. **Wineries** in these villages offer stress-free tastings. (More serious tasters should consider these wineries: Lucien Jacob in Echevronne, tel. 03 80 21 91 50, SE; Domaine Thevenot Le Brun in Marey-les-Fussey, tel. 03 80 62 91 64, NSE; and Marcel Fribourg in Villers la Faye, tel. 03 80 62 91 74, NSE.) Then head west over the hills to Pont d'Ouche. At Pont d'Ouche follow the canal toward Châteauneuf-en-Auxois. In about 10 minutes you'll see the brooding castle.

Châteauneuf's medieval **château** towers over the valleys below. The village huddles securely in the shadow of the castle and merits a stroll. Park at the lot in the upper end of the village and don't miss the panoramic viewpoint near the parking lot. Walk into the château's courtyard (25F, daily 10:00–12:00, 14:00–19:00, the interior is skippable, English handout).

Signs behind Châteauneuf lead to La Bussière's **abbey**, which was founded in the 13th century by Cistercian monks but goes largely unnoticed by tourists today. Stroll the lovely gardens, check out the refectory (look for door in rear of main building marked "Accueil;" enter and walk upstairs), and consider the cheap 90F dinner (includes wine, must call to reserve, tel. 03 80 49 02 29). Ask for the key to the *vieux pressoir* (old press).

The scenic return to Beaune is via Pont d'Ouche (toward Bligny sur Ouche) where you turn left, go uphill through Bouil-land, and then downhill through Savigny-les-Beaune.

Sleeping and Eating in or near Châteauneuf-en-Auxois

(6.50F = about $1, country code: 33, zip code: 21320)
Hostellerie du Château**, in Châteauneuf, offers rooms in two locations. Its main building ("Hotel") is a better value than its annex up the street called "La Residence." Many rooms in the "Hotel" are half-timbered and have views of the château next door; the tiny top-floor doubles are adorable (Db-280–395F,

T/QB-435F). "La Residence" has larger rooms, comfortable but pricier (D-435F, Tb-480F). The restaurant serves good *menus* from 140F (tel. 03 80 49 22 00, fax 03 80 49 21 27, www.hostellerie-chateauneuf.com).

Charming **Annie Bagatelle**, at the upper end of the village, has four beautiful rooms (2 with lofts); look for the green plaque (Db-280–360F, tel. 03 80 49 21 00, fax 03 80 49 21 49, SE a little).

To sleep floating on a luxury hotel barge at two-star prices with views up to Châteauneuf's brooding castle, find the canal-front village of Vandenesse-en-Auxois. Here the *Lady A* barge offers tight, cozy rooms. Friendly Lisa cooks an elaborate dinner upon request for 140F, including wine (Sb-250F, Db-300F, includes breakfast, call way ahead in summer, tel. 03 80 49 26 96, fax 03 80 49 27 00, SE). The *écluse* (lockhouse) at the bridge offers small groceries, wine tastings, and inexpensive *chambres*—**Chez Monique et Pascal** (Sb/Db-250F, Tb-300F, tel. 03 80 49 27 12, fax 03 80 49 26 05).

Three Châteauneuf restaurants offer Burgundian cuisine at fair prices: **La Grill du Castel** (meal-sized salads, great escargots, *boeuf bourguignonne*, CC:VM, tel. 03 80 49 26 82); **L'Orée du Bois Crêperie** (friendly and inexpensive); and the country elegant **Hostellerie du Château** (see above), where I splurge for dinner.

SEMUR-EN-AUXOIS
If you have time for one more night in Burgundy, spend it here. This overlooked town feels real and unspoiled. There are no important sights to digest—just a seductive jumble of Burgundian alleys and courtyards perched above the meandering Armancon River—all beautifully illuminated after dark. About 40 minutes from the famous church in Vezelay, and two hours from Paris, Semur makes an ideal first- or last-night stop on your trip.

Tourist Information: The informative TI is across from Hôtel Côte d'Or at Semur's medieval entry (Mon–Sat 9:00–19:00, Sun 10:00–12:00, 15:00–18:00, off-season closes earlier and on Sun, 2 place Gaveau, tel. 03 80 97 05 96). Pick up their city-walks brochure, bike routes, and information on the many area sights.

The town has two sights—the Church of Notre Dame, which dominates its small square, and the small Municipal Museum. But Semur is best experienced by following the TI's walking tours. The longer yellow route gets you down to the river and up to good views over Semur.

Sights—Near Semur-en-Auxois
▲▲**Vezelay**—This pretty little hill town, about 40 minutes northwest of Semur, is famous for its best-anywhere Romanesque Basilica of St. Madeleine. Built to honor its famous relics, the bones of Mary Magdelene, this is one of Europe's largest and

best-preserved Romanesque churches. Its beauty is its simplicity.
To appreciate this, compare it to another of the same era, Notre-
Dame de Paris. Vezelay's appeal lies in the color of the stone
and the absence of distracting decoration. The view from
behind the church is sublime. Train travelers must go to nearby
Semicelles and catch a bus from there (6/day, 30 min). Vezelay's
TI is near the church (rue St. Pierre, tel. 03 86 33 23 69).
Abbey of Fontenay—This marvelous Cistercian abbey would
be a three-star sight if you weren't forced into a long tour
(French only) to see it. More like a small town than an abbey,
Fontenay offers the complete picture of a medieval abbey
with many interesting buildings to visit (40F, daily 10:00–17:00,
20-minute drive from Semur via Montbard, no bus, 80F taxi
from Montbard).

Sleeping and Eating in Semur-en-Auxois
(6.50F = about $1, country code: 33, zip code: 21140)
Hotels and restaurants are a good value here. **Hôtel les
Cymaises**** has a quiet courtyard, private parking, and gives
three-star comfort for the price of two (Sb-310F, Db-340F, Tb-
410F, CC:VM, 7 rue du Renaudot, tel. 03 80 97 21 44, fax 03 80
97 18 23). The simple and unspoiled **Hôtel des Gourmets*** is
good for those on a tight budget and seeking a good restaurant
(D-130–160F, Db-210F, T/Q-180F, room for up to 6 people-
320F, CC:VMA, 4 rue Varenne, tel. 03 80 97 09 41, fax 03 80 97
17 95). Semur is surrounded by *chambres d'hôte*. Friendly British
ex-pat **Roger Collins** has four fine rooms in nearby Villars-
Villenotte (Db-300F, tel. 03 80 96 65 11, fax 03 80 97 32 28).

Eating: Franco-American-owned **Le Calibressan** offers fine
menus and coziness from 90F; say hello to Jill (closed Sun–Mon,
16 rue Fevret, tel. 03 80 97 32 40). Tiny, reasonable **Les Minimes**
is a local institution (closed Sun–Mon, 39 rue des Vaux, tel. 03 80
97 26 86). **L'Entracte** is where everybody goes for pizza, pasta,
salads, and more in a relaxed atmosphere (open daily, 4 rue
Fevret). The historic *charcuterie* across from the church is ready
to supply your dinner picnic.

Transportation Connections—
Semur-en-Auxois
By bus: 3 buses/day connect with TGV trains in Montbard
(20 min), and 3/day serve **Dijon** (1 hr); tel. 03 80 42 11 00.

ALSACE AND NORTHERN FRANCE

The French province of Alsace stands like a flower-child referee
between Germany and France. Bounded by the Rhine on the east
and the softly rolling Vosges Mountains on the west, this is a lush
land of Hanzel and Gretel villages, sprawling vineyards, and
appealing cities. Food and wine are the primary industry, topic of
conversation, and perfect excuse for countless festivals.

Alsace has changed hands several times between Germany
and France because of its location, natural wealth, naked vulnera-
bility, and the fact that Germany thinks the mountains are the
natural border while France thinks the Rhine is. Having been a
political pawn for 1,000 years, Alsace has a hybrid culture—locals
who swear do so bilingually, and the local cuisine features sauerkraut and fine wine. If you're traveling in December, come here
for France's most celebrated Christmas markets and festivals.

Strasbourg is a big-city version of Colmar, worth a stop for
its grand cathedral. The humbling battlefields of Verdun and the
bubbly vigor of Reims in northern France are closer to Paris than
Alsace and follow logically only if your next destination is Paris.

Planning Your Time

Set up in or near Colmar. Allow most of a day for Colmar and a
full afternoon for the Wine Road (Route du Vin). If you have one
day, wander Colmar's sights until after lunch and then set out for
the Route du Vin. Urban Strasbourg has a soaring cathedral and a
lovely center city. If you can spare an extra half day, spend it
there, but with limited time, skip it. Reims and Verdun are doable
by car as stops between Paris and Colmar—if you're speedy. Train
travelers with only one day between Colmar and Paris must
choose Reims or Verdun.

Reims, Verdun, and Colmar

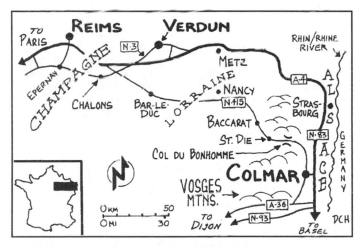

Getting around the Alsace

Trains link Colmar and Strasbourg hourly in 50 minutes. Buses and minivan excursions radiate from Colmar to villages along the Route du Vin, and you can rent bikes in Colmar and Turckheim if you prefer to pedal (for details on all of these options, see "Route du Vin," below).

Cuisine Scene—Alsace

Alsatian cuisine is a major tourist attraction in itself. The German influence is obvious—sausages, potatoes, onions, and sauerkraut. Look for *choucroute garni* (sauerkraut and sausage—although it seems a shame to eat it in a fancy restaurant), the more traditionally Alsatian *baeckeanoffe* (potato, meat, and onion stew), *rösti* (an oven-baked potato and cheese dish), fresh trout, and foie gras. At lunch, or for a lighter dinner, try a *tarte à l'oignon* (like an onion quiche but better) or *tarte flambée* (like a thin-crust pizza with onion and bacon bits). If you're picnicking, buy some stinky Münster cheese. Dessert specialties are *tarte Alsacienne* (fruit tart) and *glace Kugelhopf* (a light cake mixed with raisins, almonds, dried fruit, and cherry liqueur).

Alsatian Wines

Alsatian wines are named for their grapes, unlike in Burgundy or Provence, where wines are commonly named after villages, or in Bordeaux, where wines are commonly named after châteaus. White wines dominate in the Alsace. The following wines are made entirely of that grape variety: Sylvaner (fairly light, fruity, and inexpensive), Riesling (more robust than Sylvaner but drier than the German style you're probably used to), Gerwürtztraminer (spicy, with a powerful bouquet; good with pâtés and local cheeses), Muscat (very dry, with a distinctive bouquet and taste; best as a before-dinner wine), Tokay/Pinot Gris (more full-bodied than Riesling but fine with many local main courses), Pinot Noir (the local red is overpriced; very light and fruity and generally served chilled), and the tasty Crèmant d'Alsace (the region's good and inexpensive champagne). You'll also see *eaux-de-vie*, powerful fruit-flavored brandies; try the *framboise* (raspberry) flavor.

COLMAR

Colmar is a well-pickled old place of 70,000 residents offering a few heavyweight sights in a warm, mid-size-town package. Historic beauty was usually a poor excuse to be spared the ravages of World War II, but it worked for Colmar. The American and British military were careful not to bomb the half-timbered old burghers' houses, characteristic red- and green-tiled roofs, and cobbled lanes of Alsace's most beautiful city.

Today Colmar thrives with colorful, half-timbered buildings, impressive art treasures, and German tourists. Schoolgirls park their rickety horse carriages in front of the city hall, ready to give visitors a clip-clop tour of Old Town. Antique shops welcome browsers, and hotel managers run down the sleepy streets to pick up fresh croissants in time for breakfast.

There isn't a straight street in Colmar. Thankfully, most streets are pedestrian-only and it's a lovely town to be lost in. Navigate by the high church steeples and the helpful signs directing visitors to the various sights.

Orientation

For tourists, the town center is place Unterlinden (a 15-minute walk from the train station), where you'll find the TI, a major museum, and a huge and handy Monoprix department store and supermarket (Mon–Sat 8:30–20:30, closed Sun). Every city bus starts or finishes on place Unterlinden.

Colmar is most crowded from May through September. Weekends are busiest (reserve ahead). The impressive music festival fills hotels the first two weeks of July and the local wine festival rages for 10 days in early August. Open-air markets bustle next to the Dominican and St. Martin Churches on Thursdays and Saturdays.

Tourist Information: The TI is next to the Unterlinden Museum on place Unterlinden. Pick up a city map, a Route du Vin map, and *Colmar Actualités*, a booklet with bus schedules. Get information about concerts and festivals in Colmar and in nearby villages, and ask about Colmar's Folklore Tuesdays (with folk dancing at 20:30 every Tue mid-May–mid-Sept on place de

l'Ancienne). The TI reserves hotel rooms and has *chambres d'hôte*
listings for Colmar and the region (April–Oct Mon–Sat 9:00–
18:00, until 19:00 July–Aug, Sun 10:00–14:00; Nov–March
Mon–Sat 9:00–12:00, 14:00–18:00, Sun 10:00–14:00, tel. 03 89
20 68 92). A public WC is 20 meters to the left of the TI.

Arrival in Colmar
By Train: To reach the center from the station (lockers available),
walk straight out, turn left on avenue de la République, and keep
walking (15-min walk). Buses #1, #2, and #3 each go from the station
to the TI (about 5.70F, pay the driver). Allow 55F for a taxi to a hotel in central Colmar. The bus stops here for Route du Vin villages.

    By Car: Follow signs to *"centre-ville"* then "place Rapp."
There are several handy pay lots (under place Rapp) and (for now)
a huge free lot at parking du Musée Unterlinden (across from
Primo 99 hotel). Several hotels have private parking, and those
that don't can advise you where to park.

Helpful Hints
Tours: The TI organizes walking tours of the Old Town for 25F
and of the Unterlinden Museum for 20F (daily in summer, weekends only in other months). You can also hire a private guide for a
walking tour (490F, ask at TI). For minivan tours of the Route du
Vin, see "Getting around the Wine Road," below.

    Internet Access: Try Poussin Vert (37 rue de Neuf Brisach,
tel. 03 89 11 18 58) or Cafe de Haut Rhin (15-min walk from TI,
76 route d'Ingersheim, tel. 03 89 79 17 47).

    Bike Rental: Rent bikes from Cycles Geisweiller (just below
place Rapp, 6 blvd. du Champs de Mars, tel. 03 89 41 30 59) or the
less central Cyclotheque (31 route d'Ingersheim, tel. 03 89 79 14 18).

Self-Guided Tour of Colmar's Old Town
This walk is ideal after dark, when many of Colmar's pedestrian
streets and important monuments are illuminated by mood-setting
colored lights. Look for handy information plaques with English
explanations at various points throughout this walk.

    The importance of 15th- to 17th-century Colmar is clear as
you wander its pedestrian-friendly old center, which is decorated
with 45 buildings classified as historic monuments. Back in feudal
times, most of Europe was fragmented into chaotic little prince-
doms and dukedoms. Merchant-dominated cities (the World
Trade Organizations of their day), which were natural proponents
of the formation of large nation-states, banded together to form
"trading leagues." The **Hanseatic League** was the superleague of
northern Europe. Prosperous Colmar was a member of a smaller
league of 10 Alsatian cities called the Decapolis (founded 1354).
Delegates of this group met in Colmar's Old Custom House.

Start your tour at the **Old Custom's House** (Koifhus). Walk under it to the place de l'Ancienne Douane and face the Bertholdi statue—arm raised, à la *Statue of Liberty*. The place de l'Ancienne Douane is the festive site of outdoor wine tasting many summer evenings. The soaring, half-timbered commotion of higgledy-piggledy rooftops just beyond marks the **Tanners' Quarters**. These 17th- and 18th-century rooftops competed to get space in the sun to dry their freshly tanned hides; the nearby river channel got rid of waste products. Walk down to the end of rue des Tanneurs, turn right, and take the first left along the stream and you'll come to the old market hall (fish, produce, and other products were brought here by flat-bottomed boat). Cross the canal and turn right and you'll enter **La Petite Venise** quarter, a bundle of Colmar's most colorful houses lining the small canal. This tourist-popular area is well lit and even cuter at night.

Double back to the Old Custom House via rue des Écoles. From the Custom House, walk up rue des Marchands (Merchants' Street). Those overhanging roofs you're walking under were a medieval tax dodge. Since houses were taxed on square footage at street level, owners would expand tax-free up and over the street. In two blocks you'll come face to face with the **Pfister House**, a richly decorated merchant's house from 1537 with an external spiral staircase turret and painted walls showing the city folk's taste for Renaissance humanism (the wine shop on the ground floor is Colmar's best). The man carved into the side of the building next door (to the left) was a drape maker; he's shown holding a bar, Colmar's measure of about one meter. (In the Middle Ages it was common for cities to have their own length for a meter.) One more block on the left is the **Bartholdi Museum** (described below). A passage to the right leads to Colmar's Cathedral St. Martin. Compare this soaring structure with the typically sober Dominican Church (housing Schongauer's *Virgin in the Rosebush*, described below), a few blocks toward the TI. The **House of Heads** on rue des Têtes near the TI is Colmar's other famous merchant's house; it was built in 1609 and is decorated with 105 faces and masks. From here it's a short walk to the TI and the Unterlinden Museum.

Sights—Colmar
▲▲▲**Unterlinden Museum**—Colmar's touristic claim to fame, this is one of my favorite museums in Europe. Its extensive yet manageable collection ranges from Roman Colmar to medieval wine-making exhibits and from traditional wedding dresses to paintings that give vivid insight into the High Middle Ages.

The highlight of the museum (and, for me, the city) is Grünewald's gripping *Isenheim Altarpiece*, actually a series of three different paintings on hinges that pivot like shutters (study

Colmar

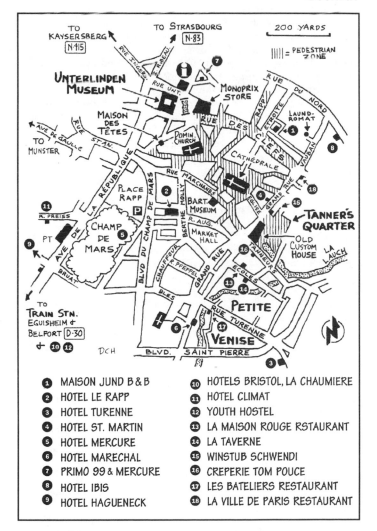

❶	MAISON JUND B & B	
❷	HOTEL LE RAPP	
❸	HOTEL TURENNE	
❹	HOTEL ST. MARTIN	
❺	HOTEL MERCURE	
❻	HOTEL MARECHAL	
❼	PRIMO 99 & MERCURE	
❽	HOTEL IBIS	
❾	HOTEL HAGUENECK	
❿	HOTELS BRISTOL, LA CHAUMIERE	
⓫	HOTEL CLIMAT	
⓬	YOUTH HOSTEL	
⓭	LA MAISON ROUGE RSTAURANT	
⓮	LA TAVERNE	
⓯	WINSTUB SCHWENDI	
⓰	CREPERIE TOM POUCE	
⓱	LES BATELIERS RESTAURANT	
⓲	LA VILLE DE PARIS RESTAURANT	

the little model on the wall, explained in English). Designed to help people in a medieval hospital endure horrible skin diseases (such as St. Anthony's Fire, later called rye ergotism) long before the age of painkillers, it's one of the most powerful paintings ever produced.

Stand like a medieval peasant in front of the centerpiece and let the agony and suffering of the Crucifixion drag its fingers down your face. The point—Jesus' suffering—is drilled home: the weight of his body bending the crossbar, his elbows pulled from their sockets by the weight of his dead body, his mangled feet, the grief on Mary's face. In hopes that the intended viewers— the hospital's patients—would know that Jesus understands their suffering, he was even painted looking like he, too, had a skin disease. Study the faces and the Christian symbolism.

The three scenes of the painting changed with the seasons of the church year. The happy ending—a psychedelic explosion of Resurrection joy—is the spiritual equivalent of jumping from the dentist's chair directly into a Jacuzzi. The last two panels, showing the meeting of St. Paul the hermit and St. Anthony, are the product of a fertile imagination and the stuff nightmares are made of.

There's more to the museum. Ringing the peaceful cloister is a fine series of medieval church paintings and sculpture and a room filled with old winepresses. Downstairs you'll find Roman and prehistoric artifacts. The upstairs contains local and folk history, with everything from medieval armor to old-time toys (35F, April–Oct daily 9:00–18:00, Nov–March Wed–Mon 9:00–17:00, closed Tue, tel. 03 89 41 89 23).

▲▲**Dominican Church**—Here is another medieval mind blower. In Colmar's Église des Dominicains, you'll find Martin Schongauer's angelically beautiful *Virgin in the Rosebush* (from 1473 but looking like it was painted yesterday) holding court center-stage. Here, Mary is shown as a welcoming mother. Jesus clings to her, reminding the viewer of the possibility of an intimate relationship with Mary. The Latin on her halo reads: "Pick me also for your child, O very Holy Virgin." Rather than telling a particular Bible story, this is a general scene...designed to meet the personal devotional needs of any worshiper. Here, nature is not a backdrop. Mary and Jesus are encircled by it. Schongauer's robins, sparrows, and goldfinches bring extra life to an already impressively natural rosebush. The contrast provided by the simple Dominican setting heightens the flamboyance of this late-Gothic masterpiece. Dominican churches were intended to be austere, as the 13th-century Catholic Church was combating a wave of heretical movements, such as the Cathars, whose message was a simpler faith (8F, daily 10:00–13:00, 15:00–18:00). This Dominican austerity is more apparent after a visit to Colmar's fancier—and Franciscan— St. Martin's cathedral.

Bartholdi Museum—This little museum recalls the life and work of the local boy who gained fame by sculpting the *Statue of Liberty*. Several of his statues grace Colmar's squares (23F, Wed–Mon 10:00–12:00, 14:00–18:00, closed Tue and Jan–Feb, in heart of Old Town at 30 rue des Marchands).

Sleeping in Colmar
(6.50F = about $1, country code: 33, zip code: 68000)
Sleep Code: **S** = Single, **D** = Double/Twin, **T** = Triple, **Q** = Quad,
b = bathroom, **t** = toilet only, **s** = shower only, **CC** = Credit Card
(Visa, MasterCard, Amex), **SE** = Speaks English, **NSE** = No
English, * = French hotel rating system (0–4 stars).

Hotels are fairly expensive and are jammed on weekends in
May, June, September, and October. Plan ahead. July and August
are busy, but there are always rooms—somewhere. Should you have
trouble finding a room in Colmar (the TI can help), look in a nearby
village where small hotels and bed-and-breakfasts are plentiful and
see my recommendations under "Sleeping in Eguisheim," below.

The only central **Laundromat** is near Maison Jund (see
"Sleeping in Colmar," below) at 1 rue Ruest, just off the pedestrian street rue Vauban (usually open daily 8:00–21:00).

Maison Jund offers my favorite budget beds in Colmar. This
easygoing B&B is the home of a wine maker. The ramshackle yet
magnificent half-timbered home feels like a medieval tree house
soaked in wine and filled with flowers. The rooms are simple, but
adequately comfortable, spacious, and equipped with kitchenettes.
Rooms are generally available only from April to mid-September,
with the cheapest rooms available in summer only (D-170F,
Db/Tb-210–250F, 12 rue de l'Ange, tel. 03 89 41 58 72, fax 03 89
23 15 83, e-mail: mjund@terre-net.fr). Leave your car at the lot
across from the Primo 99 hotel, walk from Unterlinden Museum
past Monoprix, and veer left on rue des Clefs, left on rue Etroite,
and right on rue de l'Ange. This is not a hotel, so there is no real
reception, though friendly Myriam (SE) seems to be around,
somewhere, most of the time.

Hôtel Le Rapp, just off place Rapp, with 40 modern,
just-large-enough rooms, a small basement pool, a sauna, a *hamman*
(bath), and a cozy indoor/outdoor bar-café, is the best-located two-
star hotel in Colmar. It's well run and family friendly, with a big
park one block away (Sb-300–330F, Db-385–450F, Tb-515–555F,
CC:VMA, good buffet breakfast, 1 rue Berthe-Molley, tel. 03 89 41
62 10, fax 03 89 24 13 58, www.rapp-hotel.com, SE). Its restaurant
serves a classy Alsatian *menu* with impeccable service (closed Fri).

Hôtel Turenne is a good value with 83 rooms in a historic
building a 10-minute walk from the city center and 15 minutes
from the train station. It's on a busy street with easy parking,
cable TV, and a cozy bar. Rooms are bright, pastel, and comfortable; ask for one on the non-street side (Sb-250–340F, Db-340F–
400F, Tb-400F, family-friendly studios-620F, CC:VMA, parking-
25F, from train station walk straight out on avenue Raymond
Poincaré and turn left on rue des Americains, 10 route du Bale,
tel. 03 89 21 58 58, fax 03 89 41 27 64, www.turenne.com, SE).
A third of the rooms are nonsmoking.

Hôtel St. Martin***, next to the Custom House, is a classy family-run place that began as a coaching inn (since 1361). It's small and has traditional yet well-equipped rooms woven into its antique frame. Half of its 24 rooms are in the annex, opposite a peaceful courtyard. While just as comfortable, these cheaper rooms have showers instead of tubs and no elevator or air-con (Sb-330–590F, Db-380–760F, Tb-600–840F, CC:VMA, free public parking nearby, 38 Grand Rue, tel. 03 89 24 11 51, fax 03 89 23 47 78, www.hotel-saint-martin.com, Winterstein family SE).

At the two central and painfully modern **Mercure Hôtels**, you can sleep comfortably for about the same money as Hôtel St. Martin without a hint of the Old World (Sb-535F, Db-600F, extra person-100F, CC:VMA, air-con, easy parking). The Champs de Mars Mercure is better, just off place Rapp on 2 avenue de la Marne (tel. 03 89 21 59 59, fax 03 89 21 59 00, e-mail: H1225@accor-hotels.com). The other is near the Unterlinden Museum on 5 rue Golbery (tel. 03 89 41 71 71, fax 03 89 23 82 71, e-mail: H0978@accor-hotels.com).

Hôtel Maréchal**** provides four-star comfort in a *très* romantic building at surprisingly fair rates in the heart of la Petite Venise (Sb-500–600F, Db-700–800F, with Jacuzzi-1,100F, extra bed-150F, CC:VMA, 4 place des Six Montagnes Noirs, tel. 03 89 41 60 32, fax 03 89 24 59 40, www.hotel-le-marechal.com).

Primo 99**, near Unterlinden Museum, is a French prefab hotel—a modern, cheap, efficient, bright, nothing-but-the-plastic-and-concrete-basics place to sleep for those to whom ambience is a four-letter word. It's one of Colmar's few budget deals (S/D/T-165F, Sb-275F, Db-310F, third person-50F, CC:VM, 5 rue des Ancêtres, free parking in big square in front, rooms held until 18:30 if you call, friendly staff, tel. 03 89 24 22 24, fax 03 89 24 55 96, e-mail: hotel-primo-99@rmcnet.fr, SE). Half the beds have footboards—a problem if you're taller than six foot two.

Hôtel IBIS**, on the ring road, sells modern, efficient comfort with pleasant rooms but small bathrooms (Sb-325F, Db-360F, extra person-60F, CC:VM, parking-40F, 11 rue St. Eloi, tel. 03 89 41 30 14, fax 03 89 24 51 49).

Hôtel Hagueneck** is the cheapest two-star place in Colmar, with good rooms in a small manor home and easy parking. It's a five-minute drive from the station over the tracks on the road to Epinal and a 30-minute walk from the city center (Db-230F, Tb-300F, Qb-350F, CC:M, 83 avenue du General-de-Gaulle, tel. 03 89 80 68 98, fax 03 89 79 55 29).

Sleeping near the Train Station

Hôtel Bristol** couldn't be closer to the station and, in spite of its Best Western plaque, has some character with grand public spaces and comfortable rooms (Sb-420–620F, Db-420–770F,

most Db-about 460F, CC:VMA, 7 place de la Gare, tel. 03 89 23
59 59, fax 03 89 23 92 26, www.rmcnet.fr/bristol).

La Chaumière*, on a big street two blocks from the station,
is above a truly French café. The simple rooms surround a courtyard and are much quieter off the street (S-170F, Sb-240F,
D-190F, Db-230–250F, CC:VM, parking-25F, walk straight
out of the station and turn left on avenue de la République,
74 avenue de la République, tel. 03 89 41 08 99).

Hôtel Climat's** uninspired but sufficient rooms will do in a
pinch (Db-320F, Tb-390F, CC: VM, 10 min from station, 1 block
off place Rapp, 7 avenue Jacques Preiss, tel. 089 41 34 80, fax 03
89 41 27 84).

Colmar's youth hostel is less central (dorm bed-70F, sheets-
20F, breakfast included, cheap dinners, office open 7:00–9:00,
17:00–23:00, 15-min walk from station, turn left out of station
and cross over tracks or take bus #4, 2 rue Pasteur, tel. 03 89 80
57 39, fax 03 89 80 76 16).

Eating in Colmar
(Also see "Eating in Eguisheim," below.)

For reasonably priced, good, traditional Alsatian cuisine,
try La Maison Rouge (90 and 130F *menus*, closed Sun, 9 rue des
Écoles, tel. 03 89 23 53 22). Nearby, La Taverne serves *tartes
flambées* and other regional specialties (closed Sun, 2 impasse de
la Maison Rouge, tel. 03 89 41 70 33). Join the fun in wood-cozy
ambience at Winstub Schwendi; try one of their robust 50F Swiss
rösti plates (facing Old Custom House at 3 Grand Rue). For crepes
and salads with atmosphere, eat at Crêperie Tom Pouce (daily,
10 rue des Tanneurs). For canal-front dining, head into La Petite
Venise to the bridge on rue Turenne, where you'll find a pizzeria,
a *winstub*/café (both cheap), and a fine but somewhat pricey canal-
level restaurant, Les Bateliers. Closer to the Unterlinden
Museum, La Ville de Paris is reasonable, friendly and serves
Alsatian dishes (place Jeanne d'Arc, tel. 03 89 24 53 15).

Hôtel Restaurant Le Rapp is my dress-up, high-cuisine
splurge. I comb my hair, spit out my gum, and savor a slow,
elegant meal served with grace and fine Alsatian wine (*menus* start
at 100F, the *baeckeanoffe* is great, good salads, closed Fri, air-con,
1 rue Berthe-Molley, tel. 03 89 41 62 10, SE).

Pâtisserie Salon de Thé Kuhn, just across the photo-perfect
bridge in La Petite Venise, serves (to go or eat there) melt-in-your-
mouth quiches, *tarte flambées*, and salads (closed Mon, open until
22:00, until 19:00 off-season, on place des Six Montagnes Noires).

Transportation Connections—Colmar
By train to: Strasbourg (hrly, 50 min), Reims (10/day, 6–8 hrs,
2 transfers), Dijon/Beaune (6/day to Dijon, 4.5 hrs, transfer in

Besançon; add 30 min to Beaune), **Paris**' Gare de l'Est (10/day, 5.5 hrs, transfer in Strasbourg or Mulhouse), **Amboise** (8/day, 9 hrs, transfer in Paris), **Basel**, Switzerland (8/day, 1 hr), **Karlsruhe**, Germany (3/day, 90 min, via Strasbourg; from Karlsruhe it's 90 min to Frankfurt, 3 hrs to Munich).

Route du Vin (The Wine Road)

Alsace's Route du Vin is an asphalt ribbon tying 90 miles of vineyards, villages, and feudal fortresses into an understandably popular tourist package. The generally dry, sunny climate has made for good wine and happy tourists since Roman days. Colmar and Eguisheim are ideally located for exploring the 30,000 acres of vineyards blanketing the hills from Marlenheim to Thann. If you have only a day, focus on towns within easy striking range of Colmar. Top ones are Eguisheim, Kaysersberg, Hunawihr, Ribbeauvillé, and the too-popular Riquewihr. (As you tour this region, you'll see storks' nests—some weighing over 1,000 pounds—on many church spires and city halls, thanks to a campaign to reintroduce the birds to this area.) Get a map of the Route du Vin from any TI.

Most towns have wineries that give tours (some charge a fee). The modern cooperatives at Eguisheim, Bennwihr, Hunawihr, and Ribbeauvillé, created after the destruction of World War II, provide a good look at a more modern and efficient method of production. Try the tasty Muscat and Gerwürtztraminer wines. Crèmant, the Alsatian "champagne," is very good—and much cheaper. The French term for headache, if you really get "Alsaced," is *mal à la tête*.

Getting around the Wine Road

Pick up a Michelin regional map before heading out.

By Bus: Public buses connect Colmar's train station with most of the villages along the Route du Vin. The schedules are fairly convenient, but close to nonexistent on Sunday (Mon–Sat schedules from Colmar to Eguisheim: 6/day, 5 min; to Kaysersberg: hrly, 30 min; to Riquewihr, Bennwihr, Hunawihr, and Ribbeauvillé: 6/day, 30–45 min; to Turckheim: 6/day, 20 min). Get schedules from the TI and buy tickets from the driver.

By Tour: A minibus tour company, Les Circuits d'Alsace, organizes day trips around the Alsace (Mon–Fri 9:00–12:30, 14:00–18:30, Sat 9:00–13:00, across from train station at 6 place de la Gare, tel. 03 89 41 90 88).

By Bike: The Wine Road's level terrain makes biking a good option. In Colmar, try Cycles Geiswiller (6 blvd. du Champs de Mars, tel. 03 89 41 30 59) or Cyclothèque (31 route d'Igersheim, tel. 03 89 79 14 18). Or, to save yourself the ride out of Colmar, you can rent a bike in Turckheim (84 Grand Rue, tel. 03 89 27 06 36) on the Route du Vin. Turckheim, Kaysersberg, Riquewihr,

Alsace's Wine Road

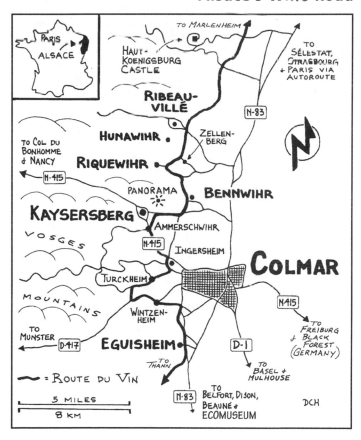

PARIS
ALSACE

TO MARLENHEIM

HAUT-
KOENIGSBURG
CASTLE

TO
SÉLESTAT,
STRASBOURG
& PARIS VIA
AUTOROUTE

RIBEAU-
VILLÉ

N-83

HUNAWIHR

ZELLEN-
BERG

TO COL DU
BONHOMME
& NANCY

RIQUEWIHR

N-415

PANORAMA

BENNWIHR

KAYSERSBERG

AMMERSCHWIHR

VOSGES

N-415

INGERSHEIM

COLMAR

TURCKHEIM

N-415

TO
FREIBURG
& BLACK
FOREST
(GERMANY)

MOUNTAINS

WINTZEN-
HEIM

TO
MUNSTER

D-417

EGUISHEIM

D-1

TO
THANN

TO
BASEL &
MULHOUSE

= ROUTE DU VIN

5 MILES

8 KM

N-83

TO
BELFORT, DIJON,
BEAUNE &
ECOMUSEUM

DCH

and Hunawihr make good biking destinations (get advice and a good map from a bike shop and avoid major roads; leave Colmar on bike path following directions under "By Car," below).

By Car: To reach the Wine Road, leave Colmar from the station following signs to Epinal. In Ingersheim turn right (north) on D-10 for Riquewihr, Hunawihr, and Ribeauvillé, or follow N-415 to Kayserberg. Look for *Route du Vin* signs. For Eguisheim, leave Colmar on N-83 toward Belfort.

By Foot: A few signed walking trails connect Route du Vin villages through the vineyards (get info at local TIs), and hikers can climb to the higher ruined castles of the Vosges Mountains (Eguisheim and Ribeauvillé are good bases). Kayserberg to Riquewihr is a pleasant one- to two-hour walk (return by bus).

Eguisheim

Just a few kilometers (a flat and easy bike ride) from Colmar, this flowery little town is ideal for a relaxing lunch and makes a good small-town base for exploring Alsace. It's a cinch by car (easy parking) and accessible by bus (6/day, 10 min, departs Colmar's train station). The helpful **TI** on the street that bisects the town has information on accommodations, festivals, walks in the vineyards, and hikes into the Vosges (April–Sept daily 9:00–12:00, 14:00–18:00; Oct–March closed Sun–Mon, 22 Grand Rue, tel. 03 89 23 40 33). Eguisheim is best explored by walking around its narrow circular road (rue des Remparts) and then cutting through the middle. Visit the colorful little church and one of Eguisheim's countless cozy **wineries** or the big and modern **Wine Cooperative** (Wolfberger, Cave Vinicole d'Eguisheim, daily 8:00–12:00, 14:00–18:00, folklore and tastings in summer Wed 17:00–19:00, 6 Grand Rue, tel. 03 89 22 20 20). If you have a car, follow signs up to Les Husseren and Les 5 Châteaux for a pleasant walk to the **ruined castle towers** and a good view of the Vosges above and vineyards below. Without wheels, stroll above the town into the vineyards above Eguisheim for good views (TI has a map).

Sleeping and Eating in Eguisheim
(6.50F = about $1, country code: 33, zip code: 68420)
Chambres d'Hôte: While none of the owners speak English, they're creative at communicating. Please remember to cancel if you reserved and can't make it.

Your Alsatian grandmother **Madame Hertz-Meyers** welcomes you with big rooms in a mansion surrounded by vineyards only 75 meters from the village center. Rooms in the main house are perfect for families and are better than her two modern apartments (Sb-235F, Db-290–320F, Tb-425F, includes breakfast, 3 rue Riesling, no sign, tel. 03 89 23 67 74, fax 03 89 23 99 23). Serious **Madame Dirringer**'s five spacious rooms face a traditional courtyard (Db-200–215F, breakfast-30F, 11 rue Riesling, tel. 03 89 41 71 87). It's hard to imagine a better location, more comfortable rooms, or a more charming owner than **Monique Freudenreich** (Db-250F, includes breakfast, 1 block from TI, 4 cour Unterlinden, tel. & fax 03 89 23 16 44). Gentle **Madame Bombenger**'s modern home has nice views into the vineyards and over Eguisheim (Db-250F, includes breakfast, 3 rue de Trois Pierres, tel. & fax 03 89 23 71 19). The **Stockys** offer comfortable rooms (Db-165–185F, 24 rue de Colmar, tel. 03 89 41 68 04).

Hotels: Eguisheim also has hotels for every taste and budget. The simple, funky, and fun **Auberge de Trois Châteaux** is creaky, wood-beamed, and unpolished, and its rooms are a steal (Db-140–210F, Tb-170–240F, 26 Grand Rue, tel. 03 89 23 11 22). At the other extreme, snazzy **Hostellerie du Château***** is ideally located in front of the church and provides stylish, contemporary luxury (Sb-410F, Db-500–580F, 2 rue du Château St. Leon IX, tel. 03 89 23 72 00, fax 03 89 41 63 93). The picturesque **Auberge Alsacienne***** has small, unimaginative but comfortable rooms (Db-300–420F, 12 Grand Rue, tel. 03 89 41 50 20, fax 03 89 23 89 32). Overlooking the village, the modern yet tasteful **Hôtel St. Hubert***** offers polished comfort, an indoor pool and sauna, vineyards out your window, and free pickup at Colmar's train station if you let them know your arrival time well in advance (Db-400–610F, extra bed-100F, 6 rue des Trois Pierres, tel. 03 89 41 40 50, fax 03 89 41 46 88, www.Hotel-St-Hubert.com).

Eating in Eguisheim: Auberge de Trois Châteaux is cozy and ideal for an inexpensive dinner (closed Tue–Wed, 26 Grand Rue). **Auberge du Rempart** has good *tarte flambée* and outdoor tables surrounding a fountain with monster fish (near TI, 3 rue du Rempart Sud). **Au Vieux Porche** is the place to go for a splurge (closed Tue, 16 rue des 3 Châteaux, tel. 03 89 24 01 90, fax 03 89 23 91 25).

More Sights—The Wine Road

These sights are listed from south to north.

Turckheim—This pleasant town, with a small castle, is just enough off the beaten path to be overlooked.

Kaysersberg—Albert Schweitzer's hometown is cute but feels overrun much of the year. Climb to the castle (under long-term renovation), browse the boutiques, and enjoy the colorful jumble of 15th-century houses and the stork's nest near the fortified town bridge. Drop by Dr. Schweitzer's house (10F, closed 12:00–14:00), check out the church and its notable 400-year-old altarpiece, taste some wine, and wander into nearby vineyards. Kaysersberg's TI is inside Hôtel de Ville (tel. 03 89 78 22 78). Walking trails through the vineyards to Riquewihr (1.5–2.5 hrs) and other Route du Vin towns are well-marked; walk under the arch (10 meters to the right of the TI as you face it) and you'll see signs.

Alsatian Panorama at WWII Monument—This remarkable viewpoint, easiest to reach by car, is at the WWII monument and military cemetery (also called Negrophile Nationale or Cimitière Militaire). The spectacular setting, best at sunset, houses a monument to the American divisions that helped liberate Alsace in World War II (find the American flag); a beautiful cemetery to French and North African soldiers who died in the cause; and a brilliant panorama of the southern section of the Route du Vin and into Germany.

To find this poorly marked place, go to Sigolsheim (between Kaysersberg and Bennwihr). The road to the panorama leaves from the center of Sigolsheim (look for French flags at Pierre Sparr winery and follow small signs to Cimitière Militaire or

Negrophile Nationale). After you check out the monument to the Americans, take the small road to the top to find the viewpoint and cemetery.

Riquewihr—Overly picturesque, this walled village is crammed with tourist shops, cafés, galleries, cobblestones, and flowers. Try the excellent tasting and tour at Caves Dopff et Irion (Cour du Château, tel. 03 89 47 92 51, TI tel. 03 89 47 80 80).

Zellenburg—This town has an impressive setting and is worth a quick stop for the views from either side of its narrow perch.

Hunawihr—This bit of wine-soaked Alsatian cuteness is far less visited than its more famous neighbors and comes complete with a 16th-century **fortified church** that today is shared by Catholics and Protestants (the Catholics are buried next to the church; the Protestants are buried outside the church wall). Park below the church at the small lot with picnic tables and follow the trail up to the church, then loop back through the village. Kids will enjoy Hunawihr's small **stork park** (Parc des Cygognes, 35F, April–Nov daily 10:00–12:00, 14:00–18:00, other animals take part in the afternoon shows). If you spend the night, try the charming and creaky **Relais du Poete** (Db-230F, fun restaurant and outdoor terrace, 6 rue du Nord, tel. 03 89 73 60 14, fax 03 89 73 36 86). You'll also find a few *chambres d'hôte* and a good wine cooperative in Hunawihr. Eat well at the **Wistub Suzel** near the church (closed Tue, 2 rue de l'Eglise, tel. 03 89 73 30 850).

Ribbeauvillé—Come here to hike. Two brooding castles hang above this pleasant town, seldom visited by Americans. The steep castle trail leaves from the top of the town (at Hôtel Trois Châteaux, park in city lot here). Allow 45 minutes one-way, or just climb 10 minutes for a view over the town.

STRASBOURG

Strasbourg is urban Alsace at its best. One of France's most appealing big cities, Strasbourg is a young, lively mix of 50,000 bicycling university students, meandering waterways, and pedestrian-only streets. Situated on the west bank of the Rhine River, Strasbourg provides the ultimate blend of Franco-Germanic culture, architecture, and ambience. The highlight is its brilliant cathedral. Since 1949 Strasbourg has been home to the European Parliament. Today it shares its administrative responsibilities for the European Union with Brussels.

   Tourist Information: There are two TIs. One is at the train station (daily 9:00–18:00); the main office is at 17 place de la Cathédrale (daily 9:00–19:00, tel. 03 88 52 28 28). Call ahead for a schedule of walking tours in English. Skip the free map. Buy the 3F city map; it describes a decent walking tour of the city's center in English.

Arrival in Strasbourg

By Train: After stopping by the TI at the station, take the slick tram (7F, direction: Illkirch) to the Grande Rue stop. Or walk 15 minutes straight up rue Marie Kuss to rue Gutenberg to the center.

By Car: Follow "centre-ville/cathédrale" signs and park as close to the center as you can. Parking lots are well marked— place Gutenberg and place du Château are most convenient, though the larger Austerlitz lot works fine.

Sights—Strasbourg

▲▲**Strasbourg Cathedral (Cathédrale de Notre Dame)**—Made out of pink sandstone, this uniquely Alsatian cathedral with its soaring single spire is, well—awesome. The delicate Gothic style of the cathedral (begun in 1277) is another Franco-German mixture that somehow survived the French Revolution, the Franco-Prussian war, World War I, and World War II. Enter and walk about halfway down the center and take a seat. The stained glass on the lower left shows various rulers of Strasbourg, while the stained glass on your right is the Bible for the poor (the illiterate). Walk to the choir and stare at the stained-glass image of Mary and find the European Union flag at the top. In the right transept is a high-tech 15th-century astronomical clock (restored in 1883), operating every 15 minutes (best on the half hour). For 20F you can climb 330 steps up the tower for an amazing view (cathedral open daily 7:00–11:40, 12:45–19:00, tower open daily April–Sept 9:00–18:30, Oct–March 9:00–16:30). Before leaving this area, stroll the impressive network of pedestrian streets that connect the cathedral with the huge place Kleber (home to various outdoor markets depending on the day of the week).

Museums Near the Cathedral—These museums are interesting only for aficionados. The Palais Rohan houses three museums: Museum of Decorative Arts, Museum of Fine Arts, and the Archeological Museum (20F/museum, 40F for all 3, Wed–Mon 10:00–18:00, closed Tue, 2 place du Château). Some may be interested in the Museum of the Cathedral (Musée de l'Oeuvre Notre Dame, 20F, 3 place du Château, Tue–Sun 10:00–18:00) or the Museum of Alsace's costumes and cultural exhibits (Musée Alsacien, 20F, Wed–Mon 10:00–18:00, 23 quai St. Nicholas).

La Petite France—Laced with canals, half-timbered homes, and cobblestones, this area was meant for meandering. To reach La Petite France, walk to place Gutenberg then follow pedestrian-only rue Grande. Wander deep —the best cafés line the canal on quai de la Bruche, and the small parks that lie between the canals are picnic-and siesta-perfect (cross bridge at rue des Moulins to reach the parks). Climb the grassy wall (Barrage Vauban) for a great view back over Strasbourg's center and waterways. The glass structure behind you is the new modern-art museum (interesting more for its architecture than its collection).

Boat Ride on the Ill River—Big, open-deck boats do a loop trip on the Ill River, giving you a different and interesting perspective on the city (adult-41F, child-21F, 75 min, boats depart from river side of Palais Rohan).

Sleeping in Strasbourg
(6.50F = about $1, country code: 33, zip code: 67000)

Hôtel Cathédrale*** occupies the best location, facing the cathedral, and offers all the comforts—for a price (Db-360–800F, CC:VM, parking-100F, 12 place de la Cathédrale, tel. 03 88 22 12 12, fax 03 88 23 28 00, www.Hotel-Cathedrale.fr). **Hôtel des Suisses****, across from the cathedral's right transept and off place du Château, is a central and solid two-star value (Db-400–460F, CC:VM, 2 place de la Rape, tel. 03 88 35 22 11, fax 03 88 25 74 23, www.strasbourg.com/hotel-suisse/).

Transportation Connections—Strasbourg
Strasbourg makes a good side trip from Colmar or stop on the way to or from Paris.

By train to: Colmar (hrly, 50 min); **Paris'** Gare de l'Est (10/day, 4.5 hrs); **Karlsruhe**, Germany (3/day, 50 min); **Basel**, Switzerland (hrly, 2 hrs).

VERDUN
Little remains in Europe today to remind us of World War I, but Verdun provides a fine tribute to the million-plus lives lost in the battles fought here. While the lunar landscape of World War I is now forested over, countless craters and trenches are visible (look into the woods as you drive). Millions of live bombs lie in vast cordoned-off areas. Drive through the eerie moguls surrounding Verdun, stopping at melted-sugar-cube forts and plaques marking where towns once existed. With two hours and a car, or a full day and a bike (and a strong heart), you can see the most stirring sights and appreciate the tremendous scale of the battles. The town of Verdun is not your destination but a starting point for your visit into the nearby battlefields.

Tourist Information: The TI is on place Nation (May–Sept daily 8:30–18:30, Oct–April closed 12:00–14:00 and at 18:00, closes at 17:30 in winter, tel. 03 29 86 14 18).

Arrival in Verdun
By Train: Walk straight out of the station and down avenue Garibaldi to the town center.

By Car: Follow signs to "centre-ville," "place Nation," and "Porte Chatel" and you'll pass the TI just before crossing the river.

Verdun

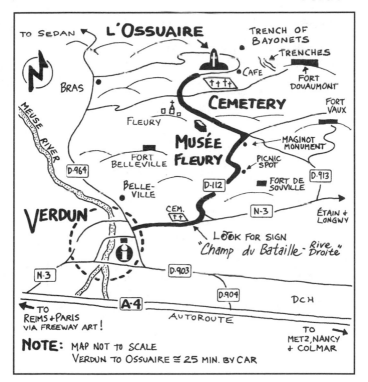

TO SEDAN ← L'OSSUAIRE
TRENCH OF BAYONETS
TRENCHES
CAFE
FORT DOUAUMONT
BRAS
†† ††
CEMETERY
FORT VAUX
FLEURY
MUSÉE FLEURY
MAGINOT MONUMENT
FORT BELLEVILLE
PICNIC SPOT
D-964
D-112
D-913
BELLE-VILLE
FORT DE SOUVILLE
VERDUN
CEM. ††
N-3
ÉTAIN + LONGWY
LOOK FOR SIGN "Champ du Bataille - Rive Droite"
N-3
D-903
TO REIMS + PARIS VIA FREEWAY ART!
A-4
D-909
DCH
AUTOROUTE
TO METZ, NANCY + COLMAR
MEUSE RIVER

NOTE: MAP NOT TO SCALE
VERDUN TO OSSUAIRE ≅ 25 MIN. BY CAR

Getting around the Verdun Battlefield

The TI has good maps of the battlefields. French-language minivan tours of the battle sites are available June through September and leave the TI around 14:00 (guides usually speak some English). You can rent a bike opposite Verdun's train station at **Cycles Flavenot** (tel. 03 29 86 12 43). To reach the battlefields by car or bike (about 30 kilometers round-trip), take D-112 from Verdun (look for signs to Douaumont) and then take D-913 to Douaumont.

The battlefield remains are situated on two sides of the Meuse River; the Rive Droite has more sights. By following signs to Fort Douaumont and the Ossuaire, you'll pass Musée Fleury.

Sights—Verdun

▲▲**Battlegrounds**—The most compelling sights are Mémorial-Musée de Fleury, l'Ossuaire, and Fort Douaumont. Start with **Mémorial-Musée de Fleury**, built around an impressive recreation of a battlefield, hard-hitting photos, weapon displays, and a worthwhile 15-minute movie narrated in English with headphones (20F, March–Dec 9:00–18:00, closes at 17:00 in winter). The museum is built on the site of a village (Fleury) that was obliterated during the fighting.

L'Ossuaire is the tomb of 130,000 French and Germans whose last homes were the muddy trenches of Verdun (March–early Sept daily 9:00–18:00, late-Sept–Feb closes 12:00–14:00 and at 17:30). Look through the low windows for a bony memorial to those whose political and military leaders asked them to make the "ultimate sacrifice" for their countries. Enter the monument and experience a humbling and moving tribute. Ponder a war that left half of all the men in France aged 15 to 30 dead or wounded. Climb the tower for a territorial view (6F) and don't miss the thought-provoking 20-minute film (17F, 20F includes tower, closed Nov–March; theater in basement, ask for English version). The little 2F picture boxes in the gift shop are worth a look if you don't visit the Mémorial-Musée de Fleury (turn through all the old photos before time expires).

Before leaving, walk to the cemetery and listen for the eerie buzz of silence and peace. You can visit the nearby **Tranchée des Baionnettes**, where an entire company of soldiers was buried alive in their trench (the soldiers' bayonets remained above ground until recently).

The nearby **Fort Douaumont** was a strategic command center for both sides at various times. It's more interesting from the outside than the inside (walk on top and notice the round, iron-gun emplacements that could rise and revolve). A walk inside (17F) completes the picture, with long, damp corridors and a German memorial where 1,600 Germans were killed by a single blast. Halfway between l'Ossuaire and Fort Douaumont (on either side of the road) are clearly visible trenches. *Village Détruit* signs indicate where villages were entirely destroyed; only monuments remain to mark their existence.

Citadelle Souterraine—This is a disappointing train ride through the tunnels of the French Command in downtown Verdun. While it tries to re-create the Verdun scene, it's not worth your time.

Transportation Connections—Verdun
By train to: Colmar (10/day, 6–8 hrs, 2 transfers), **Reims** (5/day, 3 hrs, transfer in Chalons-sur-Marne), **Paris**' Gare de l'Est (5/day, 3 hrs, transfer in Chalons-sur-Marne).

REIMS
Deservedly famous for its cathedral and champagne, contemporary Reims (rhymes with France) is a prosperous, modern city. Rebuilt after being leveled in World War I, Reims is 90 minutes from Paris by car or train and makes a good

day trip or handy stop for travelers en route elsewhere. Most sights of interest (champagne caves included) are within a 20-minute walk from the cathedral.

To best experience today's Reims, wander the thriving shopping streets between the cathedral and the train station. Rue de Vesle, rue Condorcet, and place d'Erlon are best.

Tourist Information: The TI is just outside the cathedral's left transept (Easter–mid-Oct Mon–Sat 9:00–19:00, Sun 10:00–18:00; mid-Oct–Easter Mon–Sat 9:00–18:00, Sun 9:00–17:00, free map shows champagne caves, tel. 03 26 77 45 25). Ask about tours of the cathedral in English (generally summer afternoons only, 90 min; audioguide tour available any time).

Arrival in Reims

By Train: Walk out of the station (lockers available), cross the huge boulevards Joffre and Foch, and stroll up to the pedestrian place Drouet d'Erlon. Turn left on rue Condorcet, then right on rue Talleyrand to reach the cathedral.

By Car: Just follow the "cathédrale" signs and park nearby (easiest behind the cathedral).

Sights—Reims

▲▲▲**Cathedral**—The cathedral of Reims is a glorious example of Gothic architecture, with the best west portal (inside and outside) anywhere. (Since medieval churches always face east, you enter the west portal.) Clovis, the first king of the Franks, was baptized here in 496 A.D. (thus determining France's religion), and ever since Reims' cathedral has served as the coronation place of French kings and queens. It houses many treasures, great medieval stained glass, and a lovely modern set of Marc Chagall stained-glass windows from 1974 on the east end. Joan of Arc led a reluctant Charles VII here to be coronated in 1429; the event rallied the French to push the English out of France and end the Hundred Years' War. English explanations are along the right aisle (daily 7:30–19:30).

▲**Champagne Tours**—Reims is the capital of the Champagne region. While the bubbly stuff's birthplace was closer to Epernay, you can tour a champagne cave right in Reims. All charge for tastings and are open daily. Most close for lunch from noon to 14:00 and around 17:00.

The **Taittinger Company** does a great job trying to convince you they're the best (walk 10 min up rue de Barbatre from cathedral to 9 place St. Nicaise, tel. 03 26 85 84 33). After seeing their movie (in comfortable theater seats), follow your guide down into some of the five kilometers of chilly chalk caves, many dug by ancient Romans. Popping corks signal when the tour's done and the tasting's begun (35F, includes tasting, daily 9:30–12:00, 14:30–16:30).

One block beyond Taittinger, on place des Droits de l'Homme, are several other champagne caves. **Piper Heidsieck** offers a snazzy train-ride tour and tasting (40F, 51 boulevard Henri-Vasnier, call first, tel. 03 26 84 43 44).

Sights—Near Reims

Epernay—Champagne purists may want to visit Epernay (26 kilometers away, well-connected to Paris and Reims), where the granddaddy of champagne houses, **Moët et Chandon**, offers tours daily, except from noon to 14:00 (35F with tasting, tel. 03 26 51 21 00). According to the story, it was near here that, in about 1700, the monk Dom Perignon, after much fiddling with double fermentation, stumbled onto this bubbly treat. On that happy day he ran through the abbey shouting, "Brothers, come quickly… I'm drinking stars!"

Route de la Champagne—Drivers can joyride through the scenic and prestigious vineyards just south of Reims. Follow D-9 south to Cormontreuil, then Louvois, then Bouzy, to see the chalky soil and vines that produce Champagne's costly wines. Many of the villages have small hotels if you'd like to sleep surrounded by vineyards.

Sleeping in Reims
(6.50F = about $1, country code: 33, zip code: 51100)

There are scads of hotels on the pedestrian place Drouet d'Erlon. The basic, modern, and friendly **Hôtel des Arcades**** is the best value (Sb-250F, Db-270F, 16 passage Sube, tel. 03 26 88 63 74, fax 03 26 40 66 56). **Grand Hôtel Continental***** offers reasonable three-star comfort (Sb-330–400F, Db-330–630F, CC:VM, parking-30F, 93 place Drouet d'Erlon, tel. 03 26 40 39 35, fax 03 26 47 51 12, www.grandhotelcontinental.com).

Transportation Connections—Reims

By train to: Epernay (8/day, 30 min), **Verdun** (5/day, 3 hrs, transfer in Chalons-sur-Marne), **Paris**' Gare de l'Est (10/day, 90 min), **Colmar** (10/day, 6–8 hrs, 2 transfers).

BELGIUM

- 12,000 square miles (a little larger than Maryland)
- 10 million people (833 people per square mile)
- 45 Belgian francs = about $1

Belgium falls through the cracks. Nestled between Germany, France, and Britain and famous for waffles, sprouts, and endive, it's no wonder many travelers don't even consider a stop here. But many who visit remark that Belgium is one of Europe's best-kept secrets. There are tourists—but not as many as the country's charms merit.

Belgium and the Netherlands

The country is split between the French-speaking Walloons in the south and the Dutch-speaking Flemish people (60 percent of the population) in the north. Talk to locals to learn how deep the cultural rift is. The capital city, Brussels, while mostly French-speaking, is officially bilingual. There is a small minority of German-speaking people, and, because of Belgium's international importance, more than 25 percent of its residents are foreigners.

It is in Belgium that Europe comes together: where Romance languages meet Germanic languages, Catholics meet Protestants, and the BeNeLux union was established, planting the seed 40 years ago that today is sprouting into the unification of Europe. Belgium flies the flag of Europe more vigorously than any place in Europe.

Bruges and Brussels are the best two first bites of Belgium. Brussels is one of Europe's great cities and the capital of the European Community. Bruges is a wonderfully preserved medieval gem that expertly nurtures the tourist industry, bringing the town a prosperity it hasn't enjoyed since 500 years ago, when—as one of the largest cities in the world—it helped lead northern Europe out of the Middle Ages.

Belgians brag that they eat as much as the Germans and as well as the French. They are the world's leading beer consumers and among the world's leading carnivores. In Belgium, never bring chrysanthemums to a wedding. And tweaking little kids on the ear is considered rude.

Ten million Belgians are packed into 12,000 square miles (roughly the size of Maryland). At 833 people per square mile, it's the second most densely populated country in Europe (after the Netherlands). This population concentration, coupled with a dense and well-lit rail and road system, causes Belgium to shine at night when viewed from space, a phenomenon NASA astronauts call the "Belgian Window."

Belgium's rail system is tops, and its various rail deals are worth considering. The second-class Multipass gives groups of three to five people any two trips in Belgium. Three people pay 1,320BF, four pay 1,490BF, and five pay 1,650BF; at least one of the Multipass users must be age 26 or older. People under age 26 can get a Go Pass: 1,490BF for 10 rides anywhere in Belgium. (The one-way Brussels-Bruges fare is 390BF per person.) Seniors age 60-plus can get any six rides for 1,320BF (second class) or 2,030BF (first class). Expect a modest increase in pass prices in February. Those traveling on the weekend should ask for the weekend discount for round-trips (40 percent off for 1 person, 60 percent off for any traveling companions).

BRUGES
(BRUGGE)

With Renoir canals, pointy gilded architecture, time-tunnel art, and stay-awhile cafés, Bruges is a heavyweight sightseeing destination as well as a joy. Where else can you ride a bike along a canal, munch mussels, wash them down with the world's best beer, savor heavenly chocolate, and see Flemish Primitives and a Michelangelo, all within 300 meters of a bell tower that rings out "Don't worry, be happy" jingles every 15 minutes? And there's no language barrier.

The town is Brugge (broo-gha) in Flemish, Bruges (broozh) in French and English. Before it was Flemish or French, the name was a Viking word for "wharf" or "embarkment." Right from the start, Bruges was a trading center. In the 11th century the city grew wealthy on the cloth trade. By the 14th century Bruges' population was 40,000, in a league with London and one of the largest cities in the world. At the time, Bruges was the most important cloth market in northern Europe. In the 15th century Bruges was the favored residence of the powerful Dukes of Burgundy. Commerce and the arts boomed. The artists Jan van Eyck and Hans Memling had studios here. But by the 16th century the harbor had silted up, and the economy collapsed. The Burgundian court left, Spain conquered Belgium in 1548, and Bruges' golden age abruptly ended. For generations Bruges was known as a mysterious and dead city. In the 19th century a new port, Zeebrugge, brought renewed vitality to the area. And 20th century tourists discovered the town. Today Bruges prospers because of tourism: It's a uniquely well-preserved Gothic city and a handy gateway to Europe. It's no secret, but even with the crowds it's the kind of city where you don't mind being a tourist.

Planning Your Time

Bruges needs at least two nights and a full, well-organized day. Even nonshoppers enjoy browsing here, and the Belgian love of life makes a hectic itinerary seem a little senseless. With one day, the speedy visitor could do this: 9:30–Climb the belfry, 10:00– Tour the Burg sights (visit the TI if necessary), 11:30–Take a boat tour, 12:15–Walk to the brewery, have lunch, and catch the 13:00 tour, 14:30–Walk through the Begijnhof, 15:00–Tour the Memling Museum (6 paintings), 15:45–See the Michelangelo in the church, 16:00–Tour the Groeninge Museum (closes at 17:00). Rent a bike for an evening ride through the quiet backstreets (or take a 1,000BF half-hour horse-and-buggy tour). Lose the tourists and find a dinner. (If this schedule seems insane, skip the belfry and the brewery—or stay another day.)

Orientation (area code: 050)

The tourists' Bruges (you'll be sharing it) is contained within a one-kilometer-square canal, or moat. Nearly everything of interest and importance is within a cobbled and convenient swath between the train station and Market Square (a 15-min walk).

Tourist Information: The main office is on Burg Square (Mon–Fri 9:30–18:30, Sat–Sun 10:00–12:00, 14:00–18:30, off-season closes at 17:00, lockers and money-exchange desk, tel. 050/448-686, public WC in courtyard). The other TI is at the train station (Mon–Sat 10:30–13:15, 14:00–18:30, closed Sun and off-season at 17:30, www.brugge.be). Both TIs sell a great 25BF all-inclusive Bruges visitors guide with a map and listings of all of the sights and services. The free *Exit* includes a monthly calendar of the many events the town puts on to keep its hordes of tourists entertained. It's in Dutch but almost readable (i.e., van Gershwin tot Clapton). Skip the TI's "combo" museum ticket. They also have train-schedule information and specifics on the various kinds of tours available. Bikers will want the *5X on the Bike around Bruges* map/guide, which sells for 50BF and shows five routes through the countryside.

Internet Access: The relaxing Coffee Link, with mellow music and pleasant art, is located between the train station and the center of town (60BF/15 min, Mon–Sat 10:00–21:30, Sun 13:30–18:30, across from Church of Our Lady at Mariastraat 38).

Arrival in Bruges

By Train: From the train (and from the TI near the station), you'll see the square belfry tower marking the main square. Upon arrival, stop by the station TI (has lockers) to pick up the Bruges visitors guide (map in centerfold). There are no ATMs at the station, but you can change money at ticket windows. Buses marked "CENTRUM" speed to the Market Square (40BF ticket, buy from driver, good for 1 hr). Buses #4 and #8 go farther, near the recommended Carmerstraat-area hotels. The taxi fare to most hotels is 250BF. It's a 15-minute walk from the station to the center: Cross the busy street and canal in front of the station, head up Oostmeers, and turn right on Steenstraat to reach Market Square. You could rent a bike at the station for the duration of your stay (350BF/day with a 500BF deposit, tel. 050/302-328), but other bike-rental shops are closer to the center (see "Bruges Experiences," below).

By Car: Park at the train station for just 100BF per day; show your parking receipt on the bus to get a free ride into town. The pricier underground parking garage at t'Zand costs 350BF per day.

Helpful Hints
The information number for all **museums** is 050/448-711. October through March is off-season (when some museums close on Tuesday).

You can change traveler's checks at **Best Change** (daily 9:00–21:00, until 19:00 in winter, just off Market Square on Steenstraat). The **post office** is on Market Square near the belfry (Mon–Fri 9:00–19:30, Sat 9:30–12:30, tel. 050/331-411).

Shops are open from 9:00 to 18:00, a little later on Friday. Grocery stores are usually closed on Sunday. **Market day** is Wednesday morning (Market Square) and Saturday morning (t'Zand). On Saturday and Sunday afternoons, there's a flea market along Dijver in front of the Groeninge Museum.

Sights—Bruges
Bruges' sights are listed here in walking order, from Market Square to the Burg to the cluster of museums around the Church of Our Lady to the Begijnhof (10-min walk from beginning to end). Like Venice, the ultimate sight is the town itself, and the best way to enjoy that is to get lost on the backstreets away from the lace shops and ice-cream stands.

Market Square (Markt)—Ringed by banks, the post office, lots of restaurant terraces, great old gabled buildings, and the belfry, this is the modern heart of the city. Most city buses go from here to the station. Under the belfry are two great Belgian French fry stands, a quadrilingual Braille description, and a metal model of the tower. In its day, a canal went right up to the central square of this formerly great trading center. **Geldmuntstraat**, just off the square, is a delightful street with many fun and practical shops and eateries.

▲▲**Belfry (Belfort)** Most of this bell tower has stood over Market Square since 1300. In 1486 the octagonal lantern was added, making it 88 meters high—that's 366 steps (daily 9:30–17:00, Oct–March closed 12:30–13:30, ticket window closes 45 min early, WC in courtyard). The view is worth the climb and

Bruges

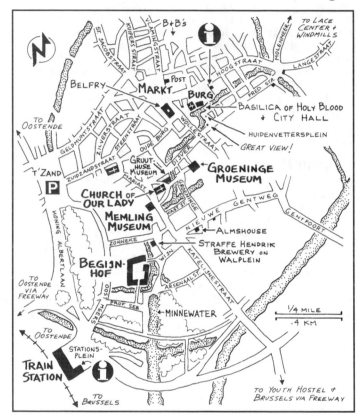

the 100BF. Survey the town. On the horizon you can see the towns along the coast. Just before you reach the top, peek into the carillon room. The 47 bells can be played mechanically with the giant barrel and movable tabs (as they do on each quarter hour), or with a manual keyboard (as it does for regular concerts) with fists and feet rather than fingers. Be there on the quarter hour, when things ring. It's *bellissimo* at the top of the hour. Carillon concert times are listed at the base of the belfry (usually Mon, Wed, and Sat at 21:00 and Sun at 14:15). Back on the square, with your back to the belfry, turn right onto pedestrian-only Breidelstraat and thread yourself through the lace and *wafels* to Burg Square.

▲▲**Burg Square**—The opulent square called Burg is Bruges' civic center, historically the birthplace of Bruges and the site of the ninth-century castle of the first Count of Flanders. Today it's the scene of outdoor concerts and home of the TI (with a 10BF WC). It's surrounded by six centuries of architecture. Sweeping counterclockwise 360 degrees, you'll go from Romanesque (the round arches and thick walls of the brick basilica in the corner, best seen inside the lower chapel) to the pointed Gothic arches of the City Hall (with its "Gothic Room") to the well-proportioned Renaissance windows of the Old Recorder's House (next door, under the gilded statues) and past the TI and the park to the elaborate 17th-century Baroque of the Provost's House. Complete your spin and walk to that corner.

▲**Basilica of the Holy Blood**—Originally the Chapel of Saint Basil, it is famous for its relic of the blood of Christ, which, according to tradition, was brought to Bruges in 1150 after the Second Crusade (and is displayed only during Friday worship services). The lower chapel (through the door labeled "Basiliek") is dark and solid—a fine example of Romanesque style (with some beautiful statues). The upper chapel (separate entrance, climb the stairs) is decorated Gothic and usually accompanied by appropriately contemplative music. A 10BF English flier tells about the relic, art, and history. The small but sumptuous Basilica Museum (well described in English) contains the gem-studded hexagonal reliquary (c. 1600) that carries the relic on its yearly Ascension Day trip through the streets of Bruges (museum is next to upper chapel, 40BF, daily 9:30–12:00, 14:00–18:00; shorter hours and closed Wed afternoon off-season).

▲**City Hall's Gothic Room**—Your ticket gives you a room full of old town maps and paintings and a grand, beautifully restored "Gothic Hall" from 1400. Its painted and carved wooden ceiling features hanging arches (explained by an English flier). Notice the New Testament themes carved into the circular "vault keys." The wall murals are late-19th-century Romantic paintings of episodes from the city's history (described in the flier). The free ground-level lobby (closed on weekends) is a picture gallery of Belgium's colonial history, from the Spanish Bourbon king to Napoleon (150BF, includes audioguide and admission to Renaissance Hall, daily 9:30–17:00, Burg 12).

Renaissance Hall (Brugse Vrije)—This is just one ornate room with an impressive Renaissance chimney. If you're into heraldry, the symbolism, explained in the free English flier, makes this worth a five-minute stop. If you're not, you'll wonder where the rest of the museum is (150BF, includes admission to City Hall, daily 9:30–17:00, entry in the corner of the square).

From Burg to Fish Market to View—From Burg, walk under the Goldfinger family down Blinde Ezelstraat. Just after you cross the bridge, the persistent little fish market (*Vismarkt*, fresh North Sea catch sold Tue–Fri 6:00–13:00) is on your left. Take an immediate right to Huidevettersplein, a tiny, picturesque, restaurant-filled square. Continue a few steps to Rozenhoedkaai Street, where you can get a great photo of the belfry reflected in the canal. Can you see its tilt? It leans about four feet. Down the canal (past a flea market on weekends) looms the huge spire of the Church of Our Lady (tallest brick spire in the Low Countries). Between you and the church are the next three museums.

▲▲▲**Groeninge Museum**—This diverse and classy collection shows off mostly Flemish art from Memling to Magritte. Rooms 1 through 18 take you from 1400 to 1945. While it has plenty of worthwhile modern art, the highlights are its vivid and pristine Flemish Primitives. (*Primitive* here means before the Renaissance.) Flemish art is shaped by its love of detail, its merchant patrons' egos, and the power of the Church. Lose yourself in the halls of Groeninge: Gaze across 15th-century canals, into the eyes of reassuring Marys, and through town squares littered with leotards, lace, and lopped-off heads (250BF, daily 9:30–17:00, Oct–March closed Tue, Dijver 12). The **Brangwyn Museum** (Arentshuis), next door, is only interesting if you are into lace or the early-20th-century art of Brangwyn (80BF, daily 9:30–17:00, off-season closed Tue, Dijver 16).

▲**Gruuthuse Museum**—A wealthy brewer's home, this is a sprawling smattering of everything from medieval bedpans to a guillotine. There's no information inside, so to understand the crossbows, dark old paintings, and what a beer merchant's doing with box seats peeking down on the altar of the Church of Our Lady next door, you'll have to buy or browse through the 600BF guidebook (130BF, daily 9:30–17:00, Dijver 17). Leaving the museum, contemplate the mountain of bricks towering 120 meters above as they have for 600 years.

▲▲**Church of Our Lady**—The church stands as a memorial to the power and wealth of Bruges in its heyday. A delicate *Madonna and Child*, by Michelangelo, is near the apse (to the right if you're facing the altar). It's said to be the only Michelangelo statue to leave Italy in his lifetime (thanks to the wealth generated by Bruges' cloth trade). If you like tombs and church art, pay to wander through the apse (70BF, Michelangelo free, art-filled apse Mon–Fri 10:00–12:00, 14:00–17:00, closes at 16:00 on Sat, Sun 14:00–16:00, closes off-season at 16:30, on Mariastraat).

▲▲**St. Jans Hospital/Memling Museum**—Across the street from the Church of Our Lady is a medieval hospital with six much-loved paintings by the greatest of the Flemish Primitives, Hans Memling. His *Mystical Wedding of St. Catherine* triptych deserves a close look. Catherine and her "mystical groom," the baby Jesus, are flanked by a headless John the Baptist and a pensive John the Evangelist. The chairs are there so you can study it. If you understand the Book of Revelations, you'll understand St. John's wild and intricate vision. The Reliquary of St. Ursula, an ornate little mini-church in the same room, is filled with

impressive detail (100BF, daily 9:30–17:00, off-season closed
Wed, Mariastraat 38).

▲▲**Straffe Hendrik Brewery Tour**—Belgians are Europe's beer
connoisseurs. This fun and handy tour is a great way to pay your
respects. The happy gang at this working family brewery gives
entertaining and informative 45-minute, four-language tours (usually
by friendly Inge, 150BF including a beer, piles of very steep steps, a
great rooftop panorama, daily on the hour 11:00–16:00, 11:00 and
15:00 are your best times to avoid groups, Oct–March 11:00 and
15:00 only, 1 block past church and canal, take a right down skinny
Stoofstraat to #26 on Walplein square, tel. 050/332-697). At Straffe
Hendrik ("Strong Henry") they remind their drinkers: "The components of the beer are vitally necessary and contribute to a well-bal-
anced life-pattern. Nerves, muscles, visual sentience, and a healthy
skin are stimulated by these in a positive manner. For longevity and
lifelong equilibrium, drink Straffe Hendrik in moderation!"

Their bistro, where you'll be given your included-with-the-
tour beer, serves a quick and hearty lunch plate (the 170BF "bread
with pâté and vegetables" is the best value, although the 250BF
"meat selection and vegetables" is a beer-drinker's picnic for 2).
On sunny summer days they offer a barbecue and salad bar for
350BF. You can eat indoors with the smell of hops or outdoors
with the smell of hops. This is a great place to wait for your tour
or to linger afterward. From here the lacy cuteness of Bruges
crescendos as you approach the Begijnhof.

▲▲**Begijnhof**—For military (and various other) reasons, there
were more women than men in the medieval Low Countries.
Towns provided Begijnhofs (buh-HINE-hofs), dignified places
in which these "Begijns" could live a life of piety and service
(without having to take the same vows a nun would). You'll find
Begijnhofs all over Belgium and Holland. Bruges' Begijnhof—
now inhabited not by Begijns but by Benedictine nuns—almost
makes you want to don a habit and fold your hands as you walk
under its wispy trees and whisper past its frugal little homes.
For a good slice of Begijnhof life, walk through the simple
museum (Begijn's House, left of entry gate, 60BF with English
flier, daily 10:00–12:00, 13:45–17:00, shorter hours off-season).

Minnewater—Just south of the Begijnhof is Minnewater, an
idyllic, clip-clop world of flower boxes, canals, swans, and tour
boats packed like happy egg cartons.

Almshouses—Walking from the Begijnhof back to the center,
you might detour along Nieuwe Gentweg to visit one of about
20 almshouses in the city. At #8, go through the door dated 1613
(free) into the peaceful courtyard. This was a medieval form of housing for the poor. The rich would pay for someone's tiny room here
in return for lots of prayers. The Diamond Museum (at the start of
Nieuwe Gentweg) is less interesting than an encyclopedia (200BF).

Bruges Experiences

Chocolate—Bruggians are connoisseurs of fine chocolate. You'll be tempted by chocolate-filled display windows all over town. Godiva is the best big-factory/high-price/high-quality local brand, but for the finest small-family operation, drop by **Maitre Chocolatier Verbeke**. While Mr. Verbeke is busy downstairs making chocolates, Mrs. Verbeke makes sure customers in the shop get the chocolate of their dreams. Ask her to assemble a bag of your favorites (the smallest amount sold is 100 grams—about seven pieces—for 90BF). Most are pralines, which means they're filled. While the "hedgehogs" are popular, be sure to get a "pharaoh's head." Pray for cool weather, since it's closed when it's very hot. (Open at least in the mornings on Tue, Wed, Fri, and Sat; open cooler afternoons as well, a block off Market Square at Geldmuntstraat 25, can ship overseas except during hot summer months, tel. 050/334-198.)

Lace and Windmills by the Moat—A 10-minute walk from the center to the northeast end of town brings you to four windmills strung out along a pleasant grassy setting on the "big moat" canal (between Kruispoort and Dampoort, on Bruges side of the moat). One of the windmills (St. Janshuismolen) is open to visitors (40BF, daily 9:30–12:30, 13:30–17:00, closed Oct–April, at the end of Carmersstraat).

To actually see lace being made, drop by the nearby Lace Centre, where ladies toss bobbins madly while their eyes go bad (60BF includes afternoon demonstrations and a small lace museum called Kantcentrum, as well as the adjacent Jerusalem church; Mon–Fri 10:00–12:00, 14:00–18:00, until 17:00 on Sat, closed Sun, Peperstraat 3). The Folklore Museum, in the same neighborhood, is cute but forgettable (80BF, daily 9:30–17:00, Oct–March closed Tue, Rolweg 40). To find either place, ask for the Jerusalem church.

▲▲**Biking**—While the sights are close enough for easy walking, the town is a treat to bike through, and you can get away from the tourist center. Consider a peaceful evening ride through the backstreets and around the outer canal. Rental shops have maps and ideas. The TI sells a handy *5X on the Bike around Bruges* map/guide for 50BF; it narrates five different bike routes (18–30 kilometers) through the idyllic countryside nearby. The best trip is 30 minutes along the canal out to Damme and back. The Netherlands/Belgium border is a 40-minute pedal beyond Damme. Two shops rent bikes in the center of town (100–110BF for 1 hr, 200–225BF for 4 hrs, or 325BF/day). Both offer free city maps and child seats. **Popelier Eric's** doesn't require a deposit and sells a good map of the countryside for 75BF (daily 9:00–21:00 in summer, 10:00–19:00 in winter, 50 meters from Church of Our Lady at Mariastraat 26, tel. 050/343-262). **'T Koffieboontje** asks for a 1,000BF deposit, your

passport, or a credit-card imprint (also rents mountain and tandem
bikes, Hallestraat 4, closer to belfry, tel. 050/338-027). The less
central **De Ketting** rents bikes for less (150BF/day, daily 9:00–
19:00, Gentpoortstraat 23, tel. 050/344-196).

Tours of Bruges

→ **Bruges by Boat**—The most relaxing and scenic (if not informative) way to see this city of canals is by boat, with the
captain narrating. Boats leave from all over town (190BF, 4/hrly,
10:00–18:00, copycat 30-min rides). Boten Stael (just over
the canal from the Memling Museum) offers a 30BF discount
with this book.

City Minibus Tours—"City Tour Bruges" gives 50-minute/
380BF rolling overviews of the town in an 18-seat, two-skylight
minibus with dial-a-language headsets and video support.
The tour leaves hourly (on the hr, 10:00–19:00 in summer,
until 18:00 in spring and fall, less in winter) from Market
Square. The narration, while clean, is slow-moving and boring.
But the tour is a lazy way to cruise by virtually every sight
in Bruges.

Walking Tours—Local guides walk small groups through the
core of town daily in July and August (150BF, depart from TI at
15:00). The tours, while earnest, are heavy on history and in two
languages, so they may be less than peppy. Still, to propel you
beyond the pretty gables and canal swans of Bruges, they are
good medicine. A private guided tour costs 1,500BF (reserve at
least 3 days in advance through the TI).

Bus Tours of Countryside—Quasimodo Tours offers those
with extra time two excellent all-day tours through the rarely
visited Flemish countryside. The "Flanders Fields" tour concen-
trates on World War I battlefields, trenches, memorials, and
poppy-splattered fields (Sun, Tue, and Thu 9:00–16:30). The
other is "Triple Treat": the port of Damme, a castle, a monastery, a brewery, and a chocolate factory as well as a sampling of
the treats—a waffle, chocolate, and beer (Mon, Wed, and Fri
9:00–16:00). Hardworking Lote leads all the tours himself, in
English only (1,500BF, 1,200BF if under 26, CC:VM, 29-seat
nonsmoking bus, includes lunch, lots of walking, pickup at your
hotel or the train station, tel. 050/370-470 to book, fax 050/
374-960, www.quasimodo.be).

Bruges by Bike—The Backroad Bike Company leads daily
bike tours through the nearby countryside at 10:00, 13:00, and
19.00 (550 650BF, 30 km, 3 hrs, tel. 050/370-470). Shorter,
longer, and evening tours are available.

Bus and Boat Tour—The Sightseeing Line offers a bus trip
to Damme and a boat ride back (660BF, April–Sept daily at
14:00 and 16:00, 2 hrs, leaves from Market Square).

Sights—Near Bruges

Dolfinarium—At Boudewijnpark, just outside of town, dolphins make a splash several times a day (call for show times—tel. 050/383-838, 280BF for 40-min show, Debaeckestraat 12, www.boudewijnpark.be). The theme park's roller-skating rink is open in the afternoon (and turns into an ice-skating rink off-season). From Bruges, catch the "Sint Michiels" bus #7 or #17 from Kuipersstraat.

Flanders Fields—This World War I museum, 60 kilometers southwest of Bruges, provides a moving look at the battles fought near Ieper (Ypres in French). Use interactive computers to trace the wartime lives of individual soldiers and citizens. Powerful videos and ear-shattering audio complete the story (250 BF, April–Sept daily 10:00–18:00, Oct–March Tue–Sun 10:00–17:00, Grote Markt 34, Ieper, tel. 057/228-584, fax 057/218-589, www.inflandersfields.be). From Bruges, catch a train to Ieper via Kortrijk (2 hrs). Drivers follow A17 to Kortrijk, then take A19 to Ieper.

Sleeping in Bruges

(45BF = about $1, country code: 32, area code: 050, zip code: 8000)

Sleep Code: **S** = Single, **D** = Double/Twin, **T** = Triple, **Q** = Quad, **b** = bathroom, **t** = toilet only, **s** = shower only, **CC** = Credit Card (**V**isa, **M**asterCard, **A**mex). Everyone speaks English.

Most places are located between the train station and the old center, with the most distant (and best) being a few blocks beyond Market Square to the north and east. B&Bs offer the best value. All include breakfast, are on quiet streets, and (with a few exceptions) keep the same prices throughout the year. Bruges is most crowded Friday and Saturday evenings Easter through October—with July and August weekends being worst. Otherwise, finding a room is easy.

You'll find a **Laundromat** at Gentportstraat 28 (daily 7:00–22:00, English instructions, machines use 20BF coins; you'll need about 14 total) or at Mr. Wash (near Hotel Hansa on St. Jakobsstraat).

Hotels

Hansa Hotel offers 24 rooms in a completely modernized old building. It's tastefully decorated in elegant pastels and has all the amenities. It's a great splurge (Db-4,520–5,970BF depending on room size, extra bed-1,250BF, suites available, CC:VMA, air-con, nonsmoking, elevator, Niklaas Desparsstraat 11, a block north of Market Square, tel. 050/338-444, fax 050/334-205, www.hansa.be, e-mail: information@hansa.be, cheery and hard-working Johan and Isabelle).

Hotel Aarendshuis, an old merchant's mansion, is well worn but comfortable. It's family run and has 25 spacious rooms, dingy carpets, chandeliered public places, and a small garden (prices vary with size and luxury: Sb-2,700BF, Db-3,000–4,000BF, Tb-4,000BF, Qb-4,500BF, kids under 10 free, car park-400BF, CC:VMA, elevator, 2 blocks off Burg Square at Hoogstraat 18, tel. 050/337-889, fax 050/330-816, e-mail: hotelaarendshuis @village.uunet.be).

Hotel Cordoeanier, another family-run place, rents 22 bright, simple, modern rooms on a quiet street two blocks off Market Square (Sb-1,950BF, Db-2,300BF, Tb-2,900–3,200BF, Qb-3,400BF, 5b-3,900BF, CC:VM, nearly free Internet access, Cordoeanierstraat 16, tel. 050/339-051, fax 050/346-111, www .cordoeanier.be, Kris and Veerie). **Hotel Nicolas** is equally central and even cheaper but smoky and not the same value (Sb-1,800BF, Db-2,100BF, CC:VMA, elevator, next to Hotel Hansa at N. Desparsstraat 9, tel. 050/335-502, fax 050/343-544).

Hotel Cavalier, which has more stairs than character, serves a hearty buffet breakfast in a royal setting (Sb-2,900BF, Db-2,400BF, Tb-3,000BF, Qb-3,300BF, 2 lofty "backpackers' doubles" on the 4th floor-1,600BF or 1,800BF with WC, CC:VMA, Kuipersstraat 25, tel. 050/330-207, fax 050/347-199, e-mail: hotel.cavalier@skynet.be, run by friendly Viviane De Clerck).

Hotel Botaniek has three stars, nine small rooms, and a quiet location a block from Astrid Park. This friendly hotel is basic, small, and comfy (Sb-2,600BF, Db-3,000BF, Tb-3,600BF, Qb-4,000BF, CC:VMA, Waalsestraat 23, tel. 050/341-424, fax 050/345-939, e-mail: hotel.botaniek@ping.be).

Hotel Rembrandt-Rubens has 15 rooms in a creaky 500-year-old building with tipsy floors, a mysterious floor plan, tacky rooms, ancient dippy beds, elephant tusks, a gallery of creepy old paintings, and probably the Holy Grail in a drawer somewhere (S-1,100BF, Ss-1,500BF, one D-1,600BF, Ds-2,100BF, Db-2,400BF, Tb-3,000BF, Qb-3,900BF, locked up at 24:00, on a quiet square between the Memlings and the brewery at Walplein 38, tel. 050/336-439, fax 050/677-780). The breakfast room (which must have been the knights' hall) overlooks a canal (while Rembrandt and Rubens overlook you from an ornately carved and tiled 1648 chimney). There's a little warmth behind Mrs. De Buyser's crankiness. The hotel has been in her family for 50 years.

Hotel Adornes, a great value, has 20 comfy new rooms with full, modern bathrooms in a 17th-century canalside house. They offer free parking, free loaner bikes, and a cellar game and video lounge (Db-3,000–3,800BF depending upon size, CC:VMA, elevator, near Van Nevel B&B, below, and Carmersstraat at St. Annarei 26, tel. 050/341-336, fax 050/342-085, e-mail. hotel .adornes@proximedia.be, Nathalie runs the family business).

Hotel De Pauw is tall, skinny, and family run, with straight-forward rooms on a quiet street across from a church (2 top-floor

Bruges Center Hotels

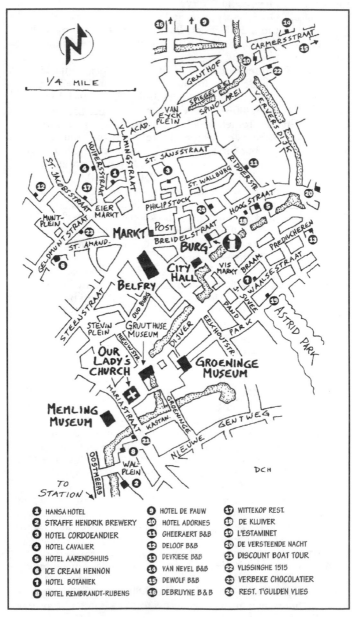

1/4 MILE

DCH

❶ HANSA HOTEL	❾ HOTEL DE PAUW	⓱ WITTEKOP REST.
❷ STRAFFE HENDRIK BREWERY	❿ HOTEL ADORNES	⓲ DE KLUIVER
❸ HOTEL CORDOEANDIER	⓫ GHEERAERT B&B	⓳ L'ESTAMINET
❹ HOTEL CAVALIER	⓬ DELOOF B&B	⓴ DE VERSTEENDE NACHT
❺ HOTEL AARENDSHUIS	⓭ DEVRIESE B&B	㉑ DISCOUNT BOAT TOUR
❻ ICE CREAM HENNON	⓮ VAN NEVEL B&B	㉒ VLISSINGHE 1515
❼ HOTEL BOTANIEK	⓯ DEWOLF B&B	㉓ VERBEKE CHOCOLATIER
❽ HOTEL REMBRANDT-RUBENS	⓰ DEBRUYNE B&B	㉔ REST. T'GULDEN VLIES

D-1,950BF, Db-2,200–2,550BF, CC:VM, free and easy parking, cable TV and phones, Sint Gilliskerkhof 8, tel. 050/337-118, fax 050/345-140, www.hoteldepauw.be, Philippe and Hilde).

Hotel Egmond is quietly located in the middle of the placid Minnewater. Its 18th-century rooms have all the comforts (Sb-3,600BF, Db-4,200BF, Tb-5,200BF, CC:VM, Minnewater 15, tel. 050/341-445, fax 050/342-940, www.egmond.be).

Crowne Plaza Hotel Brugge is the most modern, comfortable, and central hotel option. Each of its 96 air-conditioned rooms comes with a magnifying mirror and trouser press (rack rate: Db-8,300BF, prices drop as low as 5,500BF on weekdays and off-season, CC:VMA, elevator, pool, Burg 10, tel. 050/446-844, fax 050/446-868, www.crowneplaza.com).

Near Train Station: The **Hotel t'Keizershof** is a dollhouse of a hotel that lives by its motto, "Spend a night, not a fortune." It's simple and tidy, with seven small, cheery, old-time rooms split between two floors, a shower and toilet on each (S-950BF, D-1,400BF, T-2,100BF, Q-2,500BF, free and easy parking, laundry service-300BF, Oostmeers 126, a block in front of train station, tel. 050/338-728, e-mail: hotel.keizershof@12move.be, run by Stefaan and Hilde).

Bed-and-Breakfasts

These places, run by people who enjoy their work, offer the best value. Each is central and offers lots of stairs and three or four doubles you'd pay 4,000BF for in a hotel. Parking is generally easy on the street.

Koen and Annemie Dieltiens are a friendly couple who enjoy getting to know their guests and sharing a wealth of information on Bruges. You'll eat a hearty breakfast around a big table in their bright, homey, comfortable house. In April they'll move several blocks away, but will keep the same contact information (S-1,300BF, Sb-1,700BF, D-1,600BF, Db-1,900BF, T-2,100BF, Tb-2,400BF, Qb-2,900BF, 1-night stays pay 200BF extra per room, nonsmoking, Sint-Walburgastraat 14, 3 blocks east of Market Square, moving on April 2 to Waalse Straat 40, 3 blocks southeast of Burg Square, tel. 050/334-294, fax 050/335-230, http://users.skynet.be/dieltiens, e-mail: koen.dieltiens@skynet.be). The Dieltiens also rent a cozy studio and apartment for two to six people in a nearby 17th-century house (2 pay 13,300BF per week for studio, 14,700BF for apartment, prices higher for shorter stays and more people, cheaper off-season).

Paul and Roos Gheeraert live on the first floor while their guests take the second. This neoclassical mansion with big, bright, comfy rooms is another fine value (Sb-1,700BF, Db-1,900BF, Tb-2,400BF; rooms have coffeemakers and fridges; Ridderstraat 9, 4 blocks east of Market, tel. 050/335-627, fax 050/345-201, e-mail: paul.gheeraert@skynet.be). They also rent three modern, fully-equipped apartments and a large loft nearby (minimum 3 nights, view at http://users.skynet.be/brugge-gheeraert).

Chris Deloof's big, homey rooms are a good bet in the old center. Check out the fun, lofty A-frame room upstairs (Sb-1,800BF, Db-1,900–2,100BF, pleasant breakfast room, nonsmoking, Geerwijnstraat 14, tel. & fax 050/340-544, www.sin.be/ chrisdeloof, e-mail: chris.deloof@ping.be). Chris also rents a nearby apartment, great for a family or group (Qb-3,500BF).

The **Van Nevel family** rents two attractive top-floor rooms with built-in beds in a 16th-century house (S-1,300–1,600BF, D-1,600–1,900BF, T-2,500BF, includes breakfast, CC:VM but cash preferred, nonsmoking, Carmersstraat 13, 10-min walk from Market Square, tel. 050/346-860, fax 050/347-616, http://home.worldonline.be/~rvanneve, e-mail: Robert .VanNevel@advalvas.be). Robert enthusiastically shares the culture and history of Bruges with his guests.

Yvonne De Vriese rents three tidy B&B rooms on a corner overlooking two canals (1 S-1,000BF, D-1,500BF, Db-1,800BF, third or fourth person-500BF extra, breakfast served in your room, CC:VMA, Predikherenstraat 40, 4 blocks east of Burg Square, take bus #6 or #16 from station and get off at the first stop on Predikheren Rei, tel. 050/334-224, fax 050/336-491).

Arnold Dewolf's B&B is in a stately, quiet neighborhood (D-1,400BF, T-1,800BF, Q-2,200BF, family-friendly, near windmills, Oostproosse 9, tel. 050/338-366). From the train station, take bus #4 to Sasplein. Walk to the path behind the first windmill and turn left on Oostproosse.

Debruyne B&B, run by Marie-Rose and architect Ronny Debruyne, offers artsy, original decor and genuine friendliness (Db-1,900BF, Tb-2,400BF, Qb-2,900BF, 1-night stay-200BF extra per room, 5-min walk north of Market Square, Lange Raamstraat 18, tel. 050/347-606, fax 050/340-285, www .bedandbreakfastbruges.com).

Hostels

Bruges has several good hostels offering beds for around 400 to 450BF in two- to eight-bed rooms (singles go for around 600BF). Pick up the hostel info sheet at the station TI. The new American-style **Charlie Rockets** bar and hostel is the liveliest and most central (56 beds, 500BF per bed, 2–6 per room, Hoogstraat 19, tel. 050/330-660). These hostels are small, loose, and central: the dull **Snuffel Travelers Inn** (Ezelstraat 47, tel. 050/333-133), **Bauhaus International Party Hotel** (Langestraat 135, tel. 050/ 341-093), and the funky **Passage** (Dweerstraat 26, tel. 050/340- 232; its hotel next door rents 1,400BF doubles).

Eating in Bruges

Specialties include mussels cooked a variety of ways (one order can feed 2 people), fish dishes, grilled meats, and French fries. Touristy places on the square come with great views and are affordable; candle-cool bistros flicker on backstreets. Don't eat before 19:30 unless you like eating alone. Tax and service are always included.

Wittekop is very Flemish—a cluttered, laid-back, old-time place specializing in the beer-soaked equivalent of beef bourguignonne (395–675BF main courses, Tue–Sat 18:00–24:00, closed Sun–Mon, terrace in the back, Sint Jakobsstraat 14, tel. 050/332-059).

De Kluiver is a pub serving hot snacks, light 400BF meals, and great "seasnails in spiced bouillon" simmered in a whispering jazz ambience (Wed–Mon 18:00–01:00, closed Tue, Hoogstraat 12, tel. 050/338-927).

Pannekoekenhuisje, the little pancake house, is a cute restaurant serving delicious, inexpensive pancake meals (daily 12:00–21:00, just off Geldmuntstraat at Helmstraat 3, tel. 050/340-086). In 2001, enthusiastic chefs Mario and Rik open **The Flemish Pot** next door, offering vintage Flemish cuisine and homemade *wafels*.

Lotus Vegetarisch Restaurant serves good veggie lunches only (300BF plates, Mon–Sat 11:45–13:45, closed Sun, just off Burg at Wapenmakersstraat 5, tel. 050/331-078).

Two youthful, trendy, jazz-filled eateries: For hearty budget spaghetti (230BF), head for **L'Estaminet**, on the northern border of peaceful Astrid Park (11:30–3:00, closed Mon afternoon and all day Thu, Park 5). Or try **De Versteende Nacht Jazzcafe** on Langestraat 11 (500BF meals, Tue–Sat 19:00–02:00, closed Sun–Mon).

Vlissinghe 1515, the oldest pub in town, serves hot snacks in a great atmosphere (open from 11:30 on, closed Tue, Blekersstraat 2). **Restaurant 't Gulden Vlies**, just off Burg, is good for a late dinner (650BF plates, closed Mon–Tue, Mallebergplaats 17, tel. 050/334-709).

Restaurant de Eetkamer (the living room) offers stay-a-while elegance, fine service, and fine food (daily 12:00–14:30, 18:30–23:00, just south of Markt, Eeekhout 6, tel. 050/337-886). Drop by **Bistro De Schaar** for good food and fun atmosphere (Fri–Wed 12:00–14:30, 18:00–23:00, Hooistraat 2, tel. 050/335-979).

Picnics: Geldmuntstraat is a handy street when you're hungry. A block off Market Square, **Pickles Frituur** serves the best sit-down fries in town (Mon–Sat 11:00–24:00, closed Sun). A block farther, past the Verbeke chocolate shop, **Nopri Supermarket** is great for picnics (push-button produce pricer lets you buy as little as one mushroom, Mon–Sat 9:00–18:30, closed Sun). The small

Delhaize grocery is on Market Square opposite the belfry (Mon–Sat 8:00–12:00, 13:30–18:00, closed Sun). **Selfi** has cheap sandwiches to go (Breidelstraat 16, between Burg and Market Square). For midnight munchies, you'll find Indian-run corner grocery stores.

Frietjes: These local French fries are a treat. Proud and traditional *frituurs* serve tubs of fries and various local-style shish kebabs. Belgians dip their *frietjes* in mayonnaise, but ketchup is there for the Yankees (along with spicier sauces). For a quick, cheap, and scenic meal, hit a *frituur* and sit on the steps or benches overlooking Market Square, about 50 meters past the post office.

Beer: Belgium boasts more than 350 types of beer. Straffe Hendrik ("Strong Henry"), a potent and refreshing local brew, is, even to a Bud Lite kind of guy, obviously great beer. Among the more unusual of the others to try: Dentergems (with coriander and orange peel) and Trappist (a dark, malty, monk-made beer). Non–beer drinkers enjoy Kriek (a cherry-flavored beer) and Frambozen Bier (raspberry-flavored beer). Each beer is served in its own unique glass. Any pub carries the basic beers, but for a selection of more than 300 types, drink at **t'Brugs Beertje** (16:00–01:00, closed Wed, Kemelstraat 5). When you've finished those, step next door, where **Dreupel Huisje "1919"** serves more than 100 Belgian gins and liqueurs (closed Tue). Another good place to gain an appreciation of the Belgian beer culture is **de Garre**. Rather than a noisy pub scene, it has a sit-down-and-focus-on-your-friend-and-the-fine-beer ambience (huge selection, off Breidelstraat, between Burg and Markt, on the tiny Garre alley, daily 12:00–24:00, tel. 050/341-029).

Belgian Waffles: While Americans think of "Belgian" waffles for breakfast, the Belgians (who don't eat waffles or pancakes for breakfast) think of *wafels* as Liege-style (dense, sweet, eaten plain and heated up, served take-away) and Brussels-style (lighter, often with powdered sugar or whipped cream and fruit, served in tea-houses). For the best Liege-style *wafels* in town, drop by **Ice Cream Hennon** for a Luikse Wafel (50BF, daily 10:00–24:00, across from Nopri Supermarket, corner of Guldmuntstraat and Sind Amandstraat). Hennon's *wafels* and ice cream (18 flavors) are extremely fresh and tasty.

Transportation Connections—Bruges

From Brussels, all of Europe is at your fingertips (see "Brussels Connections," next chapter). Train info: tel. 050/382-382.

By train to: Brussels (2/hrly, at :33 and :59, 1 hr), **Ghent** (4/hrly, 40 min), **Ostende** (3/hrly, 15 min), **Köln** (6/day, 4 hrs), **Paris** (hrly via Brussels, 2.5 hrs, 420BF supplement for Eurail), **Amsterdam** (hrly, 3.5 hrs).

Trains from England: Bruges is an ideal "welcome to Europe" stop after London. Take the Eurostar train from London to Brussels under the English Channel (10/day, 3 hrs), then transfer to Bruges (hrly, 1 hour). Or, if you'd prefer to cross the Channel by boat, catch the London-to-Dover train (2 hrs, from London's Victoria station), then the catamaran to Ostende (2 hrs; train station at Ostende catamaran terminal), then the Ostende-to-Bruges train (15 min). Five boats run daily (1,650BF one-way, same price for cheap five-day return ticket, call to reserve a seat and pay at the dock, CC:VMA, tel. 059/559-955).

BRUSSELS

Brussels, the capital of Belgium, is also the capital of Europe. Since World War II it's been the convenient home of both NATO and the "government of Europe," working busily to move things toward unity. And it's Europe's linguistic hinge, too (60 percent of all Belgians speak the Germanic Flemish, and 40 percent speak the Romantic French). It's easy to miss Brussels as you zip from Amsterdam to Paris on the train, but those who stop are pleasantly surprised by its rich chocolatey mix of food and culture.

Brussels, like Belgium, is officially bilingual. Most maps and signs here list place-names in French and Flemish (Dutch). Since 80 percent of the people in Brussels speak French, I normally list only the French names in this chapter.

Planning Your Time

Brussels is low on great sights and high on ambience. On a quick trip, a day and a night are enough for a good first taste. It could even be done as a day trip from Bruges (1 hr away by train) or a stopover on the Amsterdam-Paris ride (hrly trains). The main reason to stop—La Grand Place—takes only a few minutes to see. With very limited time, skip the indoor sights and enjoy a coffee or a beer on the square. Even travelers not "into art" can spend an enjoyable three hours at Brussels' ancient- and modern-art museums. If you do the auto and military museums (side by side), plan on a three-hour trip from the town center. If you're in Brussels on a Monday, when most sights are closed, consider the Auto World, Atomium, shopping, a walking tour, or a minibus tour. Most important, this is a city to browse and wander.

Brussels

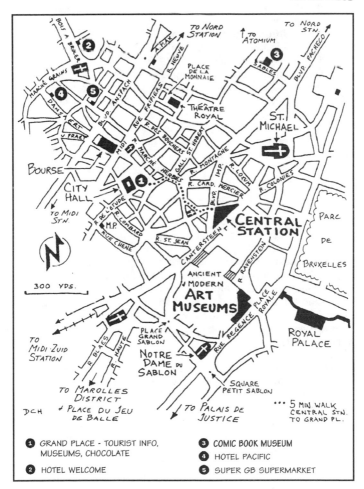

1 GRAND PLACE - TOURIST INFO, MUSEUMS, CHOCOLATE

2 HOTEL WELCOME

3 COMIC BOOK MUSEUM

4 HOTEL PACIFIC

5 SUPER GB SUPERMARKET

Orientation (area code: 02)

Central Brussels is defined by a ring of roads (which replaced the old city wall) called the Pentagon. All hotels and nearly all the sights I mention are within this circle. The epicenter is the main square (La Grand Place), TI, and Central Station (3 blocks away). To get to La Grand Place from Central Station, walk downhill from the station (through the arch in Le Meridien Hôtel across the street) and turn right; after a block, you'll reach a small square with a fountain. For La Grand Place, turn left at the far end of the square; for the TI, continue straight past the square for one block. For the restaurant streets, take the first right (an alley) past the TI (see "Eating," below).

Tourist Information: Although the office at rue du Marché-aux-Herbes 63 is for all of Belgium, it does Brussels just fine (Mon–Fri 9:00–19:00, Sat–Sun 9:00–13:00, 14:00–19:00, Sept–June closes at 18:00 and Sun afternoon, downhill 3 blocks from Central Station, tel. 02/504-0390; 2 fun Europe stores are across the street). Another TI is in the city hall in La Grand Place (daily 9:00–18:00, closed Sun off-season, tel. 02/513-8940). Among their countless fliers, pick up "Brussels, Yours to Discover," the weekly *What's On*, a city map, and a public transit map. Ask about the new Visit Brussels hop-on hop-off bus. The 70BF *Brussels Guide & Map* booklet is worthwhile if you want a series of neighborhood walks and a more complete explanation of the city's many museums. If your next destination is Bruges, get your Bruges map here.

Arrival in Brussels

By Train: Brussels can't decide which of its three stations (Central, Nord, and Midi) is the main one. Most international trains leave and land at the Nord and Midi Stations. The Eurostar leaves from Midi Station (also called Zuid or South), getting you to London in three hours. The area around the Midi Station is a rough-and-tumble immigrant neighborhood (with a towering Ferris wheel); the area around the Nord Station is a seedy red-light district. Central Station has handy services (grocery store, fast food, a luggage storage, waiting rooms, and so on) and is nearest to the sights. Normally only Belgian and Amsterdam trains stop at Central. Don't assume your train stops at more than one station. Confirm your plan with the conductor.

Trains zip under the city, connecting all three stations every two minutes or so. It's an easy three-minute chore to connect from Nord or Midi to Central. As you wait on the platform for your train, look at the track notice board that tells which train is approaching. They zip in and out constantly. Anxious travelers often board the wrong train on the right track.

By Plane: Shuttle trains run between the three stations (Midi, Central, and Nord) and Brussels International Airport, 14 kilometers away (100BF, 4/hrly, 25 min). Airport info can connect you to your airline desk: tel. 02/753-3913.

Getting around Brussels

Most of Brussels' sights are walkable. For a few of the sights, such as the auto and military museums, take the Métro. The TI's free "Métro Tram Bus Plan" is excellent. The integrated system uses one 50BF ticket that's good for one hour (notice the time when you first stamp it; buy tickets on bus or at Métro stations). The

La Grand Place

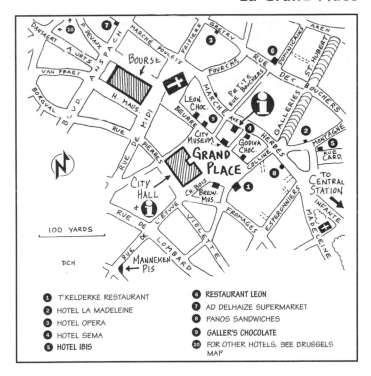

1. T'KELDERKE RESTAURANT
2. HOTEL LA MADELEINE
3. HOTEL OPERA
4. HOTEL SEMA
5. HOTEL IBIS
6. RESTAURANT LEON
7. AD DELHAIZE SUPERMARKET
8. PANOS SANDWICHES
9. GALLER'S CHOCOLATE
10. FOR OTHER HOTELS, SEE BRUSSELS MAP

deals (5 tickets/240BF, 10 tickets/350BF) are available at TIs, newsstands, and Métro stations. TIs also sell a one-day ticket for 140BF (cheaper than 3 rides, transit info: tel. 02/515-2000).

The new Visit Brussels hop-on hop-off bus makes a 12-stop circuit, allowing you to hop off, see a sight, and catch the next bus (490BF/24 hours, daily April–Sept, Oct–March Fri–Sun only, includes discounts to various sights, tel. 02/513-7744, www .brussels-city-tours.com). For information on guided nonstop tours, see "Tours of Brussels," below.

Sights—Brussels

▲▲▲**La Grand Place**—Brussels' main square, aptly called La Grand Place, is the heart of the old town and Brussels' greatest sight. Any time of day it's worth swinging by to see what's going on. Concerts, flower markets, sound-and-light shows, endless people watching—it entertains (as do the streets around it).

The museums on the square are well-advertised but dull. The **Hôtel de Ville**, or city hall, with the tallest spire, is the square's centerpiece but no big deal to see (100BF, visits only by 30-min tours, Tue 11:30 and 15:15, Wed 15:15, and Sun 12:15; Oct–March Tue 11:30 and 13:15, Wed 15:15, no Sun tour). The **City Museum**, opposite the city hall, is in a neo-Gothic building (1875) called "the King's House" (in which no king ever lived). The top floor has an entertaining room full of costumes the *Manneken* statue has pissed through; the middle floor features maps and models of old Brussels; and the bottom floor has a few old paintings and tapestries (100BF, Tue–Fri 10:00–17:00, Sat–Sun 10:00–13:00, closed Mon). Opposite the King's House is the **Brewery Museum**, with one room of old brewing para-phernalia and one room of new (all explained in Flemish and French). It's pretty lame... but a good excuse for a beer (100BF including an unnamed local beer, daily 10:00–17:00). The <u>Chocolate Museum</u>, next door, is a delightful concept. But offering a meager set of displays, a second-rate video, a look at a "chocolate master" at work, and a choco-sample for 200BF, it's way overpriced (Tue–Sun 10:00–17:00, 13 Grand Place). For many, the best thing about La Grand Place is **chocolate** at Godiva's, Leonidas, or Galler's. Each has an inviting display case of 20 or so chocolates and sells a minimum of 100 grams—your choice of six to eight pieces. Most consider Godiva the very best (hand-made, 130BF/100 grams). But most locals sacrifice 10 percent in quality to double their take by getting their fix at Leonidas (machine-made, 50BF/100 grams, white is their specialty). Galler's chocolate, the royal favorite, rivals Godiva. Only their display includes English descriptions, so you'll know what you're enjoying (next to Leonidas at rue au Beurre 44, handmade, 110BF/100 grams).

Manneken-Pis—Brussels is a great city, but its mascot (apparently symbolizing the city's irreverence) is a statue of a little boy urinat-ing. For the story about this little squirt, read a postcard stand. It's three short blocks off the Grand Place, but for exact direc-tions, I'll let you ask a local, "*Où est le* Manneken-Pis?" He may be wearing some clever outfit. By tradition, costumes are sent to Brussels from around the world. Cases full of these are on display in the City Museum (described above).

Lace and Costume Museum—This is worthwhile only to those who have devoted their lives to the making of lace (100BF, Mon–Tue and Thu–Fri 10:00–12:30, 13:30–17:00, Sat–Sun 14:00–16:30, closed Wed, Violette 6, a block off La Grand Place).

▲▲▲**Museum of Ancient Art and Modern Art**—These are two separate museums, now connected by a tunnel and covered by the same ticket. The Ancient Art museum, featuring Flemish and Belgian art of the 14th to 18th centuries, is packed with a dazzling collection of masterpieces by Van der Weyden, Breughel, Bosch, and Rubens. Start your visit with the free 30-minute video featur-ing a handful of Flemish masterpieces, enabling you to go through

the museum understanding these as if you were an art historian.
Consider the 100BF "Twenty Masterpieces of the Art of Painting—A Brief Guided Tour" booklet. Tour the rooms of this
museum in numerical order (starting with 10). Highlights are room
31—busy with Breughel—and rooms of Rubens (with delightful
mini-cartoons used as designs to produce the big canvases).

The Museum of Modern Art gives an easy-to-enjoy walk
through the art of the 19th and 20th centuries. Highlights include
David's famous neoclassical portrait of Marat (1793; 2 floors
underground, press "-2" in elevator), the stirring Social Realism
of the early industrial age, and the surreal fantasies of Rene and
Georgette Magritte.

One ticket works for both museums (150BF, worthwhile
20BF map of ancient- and modern-art museums complex, Tue–
Sun 10:00–17:00, closed Mon, half the rooms close for lunch
12:00–13:00, the other half close 13:00–14:00, decent cafeteria
with salad bar, rue de la Regence 3, tel. 02/508-3211).

▲**Belgian Centre of the Comic Strip**—This strip joint is
housed in an industrial warehouse designed by Horta, the local
Art Nouveau great. It's free to get inside to visit the brasserie
and bookstore. Upstairs in the comics museum, only Belgians
get the jokes (200BF, Tue–Sun 10:00–18:00, closed Mon, rue des
Sables 20, tel. 02/219-1980).

Sights—Away from the Center
▲**Park of the Cinquantenaire**—This park sprawls out from under
a massive triumphal arch, which was built in 1880 to celebrate the
50th anniversary of Belgian independence. While precious few of
the governmental buildings of the European Union (EU) are visually
exciting, you can emerge from the Métro at the Schuman stop to be
surrounded by the political headquarters of a more or less united
Europe. The huge, star-shaped Berlaymont Building (built in 1963
to house the Commission of the European Union) was polluted by
asbestos insulation and is now empty and being renovated. From
there, walk 10 minutes through the park to the AutoWorld and
military museums (under giant arch). The next Métro stop (Merode)
is closer to the museums.
▲**AutoWorld**—Starting with Mr. Benz's motorized tricycle of
1886, you'll walk through a giant hall filled with 400 historic cars.
It's well described in English (200BF, daily 10:00–18:00, until
17:00 off-season, in Palais Mondial, Parc du Cinquantenaire,
Métro: Merode, tel. 02/736-4165).
▲**Royal Museum of the Army and Military History**—Wander
through a vast collection of 19th-century weaponry and uniforms
and a giant hall dedicated to airplanes of war (free, Tue–Sun 9:00–
12:00, 13:00–16:30, closed Mon, tel. 02/737-7811). There's a good
display from the Belgian struggle for independence (early 1800s).

Museum of Natural Sciences—Dinosaur enthusiasts come here for the world's largest collection of iguanodon skeletons (150BF, Tue–Fri 9:30–16:45, Sat–Sun 10:00–18:00, closed Mon, rue Vautier 29, bus #34 from Bourse Stock Exchange, tel. 02/627-4238).

Royal Museum of Central Africa—Remember the Belgian Congo? Brussels has an excellent museum of the Congo and much more of Africa (ethnography, sculptures, jewelry, colonial history, flora, and fauna) an hour from the center. Take Métro 1A to Montgomery and then catch tram #44 to its final stop, Tervuren. From there walk 200 meters through the park to a palace (80BF, Tue–Fri 10:00–17:00, weekends until 18:00, closed Mon, tel. 02/769-5211).

Antoine Wiertz Museum—This 19th-century artist painted some of the world's largest canvases, with themes from biblical to political (free, 10:00–12:00, 13:00–17:00, closed Mon and every other weekend, rue Vautier 62, bus #34 from Bourse Stock Exchange, tel. 02/648-1718).

Atomium—This giant molecule, with escalators connecting the various "atoms" and a restaurant with a view in the top sphere, was the symbol of the 1958 Universal Exhibition held in Belgium (200BF, daily 9:00–19:30, 10:00–17:30 off-season, Métro: Heizel, tel. 02/474-8977). Today it's the cheesy nucleus of a park on the edge of town that has the kid-pleasing **Mini-Europa**, with 1:25-scale models of 300 famous European buildings (420BF, discounts for kids, daily 9:30–19:00, Fri–Sun until 23:00, closes earlier off-season, tel. 02/474-1311).

Tours of Brussels

Human Profile of Brussels Minibus Tour—This company, which takes eight visitors on three-hour tours, has a sincere commitment to teaching an understanding of Brussels (1,000BF, mid-March–Oct daily at 10:00 and 14:00, 10 Grand Place, tel. 02/715-9120).

De Boeck's City Tours—This typical three-hour, guided bus tour provides the handiest way to get the grand perspective on Brussels (800BF, starts with a walk around La Grand Place before jumping on a tour bus at rue de la Colline 8, daily in-season at 10:00, 11:00, 13:30, and 14:30; off-season, 10:00, 11:00, and 14:30; buy tickets a block off La Grand Place at rue de la Colline 8 or at TI, tel. 02/513-7744). You'll see (and learn about) the Royal Palace, Atomium, and the European Union Headquarters.

Chatter Tour—This 2.5-hour tour, at its best, makes hard-to-understand Brussels more than a collection of sights. But some guides are disappointingly short on chatter. You'll be on your feet much of the time (with some limited use of public transportation). The groups are small, and the better guides explain the delicate balance between French and Flemish through the architecture and art of the city. Starting with medieval and moving through modern styles, this is a study in how a region in an almost-perpetual state of flux until the 19th century somehow managed to find some cohesion and create a modern state. Of special interest is the late-19th-century Art Nouveau style, especially as pioneered by Belgian Victor Horta. You'll see several of his buildings (300BF, 250BF for hostelers who buy tickets at their hostel, mid-June–mid-Sept daily at 10:00, meet at Galeries Royales Saint-Hubert, rue Marché-aux-Herbes 90, near La Grand Place, tel. 02/673-1835). They also offer other tours.

Sleeping in Brussels
(45BF = about $1, country code: 32, area code: 02, zip code: 1000)
Sleep Code: **S** = Single, **D** = Double/Twin, **T** = Triple, **Q** = Quad, **b** = bathroom, **t** = toilet only, **s** = shower only, **CC** = Credit Card (**V**isa, **M**asterCard, **A**mex). Everyone speaks English. Prices include breakfast unless noted otherwise.

Like everything else, hotel prices are high in central Brussels. You have three budget options: modern hostels with double rooms, safe but dingy old places, and business hotels offering summer or weekend specials. September is very crowded, and finding a room without a reservation can be impossible.

Business Hotels with Summer Rates
The fancy (5,000–6,000BF) hotels of Brussels survive off the business and diplomatic trade. They are desperately empty in July and August (sometimes June, too) and on weekends (most Fri, Sat, and Sun nights). If you ask for a summer rate you'll save about a third. If you go through the TI, you'll save up to two-thirds. Four-star hotels in the center abound with summer rates between 2,500 and 3,000BF. If you are willing to sink as low as three stars, you'll probably get a double with enough comforts to keep a diplomat happy, including a fancy breakfast, for as low as 2,000BF.

While the TI assured me that every day in July and August there are tons of business-class hotel rooms on the push list, you can book in advance by calling the BTR room-booking service (tel. 02/513-7484). You will, however, get an even bigger discount by just showing up at the TI (for same-day booking only). In July and August I would arrive without a reservation, walk from the Central Station down to the TI, and let them book me a room within a few blocks. These seasonal rates apply only to business-class hotels. Because of this, budget accommodations, which charge the same throughout the year, go from being a good value one day to a bad value the next. I like the first three listings best.

Hotels near La Grand Place
Hôtel Welcome is farthest away from the Grand Place (a 10-min walk) but is the best value. Just renovated by a bundle

of hospitality energy named Meester Smeester, it offers small but business-class rooms. With just 10 rooms, it brags it's the smallest hotel in Brussels (small Sb/Db-2,600BF, Db-2,900–3,600BF, larger Db-4,500BF rooms are draped in elegance and overlook the square, extra bed-500BF, breakfast-250BF, CC:VM, free parking, will pick up guests at airport for a fee, at Ste. Catherine Métro stop on a characteristic old square, 23 Quai au Bois a Bruler, tel. 02/219-9546, fax 02/217-1887, www.hotelwelcome.com, Sophie and Michael Smeester). Guests get a 5 percent discount at the pricey attached restaurant, La Truite d'Argent.

Hôtel La Madeleine, on the small square between the station and La Grand Place, is comfortable and hotelesque, with 52 fine rooms (S-1,695BF, no shower at all for this room; Sb-3,100BF, Db-3,400BF, Tb-4,400BF, CC:VMA, elevator, rue de la Montagne 22, tel. 02/513-2973, fax 02/502-1350).

Hôtel Pacific is gently run by Paul Powells, whose motto is "safe, clean, and cheap." While the charming breakfast room is from the 19th century, the ramshackle upstairs feels like a Jackson Pollock thrift shop. Even with the wrinkly linoleum and funky furnishings, Paul gives the place an enjoyable calmness (S-1,100BF, D-2,300BF, Ds-2,250BF, T-2,550BF, includes a cheese-omelet breakfast, nonsmoking, showers-100BF, elevator, 24:00 curfew, easy phone reservations, rue Antoine Dansaert 57, tel. 02/511-8459).

Hôtel Ibis, perfectly situated halfway between the station and La Grand Place, is a huge modern place offering quiet, simple, industrial-strength yet comfy rooms (Db-4,300BF, extra person-500BF, breakfast-300BF, CC:VMA, air-con, elevator, smoke-free rooms, Grasmarkt 100, tel. 02/514-4040, fax 02/514-5067, www.ibishotel.com).

Hôtel Opera, on a great people-filled street near the Grand Place, is professional, dark, and classy, with street noise and 49 boxy rooms (Sb-2,650BF, Db-3,150BF, Tb-3,650BF, Qb-4,200BF, CC:VMA, includes breakfast buffet, courtyard rooms are quieter, elevator, Internet access, rue Gretry 53, tel. 02/219-4343, fax 02/219-1720, e-mail: hotel.opera@skynet.be).

Hôtel Floris, with wood floors and some beamed ceilings, has 11 spacious and comfy rooms just off La Grand Place and right across from the TI (Sb-3,300–5,400BF, Db-3,700–5,800BF, third person-1,200–2,500BF, CC:VMA, elevator, rooms have phones and cable TV, 24-hr desk, tel. 02/514-0760, fax 02/ 548-9039, e-mail: hotel.ustel@ping.be).

Hostels

Three classy and modern hostels, in buildings that could double as small, state-of-the-art, minimum-security prisons, are within a 10-minute walk of Central Station. Each accepts people of all ages, serves cheap hot meals, and charges about the same (S-820BF,

D-1,200BF, beds in quads-510BF, beds in bigger dorms-430BF, sheets-130BF; nonmembers pay up to 100BF extra). All rates include breakfast and showers down the hall. **Breughel Hostel**, a fortress of cleanliness, is handiest and most comfortable. Twenty-two of its rooms are bunk-bed doubles (open 7:00–10:00, 14:00–01:00, CC:VM, midway between Midi and Central Stations, behind Chapelle church, rue de St. Esprit 2, tel. 02/511-0436, fax 02/512-0711, e-mail: jeugdherberg.bruegel@ping.be). **Sleepwell**, surrounded by high-rise parking lots, is also comfortable (S-695BF, D-1,140BF, T-1,500BF, cheaper beds in larger rooms, sheets-125BF, CC:VM, includes breakfast, nonsmoking, 03:00 curfew, laundry nearby, offers Internet access and walking tours-100BF/person, rue de Damier 23, tel. 02/218-5050, www.sleepwell.be, e-mail: info@sleepwell.be). **Jacques Brel** is a little farther out but still a reasonable walk from everything (S-800BF, D-1,170BF, T/Q-495BF per person, bed in dorm-420BF, sheets-125BF, CC:VM, includes breakfast, no curfew, nonsmoking rooms, laundry available, Internet access, rue de la Sablonniere 30, tel. 02/218-0187, e-mail: brusselsbrel@laj.be).

Eating in Brussels

Eat mussels in Brussels. They're served everywhere. You get a big-enough-for-two bucket and a pile of fries. Use one empty shell to tweeze out the rest of the mussels. When the mollusks are in season, from about July 15 through April, you'll get the big Dutch mussels. Locals take a break in May and June, when only the puny Danish variety is available. For an atmospheric cellar just off the Grand Place, step into the **t'Kelderke** (daily 12:00–2:00, La Grand Place 15, tel. 02/513-7344). It serves local specialties, including mussels (a splittable two-kilo bucket of *moules* for 625BF). Locals claim the best mussels are served at the touristy **Restaurant Leon**, which offers a small "Formula Leon" 475BF *menu* of a small bucket, fries, and a beer (daily from 12:00, rue des Bouchers 18, tel. 02/511-1415).

Brussels' **restaurant streets** are touristy but fun (exit left from TI on rue Marché-aux-Herbes and take the first right). Many of these restaurants take advantage of tourists by tacking on extra charges.

If Brussels puts you in an Art Nouveau mood, have a meal or coffee at the city's most atmospheric hangout, **De Ultieme Halluci-natie** (exotic 400–750BF meals, Mon–Fri 11:00–3:00, Sat from 16:00, closed Sun, beautiful patio, rue Royale 316, tel. 02/217-0614).

You'll find *frites* (French fries) and sandwich shops throughout Brussels. **Panos** has good, cheap sandwiches (on Grasmarkt, across from entrance of Galleries Royales St. Hubert).

Two **supermarkets** are about a block from the Bourse Stock Exchange and a few blocks from La Grand Place. The **AD Delhaize** is at the intersection of Anspachlan and Marché-aux-Poulets

(Tue–Sat 9:00–20:00, Mon from 13:00, Sun 9:00–13:00), and the **Super GB** is a half block away at Halles and Marché-aux-Poulets (Mon–Sat 9:00–19:00, closed Sun).

Transportation Connections—Brussels

By train to: Bruges (2/hrly, at :04 and :30 past each hour, 50 min), **Amsterdam** (hrly, at :46 after each hour, 3 hrs), **Berlin** (7/day, 9 hrs, night train available), **Bern** (5/day, 8 hrs, night train available), **Frankfurt** (9/day, 5 hrs), **Munich** (9/day, 9 hrs), **Rome** (4/day, 15–17 hrs), **Paris** (fast trains zip to Paris—hrly, 90 min— it's best to book by 20:00 the day before or risk limited availability on same day, comes with a supplement of 420BF/second class, 630BF/first class—even for railpass holders. There's one slow, 4-hr, no-supplement train a day). Train info: tel. 02/525-9494 (long wait), international train info: tel. 0900-95-777.

To London: Brussels and London are now just three 140-mile-per-hour hours apart by Eurostar train (10/day, under the English Channel in 20 min). For the latest prices, call U.S. tel. 800/EUROSTAR, or Belgian tel. 0900-10366, or visit www.raileurope.com or www.eurostar.co.uk (you can order online at either site). In 2000, "full-fare" tickets cost $239 for first class and $159 for second class. Full-fare tickets are exchangeable and fully refundable even after your departure date. The cheaper "Leisure" tickets cost $199 for first class and $119 for second class; these are nonrefundable but exchangeable up to three days before departure. Cheaper 7- and 14-day advance-purchase tickets are sometimes available if you order your ticket in Europe (can call from home). To order your ticket by phone, call Belgian tel. 0900-10366 for Eurostar information and 0900-10177 to reserve (expensive toll line costs 20BF/min from pay phone and 60BF/min from hotel); you can either pay with a credit card or simply reserve a seat (and pay at the station at least an hour before the train leaves).

You can also buy your Eurostar tickets in the United States (tel. 800/EUROSTAR) or at any major train station in Europe. If you buy tickets in person in Belgium, go to a major train station rather than a travel agency; you'll get your tickets immediately (travel agencies can't deliver until the next day).

Another option is the sloooow train and ferry combination (8/day, 4.5–7.5 hrs). Or save a little money by riding a Eurolines bus ($46 one-way, $71 round-trip, tel. 02/203-0707 in Brussels).

By plane: Virgin Express flies cheap between Brussels and London (hrly, starting at $72), Milan, Rome, Nice, Barcelona, Madrid, Ireland, and Copenhagen (Belgian tel. 02/752-0505, www.virgin-express.com). Airport info: tel. 0900-70000.

THE NETHERLANDS

- 14,000 square miles (a little larger than Maryland)
- 15 million people (1,150 per square mile, 15 times the population density of the United States)
- 1 guilder = about 40 cents

The Netherlands, Europe's most densely populated country, is also one of its wealthiest and best-organized. A generation ago, Belgium, the Netherlands, and Luxembourg formed the nucleus of a united Europe when they joined economically to form BeNeLux.

Efficiency is a local custom. The average income is higher than that in the United States. Though only 8 percent of the labor force is made up of farmers, they cultivate 70 percent of the land, and you'll travel through vast fields of barley, wheat, sugar beets, potatoes, and flowers.

"Holland" is just a nickname for the Netherlands. North Holland and South Holland are the largest of the 12 states that make up the Netherlands. The word Netherlands means "low-lands." Half the country is below sea level, reclaimed from the sea (or rivers). That's why the locals say, "God made the Earth, but the Dutch made Holland." Modern technology and plenty of Dutch elbow grease have turned much of the sea into fertile farmland. While a new, 12th state—Flevoland, near Amsterdam—has recently been drained, dried, and populated, Dutch reclamation projects are essentially finished.

The Dutch generally speak English, pride themselves on their frankness, and like to split the bill. Traditionally, Dutch cities have been open-minded, loose, and liberal (to attract sailors in the days of Henry Hudson). And today, Amsterdam is a capital of alternative lifestyles—a city where "victimless crime" is a contradiction in itself. While Amsterdam has its quiet sides, many enjoy more sedate Dutch evenings by sleeping in a small town nearby and side tripping into the big city.

The Dutch guilder (f, for its older name, florin) is divided into 100 cents (c). There are about f2.50 in a U.S. dollar (f2.50 = $1). To roughly convert Dutch prices into dollars, divide by two, then subtract 10 percent of the original price (f98 = about $40).

The country is so small, level, and well covered by trains and buses that transportation is a snap. Major cities are connected by speedy trains that come and go every 10 or 15 minutes. Connections are excellent, and you'll rarely wait more than a few minutes. Round-trip tickets are discounted. Buses take you where trains don't, and bicycles take you where buses don't. Bus stations and bike-rental shops cluster around train stations. The national bus system, both within and between cities, runs on a uniform "strip card" system (though single-ride tickets are also available). You can buy various strip cards on the bus or more cheaply (15 strip cards, f12.25) at train stations, post offices, and some tobacco shops. If you're caught riding without a card, you have to take off your clothes.

Holland is a biker's dream. The Dutch, who average four bikes per family, have put small bike roads (with their own traffic lights) beside every big auto route. You can rent bikes at most train stations and drop them off at most others. (You can take bikes on trains, outside of rush hour, for f10.)

Smaller shops are open from 9:00 to 18:00 and until 21:00 on Thursdays (closed Sun). Larger stores and supermarkets are open weekdays from 8:00 to 20:00 and until 17:00 on Saturdays (closed Sun). The businesslike Dutch know no siesta, but many shopkeepers take Monday mornings off.

The best "Dutch" food is Indonesian (from the former colony). Find any Indisch restaurant and experience a *rijsttafel* ("rice table"). With as many as 30 spicy dishes, a rijsttafel can be split and still fill two hungry tourists. *Nasi rames* is a cheaper, smaller version of a rijsttafel. Local taste treats are cheese, pancakes (*pannenkoeken*), Dutch gin (*jenever*, pronounced "ya nayver"), light pilsner beer, and "syrup waffles" (*stroopwafel*). Yogurt in Holland (and throughout northern Europe) is delicious and drinkable right out of its plastic container. *Broodjes* are sandwiches of fresh bread and delicious cheese—cheap at snack bars, delis, and *broodje* restaurants. For cheap fast food, try a Middle Eastern *shwarma*, roasted lamb in pita bread. Breakfasts are big by continental standards. Lunch and dinner are served at American times.

Experiences you owe your tongue in Holland: a raw herring (outdoor herring stands are all over), lingering over coffee in a "brown café," an old *jenever* with a new friend, and a giant rijsttafel. Tipping is not expected, but locals round the bill up (never more than 5 percent) as thanks for good service.

AMSTERDAM

Amsterdam is a progressive way of life housed in Europe's most 17th-century city. Physically, it's a city built upon millions of pilings. But, more than that, it's a city built on good living, cozy cafés, great art, street-corner jazz, stately history, and a spirit of live and let live. It has 800,000 people and as many bikes. It also has more canals than Venice and as many tourists. While Amsterdam may box your Puritan ears, this great, historic city is an experiment in freedom.

Planning Your Time

While I'd sleep in nearby Haarlem, Amsterdam is worth a full day of sightseeing on even the busiest itinerary. While the city has a couple of must-see museums, its best sight is its own breezy ambience. The city's a joy on foot. It's a breezier and faster joy by bike. And the sights are conveniently laced together by the circular tram #20. Here are the essential stops for a day in Amsterdam:

Start the day with a circular orientation tour on tram #20 (described below). Break this morning overview with a stop at the city's two great art museums: Van Gogh and the Rijksmuseum (cafeteria for lunch). Walk to Spui from the museums via Leidsestraat (or pick up tram #20 where you got off and complete the circle back to the station).

Spend midafternoon taking a relaxing hour-long canal cruise from the dock at Spui. Near Spui consider seeing the peaceful Begijnhof, Amsterdam Historical Museum, and flower market.

Visiting the Anne Frank House after 18:00 (it's open until 21:00) will save you an hour in line.

On a balmy evening, Amsterdam has a Greek-island ambience. Wander the Jordaan for the idyllic side of town and wander

down Leidsestraat to
Leidseplein for the
roaring café and people
scene. Wander the
Red-Light District
while you're at it.

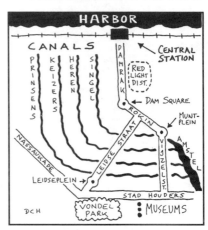

Amsterdam Overview

With extra time:
With two days in Hol-
land, I'd side trip by
bike, bus, or train to an
open-air folk museum
and visit Edam or Haar-
lem. With a third day
I'd do the other great
Amsterdam museums.
With four days I'd do
the "historic triangle"
or visit The Hague.

Orientation (area code: 020)

Amsterdam's central train station is your starting point (TI, bike
rental, and trams—including #20—fanning out to all points).
Damrak is the main street axis, connecting the station with Dam
Square (people watching and hangout center) and its Royal Palace.
From this spine the city spreads out like a fan, with 90 islands,
hundreds of bridges, and a series of concentric canals (named
"Prince's," "Gentleman's," and "Emperor's") laid out in the
17th century, Holland's golden age. Amsterdam's major sights
are within walking distance of Dam Square.

Tourist Information

Avoid Amsterdam's inefficient VVV offices if you can ("VVV"
is Dutch for tourist information office; TI in train station open
Mon–Sat 8:00–19:30, Sun 9:00–17:00). Most people wait 30 minutes
just to pick up information brochures and get a room. At the VVV
in front of the station, avoid this line by studying the display of pub-
lications for sale and going straight to the sales desk (where everyone
ends up anyway, since any information of substance will cost you).
Consider buying a city map (f4), *What's On* (f4, monthly entertainment calendar), and any of the f4 walking-tour brochures ("Discovery Tour through the Center," "The Former Jewish Quarter,"
"Walks through Jordaan"). The Amsterdam Culture & Leisure Pass,
offering free or discounted admissions to some sights and boat rides,
isn't worth the clutter or cost (f40, doesn't include Anne Frank
House). Nor does it make sense to stand in line at the VVV to buy
prepaid same-cost admissions to various Amsterdam sights.

The TI on Leidsestraat is less crowded (daily 9:00–17:00).

But for f1 a minute, you can save yourself a trip by calling the tourist information toll line at 0900-400-4040 (Mon–Fri 9:00–17:00). If you're staying in nearby Haarlem, use the helpful Haarlem TI (see next chapter) to answer most of your Amsterdam questions and provide you with the brochures.

At Amsterdam's Central Station, GWK Change has two hotel reservations windows that sell phone cards and cheaper city maps (f3) and answer basic tourist questions. The lines are shorter. They also change money, including coins, for a hefty f5 fee (near lockers, at right end of station as you leave platform).

Don't use the TI (or GWK) to book a room; you'll pay f5 and your host loses the 13 percent deposit. The phone system is easy, everyone speaks English, and the listings in this book are a better value than the potluck booking you'd be charged for at the TI.

Helpful Hints

Theft Alert: Tourists are considered green and rich, and the city has more than its share of hungry thieves—especially on trams. Wear your moneybelt.

Street Smarts: A *plein* is a square, *gracht* means canal, and most canals are lined by streets with the same name.

Shop Hours: Many shops close all day Sunday and Monday morning.

Telephones: Calling the United States from a phone booth is now very cheap—you'll get about five minutes for a dollar. Handy telephone cards (f10, f25, or f50) are sold at TIs, the GVB public-transit office (in front of station), tobacco shops, post offices, and train stations.

Internet Access: It's easy at cafés all over town. The Internet Café is a couple blocks from the station (f2.50 per 30 min, Sun–Thu 9:00–01:00, Fri–Sat 9:00–3:00, must buy at least 1 beverage, Martelaarsgracht 11, tel. 020/627-1052). A monstrous Internet café, easyEverything, has several hundred computers and cheap access (daily 24 hrs, Reguliersbreestraat 22, next to Rembrandtplein). Coffeeshops (which sell marijuana) also offer Internet access.

Arrival in Amsterdam

By Train: Amsterdam swings, and the hinge that connects it to the world is its perfectly central Central Station. Walk out the door and you're in the heart of the city. You'll nearly trip over trams ready to take you anywhere your feet won't. Straight ahead is Damrak Street, leading to Dam Square. With your back to the entrance of the station, the TI and GVB public-transit offices and circular tram #20A are just ahead and to your left.

By Plane: From Schiphol Airport, take the train to Amsterdam (6/hrly, 20 min, f6.25). If you're staying in Haarlem, take a direct express bus to Haarlem (#236 or #362, 2/hrly, 30 min, f7).

Getting around Amsterdam

The helpful GVB transit-information office is next to the TI (the glass building with revolving sign in front of train station). Its free multilingual "Tourist Guide to Public Transport" includes a transit map, explains ticket options and tram connections to all the sights, and describes the Circle Tram #20 route, listing all the stops and nearby sights (#20A goes clockwise, #20B goes counterclockwise).

By Bus, Tram, and Metro: Individual tickets cost f3 and give you an hour on the buses, trams, and metro system (on trams and buses pay as you board; buy metro tickets from machines). **Strip cards** are cheaper than individual tickets. Any downtown ride costs two strips (good for 1 hr of transfers). A card with 15 strips costs f12.25 at the GVB public-transit office, train stations, post offices, airport, or tobacco shops throughout the country; shorter strip tickets (2, 3, and 8 strips) are also sold on some buses and trams. Strip cards are good on buses all over the Netherlands (e.g., 6 strips for Haarlem to the airport), and you can share them with your partner. An f10 **Day Card** gives you unlimited transportation on the buses and metro for a day in Amsterdam; you'll almost break even if you take three trips (valid until 6:00 the following morning; buy as you board or at the GVB public-transit office, which also sells a better-value 2-day version for f15). If you get lost in Amsterdam, 10 of the city's 17 trams take you back to the central train station.

By Foot: The longest walk a tourist would take is 45 minutes from the station to the Rijksmuseum. Watch out for silent but potentially painful bikes, trams, and crotch-high curb posts.

By Bike: One-speed bikes, with "brrrringing" bells and two locks (use them both; bike thieves are bold and brazen here), rent for f10 per day at the central train station (daily 8:00–22:00, deposit of f200 or your credit-card imprint and passport required, entrance to the left down the ramp as you leave the station, tel. 020/624-8391). In the summer, arrive early or make a telephone reservation (they hold bikes until 10:30). If the station has rented all its bikes, walk 10 minutes to Rent-a-Bike Damstraat on Dam Square (f15/day, daily 9:00–18:00, deposit of f50 or credit-card imprint and I.D., Damstraat 20, tel. 020/625-5029).

By Boat: While the city is great on foot or bike, there is a "Museum Boat" and a similar "Canal Bus" with an all-day ticket that shuttles tourists from sight to sight. Tickets cost f29 (with discounts to sights worth about f5). The sales booths in front of the central train station (and the boats) offer handy free brochures with museum times and admission prices. The narrated ride takes 90 minutes if you don't get off (every 30 min in summer, every 45 min off-season, 7 stops, live quadrilingual guide, departures 10:00–17:00, discounted after 13:00 to f24, tel. 020/622-2181). If you're looking for a floating (nonstop) tour, the real canal tour boats (without the stops) give more information, cover more ground, and cost less (see "Tours of Amsterdam," below).

By Taxi: Amsterdam's taxis are expensive (f6 drop and f3 for each kilometer). Given the fine tram system, taxis are only a good value for airport connections (Schiphol Airport to Amsterdam costs f60).

By Car: Forget it—frustrating one-ways, terrible parking.

Circle Tram #20 Orientation Tour

For a ▲▲ self-guided tour, orient yourself for f3 in less than an hour by riding this designed-for-tourists circle route from the station. Catch #20A (not #20B) from tram lane (or *spoor*) #2 on the left as you leave the station. The free tourist guidebooklet—there's a stack on the desk in the transit office 50 meters away—comes with a route map and lists each stop. You could buy the f6 one-day tram #20 pass. Tram #20 runs every 10 minutes from 9:00 to 18:00 only.

0. Train Station: Leaving the station you pass both the canal bus and museum boat docks (left). The "Rondvaart" sign (right) means round-trip. Boats like these all over town offer similar one-hour city tours. Gliding up the tacky commercial cancan called the Damrak (which was once the Amstel River), you're following the same route taken by boats loaded with spices and goodies from the East Indies in the city's early trading days. The buildings across the water are Amsterdam's oldest. Behind them is the Red-Light District and the old sailor's quarter. The huge redbrick Beurs building (left) is the Dutch stock exchange.

1. The Dam Square: This is the city center, where the original dam was built across the Amstel River, giving the town its name. To your right is the Royal Palace (1655); next to it is the New Church, the coronation church of Dutch royalty. To your left is the World War I Memorial (1956), now becoming a generic peace memorial; behind that is a strip of head shops. Straight ahead is one of many "diamond polishing centers." Beyond the Dam Square you continue down Rokin. Parallel and a block to the right is the bustling Kalverstraat pedestrian shopping mall.

2. Spui Square: This marked the end of the city in the 14th century. It's near the Begijnhof and the University of Amsterdam's archaeology museum, which has a fine Egyptian collection.

3. Muntplein: This lively area is marked by the Mint Tower from 1620 (on the right). Behind that a charming flower market lines the Singel Canal (see the row of greenhouses, thriving Mon–Sat 9:00–17:00). Turning left you enter a noisy neon nightlife center.

4. Rembrandtplein: Look for Rembrandt's statue in the leafy park (right). This is the center of gay Amsterdam. You'll pass lots of discos and a Planet Hollywood, and a bridge will take you over the Amstel River. The modern brown-and-white building (left) is

Amsterdam

the city hall. Adjacent is the round Opera House. Notice the charming counterbalance bridges (right).

5. Waterlooplein: This is famous for its flea market (daily except Sun, on left). The Jewish Quarter (right) features the impressive new Jewish History Museum (renovated brick synagogues with blue-and-white banner). Crossing the bridge (funny paintings revealed when opened) you enter green Amsterdam (gardens and hothouses of University of Amsterdam all around, zoo nearby).

6. Plantage Kerklaan: Immediately to the right of this tram stop, the white facade of the old Dutch Theater (Hollandsche Schouwburg) survives. Used by Nazis as a holding zone for Jews being deported, today it's a memorial. The Dutch Resistance

Museum and the zoo are half a block to the left. Passing through many University of Amsterdam buildings, notice the "XXX" symbol of the city (the three Xs stand for the adversities the Amsterdammers have overcome throughout their history: fire, plague, and floods). Crossing the Amstel River again, see the city hall and the opera house again in the distance (right), the palatial Amstel Hotel (behind on the left), and, in the distance, Holland's tallest skyscraper—the Phillips corporate headquarters.

7. Frederiksplein: Notice the houseboats; they're a common sight in Amsterdam. Also in Frederiksplein, you'll see the huge Albert Cuyp Market, perhaps the town's most interesting market, showing off the ethnic mix daily except Sunday. Now, passing through a nondescript area, notice how the city works: Shops at street level—with homes above—keep neighborhoods vital, people-friendly, and safe. Bike lanes even have their own little traffic lights. New buildings still lean out and come with planks and pulleys for hoisting furniture past too-narrow stairways. Many of these are brick and built in the Art Deco "Amsterdam School" from the 1920s—a time when architects considered entire blocks as integrated works of art. Notice street signs with the district listed. You're in the *oud-zuid* (old south) quarter. Mail slots have green and orange decals saying yes or no to junk mail. And now public phone booths stand next to curbside computers for Internet access (locals use prepaid "chip cards"—the first step toward the cash-free society of the future—to access things such as these).

8. Museumplein: A huge park (right) leads to the grand red-brick Rijksmuseum (built in 1885 by the same guy who designed Central Station). The new addition to the Van Gogh Museum (opened 1999) juts into the park in the foreground. The Concertgebouw (on the left) is Amsterdam's main concert hall. A huge underground parking lot keeps things uncluttered.

9. Van Baerlestraat: Rounding the corner, you stop at the Stedelijk Modern Art Museum (right) and the Van Gogh Museum (see crowd on right). An ice rink (right) faces the Coster Diamond House (left).

10. Hobbenmastraat: This is the stop for the Rijksmuseum (right). A fancy gate marks the entrance to the sprawling, in-love-with-life Vondelpark (left). Pass a casino (right) as you cross a canal and enter the noisy, people-filled Leidseplein area.

11. Leidseplein: Your tram just skirts Amsterdam's liveliest café, people-watching, and entertainment district. Be sure to loiter in Leidseplein later on. The huge modern parking lot (Texaco station, left) marks the line between the protected old town (right) and the anything-goes new one (left). Turning right you cut through the proud, fashionable, and trendy Jordaan district. Ahead stands the much-loved tallest church spire in town, marking the Westerkerk (West Church). Anne Frank hid out just down the street. As you continue ahead, the canal system is evident as you cross the Prince's, Keizers (kings), Herren (medieval business fat cats), and Singel Canals and head toward the back side of the Royal Palace we saw at the Dam Square. Hop out here or glide back to your starting point at the Central Station.

Sights—Amsterdam's Museum Neighborhood

▲▲▲**Rijksmuseum**—Built to house the nation's greatest art, the Rijksmuseum packs several thousand paintings into 200 rooms. To survive, focus on the Dutch masters: Rembrandt, Hals, Vermeer, and Steen. For a list of the top 20 paintings, pick up the cheap f1 leaflet "A Tour of the Golden Age" and plan your attack (or follow the self-guided tour, one of 20, in my *Mona Winks* guidebook, written with Gene Openshaw). Audioguide tours are available, allowing you to dial up descriptions of over 200 paintings (f7.50).

Follow the museum's chronological layout to see painting evolve from narrative religious art, to religious art starring the Dutch love of good living and eating, to the golden age when secular art dominated. With no local church or royalty to commission big canvases in the post-1648 Protestant Dutch republic, artists had to find different patrons. They specialized in portraits of the wealthy city class (Hals), pretty still lifes (Claesz), and nonpreachy slice-of-life art (Steen). The museum has four quietly wonderful Vermeers. And, of course, a thoughtful brown soup of Rembrandt, including *Night Watch*. Works by Rembrandt show his excellence as a portraitist for hire (*De Staalmeesters*) and offer some powerful psychological studies, such as *St. Peter's Denial*—with a betrayed Jesus in the murky background (f15, daily 10:00–17:00, great bookshop, decent cafeteria, tram #2, #5, or #20 from station, Stadhouderskade 42, tel. 020/674-7000).

▲▲▲**Van Gogh Museum**—Near the Rijksmuseum, this outstanding and user-friendly museum was opened in 1973 to house the 200 paintings owned by Vincent's younger brother Theo. Newly renovated in 1999, it's a stroll through a beautifully displayed garden of van Gogh's work and life (f15, daily 10:00–18:00, Paulus Potterstraat 7, tel. 020/570-5200). The museum also focuses on the late-19th-century art that influenced van Gogh (it happened to be in his brother Theo's collection). The new exhibition hall (included with admission) features art from 1840 to 1920. The f8.50 audioguide includes insightful commentaries about van Gogh's paintings along with related quotations from Vincent himself.

Stedelijk Modern Art Museum—Next to the Van Gogh Museum, this place is fun, far-out, and refreshing. It has mostly post-1945 art but also a sometimes-outstanding collection of Monet, van Gogh, Cézanne, Picasso, and Chagall, and a lot of special exhibitions (f10, daily 11:00–17:00, tel. 020/573-2737).

Sights—Near Dam Square

▲▲**Anne Frank House**—A virtual pilgrimage for many, this house offers a fascinating look at the hideaway of young Anne when the Nazis occupied the Netherlands. Pick up the English pamphlet at the door. Recently expanded, the exhibit now offers more thorough coverage of the Frank family, the diary, the stories of others who hid out, and the Holocaust. Why do thousands endure hour-long daytime lines when they can walk right in by arriving after 18:00? Last entrance is 20:30. Visit after dinner (f12.50, April–Aug daily 9:00–21:00, closes daily at 19:00 Sept–March, 263 Prinsengracht, tel. 020/556-7100). For an interesting glimpse of Holland under the Nazis, rent the powerful movie *Soldier of Orange* before you leave home.

Westerkerk—Near the Anne Frank House, this landmark church has a barren interior, Rembrandt somewhere under the pews, and Amsterdam's tallest steeple. It's worth climbing for the view (f3, ascend only with a guide, departures on the hour, April–Sept Mon–Sat 10:00–17:00, closed Sun, tel. 020/612-6856).

Royal Palace (Koninklijk Paleis)—The palace, right on Dam Square, was built as a lavish city hall for Amsterdam, part of the proud new Dutch Republic. Amsterdam was awash in profit from trade. When this building was constructed (around 1660), it was one of Europe's finest. Today it's the official (but not actual) residence of the queen. Its sumptuous interior is worth a look (f5, June–Aug daily 12:30–17:00, less off-season).

▲**Begijnhof**—Step into this tiny, idyllic courtyard in the city center to escape into the charm of old Amsterdam. Notice house #34, a 500-year-old wooden structure (rare since repeated fires taught city fathers a trick called brick). Peek into the hidden Catholic church, opposite the English Reformed church, where the pilgrims worshiped while waiting for their voyage to the New World (marked by a plaque near the door). Be considerate of the people who live here (free, on Begijnensteeg Lane, just off Kalverstraat between #130 and #132, pick up flyer at office near entrance).

Amsterdam Historical Museum—Offering the town's best look into the age of the Dutch masters, this creative and hardworking museum features Rembrandt's paintings, fine English descriptions, and a carillon loft. The loft comes with push-button recordings of the town bell tower's greatest hits and a self-serve carillon "keyboard" to ring a few bells yourself (f12, Mon–Fri 10:00–17:00, Sat–Sun 11:00–17:00, good-value restaurant, next to Begijnhof, Kalverstraat 92, tel. 020/523-1822). Its free pedestrian corridor is a powerful teaser.

Sights—East Amsterdam

To reach these sights from the train station, take tram #9, #14, or #20. The first six sights listed make an interesting walk.

Rembrandt's House—Rembrandt's reconstructed house is filled with exactly what his bankruptcy inventory of 1656 said he owned. You'll find no paintings but 65 of his etchings (f12.50, Mon–Sat 10:00–17:00, Sun 13:00–17:00, 10-min English video upon request, Jodenbreestraat 4, tel. 020/520-0400).

Holland Experience—Bragging "Experience Holland in 30 minutes," this show takes you traveling with three clowns through an idealized montage of Dutch clichés. There are no words but lots of images and special effects as you rock with the boat and get spritzed with perfume while viewing the tulips (f17.50, 2 enter for price of 1 with this book, or show this book and get f2.50 off the f25 combo Rembrandt's House/Experience ticket, daily 10:00–18:00, Jodenbreestraat 8, near Rembrandt's House and Waterlooplein street market, metro: Waterlooplein, tel. 020/422-2233. www.holland-experience.nl). The men's urinal is a trip to the beach. Plan for it.

Waterlooplein Flea Market—For over a hundred years, the flea market of the Jewish Quarter has raged daily except Sunday behind the Rembrandt House.

Jewish History Museum—Four historic synagogues have been joined by steel and glass to make one modern complex telling the story of the Jews in Amsterdam through the centuries (f10, daily 11:00–17:00, good kosher café, Jonas Daniel Meijerplein 2, tel. 020/626-9945).

Dutch Theatre (Hollandsche Schouwburg)—This is a moving memorial. Once a great theater in the Jewish neighborhood, this was used as an assembly hall for local Jews destined for Nazi concentration camps. On the wall, 6,700 family names pay tribute to the 104,000 Jews deported and killed by the Nazis. There's little to actually see but plenty to think about (free, daily 11:00–16:00, Plantage Middenlaan 24, tel. 020/626-9945).

▲▲Dutch Resistance Museum (Verzetsmuseum)—This is a new and impressive look at how the Dutch resisted their Nazi occupiers from 1940 to 1945. You'll see propaganda movie clips, study forged ID cards under a magnifying glass, and read of ingenious, clever, and courageous efforts to hide local Jews from the Germans (f8, Tue–Sun 12:00–17:00, closed Mon, well described in English, tram #9 or #20A from station, Plantage Kerklaan 61, tel. 020/620-2535). Amsterdam's famous zoo is just across the street.

▲Tropenmuseum (Tropical Museum)—As close to the Third World as you'll get without lots of vaccinations, this imaginative museum offers wonderful re-creations of tropical-life scenes and explanations of Third World problems (f12.50, Mon–Fri 10:00–17:00, Sat–Sun 12:00–17:00, tram #9 to Linnaeusstraat 2, tel. 020/568-8215).

Netherlands Maritime (Scheepvaart) Museum—This huge collection of model ships, maps, and sea-battle paintings fills the

Central Amsterdam

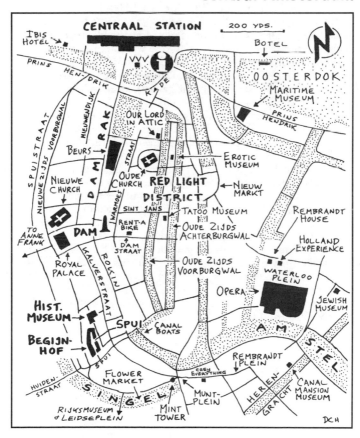

300-year-old Dutch Navy Arsenal. Given the Dutch seafaring heritage, I expected a killer museum but found it lifeless and boring. Sailors may disagree, but—even with its re-creation of an 18th-century Dutch East India Company ship manned with characters in old costumes—the museum disappoints (f14.50, daily 10:00–17:00, closed Mon off-season, English explanations, don't waste your time with 30-min movie, bus #22 or #32 to Kattenburgerplein 1, tel. 020/523-2222).

Sights—Red-Light District
Our Lord in the Attic (Amstelkring)—Near the station, in the Red-Light District, you'll find a fascinating hidden church filling the attic of a hollowed-out row of 17th-century merchants' houses.

This dates from 1661, when post-Reformation Dutch Catholics couldn't worship in public (f10, Mon–Sat 10:00–17:00, Sun 13:00–17:00, Oudezijds Voorburgwal 40, tel. 020/624-6604).
▲**Red-Light District**—Europe's most touristed ladies of the night shiver and shimmy in display-case windows between the Oudezijds Achterburgwal and Oudezijds Voorburgwal, surrounding the Oude Kerk (Old Church). Druggies make the streets uncomfortable late at night, but it's a fascinating walk at any other time after noon (S&F, f75–100).

Amsterdam has two sex museums, one in the Red-Light District and one a block in front of the train station on Damrak. While visiting one can be called sightseeing, visiting both is hard to explain. Here's a comparison:

The Red-Light District sex museum is less offensive, with five sparsely decorated rooms relying heavily on badly dressed dummies acting out the roles that women of the neighborhood play. It also has videos, phone-sex phones, and a lot of uninspired paintings, old photos, and sculpture (f5, daily 11:00–24:00, along the canal at Oudezijds Achterburgwal 54).

The Damrak sex museum goes deeper and has more rooms. It tells the story of pornography from Roman times through 1960. Every sexual deviation is uncovered in its various displays, and the nude and pornographic art is a cut above the other sex museum's. Also interesting are the early French pornographic photos and memorabilia from Europe, India, and Asia. You'll find a Marilyn Monroe tribute and some S&M displays, too (f5, daily 10:00–23:30, Damrak 18, a block in front of station).

More Sights—Amsterdam
▲**Herengracht Canal Mansion (Willet Holthuysen Museum)**—This 1687 patrician house offers a fine look at the old rich of Amsterdam, with a good 20-minute English introductory film and a 17th-century garden in back (f8, Mon–Fri 10:00–17:00, Sat–Sun 11:00–17:00, tram #1, #2, #4, #5, or #9 to Herengracht 605, tel. 020/523-1870).
Vondelpark—This huge and lively city park is popular with the Dutch—families with little kids, romantic couples, hippies sharing blankets and beers, and oldsters strolling. It's the scene of free concerts in the summer (tel. 020/523-7790).
Amsterdam Film Museum—This museum, next to Vondelpark, has a massive archive and a theater that shows a variety of films, from small foreign productions to 70-mm classics (f12.50, at least 3 showings/night, often English subtitles, Vondelstraat 69, tel. 020/523-7790, www.filmmuseum.nl).
Leidseplein—Brimming with cafés, this people- and pigeon-watching square is an impromptu stage for street artists, accordionists, jugglers, and unicyclists. Sunny afternoons are liveliest.

Stroll nearby Lange Leidsedwarsstraat (1 block north) for a taste-
bud tour of ethnic eateries from Greece to Indonesia.
Shopping—Amsterdam brings out the browser even in those who
were not born to shop. Ten general markets, open six days a week,
keep folks who brake for garage sales pulling U-ies. Shopping
highlights include Waterlooplein (the flea market); the huge Albert
Cuyp street market; various flower markets (such as the Singel
Canal market near mint tower/*Munttoren*, daily except Sun); diamond dealers (free cutting and polishing demos at shops behind the
Rijksmuseum and on Dam Square); and Kalverstraat, Amsterdam's
teeming pedestrian/shopping street (parallel to Damrak).

Tours of Amsterdam
▲▲**Canal-Boat Tour**—These long, low, tourist-laden boats leave
continually from several docks around the town for a relaxing, if
uninspiring, one-hour quadrilingual introduction to the city (f14,
2/hrly, more frequent in summer). One very central company is
at the corner of Spui and Rokin, about five minutes from Dam
Square (daily 10:00–22:00, tel. 020/623-3810). No fishing allowed—
but bring your camera. Some prefer to cruise at night, when the
bridges are illuminated.
Biking Tours—The Yellow Bike Tour company offers a city
tour (f34, 3 hrs) and a tour of the countryside (f42.50, 6 hrs, 35
km; daily April–Nov, Nieuwezijds Kolk 29, 3 blocks from train
station, tel. 020/620-6940).
Do-It-Yourself Bike Tour of Amsterdam—A day enjoying the
bridges, bike lanes, and sleepy off-the-beaten-path canals on your
own one-speed is the essential Amsterdam experience. The real
joys of Europe's best-preserved 17th-century city are the countless
intimate glimpses it offers: the laid-back locals sunning on their
porches under elegant gables, rusted bikes that look as if they've
been lashed to the same lamppost since the '60s, wasted hedonists
planted on canalside benches, happy sailors permanently moored
but still manning the deck.
    For a good day, rent a bike at the station. Head west down
Haarlemmerstraat, working your wide-eyed way down the Prinsengracht (along the canal) and detouring through the gentrified
small streets of the Jordaan area before popping out at Westerkerk
under the tallest spire in the city.
    Pedal past the palace, through Dam Square, and down
Kalverstraat (the city's bustling pedestrian mall), and poke into the
sleepy Begijnhof. Catch the hour-long cruise at Spui. Continue
down Rokin to the Mint Tower, biking along the Singel Canal
flower market to Leidsestraat. Dodge trams and people down
Leidsestraat. Enjoy the lush and peaceful Vondelpark. Then
pedal back to the Dam Square. To detour through seedy, sexy,
pot-smoking Amsterdam, roll down Damstraat and then turn

left down Oudezijds Voorburgwal through the land of Rastafarian "coffee shops," Red-Lights over black tights, and sailors lost without the sea. You'll pop out near the station.

To finish your day, escape into the countryside by hopping on the free ferry behind the Amsterdam station. In five minutes Amsterdam will be gone, and you'll be rolling through your very own Dutch painting. (See "Getting around Amsterdam," above, for info on bike rental).

Brewery Tour—The infamous Heineken brewery tours are in full slosh Monday through Friday at 9:30, 11:00, 13:00, and 14:30 (f2, 2 hrs, tours also Sat in summer; must be over age 18, tram #16, #24, or #25, Stadhouderskade 78, near Rijksmuseum, tel. 020/523-9666). Try to arrive a little early.

Wetlands Safari, Nature Canoe Tours Near Amsterdam—If you'd like to "turn your back on Amsterdam" and get a dose of the *polder* country and village life along with some exercise, consider this tour. Majel Tromp, a village girl who speaks great English, takes groups of no more than 15. The program: Meet at the VVV tourist office outside the station, catch a bus, stop for coffee, take a canoe trip with several stops, munch a village picnic lunch (included), canoe, and bus back into the big city by 14:30 (f58, May–mid-Sept Mon–Fri, call to reserve, tel. 020/686-3445 or 06/53-552-669, www.wetlandssafari.nl).

Sleeping in Amsterdam
(f1 = about 40 cents, country code: 31, area code: 020)
Sleep Code: **S** = Single, **D** = Double/Twin, **T** = Triple, **Q** = Quad, **b** = bathroom, **t** = toilet only, **s** = shower only, **CC** = Credit Card (**V**isa, **M**asterCard, **A**mex). Nearly everyone speaks English in the Netherlands, and prices include breakfast unless noted.

While I prefer sleeping in cozy Haarlem (see next chapter), those into more urban charms will find that Amsterdam has plenty of beds. Summer weekends are booked well in advance.

Sleeping near the Station
Amstel Botel, the city's only remaining "boat hotel," is a shipshape, bright, and clean floating hotel with 175 rooms (Sb-f141, Db-f159, Tb-f180, worth the extra f10 for canalside view, breakfast-f14, f40/day parking pass, CC:VMA, elevator, 400 meters from train station, on your left as you leave station, you'll see the sign, Oosterdokskade 2-4, 1011 AE Amsterdam, tel. 020/626-4247, fax 020/639-1952).

Ibis Amsterdam Hotel is a modern and efficient 180-room place towering over the station. It offers a central location, comfort, and good value without a hint of charm (Db-f298, family-f368, skip breakfast and save f24 per person, CC:VMA, book long in advance, air-con, smoke-free floors, Stationsplein 49, tel. 020/638-3080, fax 020/620-0156, www.ibishotel.com).

Amsterdam Hotels

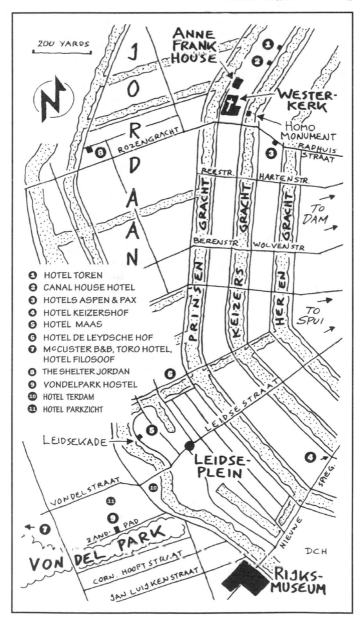

200 YARDS

N

JORDAAN

ANNE FRANK HOUSE

WESTER-KERK

Homo MONUMENT

RADHUIS STRAAT

ROZENGRACHT

REESTR.

HARTENSTR.

PRINSEN GRACHT

KEIZERS GRACHT

HEREN GRACHT

BERENSTR.

WOLVENSTR.

TO DAM

TO SPUI

❶ HOTEL TOREN
❷ CANAL HOUSE HOTEL
❸ HOTELS ASPEN & PAX
❹ HOTEL KEIZERSHOF
❺ HOTEL MAAS
❻ HOTEL DE LEYDSCHE HOF
❼ McCUSTER B&B, TORO HOTEL, HOTEL FILOSOOF
❽ THE SHELTER JORDAN
❾ VONDELPARK HOSTEL
❿ HOTEL TERDAM
⓫ HOTEL PARKZICHT

LEIDSEKADE

LEIDSE STRAAT

LEIDSE-PLEIN

SPEG.

VONDELSTRAAT

ZAND. PAD

VONDEL PARK

NIEUWE

DCH

CORN. HOOFT STRAAT

JAN LUIJKEN STRAAT

RIJKS-MUSEUM

Sleeping between Dam Square and the Anne Frank House

Hotel Toren is a chandeliered historic mansion in a pleasant, quiet canalside setting in downtown Amsterdam. This splurge is classy yet friendly, two blocks northeast of the Anne Frank House, and still run by the Toren family: Elsje, Lisa, and Eric (Sb-f240–260, Db-f260–290, Tb-f300–375, bridal suites for f425–450 make you want to get married, prices vary with view and Jacuzzi, 10 percent discount for 3 nights and cash with this book, CC:VMA, air-con, Keizersgracht 164, 1015 CZ Amsterdam, tel. 020/622-6352, fax 020/626-9705, www.toren.nl).

Well-heeled readers enjoy the similar 17th-century **Canal House Hotel**, a few doors down, for its beautiful antique interiors, candlelit evenings, and soft music (Db-f285–365, CC:VMA, elevator, Keizersgracht 148, 1015 CX Amsterdam, tel. 020/622-5182, fax 020/624-1317, www.canalhouse.nl).

Cheap hotels line the convenient but noisy main drag between the town hall and the Anne Frank House. Expect a long, steep, and depressing stairway, noisy front rooms, and quieter rooms in the back. **Hotel Aspen**, a good value for a budget hotel, is tidy, stark, and well maintained (S-f60, D-f85, Db-f130, Tb-f150, Qb-f180, no breakfast, CC:VMA, Raadhuisstraat 31, 1016 DC Amsterdam, tel. 020/626-6714, fax 020/620-0866, run by Esam, e-mail: hotelaspen@capitolonline.nl). A few doors away, **Hotel Pax** has large, plain, but airy backpacker-type rooms (S-f55-75, D-f80–125, T-f110–150, Q-f120–170, no breakfast, prices vary with size and season, CC:VMA, 2 showers for 8 rooms, Raadhuisstraat 37, tel. 020/624-9735, run by brothers Philip and Peter).

Calendula Goldbloom's B&B, run by an American couple, offers two comfortable rooms in a classy old home in a quiet Jordaan neighborhood a five-minute walk northwest of the Anne Frank House (D-f200, extra bed f60, 3-night minimum, good breakfasts, Goudsbloemstraat 132, tel. 020/428-3055, fax 020/776-0075, www.calendulas.com, Lynn and Dennis).

Sleeping in the Leidseplein Area

The area around Amsterdam's museum square (Museumplein) and the rip-roaring nightlife center (Leidseplein) is colorful, comfortable, convenient, and affordable. These three canalside places are a five- to ten-minute walk from Leidseplein.

Hotel Keizershof is wonderfully Dutch, with six bright, airy rooms in a 17th-century canal house. A steep spiral staircase leads to rooms named after old-time Hollywood stars. The enthusiastic hospitality of the De Vries family has made this place a treat for 38 years (S-f100, D-f130–140, Ds-f150, Db-f180, T-f175, Tb-f200, 3-night minimum, CC:VM, nonsmoking, classy breakfast, tram #16, #24, or #25 from station, where Keizers canal crosses

Spiegelstraat at Keizersgracht 618, 1017 ER Amsterdam, tel. 020/622-2855, fax 020/624-8412, e-mail: keizershof@vdwp.nl).

Hotel Maas is a big, well-run, elegant, quiet, and stiffly hotel-esque place (S-f125, 1 D-f145, Db-f295–345, suite-f425, prices vary with view and room size, extra person-f50, CC:VMA, hearty breakfast, air-con, elevator, tram #1, #2, #5, or #20 from station, Leidsekade 91, 1017 PN Amsterdam, tel. 020/623-3868, fax 020/622-2613, www.hotelmaas.nl).

Hotel De Leydsche Hof is canalside with simple, quiet rooms. Its peaceful demeanor almost helps you overlook the flimsy cots and old carpets (Ds-f110, Tb-f150, Qb-f200, no breakfast, near where Keizersgracht hits Leidsegracht, Leidsegracht 14, 10-min walk from Leidseplein, 1016 CK Amsterdam, tel. 020/623-2148, run by friendly Mr. Piller).

Best Western Hotel Terdam is a 90-room American-style hotel well situated on a quiet street just across the bridge from bustling Leidseplein (Db-f260–340 depending on season and air-con, CC:VMA, elevator, Tesselschadestraat 23, tel. 020/612-6876, fax 020/683-8313, www.hospitality.nl/ams).

Sleeping near Vondelpark

These options connect you with the sights via an easy tram ride, a pleasant 15-minute walk, or a short bike ride through Vondelpark.

Karen McCuster, a friendly Englishwoman, rents cozy rooms in her shoes-off home. Rooms are clean, white, and bright, with red carpeting and green plants. One room has a private rooftop patio (D-f120–160 depending on room size, includes buffet breakfast, tram #2 from station to Amstelveenseweg, Zeilstraat 22, 3rd floor, 1075 SH Amsterdam, tel. 020/679-2753, fax 020/670-4578, e-mail: p.galdermans@chello.nl).

Toro Hotel, in a peaceful residential area at the edge of Vondelpark, is your personal 19th-century hotel/mansion, with a plush lounge, elegant dining hall, and 22 rooms with TVs, safes, and phones. Rooms in the back overlook the park, canal, and garden, which is yours for relaxing. Mr. Plooy fusses over his guests (Ss-f200, Sb-f255, Db-f308, Tb-f363, CC:VMA, elevator, metered parking at door, tram #2 from station to Koningslaan, then walk to intersection of Emmalaan and Koningslaan, Koningslaan 64, 1075 AG Amsterdam, tel. 020/673-7223, fax 020/675-0031).

Hotel Filosoof greets you with Aristotle and Plato in the foyer and classical music in its lobby. Its 28 rooms are decorated with themes; the Egyptian room has a frieze of hieroglyphics. Philosophers' sayings hang on walls as thoughtful travelers wander down the halls or sit in the garden, rooted deep in discussion. The rooms are small (and split between two buildings), but the hotel is endearing (Sb-f185–215, Db-f205–235, Tb-f255–285, Qb-f275, CC:VMA, all rooms have TV and phone, elevator,

Anna Vondelstraat 6, 5-min walk from tram #1 line, get off at
Constantyn Huygenstraat, tel. 020/683-3013, fax 020/685-3750,
www.xs4all.nl/~filosoof, e-mail: filosoof@xs4all.nl).

Hotel Parkzicht is an old-time place with lots of extremely
steep stairs and 14 big plain rooms on a quiet street bordering
Vondelpark (S-f65, Sb-f95, Db-f150–175, as low as f100 in winter,
Tb-f220, Qb-f250, CC:VMA, tram #1, #2 or #5 from station,
exit Leidseplein, Roemer Visscherstraat 33, tel. 020/618-1954,
fax 020/618-0897, e-mail: hotel@parkzicht.nl).

Hostels

The Shelter Jordan is scruffy, friendly, well run, and in a great
neighborhood. These are Amsterdam's best budget beds, in 20-
bed dorms (f28, includes sheets and breakfast, maximum age 35,
nonsmoking, 02:00 curfew, near Anne Frank House, Bloemstraat
179, tel. 020/624-4717, www.shelter.nl, e-mail: jordan@shelter.nl).
It serves hot meals, runs a snack bar, offers lockers, leads nightly
Bible studies, and closes the dorms from 10:00 to 12:30. Its sister
Christian hostel, **The Shelter City**, in the Red-Light District, is
similar but definitely not preaching to the choir (f28, includes
breakfast, maximum age 35, curfew, Barndesteeg 21, tel. 020/
625-3230, e-mail: city@shelter.nl).

The city's two IYHF hostels are **Vondelpark**, Amsterdam's
top hostel (f33–49 with breakfast, S-f90, D-f135, nonmembers
pay f5 extra, lots of school groups, 4–20 beds per dorm, right on
the park at Zandpad 5, tel. 020/589-8996, fax 020/589-8955,
www.njhc.org/vondelpark) and **Stadsdoelen YH** (f33–37 with
breakfast, f5 extra without YH card, just past Dam Square,
Kloveniersburgwal 97, tel. 020/624-6832, fax 020/639-1035,
e-mail: stadsdoelen@njhc.org). While generally booked long
in advance, a few beds open up each day at 11:00.

Eating in Amsterdam

Dutch food is basic and hearty. *Eetcafés* are local cafés serving
budget sandwiches, soup, eggs, and so on. Cafeterias, *broodje*
(sandwich shops), and automatic food shops are also good
bets for budget eaters. Picnics are cheap and easy. A central
supermarket is **Albert Heijn**, at the corner of Koningsplein
and Singel Canal near the flower market (Mon–Sat 10:00–20:00,
Sun 12:00–18:00).

Of Amsterdam's thousand-plus restaurants, no one knows
which are best—especially us. I pick an area and wander. The
major action is around Leidseplein. Wander along restaurant
row: Leidsedwarsstraat. For fewer crowds and more charm, find
something in the Jordaan. The best advice: your hotel's. Most
keep a reliable eating list for their neighborhood. Here are a few
handy places to consider:

Eating near Spui in the Center

The city university's **Atrium** is a great budget cafeteria (f9 meals, Mon–Fri 11:30–14:30, 17:00–19:30; from Spui, walk west down Landebrug Steeg past the canalside Café 't Gasthuys 3 blocks to Oudezijds Achterburgwal 237, go through arched doorway on the right, tel. 020/525-3999). **Café 't Gasthuys**, one of Amsterdam's many "brown" cafés (named for their smoke-stained walls), makes good sandwiches and offers indoor or canalside seating (daily 12:00–01:00, walk west down Landebrug Steeg to Grimburgwal 7, tel. 020/624-8230).

La Place, a cafeteria on the ground floor of the Vroom Dreesmann department store, has islands of entrées, veggies, fruits, desserts, and beverages (Mon–Sat 10:00–20:00, Thu until 21:00, Sun 12:00–20:00, near Mint Tower, corner of Rokin and Muntplein, tel. 020/620-2364).

De Jaren Café ("The Years") features eclectic energy, an upstairs restaurant, and drinks at its canalside patio (daily 10:00–01:00, Nieuwe Doelenstraat 20–22, just up from Muntplein, tel. 020/625-5771).

Eating in the Train Station

The train station has a surprisingly classy budget self-service **Stationsrestauratie** on platform 1 (Mon–Sat 7:00–22:00, Sun from 8:00).

Eating near the Anne Frank House

For pancakes in a family atmosphere, try the **Pancake Bakery** (f18 pancakes, splitting is OK, offers an Indonesian pancake for those who want 2 experiences in 1, daily 12:00–21:30, Prinsengracht 191, 1 block north of Anne Frank House, tel. 020/625-1333). Across the canal, **De Bolhoed** serves serious vegetarian food (daily 12:00–22:00, Prinsengracht 60, tel. 020/626-1803). **Dimitri's** is the place for a hearty salad (f20 main course salads, daily 8:00–22:00, Prinsenstraat 3, tel. 020/627-9393).

Eating near the Rijksmuseum, on Leidseplein

The Art Deco **American Hotel** dining room serves an all-you-can-eat f16 salad bar (available 11:00–15:00, 17:00–23:00, where Leidseplein hits Singel Canal). On the café-packed street called Lange Leidsedwarsstraat, **Bojo** is a reasonably-priced Indonesian restaurant at #51 (daily from 16:00–02:00, 020/622-7434). If hunger hits in the **Rijksmuseum**, head for the cafeteria in the west wing's ground floor.

Eating near Vondelpark

Café Vertigo offers an international melange of sushi, soups, and pastas. Grab an outdoor table and watch the world spin by (daily 11:00–01:00, next to Film Museum, Vondelpark 3, tel. 020/612-3021).

Bars

Try a *jenever* (Dutch gin), the closest thing to an atomic bomb in a shot glass. While cheese gets harder and sharper with age, *jenever* grows smooth and soft. Old *jenever* is best.

Drugs

Amsterdam, Europe's counterculture mecca, thinks the concept of a "victimless crime" is a contradiction. While hard drugs are definitely out, marijuana causes about as much excitement as a bottle of beer. Throughout the Netherlands "coffee shops" are pubs selling marijuana. Menus dangling from strings look like the inventory of a drug bust. Display cases show various joints or baggies for sale. The Dutch roll a little tobacco into their joints. To avoid the tobacco, you need to get a baggie and papers. Baggies usually cost f25—smaller contents...better quality. Walk east from Dam Square on Damstraat for a few blocks and then down to Nieuwmarkt. While several touristy Bulldog Cafés are hits with tourists, less-glitzy neighborhood places (farther from the tourists) offer a better value and a more comfortable atmosphere.

Pot should never be bought on the street in Amsterdam. Well-established coffee shops are considered much safer. Up to five grams of marijuana per person per day can be sold in coffee shops. Minimum age for purchase: 18 years.

The tiny **Grey Area** coffee shop is a cool, welcoming, and smoky hole-in-the-wall appreciated among local aficionados as a seven-time winner of Amsterdam's Cannabis Cup award. Judging by the proud autographed photos on the wall, many of America's most famous heads have dropped in. You're welcome to just nurse a bottomless cup of coffee (open high noon to 21:00, closed Mon, between Dam Square and Anne Frank House at Oude Leliestraat 2, tel. 020/420-4301, www.greyarea.nl, Steven and John).

Near the corner of Leidsestraat and Prinsengracht, **Tops** coffee shop has Internet access. **Homegrown Fantasy**'s coffee shop and gallery, about two blocks northwest of Dam Square, has a gentle Dutch atmosphere, cosmic restroom, and a grow shop next door (daily 12:00–24:00, Nieuwe Zijds Voorburgwal 87a, tel. 020/627-5683).

▲**Marijuana and Hemp Museum**—This is a collection of dope facts, history, science, and memorabilia (f12.50, daily 11:00–22:00, Oudezijds Achterburgwal 148, tel. 020/623-5961). While small, it has a shocker finale: the high-tech grow room in which dozens of varieties of marijuana are cultivated in optimal hydroponic (among other) environments. Some plants stand five feet tall and shine under the intense grow lamps. The view is actually

through glass walls into the neighboring "Sensi Seed Bank"
Grow Shop, which sells carefully cultivated seeds and all the gear
needed to grow them. It's an interesting neighborhood. The
Cannabis College Foundation, "dedicated to ending the global
war against the cannabis plant through public education," is next
door at #124 (tel. 020/423-4420, www.cannabiscollege.com or
www.marijuananews.com). As you wander through the Foundation,
ponder the 400,000 Americans serving time in jail because of
U.S. marijuana laws.

Transportation Connections—Amsterdam

Amsterdam's train-information center requires a long wait. Save
lots of time by getting train tickets and information in a small-
town station or travel agency. For phone information, dial 0900-
9292 for local trains or 0900-9296 for international trains (75
cents/min, daily 7:00–24:00, wait through recording and hold...
hold...hold...).

By train to: **Schiphol Airport** (6/hrly, 20 min, f7), **Haarlem**
(6/hrly, 15 min, f12 round-trip), **The Hague** (4/hrly, 45 min),
Rotterdam (4/hrly, 1 hr), **Brussels** (hrly, 3 hrs), **Ostende** (hrly,
4 hrs, change in Roosendaal), **Paris** (5/day, 5 hrs, required fast
train from Brussels with f24 supplement; there's one slow, 4-hr,
no-supplement train a day), **London** (4/day, 10–12 hrs), **Copenhagen** (5/day, 11 hrs), **Frankfurt** (10/day, 5 hrs), **Munich** (8/day,
8 hrs, change in Mannheim), **Bonn** (10/day, 3 hrs), **Bern** (8/day,
9 hrs, change in Basel).

Amsterdam's Schiphol Airport: The airport, like most of
Holland, is English speaking, user-friendly, and below sea level.
Its banks offer fair rates (24 hrs daily, in arrival area). Schiphol
Airport has easy bus and train connections (11 kilometers) into
Amsterdam or Haarlem. The airport also has a train station of its
own. (You can validate your Eurailpass and hit the rails immediately or, to stretch your train pass, buy the inexpensive ticket today
and start the pass later.) Schiphol flight information (tel. 0900-
0141) can give you flight times and your airline's Amsterdam
number for reconfirmation before going home (f1/min to climb
through its phone tree). To reach airlines, dial KLM at 020/649-
9123 and Martainair at 020/601-1222.

HAARLEM

Cute, cozy, yet real and handy to the airport, Haarlem is a fine home base, giving you small-town, overnight warmth with easy access (15 minutes by train) to wild and crazy Amsterdam.

Haarlem is a busy Dutch market town buzzing with shoppers biking home with fresh bouquets. Enjoy the market on Saturday (general) and Monday (clothing), when the square bustles like a Brueghel painting with cheese, fish, flowers, and families. Make yourself at home here. Buy some flowers to brighten your hotel room.

Orientation (area code: 023)

Tourist Information: Haarlem's VVV, at the train station, is friendlier, more helpful, and less crowded than Amsterdam's. Ask your Amsterdam questions here (Mon–Fri 9:30–17:30, Sat 10:00–14:00, closed Sun, tel. 0900-616-1600, f1/min, helpful parking brochure, their f4 *Haarlem* magazine is not necessary).

Arrival in Haarlem: As you walk out of the train station (has lockers), the TI is on your right and the bus station is across the street. Two parallel streets flank the train station (Kruisweg and Jansweg). Head up either one and you'll reach the town square and church within 10 minutes. If you're uncertain of the way, ask a local person, "*Grote Markt?*" ("Main Square?"), and they'll point you in the right direction.

Helpful Hints

The handy GWK change office at the station offers fair exchange rates (Mon–Fri 8:00–20:00, Sat 9:00–18:00, Sun 10:00–17:00). The train station rents bikes (f10/day, f100 deposit and passport number, Mon–Sat 6:00–24:00, Sun 7:30–24:00). For Internet

access (f7.50/30 min), nonguests are welcome to use Hotel
Amadeus' computer (facing Market Square) and nonsmokers
are welcome at High Times (Lange Veerstraat 47).

Sights—Haarlem

▲▲**Market Square (Grote Markt)**—Haarlem's market square is
the town's delightful centerpiece. To enjoy a coffee or beer here
simmering in Dutch good living is a quintessential European
experience. In a recent study, the Dutch were found to be the
most content people in Europe. And later, the people of Haarlem
were found to be the most content in the Netherlands. Observe.
Just a few years ago trolleys ran through the square and cars were
parked everywhere. But today it's a people zone, with market stalls
filling the square on Mondays and Saturdays and café tables on
others. The local drunk used to hang out on the bench in front
of the town hall, where he'd expose himself to newlyweds. The
Dutch, rather than arrest the man, moved the bench. The big
statue in the square is of Coster, the man only Haarlemers think
invented printing. The little shops around the cathedral have long
been church owned and rented to bring in a little cash. The fine
building nearest the cathedral is the old meat hall—decorated
with carved bits of early advertising.

▲**Church (Grote Kerk)**—This 15th-century Gothic church (now
Protestant) is worth a look, if only for its Oz-like organ (from
1738, 30 meters high, its 5,000 pipes impressed both Handel and
Mozart). Note how the organ, which fills the west end, seems to
steal the show from the altar. Pick up the English flyer, which lists
spots of interest, including Frans Hals' tomb (under black lantern
in choir). To enter, find the small "Entrée" sign behind the church
(f2.75, Mon–Sat 10:00–16:00). Consider attending (even part of)
a concert to hear Holland's greatest pipe organ (regular free
concerts Tue at 20:15 mid-May–mid-Oct, additional concerts
Thu at 15:00 July–Aug, confirm schedule at TI).

▲▲**Frans Hals Museum**—Haarlem is the hometown of Frans
Hals, and this refreshingly easy museum—an almshouse for old
men back in 1610—displays many of his greatest paintings (f10,
Mon–Sat 11:00–17:00, Sun 12:00–17:00, tel. 023/511-5775). Enjoy
lots of Frans Hals group portraits (rooms 21, 26, 28) and take-me-
back paintings of old-time Haarlem (room 22). Peter Brueghel the
Younger's painting *Proverbs* (outside room 24) illustrates 72 old
Dutch proverbs. To peek into old Dutch ways, identify some with
the help of the English-language key.

History Museum—Across the street from the Frans Hals
Museum, this small, free museum gives a peek into old Haarlem.
Request the English version of the 10-minute video. Study the
large-scale model of Haarlem in 1822 before the town's fortifications were demolished (Tue–Sat 12:00–17:00, Sun 13:00–17:00,

Haarlem

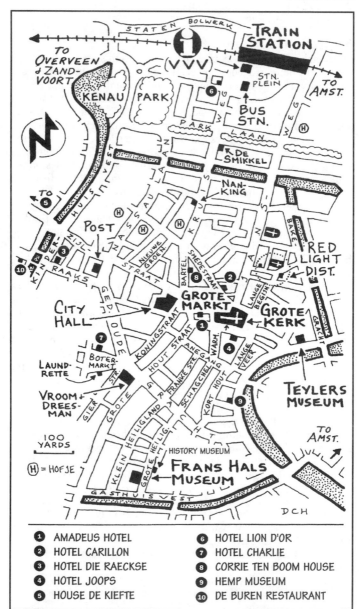

1 AMADEUS HOTEL		**6** HOTEL LION D'OR
2 HOTEL CARILLON		**7** HOTEL CHARLIE
3 HOTEL DIE RAECKSE		**8** CORRIE TEN BOOM HOUSE
4 HOTEL JOOPS		**9** HEMP MUSEUM
5 HOUSE DE KIEFTE		**10** DE BUREN RESTAURANT

closed Mon, Groot Heiligland 47, tel. 020/542-2427). The adjacent architecture museum (also free) is of conceivable interest to architects.

Corrie Ten Boom House—Haarlem is home to Corrie Ten Boom, popularized by *The Hiding Place*, an inspirational book and movie about the Ten Boom family's experience hiding Jews from Nazis. The Ten Boom House is open for 60-minute English tours (donation accepted, April–Oct Tue–Sat 10:00–16:00, Nov–March Tue–Sat 11:00–15:00, closed Mon, 50 meters off Market Square at Barteljorisstraat 19, the clock-shop people get all wound up if you go inside—wait at the door, where tour times are posted, tel. 023/531-0823). The Ten Boom family had for generations hosted a prayer meeting for peace here for Jews and Christians. On the 100th anniversary of the prayer meetings, the Gestapo came, looking for the hiding place. It's a great and inspirational story (although some may be put off by the preaching mixed in).

▲**Teylers Museum**—Famous as the oldest museum in Holland, it's interesting mainly as a look at a 200-year-old museum—fossils, minerals, and primitive electronic gadgetry. New exhibition halls (with rotating exhibits) have freshened up the place. Stop by if you enjoy mixing, say, Renaissance sketches with pickled coelacanths (f10, Tue–Sat 10:00–17:00, Sun 12:00–17:00, Spaarne 16, tel. 023/531-9010).

Canal Cruise—Making a scenic loop through and around Haarlem, these little trips are more relaxing than informative (f12.50, 70 min, 5/day, across from Teylers Museum at Spaarne 11a, tel. 023/535-7723).

Red Lights—Wander through a little red-light district as precious as a Barbie doll (2 blocks northeast of Market Square, off Lange Begijnestraat, no senior or student discounts). Don't miss the mall marked by the red neon sign reading "t'Steegje." The nearby *t'Poortje* (office park) costs f7.50.

Global Hemp Museum—More a hemp-products store and hub of Haarlem's coffee-shop action, this friendly place runs a humble hemp museum out back (shop free, museum f5, Internet access-f3/30 min, Mon–Sat 11:00–18:00, summer Sun 12:00–18:00, down the canal from Teylers Museum at Spaarne 94, tel. 023/534-9939).

Amsterdam to Haarlem Train Tour

Since you'll be commuting from Amsterdam to Haarlem, here's a tour to keep you entertained. Departing from Amsterdam, grab a seat on the right (with your back to Amsterdam, top deck if possible). Everything is on the right unless I say on the left.

You're riding the oldest train line in Holland. Across the harbor behind the Amsterdam station, the tall brown skyscraper is the corporate office of **Shell Oil**. The Dutch had the first multinational corporation (the United East India Company back in the

17th century). And today this international big-business spirit survives with companies like Shell and Phillips.

Leaving Amsterdam you'll see the cranes and ships of its harbor—sizable but nothing like the world's biggest in nearby Rotterdam.

On your left find the old **windmill**. In front of it the little garden plots and cottages are escapes for big-city people who probably don't even have a balcony.

Coming into the Sloterdijk Station (where trains connect for Amsterdam airport), you'll see huge office buildings, such as Dutch Telecom KPN. These grew up after the station made commuting easy.

A kilometer past Sloterdijk Station, about 50 meters to the right of the tracks, a yellow sign says, "Tippel Zone—open 21:00." (*Tippel* is the sound a mouse makes when it runs through the house at night.) This is a **drive-in brothel**. See the oval driveway with pink "bus stops" for browsing, the lounge building, and the blue privacy stalls behind (including 2 for bikers). The lounge has a clinic with a nurse and counselors to keep the women healthy. If a prostitute is diagnosed with AIDS, she gets a subsidized apartment to encourage her to quit the business. Shocking as this may seem to some, it's a good example of a pragmatic solution to a problem—getting the most dangerous prostitutes off the streets and combating AIDS.

Passing through a forest and by some houseboats, you enter a *polder*—reclaimed land. This is an ecologically sound farm zone, run without chemicals. Cows, pigs, and chickens run free—they're not raised in cages. The train tracks are on a dike, which provides a solid foundation not susceptible to floods. This way the transportation system functions right through any calamity. Looking out at the distant dike, remember you're in the most densely populated country in Europe. On the horizon, sleek modern windmills whirl.

Passing the tall smokestack and the Sony Music Building, find a big, unnamed, beige-and-white building. This is the **mint**, where the Dutch currency is printed (top security, no advertising). This has long been a family business. Study a bill. Even today you can read who printed it: Johan Enschede en Zonen, imp. (Johan Enschede and Sons, Inc.).

As the train slows down, you're passing through the Netherlands' biggest train-car maintenance facility and entering Haarlem. Look left. The domed building is a **prison**, built in 1901 and still in use. As you cross the Spaarne River you'll see the great **church spire** towering over Haarlem as it has since medieval times—back when a fortified wall circled the town. Hop out into one of Holland's oldest stations. Art Nouveau—decor from 1908—survives all around.

Nightlife in Haarlem

Haarlem's evening scene is great. The bars around the Grote Kerk and Lange Veerstraat are colorful and lively. You'll find plenty of music.

The best show in town: the café scene on Market Square. In good weather, café tables tumble happily out of the bars.

For trendy local crowds, consider a drink at the **Studio** (daily 12:00–02:00, on the square, next to Hotel Carillon) or **Café 1900** across from the Corrie Ten Boom House (daily 9:00–00:30, live music Sun night).

Coffee Shops: Haarlem has 16 "coffee shops" where marijuana is casually sold and smoked by easygoing noncriminal types. The **Frans Hals Coffee Shop** is one of the best established (in front of station at 46 Kruisweg). The display case–type "menu" explains what's on sale (f5 joints, f25 baggies, space cakes—but no alcohol, only soft drinks). At **High Times**, smokers can choose from 16 varieties of joints in racks behind the bar (neatly prepacked in trademarked "Joint Packs," f4-7.50, daily 12:00–23:00, Internet access, 47 Lange Veerstraat). If you don't like the smell of pot, avoid places sporting Rastafarian yellow, red, and green colors; wildly painted walls; or plants in the windows.

Crack is the wild and leathery place to go for loud music, pool, darts, and smoking (Lange Veerstraat 32). **Imperial Café and Bar** has live music Sunday through Thursday (daily 20:00–02:00, best to arrive around 00:30 on weekends, a few doors down from Crack at Korte Veerstraat 3).

Sleeping in Haarlem
(f1 = about 40 cents, country code: 31, area code: 023)

Sleep Code: **S** = Single, **D** = Double/Twin, **T** = Triple, **Q** = Quad, **b** = bathroom, **t** = toilet only, **s** = shower only, **CC** = Credit Card (**V**isa, **M**asterCard, **A**mex).

The helpful Haarlem tourist office ("VVV" at the train station, Mon–Fri 9:30–17:30, Sat 10:00–14:00, closed Sun, tel. 0900-616-1600, f1/min) can nearly always find you a f35 bed in a private home (for a f10-per-person fee plus a cut of your host's money). Avoid this if you can; it's cheaper to call direct.

Haarlem is most crowded in April, on Easter weekend, in May, and in August. Nearly every Dutch person you'll encounter speaks English. The listed prices include breakfast (unless otherwise noted) and usually include the f3.50-per-person-per-day tourist tax. To avoid this town's louder-than-normal street noises, forgo views for a room in the back. Hotels and the TI have a useful parking brochure.

For a **Laundromat**, try My Beautiful Launderette—handy, self-service, and cheap (f11 wash and dry, daily 8:30–20:30, bring coins, including 6 Dutch quarters to dry, near Vroom Dreesman department store at Boter Markt 20).

344 Rick Steves' France, Belgium & the Netherlands

Sleeping in the Center

Hotel Amadeus, on Market Square, has 15 small, bright, and basic rooms. Some have views of the square. This characteristic hotel, ideally located above an early 20th-century dinner café, is relatively quiet. Its lush old lounge/breakfast room, on the second floor, overlooks the square (Sb-f97.50, Db-f140, Tb-f180, Qb-f200, includes tax, 2-night stay and cash get you a 5 percent discount, 12-min walk from train station, CC:VMA, steep climb to lounge, then an elevator, Grote Markt 10, 2011 RD Haarlem, tel. 023/532-4530, fax 023/532-2328, www.amadeus-hotel.com, Mike takes good care of his guests).

Hotel Carillon also overlooks the town square but comes with a little more traffic and bell-tower noise. Many of the well-worn rooms are small, and the stairs are ste-e-e-p. The front rooms come with great town-square views and street noise (22 rooms, tiny loft singles-f60, Db-f142, Tb-f187.50, Qb-f210, includes tax, no elevator, 12-min walk from train station, CC:VMA, Grote Markt 27, 2011 RC Haarlem, tel. 023/531-0591, fax 023/531-4909, e-mail: fra.baars@wxs.nl). The Carillon also runs the nearby **Die Raeckse Hotel**, which has fewer stairs, less character, more traffic noise, and decent rooms (Sb-f98–115, Db-f143–171, baths cost more than showers, CC:VMA, Raaks 1, 2011 VA Haarlem, tel. 023/532-6629, fax 023/531-7937).

Hotel Joops is an innovative concept. From a reception desk in his furniture store, just behind the cathedral, Mr. Joops administers a corral of 80 rooms, all within a block of the church. He has cheap, well-worn, spacious rooms (S-f80, D-f115, T-f150) and new suites with kitchenettes (Db-f120–160, depending upon size, Tb-f165–195, breakfast—with the furniture—is f17.50 extra, save about 5 percent with cash, CC:VMA, Oude Groenmarkt 20, 2011 HL Haarlem, tel. 023/532-2008, fax 023/532-9549, www .joops.hotelinformation.com, e-mail: joops@hotelinformation.com).

Bed and Breakfast House de Kiefte, your get-into-a-local-home budget option, epitomizes the goodness of B&Bs. Marjet (mar-yet) and Hans, a fun-to-know Dutch couple who speak English fluently, rent four bright, cheery, nonsmoking rooms (with a good breakfast and travel advice) in their quiet, 100-year-old home (Ds-f100, T-f145, Qs-f175, Quint/s-f200, cash only, minimum 2 nights, family loft sleeps up to 5, very steep stairs, kid-friendly, Coornhertstraat 3, 2013 EV Haarlem, tel. 023/532-2980, cellular 06-5474-5272). It's a 15-minute walk or f14 taxi ride from the train station and a five-minute walk from the center. From Grote Markt (Market Square), walk straight out Zijlstraat and over the bridge and take a left on the fourth street.

Hotel Charlie is new and its staff eager to please. With basic rooms and a bizarre floor plan, it's only a three-minute

walk from the Markt (Sb-f100, Db-f140, Qb-f200, near launderette, Botermarkt 7, tel. 023/534-6615, fax 023/551-4488,
friendly Johnny).

Hotel Lion D'Or is a classy business hotel with all the
professional comforts and a handy location. Don't expect a warm
welcome (34 rooms, Sb-f210, Db-f275, extra beds-f50, CC:VMA,
elevator, some nonsmoking rooms, across the street from the
station at Kruisweg 34, 2011 LC Haarlem, tel. 023/532-1750,
fax 023/532-9543, www.goldentulip.nl/hotels/gtliondor).

Sleeping near Haarlem

The 300-room, very American **Hotel Haarlem Zuid** is sterile
but a good value for those interested only in sleeping and eating.
Renovated in 2000, it sits in an industrial zone, a 20-minute walk
from the center on the road to the airport (Db-f173–193 depending upon size of room, add f20 each for a 3rd or 4th person,
breakfast included or skip and save f17.50 each, CC:VMA,
elevator, easy parking, laundry service, fitness center, inexpensive
hotel restaurant, Toekanweg 2, 2035 LC Haarlem, tel. 023/
536-7500, fax 023/536-7980, www.hotelhaarlemzuid.nl, e-mail:
haarlemzuid@valk.com). Buses #5, #70, #72, and #75 connect
the hotel to the station and Market Square every 10 minutes.
Bus #80 makes runs to the beach or Amsterdam. Fast buses (#236
and #362) zip to the airport.

Pension Koning, a 15-minute walk north of the station or a
quick hop on bus #71, has five simple rooms in a row house in a
residential area (S-f45, D-f90, T-f120, 2-night minimum, includes
breakfast, Kleverlaan 179, 2023 JC Haarlem, tel. 023/526-1456).

Hostel Jan Gijzen, completely renovated and with all the
youth-hostel comforts, charges f39–43 for beds (breakfast) in
eight-bed dorms (f5 extra for nonmembers, a few D-f82, daily
7:30–24:00, Jan Gijzenpad 3, 3 kilometers from Haarlem station—
take bus #2, or a 5-min walk from Santpoort Zuid train station,
tel. 023/537-3793, fax 023/537-1176, e-mail: haarlem@njhc.org).

Eating in Haarlem

Eating between Market Square (Grote Markt) and Train Station

Enjoy an Indonesian rijsttafel feast at the **Nanking Chinese-
Indonesian Restaurant** (daily 16:00–22:00, Kruisstraat 16, a few
blocks off Grote Markt, tel. 023/532-0706). Couples eat plenty,
heartily, and cheaply by splitting a f26 Indonesian "rice table" for
one; each eater should order a drink. Say hi to gracious Ai Ping
and her daughter, Fan. Don't let them railroad you into a Chinese
(their heritage) dinner. They also do cheap and tasty takeout.

Pancakes for dinner? **Pannekoekhuis "De Smikkel"** serves

a selection of over 50 dinner (meat, cheese, etc.) and dessert pancakes. The pancakes (f18 each) are filling. With the f2.50-per-person cover charge, splitting is OK (daily 16:00–22:00, closed Mon in winter, 2 blocks in front of station, Kruisweg 57, tel. 023/532-0631).

Eat well and surrounded by trains and 1908 architecture in the classy **Brasserie Haarlem Station Restaurant** (f30 for 3 courses, daily 9:00–21:00, between tracks #3 and #6).

Eating on or near Zijlstraat
Eko Eet Café is great for a cheery, tasty vegetarian meal (f20 *menu*, daily 17:30–21:30, Zijlstraat 39, tel. 023/532-6568). Because they serve only fresh food, the *menu* gets sparse by 21:00.

Vincent's Eethuis serves the best cheap, basic Dutch food in town. This former St. Vincent's soup kitchen now feeds more gainfully employed locals than poor (f10, free seconds on veggies, friendly staff, Mon–Fri 12:00–14:00, 17:00–19:30, Nieuwe Groenmarkt 22).

The friendly **De Buren** offers handlebar-mustache fun and traditional Dutch food (such as *draadjesvlees*, beef stew with applesauce; and *oma's kippetje*, grandmother's chicken) to happy locals (f25 dinners, Wed–Sun 17:00–22:00, closed Mon–Tue, outside the tourist area at Brouwersvaart 146, follow Raaks Straat west across the canal from Die Raeckse Hotel, tel. 023/534-3364). Gerard and Marjo love their work. Enjoy their creative menu, made especially for you.

Eating between the Market Square and Frans Hals Museum
Jacobus Pieck Eetlokaal is popular with locals for its fine-value "global cuisine" (f18 plate of the day, Mon–Sat 10:00–22:00, Sun 12:00–22:00, Warmoesstraat 18, tel. 023/532-6144).

For a (f3) cone of old-fashioned French fries, drop by **Friethuis de Vlaminck** on Warmoesstraat 3 (Tue–Sat until 18:00). Notice the old-time shop sign cobbled into Warmoesstraat's brick sidewalk.

La Plume steak house is noisy with a happy, local, and carnivorous crowd (f30 meals, daily from 17:30, CC:VMA, Lange Veerstraat 1).

Bastiaan serves good "Mediterranean" cuisine in a classy atmosphere (f30 dinners, Tue–Sun from 18:00, closed Mon, CC:VMA, Lange Veerstraat 8).

De Lachende Javaan ("The Laughing Javanese") serves the best real Indonesian food in town. Their f37 rijsttafel is great (light eaters can split this extravaganza—f5 for extra plate, Tue–Sun from 17:00, closed Mon, CC:VMA, Frankestraat 25, tel. 023/532-8792).

For a candlelit dinner of cheese and wine, consider **In't Goede Uur** (Tue–Sun from 17:30, closed Mon, Korte Houtstraat 1).

For a healthy budget lunch with Haarlem's best view, eat at **La Place**, on the top floor or roof garden of the Vroom Dreesman department store (Mon–Sat 9:30–17:30, Thu until 20:30, closed Sun, on the corner of Grote Houtstraat and Gedempte Oude Gracht).

Picnic shoppers head to the DekaMarkt supermarket (Mon–Sat 8:30–20:00, closed Sun, Gedempte Oude Gracht 54, between Vroom Dreesman department store and post office).

Transportation Connections—Haarlem

By train to: Amsterdam (6/hrly, 15 min, f7 one-way, f12 same-day return, ticket not valid on "Lovers Train," a misnamed private train that runs hrly), **Delft** (2/hrly, 38 min), **Hoorn** (4/hrly, 1 hr), **The Hague** (4/hrly, 35 min), **Alkmaar** (2/hrly, 30 min), **Schiphol Airport** (2/hrly, 40 min, f10, transfer at Amsterdam-Sloterdijk); the direct buses #236 (use a strip card) and #362 (local cash) to the airport are faster (2/hrly, 30 min, f7); by taxi it's f70.

Sights—Near Haarlem and Amsterdam

The Netherlands are tiny. The sights listed below are an easy day trip by bus or train from Haarlem or Amsterdam. Match your interest with the village's specialty: flower auctions, folk museums, cheese, delft porcelain, beaches, or modern art.

▲▲**Enkhuisen's Zuiderzee Museum**—This lively, open-air folk museum in the salty old town of Enkhuizen has a "Living on Urk" village populated by people who do a convincing job of role-playing no-nonsense 1905 Dutch villagers. No one said "Have a nice day" back then. You can eat herring hot out of the old smoker and see barrels and rope made. Children enjoy the dress-up chest, the old-time game zone, and making sailing ships out of old wooden shoes (f18.50, early April–late Oct daily 10:00–17:00, free tours at 14:00, private guide for f80, tel. 0228/351-111). Take the train from Amsterdam direct to Enkhuisen, where a boat shuttles you to the museum, avoiding a pleasant 15-minute walk.

▲**Zaanse Schans**—This 17th-century Dutch village turned open-air folk museum puts Dutch culture—from cheese making to wooden-shoe carving—on a lazy Susan. Take an inspiring climb to the top of a whirring windmill (gather a group and ask for a tour). Located in the town of Zaandijk, this is your easiest one-stop look at traditional Dutch culture and the Netherlands' best collection of windmills (free, daily 8:30–18:00, until 17:00 in winter, parking f7,50/1 hr, f15/day, tel. 075/616-8218). It's 15 minutes by train north of Amsterdam; take the Alkmaar-bound train to Station Koog-Zaandijk and then walk, following the signs—past a fragrant chocolate factory—for 10 minutes.

▲▲**Aalsmeer Flower Auction**—Get a bird's-eye view of the huge Dutch flower industry. Wander on elevated walkways

Day Trips from Haarlem and Amsterdam

(through what's claimed to be the biggest building on earth) over literally trainloads of freshly cut flowers. About half of all the flowers exported from Holland are auctioned off here in six huge auditoriums (f7.50, Mon–Fri 7:30–11:00, the auction wilts after 9:30 but the warehouse swarms, gift shop, cafeteria; bus #172 from Amsterdam's station, 2/hrly, 1 hr; from Haarlem take bus #140, 2/hrly, 1 hr; tel. 0297/393-939). Aalsmeer is close to the airport and a handy last fling before catching a morning weekday flight.

▲▲▲Keukenhof—This is the greatest bulb-flower garden on earth. Each spring 6 million flowers, enjoying sandy soil behind the Dutch dunes, conspire to make even a total garden hater enjoy them. This 100-acre park is packed with tour groups daily from about March 22 to May 24 for the 2001 spring show (f20, 8:00–19:30, last tickets sold at 18:00) and from August 2 to September 16 for the 2001 summer exhibition (f15.50, 9:00–18:00, last ticket sold at 17:00, catch bus #50 or #51 from Haarlem, tel. 0252/465-555, www.keukenhof.nl). Go late in the day for the best light and the fewest groups.

The 2001 flower parade will be held April 21. This all-day parade, featuring floats decorated with blossoms instead of crepe-paper, runs through eight towns, including Lisse and Haarlem.

Zandvoort—For a quick and easy look at the windy coastline in a shell-lover's Shangri-La, visit the beach resort of Zandvoort, a breezy 45-minute bike ride or an eight-minute car or train ride west of Haarlem (from Haarlem, follow signs to Bloemendaal). South of the main beach, bathers work on all-around tans.

▲Hoorn—This is an elegant, quiet, and typical 17th-century Dutch town north of Amsterdam. Its TI can rent you a bike or give you a walking-tour brochure. Any TI offers the flier describing the "Historic Triangle," an all-day excursion from Amsterdam that connects Hoorn, Medemblik, and Enkhuizen by steam train and boat (f30 plus f6.25 for train back to Haarlem, 2/day, tel. 0229/214-862).

De Rijp—This sleepy town is worth visiting if you're driving north of Amsterdam.

Volendam, Marken, and Monnikendam—These famous towns are quaint as can be (although Volendam is too touristy).

▲Delft—Peaceful as a Vermeer painting (he was born here) and lovely as its porcelain, Delft is a typically Dutch town with a special soul. Enjoy it best by simply wandering around, watching people, munching local syrup-waffles, or daydreaming from the canal bridges. The town bustles during its Saturday antiques market (9:00–17:00). Its colorful Thursday food-and-flower market attracts many traditional villagers (9:00–17:00). The TI on the main square has a f3.50 brochure outlining Delft's sights, including a "Historical Walk through Delft" (Mon–Fri 9:00–17:30, Sat 9:00–17:30, Sun 11:00–15:00, tel. 015/212-6100). The town is a museum in itself, but if you need a turnstile, it has an impressive Army Museum (f6, Mon–Fri 10:00–17:00, Sat–Sun 13:00–17:00). Or tour the Royal Porcelain Works to watch the famous 17th-century blue delftware turn from clay into art (f5, Mon–Sat 9:00–17:00, summer Sun 9:30–17:00, tel. 015/256-9214).

▲Alkmaar—Holland's cheese capital is especially fun (and touristy) during its weekly cheese market (Friday 10:00–12:00).

▲▲Edam—For the ultimate in cuteness and peace, make tiny Edam your home. It's sweet but palatable and 30 minutes by bus from Amsterdam (2/hrly). The Edam Museum is a small, quirky house offering a fun peek into a 400-year-old home and a floating cellar (f4.50, Tue–Sat 10:00–16:30, Sun 13:30–16:30, closed in winter, on the main square). Wednesday is the town's market day (9:00–13:00). In July and August, market day includes a traditional cheese market (10:30–12:30). TI tel. 0299/315-125.

Sleeping and Eating: The **Hotel De Fortuna**, an eccentric canalside mix of flowers, a cat of leisure, a pet turtle, and duck noises, offers steep stairs and low-ceilinged rooms in several ancient buildings in the old center of Edam (Db-f185, includes breakfast, CC:VMA, garden patio, attached restaurant, Spuistraat 3, 1135 AV Edam, tel. 0299/371-671, fax 0299/371-469). The centrally located **Damhotel** (on a canal around corner from TI) has attractive, comfortable rooms with a plush feel (Sb-f115, Db-f190, Tb-f270, includes breakfast, CC:VMA, attached restaurant, Keizersgracht 1, 1135 AZ Edam, tel. 0299/371-766, fax 0299/374-031, www.damhotel.nl). The TI (tel. 0299/315-125) has a list of cheaper rooms in private homes. **Tai Wah** has take-out Chinese/Indonesian (eat in De Fortuna garden) and indoor seating (13:00–21:45, closed Tue, Lingerzijde 62, tel. 0299/371-088).

▲**Rotterdam**—This city, the world's largest port, bounced back after being bombed flat in World War II. See its towering Euromast, take a harbor tour, and stroll its great pedestrian zone (TI tel. 0900/403-4065, toll call-f1/min).

▲▲**The Hague (Den Haag)**—Locals say the money is made in Rotterdam, divided in The Hague, and spent in Amsterdam. The Hague is the Netherlands' seat of government and the home of several engaging museums. The Hague's TI is at the train station (Mon–Sat 9:00–17:30, later in summer, Sun 10:00–17:00, tel. 06/3403-5051, f1/min).

The **Mauritshuis'** delightful, easy-to-tour art collection stars Vermeer and Rembrandt (f12.50, Tue–Sat 10:00–17:00, Sun 11:00–17:00, Korte Vijverberg 8, tel. 070/302-3456). Across the pond, the **Torture Museum** (Gevangenpoort) shows the medieval mind at its worst (f8, Tue–Fri 11:00–16:00, Sat–Sun 12:00–16:00, closed Mon, required tours on the hour, last one at 16:00, ask ticket-taker if film and talk will be in English before you commit, tel. 070/346-0861). For a look at the 19th century's attempt at virtual reality, tour **Panorama Mesdag**, a 360-degree painting of nearby Scheveningen in the 1880s with a 3-D sandy-beach foreground (f9.50, Mon–Sat 10:00–17:00, Sun 12:00–17:00, Zeestraat 65, tel. 070/310-6665). The nearby **Peace Palace**, a gift from Andrew Carnegie, houses the International Court of Justice (f5, Mon–Fri, required guided tours only at 10:00, 11:00, 14:00, or 15:00, closes without warning—call ahead or check at TI, tram #7 or #8 from station, tel. 070/302-4137).

Scheveningen, the Dutch Coney Island, is liveliest on sunny summer afternoons (take tram #7). Madurodam, a mini-Holland amusement park, is a kid pleaser (f21, kids 4–11 f14, daily 9:00–17:00, until 20:00 March–June, until 23:00 July–Aug, tram #1 or #9, tel. 070/355-3900).

Utrecht—The Museum von Speelklok tot Pierement has free and necessary guided 50-minute tours on the hour demonstrating its musical clocks, calliopes, and street organs (f12, Tue–Sat 10:00–17:00, Sun 12:00–17:00, closed Mon, last tour at 16:00, 10-min walk from station, Buurkerkhof 10, tel. 030/231-2789).

▲▲**Arnhem's Open-Air Dutch Folk Museum**—An hour east of Amsterdam, Arnhem has the Netherlands' first and biggest folk museum. You'll enjoy a huge park of windmills, old farms, traditional crafts in action, and a pleasant education-by-immersion in

Dutch culture. The English guidebook (f7.50) explains each historic building (f22.50, April–Oct daily 10:00–17:00, tel. 026/ 357-6111). The park has several good budget restaurants and covered picnic areas. Its rustic Pancake House serves hearty (splittable) Dutch flapjacks.

Trains make the 70-minute trip from Amsterdam to Arnhem twice an hour (likely transfer in Utrecht). At Arnhem station, take bus #3 or, even better, #13 (faster, 4/hrly, 15 min) to the Openlucht Museum. By car from Haarlem, skirt Amsterdam to the south on E9, follow signs to Utrecht, and take A12 east to Arnhem. Just before Arnhem, take the Arnhem Nord exit "*Openluchtmuseum*" and follow signs to the nearby museum. For the Kröller-Müller Museum, follow white signs to Hoge Veluwe. ▲▲**Kröller-Müller Museum and Hoge Veluwe National Park**—Near Arnhem, Hoge Veluwe National Park is the Netherlands' largest (13,000 acres) and is famous for its Kröller-Müller Museum. This huge, striking modern-art collection, including 55 paintings by van Gogh, is set deep in the forest. The park has hundreds of white bikes you're free to use to make your explorations more fun. After you pay f9.50 at the park entrance, the museum is "free" (Tue–Sun 10:00–17:00, easy parking, tel. 055/ 378-1441). Pick up information at the Amsterdam or Arnhem TI (tel. 026/442-6767). Bus #12 connects the Arnhem train station with the Kröller-Müller Museum (March–Oct, check ahead for times as #12 runs infrequently). A visit to the park and the open-air museum makes a great day trip from Amsterdam.

APPENDIX

Whirlwind (Kamikaze) Three-Week Tour of France by Car or Train
Day   By Car
1   Fly into Paris, pick up car, visit Giverny and/or Rouen, overnight in Honfleur (save Paris sightseeing for end of trip).

2   9:00–Depart Honfleur, 10:00–Caen World War II Museum, 12:00–Drive to Arromanches for lunch and museum, 15:00–American cemetery, 16:00–Point du Hoc, 17:00–German cemetery, dinner and overnight in Bayeux.

3   9:00–Bayeux tapestry and church, 13:30–Mont St. Michel, 16:00–Drive to Dinan, 17:00–Arrive in Dinan for one Brittany stop, sleep in Dinan.

4   10:00–Depart Dinan and drive to Loire, 14:00–Tour Chambord, 17:00–Arrive in Amboise, sleep in Amboise.

5   8:45–Depart Amboise, 9:00–Chenonceau, 11:30–Cheverny château and lunch, 14:00–Possible stop in Chaumont, back in Amboise for Leonardo's house and free time in town, sleep in Amboise.

6   8:30–Depart Amboise, morning stop in Chauvigny, lunch at Mortemart, 13:30–Oradour-sur-Glane, 14:30–Drive to Beynac, 17:30–Wander Beynac or tour its castle, dinner and overnight in Beynac.

7   9:00–Browse the town and market of Sarlat, 12:00–Font de Gaume tour, 14:00–More caves, castles, or canoe extravaganza, dinner and sleep in Beynac.

8   9:00–Depart Beynac, 10:00–Short stop at Cahors bridge, 12:30–Arrive in Albi, couscous lunch, 14:00–Tour church and Toulouse-Lautrec Museum, 16:00–Depart for Carcassonne, 18:00–Explore, have dinner, and sleep in Carcassonne.

9   10:30–Depart Carcassonne, 11:00–Lastours castles or Minerve, 15:30–Pont du Gard, 16:30–Drive to Arles, 17:30–Set up for evening in Arles.

10 All day for Arles and Avignon, evening back in Arles.

11 8:30–Depart Arles, 9:00–Les Baux, 11:00–Depart Les Baux, 12:00–Lunch and wander in Isle sur la Sorgue, 14:00–Luberon hill town drive, 16:00–Depart for the Riviera, 19:00–Arrive in Nice or Antibes.

12 Sightsee in Nice and Monaco, sleep in Nice or Antibes.

13 Morning free, 12:00–Drive north, sleep at Clelles (urbanites sleep in Lyon).

14 Morning drive north, long stop in Annecy, in afternoon arrive in Chamonix. With clear weather do Aiguille du Midi.

15 All day for the Alps.

Whirlwind Three-Week Tour of France

16 9:00–Depart Chamonix, 12:00–Lunch in Brancion,
14:00–Depart, 15:00–Arrive in Beaune for Hôtel Dieu
and wine tasting, sleep in Beaune.

17 9:00–Depart for Burgundy village treats or get to Alsace
early. Arrive in Colmar after 3.5-hour drive.

18 9:00–Unterlinden Museum, 10:00–Free in town, 14:00–
Wine Road villages, evening back in Colmar.

19 8:00–Depart Colmar, 12:00–Lunch, tour Verdun battlefield,
15:00–Depart, 16:00–Arrive Reims, church and champagne,
18:00–Turn in car at Reims, picnic-dinner celebration on
train, 21:00–Collapse in Paris hotel.

20 Sightsee Paris, tour over.

Day By Train and Bus
All times are approximate. Fewer buses and trains run on Sunday.

1 Fly into Paris, find your hotel, go for an afternoon walk

2 All day to sightsee in Paris.

3 Head to Giverny in morning (about 8:00, depart Paris by
train to Vernon, check bags at station, then bus or taxi to
Giverny), early afternoon train to Rouen (check bags at

station), sightsee there, then head to Honfleur (from Rouen take late afternoon train to Le Havre—about 16:15—then catch bus to Honfleur—about 17:30), sleep in Honfleur.

4   Morning in Honfleur, midday bus to Caen then train to Bayeux, see tapestries in the afternoon. Sleep in Bayeux.

5   All day for D-Day beaches by minivan excursion or one-day car rental, late afternoon train (about 17:00) to Pontorson, taxi to Mont St. Michel, sleep on Mont St. Michel, tour abbey at night (sound-and-light show).

6   Early morning walk around the island, 9:00–Bus to Pontorson, 10:00–Train to Caen, transfer to Tours, transfer to Amboise, sleep in Amboise.

7   All day to tour the Loire, sleep in Amboise.

8   Early-morning train to Sarlat (with transfers at Tours and Bordeaux St. Jean), afternoon in Sarlat, sleep in Sarlat or Beynac (note: it's possible to visit Oradour-sur-Glane on this day; see Sarlat and Amboise "Transportation Connections").

9   All day in the Dordogne, morning train to Les Eyzies (Grotte de Font de de Gaume), taxi back, afternoon canoe trip, sleep in Sarlat or Beynac.

10   Morning train to Carcassonne (transfer in Souillac or Bordeaux and in Toulouse), afternoon wall walk, sleep in Carcassonne.

11   Morning train to Arles, sleep in Arles.

12   Morning train to Nîmes, late-morning bus to Pont du Gard (about 11:00), early-afternoon bus from Pont du Gard to Avignon (about 13:30), afternoon in Avignon, evening train back to Arles, sleep in Arles.

13   Morning bus to Les Baux (about 8:30), midday return to Arles, afternoon train to Nice, stroll the promenade, sleep on the Riviera.

14   Morning in Nice's old city, bus to Monaco, see changing of the guard and casino, return to Nice for beach time or Chagall museum, sleep in Nice.

15   Take a vacation from your vacation and spend a day on the beach. Spend part of the day in Antibes or take the bus to St. Paul-de-Vence.

16   Choose between urban or rural: Morning train to Lyon, visit Lyon, sleep there. Or take the scenic train to Digne/Grenoble and sleep in a remote mountain village en route (see "Transportation Connections—Nice").

17   Morning in Lyon, midday train to Annecy, visit Annecy, late-afternoon train to Chamonix, sleep in Chamonix.
     Or train from your remote village to Grenoble and Annecy (visit if time allows) then train to Chamonix.

18   All day to hike in the Alps, sleep in Chamonix.

19   Train to Colmar, sleep in Colmar.

20 All day in Alsace, sleep in Colmar (or evening train to
Paris if you must leave the next day).
21 Train to Paris.

"La Marseillaise"
There's a movement in France to soften the lyrics of their national
anthem. Sing it now...before it's too late.
Allons enfants de la Patrie, (Let's go, children of the fatherland,)
Le jour de gloire est arrivé. (The day of glory has arrived.)
Contre nous de la tyrannie (The blood-covered flagpole of tyranny)
L'étendard sanglant est levé, (Is raised against us,)
L'étendard sanglant est levé. (Is raised against us.)
Entendez-vous dans nos campagnes (Do you hear what's happening
in our countryside?)
Mugir les féroces soldats? (The ferocious soldiers are howling.)
Qui viennent jusque dans nos bras (They're nearly in our grasp)
Egorger nos fils et nos compagnes. (They're slitting the throats of
our sons and our women.)
Aux armes citoyens, (Grab your weapons, citizens,)
Formez vos bataillons, (Form your battalions,)
Marchons, marchons, (March on, march on,)
Qu'un sang impur (So that their impure blood)
Abreuve nos sillons. (Will fill our trenches.)

French History in an Escargot Shell
Around the time of Christ, Romans "Latinized" the land of the
Gauls. With the fifth-century fall of Rome, the barbarian Franks
and Burgundians invaded. From this unique mix of Latin and
Celtic cultures evolved today's France.

While France wallowed with the rest of Europe in medieval
darkness, it got a head start in its development as a nation-state.
In 507 Clovis established Paris as the capital of his Christian
Merovingian dynasty. Clovis and the Franks would eventually
become Louis and the French. Charles Martel stopped the spread
of Islam by beating the Spanish Moors at the Battle of Poitiers.
And Charlemagne, the most important of the "Dark Age" Frankish kings, was crowned Holy Roman Emperor in 800 by the pope.
Charles the Great presided over the "Carolingian Renaissance"
and effectively ruled a vast-for-the-time empire.

The Treaty of Verdun, which in 843 divided Charlemagne's
empire among his grandsons, marks what could be considered
the birth of Europe. For the first time, a treaty was signed in
vernacular languages (French and German) rather than in Latin.
While this split established a Franco/Germanic divide, it also
heralded an age of fragmentation. While petty princes took the
reigns, the Frankish king ruled only Île-de-France, a small region
around Paris.

Vikings, or Norsemen, settled in what became Normandy. Later, in 1066, these "Normans" invaded England. The Norman king, William the Conqueror, consolidated his English domain, accelerating the formation of modern England. But his rule also muddied the political waters between England and France, kicking off a centuries-long struggle between the two nations.

In the 12th century, Eleanor of Aquitaine (a separate country in southwest France) married Louis VII, king of France, bringing Aquitaine under French rule. They divorced, and she married Henry of Normandy, soon-to-be Henry II of England. This marital union gave England control of a huge swath of land from the English Channel to the Pyrénées. For 300 years France and England would struggle over control of Aquitaine. Any enemy of the French king would find a natural ally in the English king.

In 1328 a French king (Charles IV) died without a son. The English king (Edward III) was his nephew and naturally was interested in the throne. The French resisted. This pitted France, the biggest and richest country in Europe, against England, which had the biggest army. They fought from 1337 to 1453 in what was modestly called the Hundred Years' War.

Regional powers from within France sided with England. Burgundy actually took Paris, captured the royal family, and recognized the English king as heir to the French throne. England controlled France from the Loire north, and things looked bleak for the French king.

Enter Joan of Arc, a 16-year-old peasant girl driven by religious voices. France's national heroine left home to support the dauphin Charles VII (boy prince, heir to the throne but too young to rule). Joan rallied the French, inspiring them to ultimately throw out the English. In 1430 Joan was captured by the Burgundians, who sold her to the English, who convicted her of heresy and burned her at the stake in Rouen. But the inspiration of Joan of Arc lived on, and by 1453, English holdings on the Continent had dwindled to the port of Calais.

By 1500 a strong centralized France had emerged with borders similar to today's borders. Her kings (from the Renaissance François I through the Henrys and all those Louises) were model divine monarchs, setting the standards for absolute rule in Europe.

Outrage over the power plays and spending sprees of the kings, coupled with the modern thinking of the Enlightenment— whose leaders were the French *philosophes*—led to the French Revolution (1789) and the end of the Old Regime and its notion that some are born to rule while others are born to be ruled.

But the excesses of the Revolution led to the rise of Napoléon, who ruled the French empire as a dictator until his excesses ushered him into a South Atlantic exile. The French settled on a compromise role for their ruler. The modern French king was himself ruled by a constitution. Rather than dress in leotards and powdered wigs, he went to work in a suit with a briefcase.

The 20th century spelled the end of France's reign as a military and political superpower. Devastating wars with Germany in 1870, 1914, and 1940 and the loss of her colonial holdings left France with not quite enough land, people, or production to be a top player on a global scale.

France in the 21st century is the cultural capital of Europe and a leader in the push to integrate Europe into one unified economic power. When that happens, Paris will once again emerge as a superpower capital.

Contemporary Politics in France

The key political issues in France today are high unemployment (about 12 percent), a steadily increasing percentage of ethnic minorities, and a recognized need to compete in a global marketplace. The challenge is to address these issues while maintaining the social benefits the French expect from their government. As a result, national policies seem to conflict with each other (e.g., France supports the lean economic policies of the European Union but has recently reduced the French work week to 35 hours).

The unification of Europe has been powered by France and Germany. The 15-member European Union, which is well on its way to becoming a "United States of Europe," is dissolving borders and freeing up trade. They've established a European currency called the Euro. Some stores already have prices marked in francs and Euros (though Euros won't appear as bills and coins until 2002).

French national politics are fascinating. While only two parties dominate American politics, France has five major parties. From left to right, these include the reformed Communists (PCF-Parti Communiste Française), the moderate Socialists (PS-Parti Socialiste), the aristocratically conservative UDF (Union pour la Democratie Française), the center-right RPR (Rassemblement pour la République), and the racist Front National. In general the UDF and RPR split the conservative middle ground and the Socialists dominate the liberal middle ground. But in France (unlike the United States), coalitions are generally necessary for any party to "rule." At the fringes you'll read about the racist Front National Party, led by Jean-Marie Le Pen. Le Pen's "France for the French" platform calls for the expulsion of ethnic minorities and broader police powers. As unemployment has gone up, so has the popularity of this far-right party. Garnering 15 percent of a recent national vote, Le Pen has been able to force center-right parties farther in his direction. On the far left, the reformed Communists, still recovering from the fall of the Soviet Union, have had to work more flexibly with the less-radical Socialists and the environmental parties.

While the French president is elected by popular vote every seven years (which may be shortened to five) , he is more of a figurehead than his American counterpart. The more powerful prime minister is elected by the parliament (every three years). With five major parties, a single majority is rare—it takes a coalition to elect a prime minister. Currently the left is working together better than the right, and France has a liberal prime minister (Socialist Lionel Jospin) with a conservative president (Jacques Chirac). This "cohabitation" is similar to an American president having to deal with a Congress controlled by an opposing party.

Let's Talk Telephones

Dialing Direct

Here's a primer on making direct phone calls. For information specific to France and the Low Countries, see "Telephones and Mail" in the introduction.

Calling between Countries: Dial the international access code (of the country you're calling from), the country code (of the country you're calling), the area code (if it starts with zero, drop the zero), and then the local number. (For France, see "Europe's Exceptions," below.)

Calling Long Distance within a Country: First dial the area code (including its zero) and then dial the local number.

Europe's Exceptions: Some countries, such as France, Italy, Spain, Portugal, Norway, and Denmark, do not use area codes. To make an international call to these countries, dial the international access code (usually 00), the country code, and the local number in its entirety. OK, so there's one exception: For France, drop the initial zero of the local number. To make long-distance calls within any of these countries, simply dial the local number. (For example, within France, dial the 10-digit telephone number direct throughout the country.)

International Access Codes

When dialing direct, first dial the international access code of the country you're calling from. For the United States and Canada, it's 011. Virtually all European countries use "00" as their international access code; the only exceptions are Finland (990), Estonia (800), and Lithuania (810).

Country Codes

After you've dialed the international access code, dial the code of the country you're calling.

Austria—43	Canada—1	Estonia—372
Belgium—32	Czech Rep.—420	Finland—358
Britain—44	Denmark—45	France—33

Germany—49	Netherlands—31	Sweden—46
Greece—30	Norway—47	Switzerland—41
Ireland—353	Portugal—351	United States—1
Italy—39	Spain—34	

Calling-Card Operators

	AT&T	MCI	Sprint
France	0800-990-011	0800-990-019	0800-990-087
Belgium	0800-100-10	0800-100-12	0800-100-14
Netherlands	0800-022-9111	0800-022-9122	0800-022-9119

Telephone Directory
Useful Parisian Phone Numbers and Addresses

Emergency: Dial 17 for police
Emergency Medical Assistance: 15
Train Schedules and Reservations: 08 36 35 35 35.
Paris & France Directory Assistance (some English spoken): 12
American Church: 01 40 62 05 00
American Express: 11 rue Scribe, Mo: Opéra, 01 47 77 77 07
American Hospital: 01 46 41 25 25
American Pharmacy: 01 47 42 49 40
Office of American Services (lost passports, etc.): 01 43 12 48 45
U.S. Embassy: 01 43 12 22 22
Sunday Banks: 115 and 154 avenue des Champs-Élysées

Numbers and Stumblers

- Europeans write a few of their numbers differently than we do: 1 = 1 , 4 = 4 , 7= 7. Learn the difference or miss your train.
- In Europe, dates appear as day/month/year, so Christmas is 25/12/01.
- Commas are decimal points and decimals commas. A dollar and a half is 1,50, and there are 5.280 feet in a mile.
- When pointing, use your whole hand, palm downward.
- When counting with fingers, start with your thumb. If you hold up your first finger to request one item, you'll probably get two.
- What we Americans call the second floor of a building is the first floor in Europe.
- Europeans keep the left "lane" open for passing on escalators and moving sidewalks. Keep to the right.

Festivals in France, Belgium, and the Netherlands

January Monte Carlo Motor Rally, Monaco
Jan–Feb Carnival Celebrations, Belgium, Holland, France
April Queen's Day (April 30—street fairs, parades), Netherlands
Flower Parade, Haarlem, Netherlands

May	Festival de Versailles (arts)
	Cannes Film Festival
	Grand Prix, Monaco
	Ascension Day (religious procession), Bruges, Belgium
	Festival Jeanne d'Arc (pageants), Rouen, France
June	Festival du Marais (arts), Paris
	Holland Festival of Performing Arts, Amsterdam
	North Sea Jazz Festival, The Hague, Holland
July	Ommegang (historical pageant), Brussels
	Bastille Day (July 14—fireworks, celebrations), France
	Grand Parade du Jazz, Nice, France
	Festival d'Avignon (arts), Avignon, France
	Tour de France, (ends in Paris)
	Les Tombées de la Nuit (arts festival), Rennes, France
	Beaune International Music Festival
	Fête de la Musique—17th (free concerts celebrating summer solstice), France
	Belgian National Day (July 21—parades, feasts), Brussels
August	Canal Festival (historic fair, performances), Bruges
September	Opening of Parliament (pageantry), The Hague, Holland
	Fête d'Automne (arts festival), Paris
December	Christmas Market, Strasbourg, France

For more information on festivals and events in these countries, try the following Web sites: www.whatsgoingon.com, www.festivals.com, www.franceguide.com, and www.polydeme.fr/festivals/fr_accueil.htm (in French).

Metric Conversions (approximate)

1 inch = 25 millimeters	32 degrees F = 0 degrees C
1 foot = 0.3 meter	82 degrees F = about 28 degrees C
1 yard = 0.9 meter	1 ounce = 28 grams
1 mile = 1.6 kilometers	1 kilogram = 2.2 pounds
1 centimeter = 0.4 inch	1 quart = 0.95 liter
1 meter = 39.4 inches	1 square yard = 0.8 square meter
1 kilometer = .62 mile	1 acre = 0.4 hectare

Climate
First line, average daily low temperature; second line, average daily high; third line, days of no rain.

	J	F	M	A	M	J	J	A	S	O	N	D
FRANCE												
Paris												
	34°	34°	39°	43°	49°	55°	58°	58°	53°	46°	40°	36°
	43°	45°	54°	60°	68°	73°	76°	75°	70°	60°	50°	44°
	14	14	19	17	19	18	19	18	17	18	15	15
Nice												
	35°	36°	41°	46°	52°	58°	63°	63°	58°	51°	43°	37°
	50°	53°	59°	64°	71°	79°	84°	83°	77°	68°	58°	52°
	2322	24	23	23	26	29	26	24	23	21	21	
BELGIUM												
Brussels												
	30°	32°	36°	41°	46°	52°	54°	54°	51°	45°	38°	32°
	40°	44°	51°	58°	65°	72°	73°	72°	69°	60°	48°	42°
	10	11	14	12	15	15	14	13	17	14	10	12
NETHERLANDS												
Amsterdam												
	31°	31°	34°	40°	46°	51°	55°	55°	50°	44°	38°	33°
	40°	42°	49°	56°	64°	70°	72°	71°	67°	57°	48°	42°
	9	9	15	14	17	16	14	13	11	11	9	10

French Survival Phrases

For more user-friendly French phrases, check out *Rick Steves' French Phrase Book and Dictionary* or *Rick Steves' French, Italian & German Phrase Book and Dictionary*.

Hello (good day).	**Bonjour.**	bohn-zhoor
Do you speak English?	**Parlez-vous anglais?**	par-lay-voo ahn-glay
Yes. / No.	**Oui. / Non.**	wee / nohn
I'm sorry.	**Désolé.**	day-zoh-lay
Please.	**S'il vous plaît.**	see voo play
Thank you.	**Merci.**	mehr-see
Goodbye.	**Au revoir.**	oh vwahr
Where is...?	**Où est...?**	oo ay
...a hotel	**...un hôtel**	uhn oh-tehl
...a youth hostel	**...une auberge**	ewn oh-behrzh
	de jeunesse	duh zhuh-nehs
...a restaurant	**...un restaurant**	uhn rehs-toh-rahn
...a grocery store	**...une épicerie**	ewn ay-pee-suh-ree
...the train station	**...la gare**	lah gar
...the tourist info office	**...l'office du tourisme**	loh-fees dew too-reez-muh
Where are the toilets?	**Où sont les toilettes?**	oo sohn lay twah-leht
men / women	**hommes / dames**	ohm / dahm
How much is it?	**Combien?**	kohn-bee-an
Cheaper.	**Moins cher.**	mwan shehr
Included?	**Inclus?**	an-klew
Do you have...?	**Avez-vous...?**	ah-vay-voo
I would like...	**Je voudrais...**	zhuh voo-dray
...a ticket.	**...un billet.**	uhn bee-yay
...a room.	**...une chambre.**	ewn shahn-bruh
...the bill.	**...l'addition.**	lah-dee-see-ohn
one	**un**	uhn
two	**deux**	duh
three	**trois**	twah
four	**quatre**	kah-truh
five	**cinq**	sank
six	**six**	sees
seven	**sept**	seht
eight	**huit**	weet
nine	**neuf**	nuhf
ten	**dix**	dees
At what time?	**À quelle heure?**	ah kehl ur
Just a moment.	**Un moment.**	uhn moh-mahn
Now.	**Maintenant.**	man-tuh-nahn
today / tomorrow	**aujourd'hui / demain**	oh-zhoor-dwee / duh-man

Road Scholar Feedback for
FRANCE, BELGIUM & THE NETHERLANDS 2001

We're all in the same travelers' school of hard knocks. Your feedback helps us improve this guidebook for future travelers. Please fill this out (or use the on-line version at www.ricksteves.com/feedback), attach more info or any tips/favorite discoveries if you like, and send it to us. As thanks for your help, we'll send you our quarterly travel newsletter free for one year. Thanks! **Rick**

Of the recommended accommodations/restaurants used, which was:

Best _____

      Why? _____

Worst _____

      Why? _____

Of the sights/experiences/destinations recommended by this book, which was:

Most overrated _____

      Why? _____

Most underrated _____

      Why? _____

Best ways to improve this book:

_____

_____

I'd like a free newsletter subscription:

_____ Yes _____ No _____ Already on list

_____
Name

_____
Address

_____
City, State, Zip

_____
E-mail Address

Please send to: ETBD, Box 2009, Edmonds, WA 98020

Faxing Your Hotel Reservation

Faxing is more accurate and cheaper than telephoning. Use this handy form for your fax (or find it online at www.ricksteves.com /reservation). Photocopy and fax away.

One-Page Fax

To: _____ @ _____
       hotel   *fax*

From: _____ @ _____
          name   *fax*

Today's date: ____ /_____ /____
                 day *month* *year*

Dear Hotel _____,

Please make this reservation for me:

Name: _____

Total # of people: _____   # of rooms: _____   # of nights: _____

Arriving: ____ /_____ /____ My time of arrival (24-hr clock): _____
            day *month* *year*   (I will telephone if I will be late)

Departing: ____ /_____ /____
              day *month* *year*

Room(s):   Single___   Double___   Twin___   Triple___   Quad___

With: Toilet___   Shower___   Bath___   Sink only___

Special needs: View___   Quiet___   Cheap___   Ground Floor___

Credit card: Visa___   MasterCard___   American Express___

Card #: _____

Expiration date:_____

Name on card: _____

You may charge me for the first night as a deposit. Please fax, e-mail, or mail me confirmation of my reservation, along with the type of room reserved, the price, and whether the price includes breakfast. Thank you.

_____
Signature

_____
Name

_____
Address

_____
City   **State**   **Zip Code**   **Country**

_____
E-mail Address

INDEX

AVALON
TRAVEL
p u b l i s h i n g

BECAUSE TRAVEL MATTERS.

AVALON TRAVEL PUBLISHING knows that travel is more than coming and going—travel is taking part in new experiences, new ideas, and a new outlook. Our goal is to bring you complete and up-to-date information to help you make informed travel decisions.

AVALON TRAVEL GUIDES feature a combination of practicality and spirit, offering a unique traveler-to-traveler perspective perfect for an afternoon hike, around-the-world journey, or anything in between.

WWW.TRAVELMATTERS.COM

Avalon Travel Publishing guides are available at your favorite book or travel store.

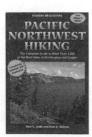

FOR TRAVELERS WITH SPECIAL INTERESTS

GUIDES

The 100 Best Small Art Towns in America • Asia in New York City
The Big Book of Adventure Travel • Cities to Go
Cross-Country Ski Vacations • Gene Kilgore's Ranch Vacations
Great American Motorcycle Tours • Healing Centers and Retreats
Indian America • Into the Heart of Jerusalem
The People's Guide to Mexico • The Practical Nomad
Saddle Up! • Staying Healthy in Asia, Africa, and Latin America
Steppin' Out • Travel Unlimited • Understanding Europeans
Watch It Made in the U.S.A. • The Way of the Traveler
Work Worldwide • The World Awaits
The Top Retirement Havens • Yoga Vacations

SERIES

Adventures in Nature
The Dog Lover's Companion
Kidding Around
Live Well

  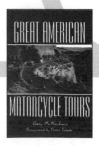

MOON HANDBOOKS provide

comprehensive coverage of a region's arts, history, land, people, and social issues in addition to detailed practical listings for accommodations, food, outdoor recreation, and entertainment. Moon Handbooks allow complete immersion in a region's culture—ideal for travelers who want to combine sightseeing with insight for an extraordinary travel experience.

USA

Alaska-Yukon • Arizona • Big Island of Hawaii • Boston • Coastal California • Colorado Connecticut • Georgia • Grand Canyon • Hawaii Honolulu-Waikiki • Idaho • Kauai • Los Angeles Maine • Massachusetts • Maui • Michigan Montana • Nevada • New Hampshire New Mexico • New York City • New York State North Carolina • Northern California • Ohio Oregon • Pennsylvania • San Francisco Santa Fe-Taos • Silicon Valley • South Carolina Southern California • Tahoe • Tennessee • Texas • Utah • Virginia Washington • Wisconsin • Wyoming • Yellowstone-Grand Teton

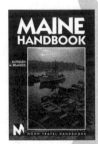

INTERNATIONAL

Alberta and the Northwest Territories Archaeological Mexico • Atlantic Canada • Australia Baja • Bangkok • Bali • Belize • British Columbia • Cabo • Canadian Rockies • Cancún Caribbean Vacations • Colonial Mexico • Costa Rica Cuba • Dominican Republic • Ecuador • Fiji Havana • Honduras • Hong Kong • Indonesia Jamaica • Mexico City • Mexico • Micronesia The Moon • Nepal • New Zealand Northern Mexico • Oaxaca • Pacific Mexico Pakistan • Philippines • Puerto Vallarta • Singapore • South Korea South Pacific • Southeast Asia • Tahiti • Thailand Tonga-Samoa • Vancouver Vietnam, Cambodia and Laos • Virgin Islands Yucatán Peninsula

www.moon.com

Rick Steves shows you where

to travel and how to travel—all while getting the most value for your dollar. His Back Door travel philosophy is about making friends, having fun, and avoiding tourist rip-offs.

Rick's been traveling to Europe for more than 25 years and is the author of 20 guidebooks, which have sold more than a million copies. He also hosts the award-winning public television series *Travels in Europe with Rick Steves*.

RICK STEVES' COUNTRY & CITY GUIDES

Best of Europe
France, Belgium & the Netherlands
Germany, Austria & Switzerland
Great Britain & Ireland
Italy • London • Paris • Rome
Scandinavia • Spain & Portugal

RICK STEVES' PHRASE BOOKS

French • German • Italian • French, Italian & German
Spanish & Portuguese

MORE EUROPE FROM RICK STEVES

Europe 101
Europe Through the Back Door
Mona Winks
Postcards from Europe

WWW.RICKSTEVES.COM

ROAD TRIP USA

Getting there is half the fun, and Road Trip USA guides are your ticket to driving adventure. Taking you off the interstates and onto less-traveled, two-lane highways, each guide is filled with fascinating trivia, historical information, photographs, facts about regional writers, and details on where to sleep and eat—all contributing to your exploration of the American road.

"Books so full of the pleasures of the American road, you can smell the upholstery."
~ BBC radio

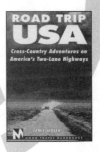

THE ORIGINAL CLASSIC GUIDE
Road Trip USA

ROAD TRIP USA REGIONAL GUIDE
Road Trip USA: California and the Southwest

ROAD TRIP USA GETAWAYS
Road Trip USA Getaways: Chicago
Road Trip USA Getaways: New Orleans
Road Trip USA Getaways: San Francisco
Road Trip USA Getaways: Seattle

www.roadtripusa.com

TRAVEL ✦ SMART®

guidebooks are accessible, route-based driving guides. Special interest tours provide the most practical routes for family fun, outdoor activities, or regional history for a trip of anywhere from two to 22 days. Travel Smarts take the guesswork out of planning a trip by recommending only the most interesting places to eat, stay, and visit.

"One of the few travel series that rates sightseeing attractions. That's a handy feature. It helps to have some guidance so that every minute counts."
~ San Diego Union-Tribune

TRAVEL SMART REGIONS

Alaska
American
Southwest
Arizona
Carolinas
Colorado
Deep South
Eastern
Canada
Florida Gulf
Coast
Florida
Georgia
Hawaii
Illinois/Indiana
Iowa/Nebraska
Kentucky/Tennessee
Maryland/Delaware
Michigan
Minnesota/Wisconsin
Montana/Wyoming/Idaho
Nevada

New England
New Mexico
New York State
Northern California
Ohio
Oregon
Pacific Northwest
Pennsylvania/New Jersey
South Florida and the Keys
Southern California
Texas
Utah
Virginias
Western Canada

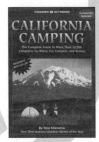

CiTY·SMaRT™

The best way to enjoy a city is to get advice from someone who lives there—and that's exactly what City Smart guidebooks offer. City Smarts are written by local authors with hometown perspectives who have personally selected the best places to eat, shop, sightsee, and simply hang out. The honest, lively, and opinionated advice is perfect for business travelers looking to relax with the locals or for longtime residents looking for something new to do Saturday night.

A portion of sales from each title benefits a non-profit literacy organization in that city.

CITY SMART CITIES

Albuquerque	Anchorage
Austin	Baltimore
Berkeley/Oakland	Boston
Calgary	Charlotte
Chicago	Cincinnati
Cleveland	Dallas/Ft. Worth
Denver	Indianapolis
Kansas City	Memphis
Milwaukee	Minneapolis/St. Paul
Nashville	Pittsburgh
Portland	Richmond
San Francisco	Sacramento
St. Louis	Salt Lake City
San Antonio	San Diego
Tampa/St. Petersburg	Toronto
Tucson	Vancouver

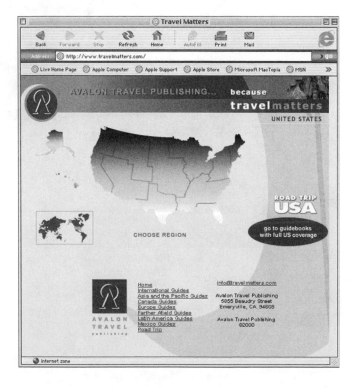

www.ricksteves.com

The Rick Steves web site is bursting with information to boost your travel I.Q. and liven up your European adventure. Including:

- The latest from Rick on what's hot in Europe
- Excerpts from Rick's books
- Rick's comprehensive Guide to European Railpasses

www.foghorn.com

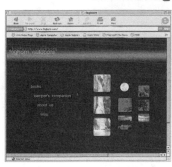

Foghorn Outdoors guides are the premier source for United States outdoor recreation information. Visit the Foghorn Outdoors web site for more information on these activity-based travel guides, including the complete text of the handy Foghorn Outdoors: Camper's Companion.

www.moon.com

Moon Handbooks' goal is to give travelers all the background and practical information they'll need for an extraordinary travel experience. Visit the Moon Handbooks web site for interesting information and practical advice, including Q&A with the author of The Practical Nomad, Edward Hasbrouck.

FREE-SPIRITED TOURS FROM

Rick Steves

Great Guides

Big Buses

Small Groups

No Grumps

**Best of Europe ■ Best of Europe II ■ Eastern Europe ■ Turkey ■ Italy ■ Britain
Spain/Portugal ■ Ireland ■ Eastern France ■ Western France ■ Village France
Scandinavia ■ Germany/Austria/Switzerland ■ London ■ Paris ■ Rome**

Looking for a one, two, or three-week tour that's run in the Rick Steves style?
Check out Rick Steves' educational, experiential tours of Europe. Rather than
seeing Europe as a spectator from a bus window, you'll be encouraged to dive into
daily life. You'll have opportunities to meet the locals, see how local transportation
and services work, and get comfortable wandering off on your own. By the end of the
tour, you'll have the knowledge and confidence it takes to travel through Europe
independently—which is what many of our tour members do before they return home.

Rick Steves' tours include much more in the "sticker price" than mainstream
tours. Here's what you'll get with a Europe or regional Rick Steves tour...

Group size: Your tour group will be no larger than 26. **Guides:** You'll have two guides
traveling and dining with you on your fully guided Rick Steves tour. **Bus:** You'll travel
in a full-size 48-to-52-seat bus, with plenty of empty seats for you to spread out and
read, snooze, enjoy the passing scenery, get away from your spouse, or whatever.
Sightseeing: Your tour price includes all group sightseeing. There are no hidden
extra charges. **Hotels:** You'll stay in small, characteristic, locally-run hotels in the
center of each city, within walking distance of the sights you came to see. **Price and
insurance:** Your tour price is guaranteed for 2001. Single travelers do <u>not</u> pay an
extra supplement (we have them room with other singles). ETBD includes prorated
tour cancellation/ interruption protection coverage at no extra cost. **Tips and
kickbacks:** All guide and driver tips are included in your tour price. Because your
driver and guides are paid salaries by ETBD, they can focus on giving you the best
European travel experience possible.

Interested? Call (425) 771-8303 or visit www.ricksteves.com for a free copy of
Rick Steves' 2001 Tours booklet!

Rick Steves' Europe Through the Back Door

130 Fourth Avenue North, PO Box 2009, Edmonds, WA 98020 USA
Phone: (425) 771-8303 ■ Fax: (425) 771-0833 ■ www.ricksteves.com

FREE TRAVEL GOODIES FROM

Rick Steves

EUROPEAN TRAVEL NEWSLETTER

My *Europe Through the Back Door* travel company will help you travel better *because* you're on a budget—not in spite of it. To see how, ask for my 64-page *travel newsletter* packed full of savvy travel tips, readers' discoveries, and your best bets for railpasses, guidebooks, videos, travel accessories and free-spirited tours.

2001 GUIDE TO EUROPEAN RAILPASSES

With hundreds of railpasses to choose from in 2001, finding the right pass for your trip has never been more confusing. To cut through the complexity, ask for my 64-page *2001 Guide to European Railpasses.* Once you've narrowed down your choices, we give you unbeatable prices, including important extras with every Eurailpass, *free:* my hour-long "How to get the most out of your railpass" video; your choice of one of my 16 country guidebooks and phrasebooks; and written advice on your one-page trip itinerary.

RICK STEVES' 2001 TOURS

We offer 16 different one, two, and three-week tours (160 departures in 2001) for those who want to experience Europe in Rick Steves' Back Door style, but without the transportation and hotel hassles. If a tour with a small group, modest family-run hotels, lots of exercise, great guides, and no tips or hidden charges sounds like your idea of fun, ask for my 48-page 2001 Tours booklet.

YEAR-ROUND GUIDEBOOK UPDATES

Even though the information in my guidebooks is the freshest around, things do change in Europe between book printings. I've set aside a special section at my website (www.ricksteves.com/update) listing *up-to-the-minute changes* for every Rick Steves guidebook.

Call, fax, or visit www.ricksteves.com to get your...

- ☑ **FREE EUROPEAN TRAVEL NEWSLETTER**
- ☑ **FREE 2001 GUIDE TO EUROPEAN RAILPASSES**
- ☑ **FREE RICK STEVES' 2001 TOURS BOOKLET**

Rick Steves' Europe Through the Back Door

130 Fourth Avenue North, PO Box 2009, Edmonds, WA 98020 USA
Phone: (425) 771-8303 ■ Fax: (425) 771-0833 ■ www.ricksteves.com

Rick Steves' Phrase Books

Unlike other phrase books and dictionaries on the market, my well-tested phrases and key words cover every situation a traveler is likely to encounter. With these books you'll laugh with your cabby, disarm street thieves with insults, and charm new European friends.

Each book in the series is 4" x 6", with maps.

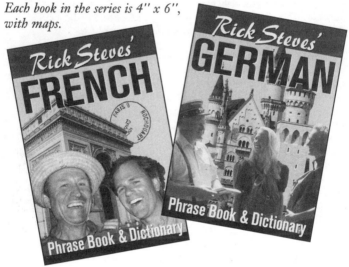

RICK STEVES' FRENCH PHRASE BOOK & DICTIONARY
U.S. $6.95/Canada $10.95

RICK STEVES' GERMAN PHRASE BOOK & DICTIONARY
U.S. $6.95/Canada $10.95

RICK STEVES' ITALIAN PHRASE BOOK & DICTIONARY
U.S. $6.95/Canada $10.95

RICK STEVES' SPANISH & PORTUGUESE PHRASE BOOK & DICTIONARY
U.S. $8.95/Canada $13.95

RICK STEVES' FRENCH, ITALIAN & GERMAN PHRASE BOOK & DICTIONARY
U.S. $8.95/Canada $13.95